SPENSER STUDIES

XVII

SPENSER STUDIES

A Renaissance Poetry Annual XVII

EDITED BY

William A. Oram   *Anne Lake Prescott*
Thomas P. Roche, Jr.

AMS PRESS
NEW YORK

SPENSER STUDIES
A RENAISSANCE POETRY ANNUAL

edited by

Anne Lake Prescott, William A. Oram, and Thomas P. Roche, Jr.

is published annually by AMS Press, Inc. as a forum for Spenser scholarship and criticism and related Renaissance subjects. Manuscripts must be double-spaced, including notes, which should be grouped at the end and should be prepared according to *The Chicago Manual of Style*. Authors of essay-length manuscripts should include an abstract of 100–150 words and provide a disk version of the article, preferably in a Windows-compatible format. One copy of each manuscript should be sent to Thomas P. Roche, Jr., Department of English, Princeton University, Princeton, NJ 08544, one copy to Anne Lake Prescott, Department of English, Barnard College, Columbia University, 3009 Broadway, New York, NY 10027-6598, and one copy to William A. Oram, Department of English, Smith College, Northampton, MA. 01063

Please send inquiries concerning subscriptions or the availability of earlier volumes to AMS Press, Inc., Brooklyn Navy Yard, Bldg. 292, Suite 417, Brooklyn, NY 11205, USA.

ISSN 0195-9468
Volume XVII, ISBN 0-404-19217-3

Contents

The Life of Virgil and the Aspiration of the "New Poet"
    M. L. DONNELLY   1
The "Secret Faith" of Spenser's Saracens
    BENEDICT S. ROBINSON   37
Despair and the Proportion of the Self
    ANDREW ESCOBEDO   75
Despair and the Composition of the Self
    BETH QUITSLUND   91
"Just Time Expired": Succession Anxieties and the
    Wandering Suitor in Spenser's *Faerie Queene*
    TY BUCKMAN   107
Busirane's Place: The House of Rhetoric
    JUDITH H. ANDERSON   133
Distressing Irena: Gender, Conquest, and Justice in Book V
    of *The Faerie Queene*
    MARY R. BOWMAN   151
Spenser, Ralegh, and the Language of Allegory
    LIN KELSEY   183
"Worme-eaten and full of canker holes": Materializing
    Memory in *The Faerie Queene* and in *Lingua*
    ALAN STEWART and GARRETT A. SULLIVAN, JR.   215
"Beeleve this butt a fiction": Female authorship, Narrative
    Undoing, and the Limits of Romance in the Second
    Part of the Countess of Montgomery's *Urania*
    CLAIRE R. KINNEY   239

Forum
251

Republicanism, Nostalgia, and the Crowd
    DAVID SCOTT WILSON-OKAMURA   253
Was Spenser Really a Republican After All? A Reply to
    David Scott Wilson-Okamura
    ANDREW HADFIELD   275

Gleanings
291

Spenser's Dedicatory Sonnets to the 1590 *Faerie Queene:* An
    Interpretation of the Blank Sonnet
        RICHARD MCNAMARA   293
Robert Parsons/Richard Verstegen and the Calling-in of
    Mother Hubberds Tale
        ANDREW HADFIELD   297

Illustrations
12–16; 48–51

Index
301

M. L. DONNELLY

The Life of Vergil and the Aspirations of the "New Poet"

Recent criticism has questioned as ahistorical the traditional view that Spenser deliberately embraced the Vergilian career path, seeing the English poet and Irish colonial functionary as moved instead by more various and worldly career goals analogous to those of contemporary place seekers like Gabriel Harvey. However, attention to the narrative of the poet's character and career usually prefixed to the published editions of Vergil's works in the Renaissance lends support to the traditional view. *The Life of Vergil* usually attributed to Aelius Donatus that Spenser would have known in any of variously accreted versions confirms the role of laureate poet as, not a modern construction, ahistorically imposed on the aspiring young English humanist intellectual, but a very specific model, quite available in the sixteenth century, though obviously not a suitable pattern for everyone. The Vergilian life has much to say about the rising poet's relations to patronage, to unexpected kinds of encyclopedic learning, to rival poetasters, and to the poet's grasp of practical ethical and political knowledge and responsibilities. Its representation of the poet's place in the definition and direction of the course of empire undercuts the argument that attribution of Vergilian laureate aspirations to Spenser wrongly aestheticizes his career and somehow places him above or outside his "determining social and political realities." To understand what role in life Spenser set out to play, it is essential to understand in detail the pattern or model held up to him for emulation by the traditional life of Vergil available in his time.

1

> Lo I the man, whose Muse whilome did maske,
> As time her taught, in lowly Shepheards weeds . . .
> (*The Faerie Queene*, Book I, Canto i, 1–2)

*I*T USED TO BE ONE of the *données* of Spenser criticism that, in passages like the epigraph above, Spenser deliberately set himself in the pattern of the Vergilian *rota*, thus unmistakably laying claim to laureate status. At the very least, in appropriating to himself the *cursus virgilianus*, Elizabeth's bard was announcing his aspirations to a high-serious and exclusive literary role—indeed, one beyond the ambitions or scope of any of his contemporaries.[1] That comfortable common-place has lately been questioned by a new generation of scholars. Joseph Loewenstein points out the awkward fact that his pastoral book was *not*, in fact, Spenser's first poetic venture, while he and Patrick Cheney both canvass those literary productions subsequent to *The Shepheardes Calender* that regrettably do not seem perfectly imitative of the Vergilian progression from pastoral through georgic to epic, without backward glance.[2] Richard Rambuss has vigorously argued against the representation of "Spenser's careerism . . . being dictated by a singleminded pursuit of laureateship along a Virgilian career trajectory from pastoral to epic," insisting that "Spenser's career goals are far more various and never strictly Virgilian."[3] Seeking not just "new readings of Spenser" but "new or alternative 'Spensers,' " Rambuss wants to debunk "a Spenser larger than his own cultural moment, . . . a poet who virtuosically [sic] stands above the impingements of determining social and political realities."[4] He seeks "a strategic decentering of 'the poetic Spenser'—a decentering to be achieved by placing him in other contexts, namely the colonial and the bureaucratic," career contexts which he believes to have been at least as central to Spenser's aspirations as his poetic ambitions.[5] Rambuss in fact implicitly equates Spenser's career path and ambitions to Donne's. He chides Arthur Marotti for falling in with other new historicists in calling Spenser a new kind of poet "despite Marotti's awareness of how another celebrated poet of the period, John Donne, regarded literature not as his vocation but more as an avocation to be used in the pursuit of mainly social rather than artistic patronage."[6]

But of course in making this comparison, Rambuss smoothly elides the very real differences between the career paths and especially the publishing patterns of the two "celebrated poets." These differences seem to me to support the continued assertion of at least a qualified assent to the Vergilian career pattern or model.[7] It is true that purely "literary" approaches to mapping Spenser's career and *oeuvre*, whether generic, stylistic, moralistic or "prophetic" in emphasis, tend to ignore attractions and pressures exerted by politics and worldly power in favor of "transcendental" values. To this result Rambuss rightly objects. But both Rambuss's focus on extra-literary career patterns, and the exclusive privileging of the literary he charges against Richard Helgerson, leave out of consideration the actual Vergilian model as known to Spenser and his contemporaries from the *Life* of The Poet. That model depicts the laureate poet as both "the best poet" and in addition, the sage, a wise and trusted counsellor at the elbow of power, the definer and inspirer of the course of empire. Spenser *does* redefine "authorial posture," and his redefinition *was* unprecedented for Tudor England, though not without precedent altogether, because Vergil had been before.

The redefinition Spenser pursued did not seek to "privilege the literary as a domain altogether apart." "Poetry" was "apart," though by no means "privileged," for Spenser's friend Gabriel Harvey and other aspiring courtiers and would-be humanist civil servants. They used literary endeavor as a tool, a mode of self-advertisement to advance a political or bureaucratic career. In contrast, in the Vergilian poet's role as practical instructor and moral guide to the nation and its leaders, Spenser's paideutic model privileged poetry as, in effect, the master discourse in the circle of the liberal arts and sciences, including *politike*. The highest kind of poetry subsumed all other merely secular arts and knowledge, and owned a public purpose. The evidence of Spenser's own writings as well as the testimony of his contemporaries make it clear that he was not setting out for himself on a career-path nor was he perceived as setting out on a career-path that had been travelled before him by Gascoigne, Whetstone, and Harvey, one that would be pursued by the ambitious Ralegh, or, at quite another social level, by Sidney, Dyer, or Greville.

In order to understand the full implication of the Vergilian career-path in mysteries of state as well as mastery of encyclopedic knowledge, what is needed at this point, I think, is closer attention to the career of Vergil as it was circulated from the late classical period down to the end of the Renaissance. This story was available in the "Life" of the Poet known to everyone who was literate, and generally prefixed to school-editions and ornate and impressive folio *Opera* alike.[8] Despite the modesty and self-effacing character of the poet in that traditional narrative, his role involved him in the highest levels of policy and statecraft, not as a minor bureaucrat and place-seeker, but as counselor and confidant of the emperor himself. Thus an understanding of the Vergilian role as depicted in the *Vita Vergiliani* known to Spenser's contemporaries helps to adjudicate the contentious debate between those recent critics whose emphasis on the poet's laureate aspirations seems to their opponents an unhistorical segregation of literature into an autonomous and transcendental realm, and those who, concentrating on social, historical, and contextual pressures, would assimilate Spenser's aims and practice to those of his ambitious friend Harvey, or the climbing Ralegh, or Sidney, or Donne.

Surprisingly little attention has been given to the actual written life of the Mantuan as a pattern and influence. To grasp the Renaissance understanding of the role of Vergil is to reflect on the *idea* of Vergil—the representation of the life and career of the poet, and its placement in social and political terms—that was inherited and cultivated by Renaissance Europeans. Spenser's epic narrator declares himself to be, first of all, one "whose Muse whilome did maske / As time her taught, in lowly Shepheardes weeds." We need to attend carefully to what Spenser's time did teach him, not only about the need for and uses of masks, but specifically about the Vergilian mask thus adopted, and the poetic role and career pattern its imitation implied. How well did the mask of Vergil fit the aspiring Elizabethan?

In expounding authors, the fourth-century commentator on the *Aeneid*, Servius, advises that two of the things to be considered are the poet's life and his intentions in writing.[9] These injunctions are clearly out of fashion today. Renaissance poetics, however, operated on a rhetorical model that declared an ethical bias and emphasized authorial intent exercised in the choice of means for moving and persuading an audience. Furthermore, the combination of the ethical concern of humanist education and ideology—"ethical" in both the senses of rhetorical *ethos* and moral emphasis, *ethike*—and the humanist preoccupation with fame ensured an intense interest in the life and character of authors. This was particularly true for the authors of certain kinds of works, especially the heroic poem. Consequently, it seems appropriate to explore the idea that following Servius' advice in looking at Vergil—or at least the conventional *idea* of Vergil in the Renaissance—might usefully illuminate Edmund Spenser's aspirations and expectations as he set out on his poetic career. Incidentally, a fuller awareness of the Vergilian model will clarify the possible range of conceptions of the poet's role available in Renaissance England.

Of course, given the lack of documentary evidence for inward commitments and states of mind, following Servius' advice in an attempt to illuminate Edmund Spenser's conception of the role he would play as he set out on his poetic career will inevitably commit us to, as Jean Brink has said, "more indirect and circumstantial means" —to analogy, inference, and, on occasion, apparent contrast with other patterns of aspiration and careerism that can be documented among the poet's contemporaries.[10] I will argue that the traditional textual representation of the life and career of Vergil circulated in the Renaissance would have been a powerful spur to emulation for young Edmund Spenser. The suggestive congruence of the life and image of the Roman Imperial poet with his own origins, character, and circumstances would inevitably have magnetized his youthful imagination. The Vergilian career pattern was then consciously chosen by the ambitious Cantabrigian as a model of aspiration and an object of imitation. This deliberate choice sets Spenser apart beyond the typical humanist imitation, veneration, and use of ancient texts, just as Vergil is set apart from other, lesser poets.

The matter of my argument is the accumulation of biographical facts and folklore retailed in typical Renaissance editions of the *Princeps poetarum*—usually, with accretions and embellishments, the Life attributed to the fourth-century grammarian, Aelius Donatus. The conception of Vergil and Vergil's place that is created and conveyed in these texts is then crystallized in various pictorial representations of The Poet on the frontispieces and titlepages of a multitude of Renaissance editions. My argument will turn on the congruencies between the facts, beliefs, connections, and attitudes carried down by these materials on the one hand, and Spenser's background, friends, patrons, and contemporary situation on the other. In the light of these congruencies, Spenser appears to have orchestrated his own career to emulate and capitalize on analogies with the traditional narrative of the Vergilian life and role. Ultimately, the Vergilian career exemplifies a particular kind of idealized patronage relationship, and is implicated in the writer's strategies concerning his relations with social and political structures, the uses of poetry and ideology, and the connections of literature and power.

The Renaissance image of Vergil was different from, and far more imposing than that of other revered classical authors, even Horace or Ovid. Vergil's primacy is manifest in the elaborateness of those great Renaissance editions, some of the handsomest books produced in the sixteenth century. Most of these full-scale editions include the "Life" of the poet attributed to Aelius Donatus. Nothing comparable exists for the other great Latin poets admired by the Renaissance. Vergil's reputation as first among poets of the highest kind was unrivalled during the period. The inspired singer and master of universal knowledge had not yet shed all the aura of magic and prophetic power in which the uncritical veneration of the intervening ages had

vested him.[11] The fascination with the poet's life and career mani-
fested in the accumulation of mythical and folkloric material in his
biography reflects this veneration.[12] The age's idealizing attitude toward the poet is only most blatantly conveyed in editions apparently
meant to be used as school texts, like the one in which Philip Melanchthon was involved.[13] Vergil was not only the best of poets, his
works and life were unrivalled teachers of wisdom and morality. The
conclusion of the sixteenth-century Jesuit editor Guellius is typical:

> I am furnished to pledge myself from the records of the Ro-
> mans, that just as much as his songs in their sweetness and
> gravity merited the favor of the Imperator, of the Julian family,
> and in the end, *virtue breaking down even envy*, of the whole
> Roman people, so, for his inborn and natural courtesy ("*comi-
> tate*"), his modesty, from which indeed he took that name he
> was known by [i.e., "Parthenias"], for his liberality, and for his
> mildness, did Maro himself deserve favor: . . . no man of his
> status or lot may be compared to him. Therefore it was not by
> chance that it should have been thought proper by that most
> prudent Imperator that the poet whom he had for the trumpet
> of his praise should be seen to have been admitted to intimate
> familiarity, whom he consulted, not about numbers only, and
> matter of philosophy, but often concerning politics, and even
> concerning handing the republic back to the people.[14]

The poet's virtue and artistry win not only access, but *familiarity*,
from the most prudent of rulers and patrons. The poet becomes his
emperor-patron's trusted counselor on matters of highest state.

If a high-minded young poet would have responded reverentially
to the memory of a man of whom Donatus could say, "truly his life
and lips and soul remained constant in such probity, that he was
called of the Neapolitan vulgar, 'Parthenias' [that is, "virginal"],"[15]
there are other details in the conventional biographical matter no less
calculated to appeal to the aspiring son of a couple who "were not
people of means,"[16] a youth eager to better himself, to move in the
circles of the great, and, not incidentally, to serve himself, as well as
his country, with his talents. From the Life, Vergil is easily construed
as the talented and fortunate outsider, a provincial who through his
abilities and virtue rose to be the intimate of the great and wealthy
patrons Asinius Pollio and Maecenas, the friend of Horace, and court
poet and trusted advisor to the Divine Augustus himself.

In Aelius Donatus and the miscellaneous half-legendary and wholly fanciful folkloric material that was picked up by the text attributed to him as it was passed down through the twelve-and-a-half centuries between his time and Spenser's, certain elements of the Vergil-story are always prominent. These include Vergil's fame and popularity with the Romans, the poet's friendship with the wealthy and power-ful of his day, his intimacy with Augustus, the comfortable circum-stances of his life as the result of his poetry and the patrons and friends it won for him, and the generous, even noble, use he made of these advantages. Finally, "Donatus" and the various Renaissance intro-ductions, commentaries, and epistles "Ad Lectorem" assert repeatedly that Vergil's poetry not only inculcates sound morals and wisdom, but shows the way to prudent policies that maintain and glorify the nation's historic *mores* and mission. His works are seen as a fountain of recondite erudition feeding the generations of learned commentators. They are not lacking in ethics, politics, economics, astronomy, geog-raphy, nor even theology. From him one can learn the customs of peoples, the situations of lands and seas, the strategems of wars, the strength to be a soldier, the force of eloquence, and the sacred rites of the gods, so that his works are indeed the promptuary of all knowl-edge.[17] In the Renaissance, the valuation of the laureate poet's work as a virtual handbook and guide to statecraft, policy, and military arts was inextricably interwoven with the image of the author's successful life and career.

The first sentence of "Donatus' " *Life* should have jumped out at Spenser: it says that the eventually famous, wealthy, influential, and revered poet was "born of middling parents" (*"parentibus modicis fuit"*), his father being variously recorded as an artisan or potter or as the servant of a wandering magus. Through his labor, Vergil's father was able to translate his family to gentility. He married the daughter of a landowner who may have brought connections with still more important figures.[18] Less tinctured with legend is the ac-count of the poet's education. He studied his elements at Cremona, and pursued his studies at Mediolanum (Milan) and Naples, giving himself vehemently to the study of the Greek and Latin languages; he was addicted to the studies of medicine and mathematics, as well.[19] It is apparent that, however humble his origins, his parents spared no sacrifice to procure for him the best education available, and that he eagerly seized that advantage.

The emblematic content of the *Life* is as powerfully attractive as the "facts" it disseminates. According to "Donatus," the poet was born in the fields, in a wayside ditch, in the region called Andes not far from Mantua north of the Po, after his mother had had a prophetic dream about giving birth to a laurel branch which, upon contact with the earth, became a mature tree and brought forth various fruits and flowers.[20] It is impossible to resist the observation, surely not lost on an alert reader of allegories, that in the dream, the emblem of the poet himself assumes the significance of the tree beneath which Tityrus sits in the first Eclogue, emblem in later iconographical tradition of imperial protection and benefaction. Emblematically, as the embodiment of the florescent and fruitful laurel tree, the poet himself becomes the adorner and sustainer of the lives of a hungry people.

Bringing Vergil to Rome after the completion of his studies, and returning from allegorical vision to folk-tale narrative, the *Life* explains how Vergil made the acquaintance of Octavian's master of the stables, and showed him how to cure various diseases incident to horses. For his "horse-sense" the scholar-poet was rewarded by the order that he should be given bread each day as one of the *stabulariis*. The story continues with two remarkable proofs of this young provincial's extraordinary judgment. First, Vergil accurately deduced from the evident marks of their ancestry the competitive prospects of supposedly prize animals given Octavian. Suitably impressed, Octavian twice ordered Vergil's bread-ration doubled as a reward. As the tale goes, at this time Octavian was much troubled concerning his own parentage, on which his political future seemed dependant. Presuming on Vergil's uncanny success in discovering the ancestry of dogs and horses by examining them, he thought perhaps this friend of his stable-master might be able to resolve his doubts concerning his own father. Accordingly, Octavian consulted with Vergil privately, asking him whether his skill could ascertain the answer to his nagging doubts about his own origins. With its developed dialogue, suspense, and emphasis on the wit of the punch-line (which is not, in truth, particularly clever), the story appears clearly the sort of thing that circulated in medieval and Renaissance collections of novelle.[21] However, we should not be too quick to dismiss such stories as representing merely the kinds of accretions a dark age would collect around the resonant names of the past—*nugas nugarorum*, "trifling speeches of good-for-nothings," as one late commentator sniffs.

These central "facts" and emphasis are repeated in almost all the Renaissance editions of Vergil. There is, first, the poet—poor, without place or status, modest, but widely and usefully learned, and without being pushy, adept at making the right connections and attracting the interest of potential patrons. Next comes the patron himself—wealthy, powerful, complaisant and liberal, but anxious, troubled in spirit, requiring advice and counsel for which there is a rich reward, and which only the poet can provide. On the one side, wit, modesty, and virtue; on the other, wealth, power, and magnanimity: the results, friendship, influence, and reward for the poet. Aspects of this constellation reappear in the life again and again, and so persistently were they taken as central to understanding and appreciating the poet, that over a hundred years after Spenser, Knightley Chetwood, in his *Life of Vergil* prefixed to Dryden's great edition, was still attempting to preserve them by supplying Augustan rationalizations and commonsensical explanations for them.[22]

Vergil's personal virtue is illustrated by the story from Asconius Pedianus that Varus so admired the poet that he wanted to share Plotia Hieria with him, but that the poet most pertinaciously abstained from intercourse with Varus' woman.[23] Intimacy with the wealthy and powerful is asserted again and again, interwoven, along with instances of his unassailable virtue, into stories about the production of his enduring works. Urged by Asinius Pollio, who was greatly loved by Vergil, and who greatly rewarded him in turn, Vergil completed the *Bucolics* in three years. When Vergil, invited to dinner with Pollio, was captivated by the beauty and diligence of the servant-boy Alexander, Pollio gave him the youth. On Cornelius Gallus, the famous orator and a better than mediocre poet, Vergil conferred the distinction of a wonderful devotion. He originally gave the fourth *Georgic*, from the middle to the end, to Gallus' praises, but afterward, when Gallus had fallen under suspicion and been executed, Augustus ordered Vergil to change that portion into the fable of Aristeus. When, shortly after the death of Marcellus, the son of Augustus' sister, Octavia, the poet was besought to read before Augustus and his court from his poem in progress, the *Aeneid*, he inserted the lines in Book Six praising the ill-fated youth (lines 860–86), reading them with such feeling that they say that Octavia fainted away from emotion. The master of pathos did quite well for this bit of courtship, too: it was ordered that a half a score sesterces be given to Vergil for each verse of his memorial. (Chetwood translates the sum as "two Thousand one Hundred Pounds, odd Money; a round Sum for Twenty Seven Verses. But they were Virgil's.")[24] The trust Augustus reposed in the poet is highlighted in the story that he consulted Vergil to decide between conflicting advice from his son-in-law, Agrippa, and his favorite, Maecenas, concerning whether he ought to restore the republic in its old form or retain sovereign power himself. (Vergil politicly, but also, according to the legend, with sound judgment of the character of the Roman people at the time, advised him to hang onto power, which of course he did.)[25]

It is this aspect of the Vergilian role that Rambuss and others critical of the idea of laureate aspirations neglect. They see the poet's

role too narrowly, perhaps in terms of the relation between poetry
and statecraft that has typically been the case in modern English-
speaking countries. The laureate role seems to them exclusively literary and aesthetic—a kind of aspiration they reject as ahistorical for
this period. But according to the lives of Vergil printed in Early
Modern editions of the poet, the Vergilian laureate was a trusted
advisor and confidante of power, indeed a kind of cabinet counselor.
His historical, ethical, and political wisdom was not merely theoretical; it was practical and applied. As F. J. Levy has asserted, the patron,
the necessary Maecenas, not only provided moral and financial support to the poet, and protected him from "the malice of evill
mouthes," but "most important, he provided the poet with access
to political power. . . . The inner sanctum was reserved for the
ruler—and the laureate. In Ben Jonson's vision of the relationship,
Augustus readily ceded part of his glory to the poet, . . . and at the
conclusion of *Poetaster*, emperor and poet together pass judgment on
the offenders."[26]

Such trusted merit in such a role issues in considerable personal
reward. The lives make much of Vergil's circumstances by the end
of his career, claiming that he received adulation in public places
scarcely inferior to that accorded Caesar, and commanded "a compe-
tent estate" at Rome. Thanks to the benefactions of friends to the
extent of 100,000 sesterces, he enjoyed a house on the Esquiline near
the gardens of Maecenas, although he more often made use of his
country retreats in Campania and Sicily. He was loved by all the best
poets of the time, Tucca, Varus, Horace, Gallus, Propertius, to whom
his extensive library was always open. He had as his executors after
his death no lesser persons than the Emperor Augustus himself and
Augustus' favorite, Maecenas, who looked after his burial at Naples
according to his direction, and set up the tomb, with his urn supported by nine pillars, over which was graven the simple distich he
had composed for himself.[27] What Renaissance humanist could ask
for more?[28]

The pictorial traditions carried down by the illustrations for Renaissance editions of Vergil, particularly titlepages and frontispieces,
confirm that the episodes and themes in Donatus's *Life* that I have
just highlighted were indeed the salient features in the poet's career
for the Renaissance. Over and over again, the pictorial traditions
present the poet's knowledge, virtue, and eloquence as opening the
doors of power, highlight the trust reposed in the poet, and emphasize
his exaltation by admiration and envy, his courtship by the wealthy
and the great, and his serenely enjoyed prestige and success.

The famous edition of Johann Gruninger, Strausborg, 1502, in which Sebastian Brant was involved, and many subsequent editions which imitated Gruninger's cuts, such as Jacobo Mareshal's Leyden edition of 1527, include in the background of the frontispiece an illustration of how Vergil first came to Augustus' attention because of his "horse-sense," a noteworthy confirmation of the centrality of this episode and the elements it embodies for sixteenth-century interests. No less significant is the representation of the poet's immortalization by the Muse in the midst of his rejoicing literary friends and chagrined poetasters, on the one hand, and his wealthy and powerful patrons, on the other (see figs. 1 [Strasbourg 1502] and 2 [Leyden 1527]).

The woodcut illustrating the Portesio Venice edition of 1510 and its cruder descendant in the 1536 edition from the press of Aurelius Pincius represent another frequently found illustrative tradition showing the laurel-crowned Vergil offering his *Aeneid* to the throned Augustus, while Maecenas and Pollio stand on either side in support. Beneath this homage to the relations among the poet, his patrons, and enthroned power, the Portesio title page also stresses the academic tradition of learning, showing the historical community of Vergil's commentators, ancient and modern together, seated at their writing-desks, quills in hand, dutifully explicating and passing on as the heritage of the ages the text of the *"Princeps poetarum"* (Fig. 3).

The last two illustrations, the plate opposite the frontispiece from the sumptuous 1654 folio of Ogilby's translation, which was taken over by the Dryden translation published by Tonson in 1697, and the Houbroken plate from the title page of Vergil's *Opera* printed by Halma, Leovardiae, 1717, are later than our period, but I include them because they illustrate the persistence of the theme of the poet's intimate connections with power in the iconographic traditions of Vergil-illustration. The Ogilby plate, designed by F. Cleyn and cut by P. Lombart, renders the dramatic moment from Vergil's public reading at court of Book VI of the *Aeneid*, when Octavia swooned—an image of the power of art in at least two senses (Fig. 4). The Halma plate continues the tradition of the triumph of true art over poetasters and false critics, presenting Vergil, at the head of a gaggle of pleased-looking Muses, addressing the throned Augustus (who is backed and surrounded by the emblems of Roman imperial power), while the flayed pretender to art, Marsyas, and the false judge, Midas, groan in dismay and grief behind the emblematic goose, left behind by the true poet in his ascent (Fig. 5).[29]

This last represents the one element prominent in the illustrations of the life of Vergil that we have not yet touched on. An antimasque

Fig. 1. Engraved titlepage of Johann Gruniger's edition of Vergil's
Opera, Strasbourg, 1502, reproduced courtesy of the Department of
Special Collections, Kenneth Spencer Research Library of the Uni-
versity of Kansas: Aitchison D2.

Fig. 2. Engraved titlepage of Jacobo Mareschal's edition of Vergil Leiden, 1527, reproduced courtesy of the Department of Special Collections, Kenneth Spencer Research Library of the University of Kansas: Aitchison E2.

Fig. 3. Virgil, *Opera* (Venice: Bernadino de Portesio, 1510), frontispiece. By permission of Princeton University Library.

Fig. 4. Plate opposite frontispiece, John Ogilby's *The Works of . . . Maro, Translated, adornd with Sculpture, and illustrated with Annotation* (London: Thomas Warren, 1657), reproduced courtesy of the Department of Special Collections, Kenneth Spencer Research Library of the University of Kansas: Aitchison G1.

Fig. 5. Houbroken plate from the engraved title page of the Halma
edition of Virgil's works, Leovardiae, 1717. Reproduced courtesy of
the Thomas Fisher Rare Book Library of the University of Toronto.

of discomfited poetasters was represented by some examples throughout the iconic tradition, from Gruninger to Houbroken. That, too,
however, is implicit in Donatus' *Life*. For Donatus also tells an alternative story of how Vergil gained Augustus' notice, involving an
attempt by an ambitious hack, Bathyllus, to take credit for Vergil's
verses, and his subsequent discomfiture through Vergil's clever ploy.
Ogilby's edition translates the traditional story in the brief "Life" at
the beginning of the volume. Vergil, dispossessed of his ancestral lands
by Augustus' resettlement of his veterans in the region of Cremona,

> went to Rome, and, to prepare his way into the Emperor's
> knowledge, affix'd this Distich upon the Court-gate.

> Nocte pluit tota, redeunt spectacula mane:
> Divisum Imperium cum *Jove* Caesar habet.
> *All Night it rains, the Shews return next day :*
> *Thus* Jove *and* Caesar *share in equal sway.*

The Author of these Verses (with which Augustus was much
pleas'd) being sought for, Bathyllus, an inferiour Poet of that
time, presented himself, and intercepted the Honours and Rewards of Virgil; who in vindication of himself, to the same
Distich annex'd four times

> Sic vos non vobis, &c.

Bathyllus unable, at the Command of Augustus to, [sic] supply
these Hemistichs, Virgil thus perform'd it.

> Hos ego versiculos feci, tulit alter honores:
> Sic vos non vobis vellera fertis oves,
> Sic vos non vobis nidificatis aves,
> Sic vos non vobis mellificatis apes,
> Sic vos non vobis fertis aratra boves.
> *"Twas I the Verses made, the Praise another had:*
> *So you not for your selves Sheep Fleeces yield,*
> *So you not for your selves Birds Harbours build,*
> *So you not for your selves Bees Honey yield,*
> *So you not for your selves Steers plow the Field.*

By this means he was taken notice of by the Emperour, into
whose favour, through the sollicitiations of Pollio and Mecoe-
nas, he was so far receiv'd that he obtain'd a Grant of the recovery of his own Estate. . . ."[30]

Bathyllus became a by-word all over Rome, and Vergil's reputation
was only enhanced by the episode. Renaissance versions of Donatus
also recount that when Vergil was told of the maledictions and enmity
of Cornificius toward himself, Vergil could not understand it, and
asked the cause, since he had never offended Cornificius, and indeed
loved him. Didn't he recall the opinion of Hesiod, he was asked: the
architect is envied by another architect, and the poet by the poet?
That Greek meant "by the bad [poet or architect]," replied Vergil,
"for the good love the learned."[31]

Thus from before Spenser's time until well past it, the title pages
and illustrations of the Renaissance editions of Vergil reflect persistently repeated and insistently highlighted themes of the myth and
model of Vergil as "*Princeps poetarum.*" The traditions present with
varying emphases anecdotes that feature wit and learning devoted to
moral and national ends; discredited "bad" poetry and rivals overgone; the patronage and indeed friendship of the greatest and wealthi-
est fellow countrymen; and the good poet's merited rewards of fame,
wealth, and political influence.

Now, it is easy to see certain broad similarities between this amal-
gam of popular legend, history, and morality, and the aspirations of
the fifth generation of English humanists—the generation of Lyly,
Harvey, and Spenser. In the background of that generation's aspirations was the idealism that had flowered in Colet and Lily, More and
Erasmus, men for whom, in G. K. Hunter's words, "the end of
education is *sapiens et eloquens pietas,* active Christian virtue rendered
effective in the service of the community by the power to write and
to speak."[32] The greatest scope for such service to the community
could of course be attained only by rising into positions of power and
influence at or near the seat of sovereignty. The Italian predecessors of
the English Humanists provided abundant models of the Humanist as
ambassador, counselor, senator or civil servant. The Italians, however,
with the exception of Petrarch, had not deliberately embarked on
emulation of the Vergilian career-path. Instead, behind the Italians
stood the pattern of another great Roman man of letters, Marcus
Tullius Cicero. Cicero affords the obvious classical career pattern of
the man of letters as civil servant, moral director, and exemplar of
virtue, on the good old Roman model.[33] But Cicero was not a poet,

and astute as his political insights were, noble as the *virtus* he incul-
cated in his ethical and philosophical writings might be, he did not
attempt to rival Homer and enshrine the *ethos* of his national culture
in an epic poem.

As Hunter has observed in his study of the humanism and courtship
of John Lyly, "the 'refocussing' of Humanist idealism on national
politics certainly meant some dislocation of the learned tradition."[34]
In all truth, Cicero's career in the final analysis proved a little too
relentlessly "careerist." The altruistic Humanist aspiration to devote
one's life to the service of one's church and state is dogged by its
dark twin: selfish personal ambition and the thirst for self-aggrandize-
ment. Too easily, climbing into positions of power and status and
gaining the appropriate trappings of such positions, which were in
fact to lay hold of the effectual *means* of service, became ends in
themselves. Thomas Cooper had complained in 1565 that the lives
of the scholar and minister of the gospel were neglected because of
the lure of the court and pursuit of a life of noble connections, power,
influence, and worldly reward. In dedicating his *Thesaurus* to the earl
of Leicester, at that time Queen Elizabeth's favorite and chancellor
of the University of Oxford, Cooper complained that the life of the
scholar is "debased to ignominy" while "parents, seeking the advantage of their own, prescribe other disciplines for their children; and
the children judge rather by popular esteem than by the inherent
dignity of the matter." Consequently,

the Universities and public schools have been promptly abandoned by the best minds; and of those who were well educated
as children but few are anxious to penetrate into the depth of
things—except for those who go on to study law or medicine.
The rest give up their studies and betake themselves to the life
of a courtier, or devote themselves to the law of the land [at
the Inns of Court] or withdraw to some other kind of pastime,
which they think will prove more profitable. . . . [Conse-
quently, the church and the schools are unfurnished with
learned preachers and teachers.] For though certain honour and
great reward is promised to those who undertake functions in
the state; the lot of rectors in churches and masters in schools
is contempt rather than praise. No wonder if many are found
seeking glory and dignity, but few following virtue and learning
when these are joined with shame.[35]

Cooper's charges would seem to be notably illustrated by the ambitions and obsessions of Spenser's friend and mentor, Gabriel Harvey. Harvey's longing for an active role in the power elite and his ambitious pursuit of place and influence were displayed transparently enough in all his relationships and suits, but his marginalia spell out his aspirations with the unreserve of a man communing with himself.[36] In his notes in his copy of *OEkonomia, seu Dispositio Regularum vtriusque Iuris in Locos Communes* (1570), Harvey noted: "The prynces Court, ye only mart of praeferment, & honour. A Goulfe of gaine. No fisshing to ye Sea. nor seruice to A King. Solum operaeprecium."[37] Harvey's ambitions for the rewards of a life of service to the state had been fostered by the early patronage and mentorship of Sir Thomas Smyth, a Pollio of his native Walden, and by the benefaction of Sir Walter Mildmay, Queen Elizabeth's chancellor of the Exchequer. Clearly, the route to preferment, which was the route to public service, private aggrandizement, and fulfillment, was through the cultivation of great and influential patrons. In 1573, Harvey had had occasion to test the principle, when he successfully invoked the intervention of the non-resident master of Pembroke Hall, John Young (later the bishop of Rochester whom Spenser served as secretary) to secure his Master of Arts degree, blocked by intramural jealousies. By 1578–79, Harvey was "well-acquainted" with Leicester, Philip Sidney, Edward Dyer, and Daniel Rogers.[38]

The typical Humanist valuation of literature as "a kind of courtship display of general secular capacity" informed Harvey's maneuverings.[39] He saw to it that his orations opening the 1574, 1575, and 1576 Easter terms as University Praelector in Rhetoric were published by Henry Bynneman. Bynneman also received for his press Harvey's contributions to the entertainment presented for Queen Elizabeth at Audley End in late July 1578 during one of her state progresses (*Gratulationes Valdinenses*, 1578), and his Humanist exchange with Spenser, published as *Three Proper, and wittie, familiar Letters* (1580), and its later successor, *Foure Letters* (1592).[40] It is a bit difficult to say whether these publications were meant to advance the humanist credentials and career ambitions of both men equally, or just how much they may have functioned as an element in the marketing of the coyly modest "Immerito." In many respects, they appear more tailored to the hopes and needs of Harvey. They did appear through the offices of his usual publisher, Bynneman, rather than the shop of Hugh Singleton, used by Spenser for his *Shepheardes Calender* the year before the first series of letters came out. Moreover, William Ponsonby had engaged in assiduous machinations to set himself up as in effect "official printer to the Sidney circle," so that if the *Letters* had been a promotion arranged by the more central figures in the Leicester-Sidney group, he would have been a likelier choice than Bynneman.[41] In any case, the published letters fit the larger humanist pattern of literary self-advertisement rather better than the specifically Vergilian model, which according to the Life seems largely dependent on a series of lucky chances, and on the promotions and good offices of others in advancing the poet to the notice of generous patronage. Even if the 1580 *Letters* were largely Harvey's gambit, however, from Spenser's point of view they might appear to function exactly as Vergil's contacts had in introducing him to public notice and giving momentum to his career.

If the first part of the specifically Vergilian model of the lowly outsider's rise to notice was valid, then apt networking was crucial. Shrewd display of one's abilities combined with discreet flattery of well-placed and powerful persons in purely literary and learned compositions ought to procure recognition and access. Access having been gained, the wide knowledge, prudence, and wisdom that fed the literary compositions might be more practically exercised in pouring into the private ear of potentially complaisant and generous patrons wisdom on the conduct of both worldly affairs and matters of state. The efficacy of such counsel would be recompensed not only by the advancement of the client's fortunes, and further employment in business of weight and trust, but also by support and protection bestowed on the heroic enterprise of the encyclopedic national epic.

Harvey and Spenser were different men on differing career paths, however close their friendship and however similar their shared ambitions of personal advancement and public service to England. After his first trials of the patronage of Leicester and the Sidney circle failed to produce for him the brilliant career-advancement he had hoped, Harvey betook himself to the study of the civil law, and thence to London in his ultimately frustrated pursuit of wealth and importance. Spenser also served Leicester in 1579–80, and was probably assisted by Leicester's patronage or the influence of someone else in Leicester's circle to a place in the service of Lord Grey in Ireland—not exactly what he had in mind at the outset, perhaps, but a stepping-stone.[42] What has appeared to scholars in retrospect an "Irish exile" may well have appeared to Spenser at the time as an opportunity. Service with Grey in Ireland certainly provided an occasion to display his politic talents where they would likely be noticed in the service of a nobleman connected with the Leicester faction. But Lord Grey's civil and military administration would also likely provide chances to improve his knowledge and experience of war, military matters, and the management of empire, all of which he would need to put in play in the composition of his national epic. Even his entry as the putative first stage of the Vergilian *rota*, his pastoral *Shepheardes Calender*, had carried a baggage of public political and religious engagement—not at all a poetry of elegant display and escapist fantasy that might merely serve to advertise the talents of an ambitious young man pursuing the larger humanist career path.[43] And unlike other ambitious young men pursuing the humanist (but not the Vergilian) career path, Spenser went on, having already sung *pascua* in *The Shepheards Calender*, to sing of *duces* in an epic poem. He reached, figuratively speaking, for Augustus' notice: the poem was dedicated "To the most high, mightie and magnificent Empresse renovvmed for pietie, vertue, and all gratiovs government Elizabeth," and was supported by dedicatory sonnets to virtually all the actual or potential Pollios and Maecenases of the Elizabethan court.[44]

The difference between Spenser and his erstwhile companion, Harvey, of course lies in the fact that Harvey, like many of his contemporaries, was merely an ambitious scholar and would-be gentleman who cultivated poetry as one more courtly accomplishment and means of self-advertisement. Literature for him and others of his ilk was only "a kind of courtship display," to be dropped after it had achieved its purpose of self-advancement. At best for them, literary flourishes might be used to confer ornament or dignity on state correspondence and public oratory, or kept as a gentlemanly pastime and amusement. Spenser, on the other hand, as Harvey himself must have recognized early on, was an unusually talented poet, one who had already been published at the age of about seventeen, one gifted and versatile enough that his elaborate, if anonymous, formal appearance as "the newe Poete" in the 1579 *Shepheardes Calender*, with all its deliberate evocation of the antecedent Vergilian model, would not merely invite mockery of his pretensions.

The image of the life and career of the Renaissance Vergil was not the appropriate pattern for every eager Elizabethan *novus homo*. We have seen how Harvey, for example, explicitly admired the role model of Cicero. For Edmund Spenser, however, the Vergilian model must have seemed at first to fit perfectly, beyond his fondest dreams. Born in London to parents "who were not people of means," (but, like Vergil's mother, claiming distant if imprecisely traceable connections to important landowners, in Spenser's case the great Spencers of Wormleighton and Althorp), well-educated as a charity-boy at the Merchant-Taylors' School under Mulcaster, where, like the Roman poet, *cum literis & Graecis & Latinis vehementissimam operam dedisset*, Spenser's family circumstances, passion for learning, and evident literary gifts all matched the model.[45] Conscious of his abilities, already making useful connections, and with such congruence of character and circumstances, how could Spenser doubt that the mantle was destined to descend to him? His genius had found approval with learned men like Harvey. By one means or another, probably through Pembroke College contacts, and possibly shortly after leaving Cambridge, as early as 1574 he had secured service in the household of Dr. John Young, who had been nonresident master of his college, and became bishop of Rochester in 1578.[46] His abilities and connections also brought him to the notice of poets and gentlemen like Dyer and Sidney, who would condescend to conversation and perusal of his writings; he came into the circle of the greatest of Elizabeth's courtiers and confidants, the earl of Leicester—who as her master of horse was something better than Vergil's *entrée*, Octavian's master of stables. As Cambridge and London and his noble and accomplished acquaintances and patrons fostered his gifts and flattered his ego with recognition and encouragement, his sense of the fitness of the Vergilian mantle would have been strengthened and confirmed at every turn. Even up through his securing a place with Lord Grey in Ireland, he could have cherished the sense of the rising trajectory of his career in congruence with the great model, for one other thing was noted in the lives of Vergil: he had never been in a hurry to win fame, he had never rushed to publish; he had always been willing to cultivate his muse in retirement and bide his time. The image of the life and career of Vergil would have seemed to Spenser to fit like a fine and well-cut glove, to be the perfect pattern realized in his own experience.

My view, then, is that at least from his days at Cambridge, Spenser quite deliberately and consciously did cultivate the imitation of the Vergilian career path. That is, he did not merely intend to use his poetic talents as a ladder by which to attain recognition and rise to a secure place, after which he could kick away the ladder. Rather, he intended poetry to be his major bid for fame, and more so, that, freighted with his wide reading and practical experience, it should be, in the words of his later successor, the means of teaching "something doctrinal and exemplary to a nation." He grandly imagined that his learned poetry could be constitutive of the terms and vocabulary of ethical discriminations, political discourse, and national and imperial ideology for his contemporaries, patrons, and empress, in imitation of the great model of the *"Princeps poetarum."*

In his attempt to shift Spenser criticism away from what he sees as a single-minded emphasis on "the poet's poet," and to redirect attention to the poet's dual career paths in his historical context, Richard Rambuss has complained of even New Historicism's tendency "to reify [Spenser's] achievement of a measure of transcendence over the historical world, over his determining social context and historical circumstances, over his own deeply personal and financial stakes in the successful colonization of Ireland."[47] While recognizing the value of Richard Helgerson's *Self-Crowned Laureates*, for example, Rambuss laments what he sees as that work's implication in this conferral of independence of historical circumstance and transcendent status: "Helgerson sees Spenser engaged in an unprecedented renegotiation of the current system of available authorial postures, a virtuosic effort to privilege the literary as a domain altogether apart from other career pursuits."[48] But, as I hope I have shown, Spenser's redefinition of "authorial posture," though unprecedented for Tudor England, certainly had ample and august precedent in the traditional image of Vergil's life and career.

Rambuss is right, however, to recoil from the aestheticization of that poet's role. From his early attachment to the Leicester circle to his late admiration of Essex, Spenser's writings as well as his career were shaped and directed by intense ideological and political commitment. Perhaps like the storied Vergil of "Donatus," Spenser was a man of a kind of virtuous naïveté, unswervingly loyal to his friends and patrons (though Vergil did change that fourth Georgic). Spenser's memorializations of Leicester in the *Complaints* volume, and the late elegy to Sidney, demonstrate his loyalty beyond the grave to his patrons and ideological heroes, a loyalty that extended far beyond the reach of any immediate utility such connections would have had for any truly worldly-wise time-server. Throughout his career he aligned himself with the anti-Spanish, pan-European Protestant crusade that Leicester's faction had dreamed of—the faction that never did succeed in gaining the driver's seat in Elizabethan state policy against the machinations of the all-sufficient Burghley and his prudent and penurious queen. Indeed, Spenser may have been quite as naïve about actual court politics as the legendary and unworldly Roman poet supposedly was.[49] But he was not himself unworldly. Near the end of his life, he was still ideologically engaged, throwing his hopes onto Essex, successor to the Leicester interest. In a move intelligible only on ideological grounds (unless purely personally motivated), Spenser at the same time cultivated Ralegh as well, Essex's rival—a dual attachment completely unsuitable, except that each was equally Protestant and anti-Spanish.[50]

His religious and ideological commitment was central to Spenser's conception of himself in the tradition of Vergil's career. Envisioning himself in that Vergilian role was possible for Spenser and not before him in England, not only because Spenser was a consummately gifted and ambitious poet (a necessary, but not sufficient, cause). The possibility arose for him because for the first time, actuated by the fervent ideology of apocalyptically militant Protestantism and under a regime in which England might not unreasonably dream of imitating Augustan Imperial glory, the necessary individual literary capabilities and aspiration came together with a proud confidence in the range and capabilities of the English language at his disposal. Neither the actual range and competence in the language, nor the boundless confidence necessary to mobilize it, had been there for even the generation of poets just before Spenser, the generation of Googe, Turberville, Sackville, and Gascoigne. The century's education, steeping youth in a classicising educational humanism, made it inevitable that such ambitions as Spenser's would be poured into just such a Roman mold as the image of Cicero, for most ambitious youth, but for Spenser, the career of Vergil, instead. The mask of "Immerito" may have been a device of prudence for the author of critical reflections on state policy and the religious establishment in *The Shepheardes Calender*. It might have been the product of authorial anxiety about giving his work over from the patronage culture of manuscript circulation among a coterie to "the stigma of print."[51] It may have been the result of a real personal diffidence, or even the deliberate imitation, again, of the natural modesty of Maro, his great predecessor and pattern. But *The Shepheardes Calender* promised, and eleven years later, the first installment of the epic *Faerie Queene* demonstrated, that in Spenser linguistic and prosodic mastery had come together with the ambitious confidence to dream big dreams.

The turn taken by his poetic career was a sadly ironic one for the Vergilian aspirant, though.[52] By the time that the bitter, satiric, disillusioned *Complaints* volume followed hard upon the first installment of the great romantic heroic poem (1591 and 1590, respectively), there was apparently good reason for the poet to fear that his career-path had fallen instead into imitation of that other Augustan poet, whose style he had so aptly imitated and overgone in many passages of the 1590 *Faerie Queene*, but whose moral tone and frivolous wit so differed from his own and the Mantuan's highmindedness. Did Spenser, laboring in his Irish offices or managing his remote Irish estates, cherishing complaints of neglected art and resentments of courtly usage, reflect ruefully on the exiled and discountenanced Ovid of Pontine exile, and the *Tristia*? Spenser's fall from the Vergilian path to worldly success and influence may have been owing partly to his historical situation compared to that of his model. Vergil was perhaps fortunate to write for a Roman ruling class decimated and exhausted by the round of civil wars just ended. Certainly the factions around Elizabeth evince both greater vitality and more persistent friction, divided counsels, and relentless jockeying for position than are found in the enervated Senate or among Augustus' surviving counselors and friends. On the other hand, we may also suspect a lack of ductility in Spenser's commitments to his early patrons and friends. Moreover, beyond stubborn personal loyalties, at home and abroad the English poet tenaciously adhered to an aggressively Protestant stance, with its concomitant dream of military adventurism. That had been the policy of Leicester and Sidney, and was the program of both the rivals, Ralegh and Essex. But those designs all came to nothing in the face of the consistent disapproval of "the rugged forhead that with graue foresight/ Welds kingdomes causes, and affaires of state" and the prudent queen. In the end, never having enjoyed the immense success and popular adulation accorded his model in the "Lives," the English moral singer, memorialist of politic and noble deeds, and would-be private counselor to his Imperial Mistress, still resembled Vergil in his early death, leaving behind some grieving patrons, and his great national epic unfinished.

Kansas State University

NOTES

I want to take this opportunity to thank the Graduate School at Kansas State University, whose Faculty Development Funds helped support the research for this study, and the staffs of the University of Toronto Thomas Fisher Library and the Kenneth Spencer Research Library at the University of Kansas, whose Aitchison Collection was particularly useful, for their assistance and courtesy in making the Renaissance editions of Vergil cited here available to me. Figures 1, 2, and 4 are reproduced courtesy of the Department of Special Collections, Kenneth Spencer Research Library, University of Kansas; figure 3 courtesy of the Princeton University Libraries, and figure 5 courtesy of the Thomas Fisher Rare Book Library at the University of Toronto. Bill Oram, Jerry Dees, and Mihoko Suzuki have read and commented on various drafts, though any errors that remain are entirely my own responsibility, as are all paraphrases and translations of the Latin texts, unless otherwise explicitly credited.

1. "It is a commonplace of the dominant strain of Spenser criticism that Spenser reaches back past these poets [Dante and Petrarch] to the more celebrated narrative model of the *cursus virgilianus*." Joseph Loewenstein, "Spenser's Retrography: Two

Episodes in Post-Petrarchan Bibliography," in *Spenser's Life and the Subject of Biography*, ed. Judith Anderson, Donald Cheney, and David A. Richardson (Amherst, MA: University of Massachusetts Press, 1996), 115. For the *rota Virgilii*, see Patrick Cheney, "Spenser's Pastorals: *The Shepheardes Calender* and *Colin Clouts Come Home Againe*" in *The Cambridge Companion to Spenser*, ed. Andrew Hadfield (Cambridge: Cambridge University Press, 2001), 79 and fig. 1.

2.   Cheney in the *Cambridge Companion* calls attention to the awkward fact of what appears to be a "return to pastoral" in *Colin Clouts Come Home Again*, published in 1595 after the first installment of the epic poem, but maintains that really "Spenser did not 'return' to pastoral because he never left it" (82). Loewenstein declares that "Spenser's various engagements with the sonnet, that most Petrarchan instrument of literary autobiography, interrupt and even resist the press of his Virgilian self-identification." Moreover, he warns, "such 'career criticism' [as insistence on the *cursus virgilianus*] smoothes over the actual "uncertainties of composition, the mystery of the next thing," making each succeeding work appear the inevitable, foreordained product of the cursus. ("Spenser's Retrography," 115; Loewenstein treats the question of Spenser's adolescent involvement with van der Noot's *Theatre of Voluptuous Worldlings*, as well as the *Complaints* volume [1591], and the 1595 *Amoretti* and *Epithalamion* volume; see also Loewenstein, "A Note on the Structure of Spenser's *Amoretti*: Viper Thoughts," in *Spenser Studies*, 8 [1987]: 311–23). However, Cheney's criticism functions within a larger context, ingeniously saving the appearances of the Vergilian pattern by explaining Spenser's actual career pattern as an extension of the Vergilian model, and an artful accommodation of its generic givens to insistent literary and cultural currents that Vergil never felt, such as Augustinian Christianity, Sannazaro's eroticisation of pastoral, Petrarchism, and Ovidian epyllion or minor epic (see esp. 82–85). But for Loewenstein, "the critical insistence on Spenser's Virgilianism is a misrepresentation, albeit a misrepresentation of Spenser's own making" ("Spenser's Retrography," 115).

3.   *Spenser's Secret Career* (Cambridge: Cambridge University Press, 1993), 4.

4.   "Spenser's Lives, Spenser's Careers," in *Spenser's Life and the Subject of Biography*, 15.

5.   Ibid., 2.

6.   Rambuss, "Spenser's Lives, Spenser's Careers," 13, citing Marotti in *Patronage in the Renaissance* (Princeton, N.J.: Princeton University Press, 1981), ed. Guy Fitch Lytle and Stephen Orgel, 208.

7.   Among many other recent critics who have maintained or further developed the concept of Spenser's pursuit of the traditional "Vergilian career trajectory," I might single out here Richard Helgerson, with whose influential *Self-Crowned Laureates: Spenser, Jonson, Milton and the Literary System* (Berkeley: University of California Press, 1983) Rambuss is particularly concerned to engage; William Allan Oram in *Edmund Spenser* (New York: Twayne Publishers, 1997); F. J. Levy, "Spenser and Court Humanism," in *Spenser's Life and the Subject of Biography*, 65–80; David Lee Miller, "Spenser's Vocation, Spenser's Career," *ELH* 50 (1983): 209–15, and *The Poem's Two Bodies: The Poetics of the 1590 Faerie Queene* (Princeton, N.J.: Princeton University Press, 1988), 29ff.; and Patrick Cheney, in the chapter on "Spenser's Pastorals" from the *Cambridge Companion*, cited above, and in *Spenser's Famous Flight:*

A Renaissance Idea of a Literary Career (Toronto: University of Toronto Press, 1993), where, "not controverting a principle that most readers will readily accept (that Spenser follows Virgil in writing pastoral and epic) . . . [but] simply extending it" (46), he conflates the Vergilian career model with two others which he labels the Ovidian and the Augustinian, to produce what he calls an "Orphic" progression (see esp. 3–22, 28–38, 48–63, 77–78). Other recent critics have maintained that, in Cheney's words, "although the poet changes his mind about the progression of the Virgilian triad, he still circumscribes his career in forms derived from that triad" (*Spenser's Famous Flight*, 260, n. 29). See also the articles in the *Spenser Encyclopedia* mentioned by Cheney, *Spenser's Famous Flight*, 260, n. 27.

8. H. Nettleship edited *Ancient Lives of Vergil, with an Essay on the Poems of Vergil in Connection with His Life and Times* (Oxford: Clarendon Press, 1879). The "Life by Suetonius, originally prefixed to the Commentary by Aelius Donatus, and usually attributed to him," printed in its "uninterpolated form" (see Nettleship "Preface," sig. B2) is on 8–21, based on the tenth century cod. Sangallensis 862. For the "apocryphal matter" or interpolations, which include many of the stories favored by the Renaissance editors and illustrators of Vergil, see the *apparatus plenus* after the text given in Iacobus Brummer, ed. *Vitae Vergilianae* (Leipzig: Teubner, 1912). For a modern translation of both the uninterpolated "Life" and the apocryphal interpolations, see the valuable on-line site, Donatus, Aelius. *Life of Virgil*. Tr. David Wilson-Okamura. 1996. Online. Internet. 10 July 2002. Available http:www.virgil.org/vitae/a-donatus.htm. For convenience, this translation will be referred to in the notes below as "Wilson-Okamura," by paragraph numbers. Wilson-Okamura supplies a useful selected bibliography, as well. For an Elizabethan translation of the "Life" as usually circulated in Renaissance editions, see "Virgils life, set foorth, as it is supposed, by Aelius Donatus, and done into English" [by Thomas Twyne], in the Phaer-Twyne translation of *The whole .xii. Bookes of the Aeneidos of Virgill* (London, 1573), sigs. A3r-C2r.

9. Servius cited by Iodovus Badius Ascensius "in opera Vergiliana, quaedam praembula seu praenotamenta scitu digna," in the 1587 Froschauer printing of Vergil's *Opera* at Tiguri (sig. *5).

10. "'All his minde on honour fixed': The Preferment of Edmund Spenser," in *Spenser and the Subject of Biography*, 46. Brink's article provides a model of carefully scrupulous use of what relevant and analogous documentation can be assembled, and judicious inference and extrapolation from that base.

11. Donatus' Oxford editor, Colin Hardie, comments on the postclassical reputation of Vergil and the climate of opinion in which his most famous biographer worked, thus:

> Then in the fourth century Vergil emerged as the most absolute philosopher, the greatest orator, the norm of grammar, the crier (or "promoter" or "huckster") of eternal Rome, vindicator of the old gods, more divine than the gods themselves, whatever might be more than a man and a poet, whose true face no man unless Dante Alighieri [at a much later time, presumably] had made out. Indeed, the Christians wanted to convert Vergil, if not to the faith of Christ (Saint Jerome, *Epistles* 53.7), then to the practice, with

Vergilian passages stitched together so that under pressure they might express the Old and New Testaments. Donatus sucked in the dark atmosphere of such an age, indeed between the dreams of soothsayers and the perplexities [or "narrowness"] of grammarians, negligent on both sides of true history" ["quarto denique saeculo Vergilius philosophus absolutissimus evadit, orator maximus, grammaticae norma, Romae aeternae praeco, deorum veterum vindex, dis ipsis divinior, quidvis potius quam homo et poeta, cuius veram tandem faciem nemo nisi Dantes Alighieri dispexit. Christiani quoque Vergilium, si minus ad fidem Christi (S. Heronym. *Ep.* 53.7), in usum sane convertere volebant, consutis centonibus Vergilianis, ut Testamenta Vetus et Novum exprimerent. Talis saeculi crassum aera, quippe inter somnia sortilegorum et angustias grammaticorum, utrorumque res gestas neglegentium, hauriebat Donatus."]

    —Hardie, *Vitae Vergilianae antiquae. Vita Donati; Vita Servii; Vita Probiana; Vita Focae; S. Hieronymi excerpta* [Oxford: E Typographaeo Clarendoniano, 1957], xxi-xxii.

Because what was printed as Donatus' *Life* in the Renaissance was the result of a wholly uncritical process of accretion and elaboration on a text probably by Suetonius in the first place, the reader should consider that wherever in this article a reference is made to "Donatus' *Life,*" the proper name should be read as if in "scare quotes." On establishment of the text and authorship, see Hardie, "Praefatio," iii-v, ix-xii.

12. Giuliano Mambelli, *Gli Annali delle Edizione Virgilianae* (Florence: Leo S. Olschki, Editore, 1954) catalogues and describes most of the editions of Vergil referred to in this piece. For examples of the Renaissance veneration of the poet reflected in the magnificence and elaboration of editions, see the Gruninger edition, Strasbourg, 1502 (Mambelli 99), reproduced at Lyons in 1517 by Jacob Sachon, and in 1529 by Jean Crespin, with the same illustrations; the Stagninus edition from Venice, 1507 (M 110), in which "Il testo e inquadrato nel commento" ("the text is framed in commentary"), whose "graziose silografie" ("graceful woodcuts") are reproduced in M 141, the 1520 Venice edition from Georgii de Rusconibus and his press; the series of Junta editions from Venice including the important 1519 edition reproducing the 1502 Gruninger illustrations (also reproduced in the Junta edition of 1515); also M 166, the François Regnault 1529 Paris edition, described by Mambelli as having "Frontespizio istoriato con episodi delle note leggende del Virgilio"; and the 1532–33 Junta edition from Venice, M166, noted by Mambelli as "assai intersessanti" because it represents the transition from Gothic illustration to the style of the Renaissance, and brings "the curious anachronism of showing Greek warriors at the siege of Troy with artillery"; finally, see the extremely handsome Junta edition—"una delle piu belle e pregiate edizioni figurate del sec. XVI"—from Venice of 1537, M 179, in which text there are one hundred thirteen woodcuts, of which thirty-five, "magnificent illustrations of the life of the fields and farms, adorn the *Georgics* and the *Eclogues,* while the rest illustrate the *Aeneid* and the works attributed to Vergil" (quotations from Mambelli).

13. E.g., the 1587 edition published by Froschauer at Tiguri (not in Mambelli; consulted at the Kenneth Spencer Research Library at the University of Kansas).

14.   [Certe, quamvis Aristoteles revocarit ab exilio pulsos a Socrate poetas, nolo
tamen hac sola auctoritate defensionem fulcire, sed nec Catulli, qui castum
mavult poetam, quam poema:] sed spondere ex Romanorum monumentis
paratus sum, Maronem non magis carminis suavitate & gravitate, gratiam Im-
peratorum, Iuliae familie, totius denique, rupta virtute invidia, populi Romani,
quam insita nativaque comitate, verecundia, a qua & cognomentum duxit,
liberalitate, mansuetudine meruisse: reculae scilicet amicis praebitorem muni-
ficum, in officiis, beneficiisque dandis ad servorum suorum eruditionem usque
nulli sui moduli, sortisque homini comparandum. Nec temere igitur a pru-
dentissimo Imperatore, quem pro tuba suae laudis habebat poeta, in intimam
familiaritatem admissus videri debet, quem non de numeris solum, & re Philo-
sophica, sed saepe de polita, de reddenda etiam populo republica, consuluerit.
    —P. Virgilius Maro, Et in eum Commentationes, & Paralipomena Germani
    Valentis Guellii, P.P. Eiusdem Virgilij Appendix, cum Josephi Scaligeri Com-
    mentariis & castigationibus. Antverpiae, Ex officina Christophori Plantini,
    Architypographi Regii. 1575.

From the editor, Guellius', defense of his efforts, sig. [*5ᵛ]. Humanist apologetics
of this sort has a general basis in the desire to respond to Plato's censure of poets,
and a specific impetus in aspersions upon Vergil's personal life and morals arising
from references to his affection for his slaves Cebetes and Alexander, and from his
account of the love of Corydon for Alexis in the second Eclogue.
15.   Repeated by Badius Ascensius in prefatory matter to the Froschauer printing of
Vergil's Opera, Tiguri, 1587, sig. [*6]; Hardie, Vitae Vergilianae antiquae, 4–5:37–38;
Wilson-Okamura 25.
16.   Alexander C. Judson, The Life of Edmund Spenser (Baltimore: The Johns Hopkins University Press, 1945), 8.
17.   "Quantum sit in eo eruditionis reconditae docti norunt commentatores; in
eo, nec ethica, nec politica, nec oeconomica, nec Astronomica, nec Geographica,
nec Theologica desiderantur; ex eo gentium mores, terrarum, ac marium situs, bel-
lorum strategemata, militare robur, facundiae vires, deorum sacra ediscuntur est
re vera Virgilius omnis eruditionis promptuarium. . . . " Alexander Ross, Virgilii
Evangelisantis Christiados Libri XIII, Londoni, Typis Iohannis Legate, sumptibus Ri-
cardi Thrale, 1638 (M1631, classed there among "Centoni Virgiliani;" widely reprinted on the Continent during the seventeenth and eighteenth centuries), (sig. A4)
18.   "Virgilius Maro parentibus modicis fuit, & praecipue patre Marone: quem
quidam opificem figulum: plures Magi cujusdam viatoris initio mercenarium: mox
ob industriam generum tradiderunt: quem cum agricolationi, reique rusticae curandis
reculam auxit." (From Tib.Clavdii Donati ad Tib. Clavdivm Maximvm Dona-
tionum Filivm, de P. Virgilii Maronis Vita, in P. Virgilii Maronis Opera; nunc emendati-
ora. Lugduni Batavorum, ex officina Elzeviriana, 1636, sig. **; text checked against
Venice Junta edition of 1537 (M179), sig. +ij). Cf. Hardie, Vitae Vergilianae antiquae,
2:1; Wilson-Okamura, unnumbered first paragraph. For the last sentence, Hardie's
Oxford text has even more significantly, "mox ob industriam generum tradiderunt,
egregieque substantiae silvis coemendis et apibus curandis auxisse reculam" [2:3–5].
19.   " . . . paulopost Neapolim transijt. Vbi cum litteris & graecis & latinis vehementissimam operam dedisset, tandem omni cura, omnique studio indulsit medi-
cinae & mathematicis" (from M 141, Publii Vergilii Bucolica, Georgica, Aeneis cum

Servii Commentariis . . . , Venetiis, G. de Rusconibus, 1520; cf. M 179, sig. +ij; parts of the text correspond to Wilson-Okamura 20, 44 [interpolations]).

20.   Hardie, *Vitae Vergilianae antiquae*, 3: 7–13. The dream is in the Rusconibus edition of 1520 (M141); also in Junta 1537 ed. (M179); Wilson-Okamura 5.

21.   M179, sig. +ij; M141, sig. aij-aij°. The "witticism" turns on the bread ration given to Vergil on Augustus' order, and then augmented. Vergil tells Augustus that his father must have been a miller. The Imperator is aghast. How does he know? Vergil says that again and again, Augustus hands out rewards of bread—which is the office either of a miller or of a miller's son. "Attente expectabat Augustus quidnam diceret. At ille, quantum ego rem intelligere possum pistoris filius es inquit. Obstupuerat Caesar & statim quo id pacto fieri potuerit, animo voluebat. Interrumpens Virgilius, audi inquit, quo pacto id conijcio. Cum quaedam enunciaverim praedixerimque quae intelligi scirique non nisi ab eruditissimis, summisque viris potuissent Tu princeps orbis, iterum & iterum panes in mercedem dari iussisti, quod quidem, aut pistoris, aut nati pistore officium erat. Aut deinceps inquit Caesar, non a pistore, sed a rege magnanimo dona feres. Placuit Caesar Caesari facetia, illumque plurimi fecit, & Pollioni commendavit." (M179, +ij; cf. Wilson-Okamura 20 [interpolations].

22.   In the story about Vergil first being noticed because of what was essentially knowledge of animal husbandry and breeding genetics, Chetwood rationalizes on cultural/historical grounds the greater cleverness of the Vergil figure compared to the Romans he advises. Chetwood observes that "the Romans knew least of Natural Causes of any civiliz'd Nation in the World: And those Meteors, and Prodigies which cost them incredible Sums to expiate, might easily have been accounted for, by no very profound Naturalist," whereas Vergil added to his native brilliance presumably both his own medical studies and whatever he may have learned of astrology and medicine from his father's lore (*The Works of John Dryden*, vol. 5, *Poems: The Works of Virgil in English, 1697* [Berkeley: University of California Press, 1987], ed. William Frost, 12). Illustrating the survival of credulity alongside enlightenment rationalization, Chetwood takes the story in Donatus as the official explanation put forth to cover Vergil's new intimacy with the future Augustus, opining that in fact, on the basis of "Predictions of *Cicero,* and *Catulus*" recounted in Suetonius' *Life of Augustus,* cap. 94, and having heard of "*Assyrian* and *Egyptian* Prophecies, (which, in truth, were no other but the *Jewish*), that about that time a great King was to come into the World," Vergil actually first won Augustus' favor at this time by predicting that he was the prophesied great ruler, and would gain the empire (*Works of John Dryden*, 5:12).

23.   Quoted in "P. Vergilii Maronis Vita per Aelium Donatum Celebrem Grammaticum Edita" in the Rusconibus edition of the *Bucolics, Georgics,* and *Aeneid,* Venice, 1520, sig. [aijv]. In other eds., as well; cf. M 179, sig. +ij.; M141 sig. aijv;Hardie, 4: 33–36.

24.   Paraphrased from passages in the *Life* that reveal the continuing fascination the intimacy of literary genius with socially and politically powerful persons exercises over lovers of literature:

Bucolica trienio Asinij Pollionis suasu perfecit . . . . Hunc Pollionem maxime amavit Maro: & dilectus ab eo magna munera tulit. Quippe qui invitatus

coenam captus pulchritudine & diligentia Alexandri Pollionis pueri eum
dono accepit . . . . C. Asinium, Cornelium Gallum oratorem clarum & poetam non mediocrem miro amore dilexit Virgilius . . . . Verum usque adeo
hunc Gallum Virgilius amarat: vt quartus Georgicorum a medio usque ad
finem eius laudem continerat, quem postea iubente Augusto in Aristaei
fabulam conmutavit . . . . Cui in multo post perfecta demum materia treis
omnino libros recitavit, secundum videlicet, quartum, & sextum. Sed hunc
praecipue ob Octaviam, quae cum recitationi interesset ad illos de filio suo
versus, Tu Marcellis eris, defecisse fertur. Atque aegre refocillata dena sester-
tia pro singulo versu Virgilio dari iussit . . . .

    —Rusconibus ed. from Venice, 1520, sigs. aiii^v-aiiij); Wilson-Oka-
mura 91.

Chetwood's comment is in *Works of John Dryden*, 5. 27.
25.   Elzevir ed., 1636, sig. [★★★6^v]; late version retold in Chetwood, *Works of John Dryden*, 5.22. See M 179, sig. +iij; M 141, sig. [a^v]; Wilson-Okamura 186 and note 3. The original debate between Agrippa and Maecenas is recounted in Dio Cassius (and reprinted in a number of Renaissance editions of Machiavelli's *The Prince*, sometimes without any clear indication that it is not somehow an appendix to that work), but in Dio, Vergil plays no part in the discussion. See *Dio's Roman History*, trans. Earnest Cary (London and Cambridge, MA: Heinemann and Harvard University Press, 1955), The Loeb Classical Library, Book LII, 78–185.
26.   F. J. Levy, "Spenser and Court Humanism," in *Spenser's Life and the Subject of Biography*, 72. Jonson's vision is firmly based on details given in Donatus' *Life*; Chetwood retails the Augustan version of this poet's dream in the Dryden/Tonson edition of 1697:

> But Learned Men then liv'd easy and familiarly with the great: *Augustus* himself would sometimes sit down betwixt *Virgil* and *Horace*, and say jeast-ingly, that he sate betwixt Sighing and Tears, alluding to the Asthma of one, and Rheumatick Eyes of the other; he would frequently Correspond with them, and never leave a Letter of theirs unanswered: Nor were they under the constraint of formal Superscriptions in the beginning, nor of violent Superlatives at the close of their Letter: The invention of these is a Modern Refinement." (sig. ★4v)
>   —*Works of John Dryden*, 5.22

27.   On his popularity and being followed by crowds, Hardie 4:37–5:41; M 141 sig. aij^v; M 179 sig. +ij: "cetera sane vita et ore et animo tam probum constat, . . . si quando Romae, quo rarissime commeabat, viseretur in publico, sectantes demon-strantesque se subterfugeret in proximum tectum;" on Augustus' and his own friends' generosity, and Vergil's houses, Hardie 5:41–45: "bona autem cuiusdam exulantis offerente Augusto non sustinuit accipere. Possedit prope centies sestertium ex liber-alitatibus amicorum habuitque domum Romae Esquiliis iuxta hortos Maecenatianos, quamquam secessu Campaniae Siciliaeque plurimum uteretur;" M 179 adds: "Quae-cunque ab Augusto peteret, repulsam nunquam habuit" (sig. +ij; also in M 141,

sig. [aij^v]. See Wilson-Okamura 39. On the library, Wilson-Okamura 186, Elzevir ed. sig. [★★★4^v], duplicated with verbal variants in M 179 and M141: "Eius biblio-theca non minus aliis doctis patebat, ac sibi: illudque Euripidis antiquam saepe usurpabat, . . . hoc est, communia amicorum esse omnia;" on Vergil's heirs, see Hardie 10:141ff.; Wilson-Okamura 138. Ogilby's unacknowledged paraphrase of Donatus and other materials in the prefatory matter of his 1654 edition includes most of these details, and concludes with the laurel tree story, which, like many of the other more fabulous "facts," is from the interpolations and does not appear in Hardie's modern edition.

28.   For two well-known examples of humanist concern with appropriate literary and monumental funerary recognition, and their relation to a survival in memory after death, see Milton's reflections on Mansus's relations with Tasso and that patron's memorial commemoration of his friend and client, described in *Manso*, and the whole impetus of *Lycidas* as literary memorial, in each case accompanied by anxious reflections by Milton concerning his own "destined urn." The most famous histori-cal re-imagination of the impulse is, of course, Browning's "The Bishop Orders his Tomb at St. Praxed's."

29.   Anne Lake Prescott suggests in a personal communication that the goose may not symbolize the stupidity of the pretenders to art, but represents instead the guard-ians of the Forum who saved Rome from the Goths, here aligned with Vergil and imperial power against bad art. The best source for more on the Renaissance Human-ist tradition of Vergil, and the pictorial representations, is Annabel Patterson, *Pastoral and Ideology: Virgil to Valéry* (Berkeley: University of California Press, 1987), ch. 2, esp. 92–106, "Sebastian Brant: Illustration as Exegesis." For Spenser and the tradition see 106–132.

30.   "The Life of Virgil" prefixed to Ogilby translation in 1654 ed., Wing V610,—pages unnumbered, without signature indication. See also Elzevir ed., 1636, sig. [★★★4^v]-[★★★5]; in M 179, sig. +iij; M 141, sig. [aiiij^v]-[av]; Wilson-Okamura 186.

31.   Elzevir ed., 1636, sig. [★★★5^v]. M179, sig. +iij; M141, sig. [av]; Wilson-Oka-mura 186.

32.   G. K. Hunter, *John Lyly* (Cambridge, MA: Harvard University Press, 1962), 24.

33.   "The figure of Cicero—*that archetypal novus homo*—promoting public virtue and putting down public vice by the power of his philosophical eloquence, was one that remained central to the education of the whole period" (Hunter, *John Lyly*, 25, emphasis mine). Spenser's friend Harvey valued highly Cicero's life and career and his conduct of his affairs as a career model. This admiration is implicit in many of his comments on the value and preeminence of Cicero's style, recorded in the *Marginalia*. Cf. particularly his comment on Cicero as a *novus homo* who made his own fortunes. See *Gabriel Harvey's Marginalia*, collected and edited by G. C. Moore Smith (Stratford-Upon-Avon: Shakespeare Head Press, 1913), 198: 4–19. In "Spenser and Court Humanism," F. J. Levy affirms Cicero's centrality to the human-ist ideal, and indeed asserts that "the Virgil of the Renaissance was himself a con-struct, made up of the ancients' ideas of the poet, moral philosopher, and orator, and owing rather more to Cicero than to Virgil himself" (74; see also 77–78).

34.   Hunter, *John Lyly*, 25

35.   Quoted from the dedication of Cooper's *Thesaurus* [1565] in Hunter, *John Lyly*, 28–29.

36.   Jon Quitslund neatly characterizes Harvey as one "for whom margins, flyleaves, and odd sheets of paper were apt to serve as hallway mirrors for a man always preparing to do something other than writing" in "Questionable Evidence in the *Letters* of 1580 between Gabriel Harvey and Edmund Spenser" in *Spenser' Life and the Subject of Biography* (84–85). A judicious and sympathetic study of Harvey's application of his learning to practical policy and affairs is to be found in Lisa Jardine and Anthony Grafton, "'Studied for Action': How Gabriel Harvey Read His Livy," *Past and Present*, No. 129 (November, 1990): 30–78.

37.   *Gabriel Harvey's Marginalia*, 142. The marginalia are relentlessly concerned with cultivating worldly knowledge, as did Marchiavelli and Aretino, in order to repair the deficiencies of "Schollars, & common youthes, euen amongst ye lustiest, & brauist courtiers" (147); with cultivating eloquence, fortitude, and audacity in place of the scholar's melancholy and retirement (e.g., 142, 143, 145, 149, 156); and with the superiority of the least of the Roman arts—industry, vigilance, shrewdness or skill in the seasons of both peace and war, and virtue both in the household and in service abroad—to the greatest of the Greek arts of letters (141). Here, too, Harvey records his anxiety that "Common Lerning, & ye name of A good schollar, was neuer so much contemn'd, & abiectid of princes, Pragmaticals, & common Gallants, as nowadayes; jnsomuch that it necessarily concernith, & importith ye learnid ether praesently to hate y^r books; or actually to insinuate, & enforce themselues, by uery special, & singular propertyes of emploiable, & necessary vse, in all affaires, as well priuate, as publique, amounting to any commodity, ether oeconomical, or politique" (151).

38.   See Virginia F. Stern, *Gabriel Harvey: His Life, Marginalia and Library* (Oxford: Clarendon Press, 1979), ch. 3, and 31.

39.   Hunter, 33, citing R. M. Sargent, *At the Court of Queen Elizabeth* (1935), 6, and Eleanor Rosenberg, *Leicester, Patron of Letters* (1955), 179, 323ff.

40.   See Stern, ch. 5, esp. 48–69, for Harvey's maneuverings for recognition, connections with Leicester and the Sidney circle, and use of published literary texts in the attempt to gain notice and advance his career. On the Spenser-Harvey correspondence, see also "letter as genre" and "letters, Spenser's and Harvey's" in *The Spenser Encyclopedia*, ed. A. C. Hamilton, et al. (Toronto: University of Toronto Press, 1990), and Jon Quitslund, "Questionable Evidence in the *Letters* of 1580 between Gabriel Harvey and Edmund Spenser," 81–98, as well as Joseph Loewenstein's treatment in "Spenser's Retrography," esp. 100–102.

41.   Joseph Loewenstein, "Spenser's Retrography," esp. 100–102.

42.   See Vincent P. Carey and Clare L. Carroll, "Factions and Fictions: Spenser's Reflections of and on Elizabethan Politics," in *Spenser's Life and the Subject of Biography*, esp. 37–39; Jean Brink, however, thinks that Harvey himself was the key link in connecting Spenser with Lord Grey, probably through his acquaintance with Sir Edward Denny; see " 'All his minde on honour fixed': The Preferment of Edmund Spenser," in *Spenser's Life and the Subject of Biography,* 46, 55–60; Brink, passim, for further details of Gabriel Harvey's career strategies.

43.   See Patrick Cheney's treatment of public themes in the pastorals, *The Cambridge Companion to Spenser*, 80–81.

44.   On biographical facts, for Harvey, see Stern, passim; for Spenser, see the now-dated *The Life of Edmund Spenser*, by Alexander Judson (Baltimore: Johns Hopkins University Press, 1945), the entry in *The Spenser Encyclopedia*, s.v. "Spenser, Edmund," by Ruth Mohl; articles in *Spenser's Life and the Subject of Biography* referred to throughout these notes, and the Chronology and convenient summary of facts and speculations in William Allan Oram, *Edmund Spenser* (New York: Twayne Publishers, 1997), xiii–xvi and 1–24.

45.   Judson, *Life of Spenser*, 1–7; Elzevir ed. 1636, sig. **v; cf. M 141, sig. Aij; M 179, sig. +ij; Wilson-Okamura, unnumbered first paragraph, and 20.

46.   Jean R. Brink, " 'All his minde on honour fixed,' " 54–55 for the early date of Spenser's service in Young's household. Thanks especially to Bill Oram for straightening out some of my chronology for Spenser's patronage connections.

47.   Rambuss, in *Spenser's Life and the Subject of Biography*, 9.

48.   Rambuss, ibid., 12.

49.   "Spenser never understood the political system at court well enough to manipulate it." F. J. Levy, "Spenser and Court Humanism," 75.

50.   See Levy, 74ff.

51.   The title, of course, of J. W. Saunders's ground-breaking essay, "The Stigma of Print: A Note on the Social Bases of Tudor Poetry," *Essays in Criticism* 1 (1951):139–64; Joseph Loewenstein develops the idea ingeniously and suggestively in "Spenser's Retrography," 119–130.

52.   "If Spenser was England's Virgil, he became a Virgil speaking from the margins rather than the center. For all its successes, his life is the biography of an outsider." William Allan Oram, *Edmund Spenser*, 2. F. J. Levy summarizes:

> To accomplish his aim, Colin needs an intermediary, a Maecenas indeed, but more than a Maecenas. A patron could open the doors to Elisa's court, and Elisa herself would serve brilliantly as the jewel at the epic's center. What was still needed, however, was a way of setting her in motion, as Virgil had Aeneas . . . . For Spenser, too, the ideal epic celebrated heroic action—in his view, the destruction of the Antichrist. As the queen could not lead the forces herself, she required a surrogate. Leicester, "the worthy whome shee loveth best," might have been able to wield "the stubborne stroke of stronger stounds [blows]" had he been turned free. Instead, with the deaths of Leicester and Walsingham, the cautious Burghley prevailed . . . . The result was that "learning lies unregarded, / And men of armes doo wander unrewarded" (*Ruines of Time*, 452–53, 440–41). In other words, in so arid a climate neither of the two components traditionally making up the perfect courtier could survive.
>
> —F. J. Levy, "Spenser and Court Humanism," 73.

BENEDICT S. ROBINSON

The "Secret Faith" of Spenser's Saracens

The Faerie Queene V.viii, Mercilla marshals her forces against "the Souldan" in a fight usually understood as an allegory of the invasion of England by Philip II's Armada. But why represent Philip II as a sultan? In this essay, I argue that Spenser assimilates Catholicism to Islam by writing together narratives of crusade with Protestant apocalyptics, which emphasized the identity of Islam and Catholicism as forms of false belief. He thereby refashioned medieval heroic poetry for a Protestant politics, offering a complex exploration of the fissures of religious identity after the Reformation. This essay forms part of a larger project arguing that English poets and playwrights responded to the roughly contemporary experiences of Ottoman expansion and Christian schism by adapting, rewriting, or resisting the conventions of "Saracen" romance. Fragments of romance echo through a variety of texts, even those seemingly remote from romance. I read this as evidence of an ongoing engagement with problems of religious and national identity in an age of Christian religious warfare and increasing diplomatic and commercial contact with the Islamic world.

NEAR THE END OF BOOK I of *The Faerie Queene*, as his Redcross Knight prepares for the final assault on the dragon, Spenser glances forward to a future battle in which his Faery Queen will face a pagan king in a kind of misplaced crusade:

> Faire Goddesse lay that furious fit aside,
> Till I of warres and bloudy Mars do sing,
> And Briton fields with Sarazin bloud bedyde,
> Twixt that great faery Queene and Paynim king.[1]

37

When was British soil stained with Saracen blood? Redcross does fight a series of Saracens in Book I, but the fights remain inconclusive and the knight of holiness abandons them in order to pursue his dragon. Not until the middle of Book V does Spenser offer this promised battle, in Arthur's fight with the "Souldan"—that is, a sultan, a "Paynim king," the archaic spelling of whose title links him to both the Islamic world and the conventional representation of that world in romance.

Saracens in fact populate *The Faerie Queene*, appearing not just in Books I and V but in every book but Book III, that is, in every book in which Arthur appears in the eighth canto to rescue the questing knights. In *The Faerie Queene*—as in so many other heroic poems of the Middle Ages and Renaissance—the action in some sense turns on the defeat of Saracens. But Spenser critics have paid very little attention to these Saracens. Even *The Spenser Encyclopedia* does not include any article on "Saracens," "Turks," or "Islam," and the Souldan himself is discussed only in the entry on Adicia, and only to argue that he represents Philip II of Spain.[2]

I do not want to deny that reading. But I do want to argue that in it the Saracen becomes invisible in ways that obscure a significant dimension of Spenser's meaning. There was plenty of reason for Spenser to think about and represent Islam. For two centuries the Ottoman empire had been expanding from a small sultanate to an empire that stretched from Hungary to North Africa and dominated much of the Mediterranean. Even the Christian victory at Lepanto in 1570 had little lasting significance, since by the following year the Turks had refurbished their fleet and used it to capture Cyprus, an event that probably still resonates in *Othello*.[3] English readers eagerly bought books describing the plight of Christians living under the Turks, while parish churches took up collections for the redemption of captives, and preachers warned against the dangers of converting to Islam, or "turning Turk." The Ottoman military advances slowed after the 1570s, but the fears inspired by the Turks did not, as "Turkish" pirates—notoriously including English renegades—raided coastlines as far away as England itself.

The significance of this Turkish threat is justly receiving growing critical attention. But I will argue that there is more to be said about Spenser's Saracens than either literary conventionality or a direct response to Turkish power allows. When Spenser figures Philip II as a sultan, he uses a Saracen to represent not only an Islamic but also a Catholic enemy: he assimilates Catholicism to Islam by writing together medieval narratives of crusade against the Saracens with Protestant apocalyptic histories, which emphasized the identity of

Islam and Catholicism as manifestations of Antichrist and forms of false belief.[4] Spenser appropriates romance for a Protestant politics, to suggest through allegory a holy war fought against multiple forms of faithlessness, and to investigate the sense of identity offered by this vision of an embattled Protestant community. In effect, the conflict of Christians and Saracens is rewritten to accommodate a third term that divides the Christian camp. Through this rewriting of romance, Spenser explores the problems of a Christendom at war with itself, and a Protestant England renegotiating its relationships with both the Catholic and Muslim worlds. What we can see here is not only one more dimension of Spenser's allegory but also and more significantly how his generic choices in *The Faerie Queene* are themselves complex interventions into the question of Christian identity in the sixteenth century.

After Luther, both Reformation and Counter-Reformation polemicists turned the representations of Islamic faithlessness against Christian enemies: both sides accused each other of fomenting schism for worldly ends, as "Mahomet" had done in his own time. As Christendom waged religious war against itself, poets like Tasso and Spenser turned to the medieval romances of crusade in an attempt to adapt that older narrative frame to the contemporary history of Christian religious war.[5] For Spenser, this meant an effort to come to terms with crusade narrative itself, both to reconceive it for a new moment, but also finally to question whether it could provide an adequate narrative within which to frame the dilemmas of Protestant faith.

This process of questioning was already embedded within medieval romance, which constantly interrogates its own terms of difference. Even in the chansons de geste—which provided the stories for a series of Middle English romances—difference is always unstable: Ganelon's complicity with the Saracens, registered in his taste for Alexandrian silk, reveals the border between self and other to be permeable, just as the noble behavior of a Saladin quietly reproves a Christendom that fails to fulfill its own aspirations.[6] Romance already offered complex considerations of identity and difference. But sixteenth-century pressures taxed its resources to the point of crisis.

In tracing Spenser's uses of crusade narrative, I want to emphasize that anyone interested in early modern representations of the Turks or of Islam must take into account the impact of the Reformation on the categories and images of Christian identity and un-Christian difference. It is essential to recognize the importance of religious imperatives for understanding the figure of "the Turk" in sixteenth- and seventeenth-century literature: the word "Turk," like the word "Saracen," primarily meant "Muslim," while to "turn Turk" meant to convert to Islam.[7] At the same time, I will argue that anyone interested in the Reformation must pay attention to the Turks. Discussions of Islam preoccupy some of the most central Reformation texts. This is not an incidental historical pressure.[8] In the Middle Ages, Christian identity was frequently articulated in opposition to Saracen faithlessness; as I hope to show, the presence of Islam in Reformation texts signals an effort to transform these older notions of religious identity for a world in which the unity of Latin Christendom had been fractured.

When Spenser evokes and transforms crusade narrative, he engages this contest over the forms of faithlessness. Attending to this dynamic expands our sense of the cultural significances of romance in the early modern period, and shows the importance of romance for thinking about Christian identity after the Reformation. I also hope to open up a historical sense of Spenser's aesthetic choices, to show how his poem, by situating itself with respect to the conventions of romance, explores the meanings those conventions could have in the post-Reformation world. Spenser's engagement with contemporary history is not only a matter of topical allegory: Spenser explores history as a problem of narrative, of the self and its action in the world, and he engages that problem through his uses of a form itself already saturated with imaginative and historical significance. In this essay I hope to draw out some of that significance.[9]

*

The "Saracen" has a long history. Originally the Roman name for the nomads of Syria and Arabia, and a word itself of uncertain origin, over the course of the Middle Ages "Saracen" became a term for all unbelievers, although one primarily associated with the Muslims. From Jerome on, the name was understood as a spurious claim to descent from Sara by a people properly identified as "Agarens," the children of Hagar; at stake in this false etymology are competing claims to election and a special relationship to the divine, claims that were put to judgment in romance.[10] In poetry, the Saracens were associated with a series of deviations: pride, blasphemy, monstrousness, cannibalism, lust, an unjust excess of wealth and power.[11] But their most recognizable trait is their idolatry. The romance Saracen worships a pantheon of gods including "Mahound," as well as "Apollin," "Jupiter le grant," "Ascarot," and "Alcaron."[12] The romances

that feature the Saracens encode, to varying degrees, a crusading impulse, a pressure for the conquest or assimilation of the Saracen that
frequently provides closure for the text. If this is clearly true of a
poem like *The Sowdone of Babylon*, it is true also of Ariosto's *Orlando
Furioso*, which, for all its irony, fits its stories into a narrative that
moves from the siege of Paris to the capture of an African city. The
presence of Saracens in the text suggests the ethos of heroic action
against the infidel, however the text negotiates that ethos.[13]

When Tasso attempted to merge romance with classical epic, he
also in a sense restored romance to the history that produced it by
taking as his subject the first crusade itself. He thereby reliteralized
the crusading impulse in romance, and at the same time suggested
the lack of fit between that heroic narrative and the reality of the
contemporary religious wars.[14] The plot of the *Gerusalemme Liberata*
strains between the linear, end-directed story of crusade and the wan-
derings and deceptions that must be overcome for crusade to be
possible: in this way the broad narrative structures of the text themselves focus attention on the ideal of unity and the problem of dissension.[15]

The narrative details of the poem also suggest the pressure of contemporary conflict on this poetry of holy war. In Canto viii, Tasso
depicts a rebellion that allegorizes how religious schism has left the
Christian nations vulnerable to the Turks. Under the influence of
the fury Alecto, the Italian knight Argillan dreams that Godfrey has
betrayed his own army. Argillan incites the soldiers against Godfrey
in a revolt whose geography identifies it with the religious politics
of the sixteenth century: Argillan himself was "bred vp in braules and
fraies" on the banks of the Tronto, a region notorious for resistance
to papal control, and his rebellion spreads to the Italians, the Swiss,
and the English.[16] Tasso thereby links political restlessness in Italy to
the Protestant nations and their refusal of papal sovereignty.

Another sequence of events in the same canto further suggests
the connection between sixteenth-century religious politics and the
problem of Islam. The canto begins with the arrival of a messenger
who relates the tragic deaths of Prince Sven of Denmark and his
soldiers at the hands of Solyman and the Turks. When the messenger
finishes his story, Godfrey laments how "so friendly and valorous a
troop one brief moment has taken away, and a little ground swal-
lowed up." Crucially, at this point Godfrey identifies the messenger
not as a Dane but a "German." The sudden disappearance of a troop
of loyal soldiers is linked to Germany, itself partly withdrawn from
Catholic Christendom by the Lutheran schism.[17] This disappearance
of the German or Danish allies, moreover, occurs when Solyman and

the Turks first appear. Facing the Turks alone, the Germans are wiped out, in a story that must have recalled for any sixteenth-century reader the contemporary expansion of the Turkish empire at the cost of the "German" one.[18] At the same time, that story heightens the significance of Argillan's "Protestant" rebellion. Crusade demands unity because otherwise the Turks will demolish each Christian kingdom one by one. Protestantism eviscerates any hope of unity.

Tasso turns the ideology of crusade against the Reformation. The contemporary history underlying this is signaled by the role of Solyman, namesake of the sixteenth-century Suleiman who fought the Habsburgs in Eastern Europe and the Mediterranean. A new crusade against the Turks would solve at once the threat of Protestant schism and of an Ottoman invasion of Italy, famously attempted in the 1480–81 capture of Otranto and again in the 1565 siege of Malta. Tasso's use of crusade history encodes a Counter-Reformation polemic that blames the Protestants for the continued power of the Turks.

The real enemy, for Tasso, is the enemy within, the susceptibility to temptation, the desire to stray, that leads his heroes from their task; his Saracens, perhaps as a result, are allowed a kind of nobility associated with classical epic, though their refusal of Christianity dooms them to suffer the loss of their world. Spenser's Saracens, on the other hand, offer little to be admired. They embody violence and faithlessness and they are punished with an equal violence that admits only the most perfunctory expressions of pity.[19] The starkness of the representation may in part explain why Spenser's Saracens have received so little commentary. But I want to suggest that if we attend to the role Spenser's Saracens play in his text, we will see a narrative complexity no less sophisticated than Tasso's representational complexity.

In *The Faerie Queene*, the path toward the moral self-fashioning of the knights repeatedly involves the overcoming of Saracens: in the eighth cantos of Books I, II, IV, V, and VI, Arthur fights Saracens and rescues the knights so that they can continue their quests. Arthur, as various critics have recognized, often functions as a figure for divine grace: he appears in the eighth canto because eight is the number of regeneration; he carries the shield of faith; and he is at various times associated with divine, redemptive power.[20] His enemies are described as Saracens in the eighth cantos even if, like Pyrochles and Cymochles in Book II, they are never so described elsewhere. As in Tasso, the Saracens are caught up with the representation of grace insofar as they are the prime objects of Arthur's divinely inspired violence.

In two crucial episodes in Book V, Spenser elaborates on these suggestions, using crusade narrative as a means of exploring the conflicts of a faith that seeks expression in active virtue. In Canto ii, Artegall learns about the crimes of Pollente, a "cursed cruell Sarazin" who keeps the passage of a bridge (V.ii.4). This figure of unjust subjection lives with his daughter Munera, who has heaped up her father's spoils until she has exceeded "many Princes" in wealth (V.ii.9). When Artegall hears of this, he seeks out Pollente and strikes off his head. Pollente dies cursing God: he is "the Carle vnblest," and both he and his daughter are called blasphemers (V.ii.12; 18–20). Spenser describes Pollente and Munera as typical Saracens: if they are, as Merlin Neff argued, figures for kinds of financial extortion that distort social hierarchy by offering power disproportionate to rank, the fight against those secular perversions of justice is imagined as a crusade.[21]

In Canto viii Spenser depicts another battle with a Saracen that reinforces the point that injustice is a religious as well as a social violation: here we see the war between Mercilla and the Souldan won for the queen of justice by Arthur and Argetall.[22] The Souldan himself is a clear figure of faithlessness, a "miscreant" who has neither "religion nor fay,/But makes his God of his vngodly pelfe,/And Idols serues" (V.viii.19). Like Pollente, he values gold over God, and in fact conflates gold with God, in his idolatry; unlike Pollente, he retains a strong religious function in that he is defeated only when Arthur resorts to the shield of faith, a weapon he has not used since Book I.[23]

The Souldan is Mercilla's great enemy, a "mighty man" who "seekes to subuert her Crowne and dignity": "her good knights" he "either spoiles, if they against him stand,/Or to his part allures, and bribeth vnder hand" (V.viii.18). On the one hand, this description suggests the sultan in Istanbul, who fought against Christian armies but also notoriously lured Christians to his cause and religion.[24] But at the same time, the description also looks to an enemy closer at hand: Philip of Spain and his Armada. A. C. Hamilton suggests that the Souldan's chariot figures the Spanish ships, the scattering of his horses the scattering of those ships, and his blasphemous "banning" the excommunication of Elizabeth, the religious and legal justification for the Armada. As René Graziani argues, the Souldan's appearance recalls Philip's *impresa*, which depicts Apollo in his chariot—an image Spenser inverts into Phaeton's wild ride.[25] If the fight with Pollente suggests that faith should result in the active struggle against injustice, the fight with the Souldan extends that sense into the political world and the war with Spain supported by the godly and by the Leicester faction at court.

The evidence for this allegory seems conclusive. But no one has explained why Philip should be allegorized as a sultan. In terms of his representation, nothing distinguishes this Saracen from any of the other Saracens in Spenser's text. Between representation and allegory, however, Spenser conflates Islam and Catholicism, suggesting that the English war against Spain was itself a kind of crusade. The idea of a crusade against Spain was not a new one: Urban II preached a holy war against the Arabs in Spain whose echoes reverberated into the seventeenth century with the ongoing expulsions of the "Moriscos," or converted Moors. English polemicists enjoyed reminding each other of Spain's Moorish history: "the *Mores*" ruled Spain for eight hundred years, Edward Daunce noted in 1590, "during which time, we must not thinke that the *Negros* sent for women out of *Aphrick*."[26] Spenser himself wrote that the Arab invasions left Spain a mongrel nation.[27] Catholic Spain was still partly Saracen, and the English loved to relate the legends of how it came to be that way.[28]

Such claims countered the rhetoric of the Armada, which called itself a crusade against heretics. The pope proclaimed indulgences for the sailors, and the ships were decorated with banners displaying crusade insignia, a fact that could not have escaped the English when they hung those banners in celebration.[29] The anti-Spanish crusade that Spenser figures in the fight of with the Souldan effectively reverses Philip's claim to be fighting a holy war. Islam and Catholicism are collapsed in the figure of the Souldan, so that Spenser can appropriate the battle of Christian against infidel for a Protestant vision of the struggle of true and false belief.[30]

The story of the fight with the Souldan tackles the same problem that Tasso did: how to imagine a holy war at a moment when Christianity was divided against itself. But while Tasso tried to solve that problem through narrative, Spenser approaches it through allegory. In this sense, the episode surely represents the culmination of the encounters between Christian and Saracen knight that extends back to the first pages of the poem. And yet, if this is so, the defeat of the Souldan is oddly decentered. It does not appear at a structurally vital moment, nor does it complete either the allegory of justice or the ongoing fight with the Saracens. The conflicts of Book V resume right afterward and remain famously unresolved. The Souldan is not even the last Saracen in *The Faerie Queene*: in the eighth canto of Book VI Arthur again fights an infidel who swears by Mahound and Termagant.

In Spenser's poem, crusade cannot bring closure to the problem of faithlessness. The Saracens are never the focus of his quests, and he never allows his knights to defeat them decisively. Tasso's narrative

constantly strains toward final victory. But Spenser decenters crusade
even as his allegory, by multiplying the forms of false belief, problematizes the representation of any single, final victory over faithlessness. It is this simultaneous use of and resistance to crusade narrative
whose stakes I hope to clarify.

★

To begin with, it is essential to recognize that Spenser is here participating in a Reformation polemic about the historical and prophetic
interpretation of Islam. The link Spenser draws between Islam and
Catholicism was licensed first of all by the medieval association of
Islam with Christian heresy, and secondly by the ways in which the
Reformation revitalized that association. In the late Middle Ages,
interest in Islam tended to move in tandem with anxiety about re-
formist tendencies in the church, because Islam was understood to
be at once alien and familiar. On the one hand, it seemed the purest
form of false religion, a religion that elevated the carnal over the
spiritual in its supposed idolatry and its denial of the divinity of
Christ. For this, the Middle Ages imagined a Muhammad who died
in filth, devoured by pigs; a Muhammad whose body was buried only
when his disciples were forced by the smell to admit that he would
not fulfill his promise to rise again; or a Muhammad who in Dante's
vision of hell was compelled to suffer a literal turning inside out, so
that the bowels and anus, the "miserable" but "vital" sack, were
given precedence over the body's "higher" parts.[31] The violent satire
expresses a logic crucial to the medieval view of Islam: Islam is a
parody and an inversion of Christian faith, associated with filth, ana-
lity, and violence.

But parody requires proximity, and Islam was also imagined to
bear an intimate relationship to Christianity. Medieval legends
claimed that Muhammad invented his religion under the tutelage of
the heretical monk Sergius, or identified Muhammad himself as a
renegade Christian, a cardinal who had been passed over for the
papacy.[32] To Dante, Muhammad was a "seminator di scandalo e di
scisma," a sower of scandal and schism. The encounter with the hell-
bound Muhammad occurs after the story of Guido da Montefeltro,
a Franciscan who hoped to have the crimes he had perpetrated on
behalf of the papacy forgiven him, but who learned too late that no
service to ecclesiastical authority can substitute for a personal faith.[33]

At the end of the encounter, the prophet tries to send a message to the heretical "Pseudo-Apostles" of Fra Dolcino, already dead at the hands of a papal army. In other words, Dante places Islam squarely between the demand for the reform of a corrupt church and the problem of heresy.

The corollary of the assertion that Islam is a Christian heresy was that Christianity itself nursed a hidden Islamicization. The author of one Lollard tract compares anyone who opposes the ready availability of scripture to "Makamete and Surgeus the monk," who "maden a lawe after ther owne malice and token sumwhat of the gosepel to a fleschly vnderstondynge."[34] The corrupt church, substituting human traditions for the gospel, imitates Islam.[35] In Islam, Christian polemicists thought they had the example of a claim to reform gone wrong, one that had produced doctrinal monstrosity, and had disguised under questions of faith the imperial ambitions of a barbaric people. Because of this rhetoric, any effort to imagine a reformed Christianity would necessarily have to come to terms with the specter of Islam, but so, too, would any effort to defend the Church in its existing form.

Catholic polemicists turned this rhetoric against the reformers. In his *Dialogue of Comfort*, written from a prison cell while awaiting execution, Thomas More used the fiction of a conversation in Budapest on the eve of the arrival of Suleiman's army in 1529 to instruct English Catholics how to prepare themselves for persecution: conversion to Protestantism More figured as conversion to Islam, and life under a Protestant national church as life under a Turkish tyrant.[36]

The reformers turned these charges back against the Catholics.[37] Luther did not mention the Turks in his 1517 Theses, but they feature in his subsequent defenses of those theses. In 1518, his discussion of the remission of sins turned into an angry argument about the theological implications of Turkish power, in which he asserted that to resist the Turks was to resist the judgment of God.[38] In *On War Against the Turks*, Luther conceded that it was the duty of Christians to resist the Turks, but he insisted that such resistance be performed in the name of secular authority, and he renewed his attack on crusade and indulgences.[39] The doctrine of holy war and the penitential system represented to him an Islamicization of Christianity. The pope, he wrote,

is not much more godly than Muhammad and looks very much like him, for he, too, pays lip service to the gospels and all the holy scriptures, but he believes that many parts of them are too difficult and impossible, and these are the very parts that the

Turks and Muhammad also consider too difficult . . . [The pope rules] not with the gospels or the word of God, but has also made a new law and Alcoran, namely, his Decretal, and this he enforces with excommunication, just as the Turk enforces his Koran with the sword.[40]

As Luther twice asserts in *Table Talk*, "The pope is the spirit of antichrist, and the Turk the flesh of antichrist."[41]

This rhetoric is registered with iconic starkness in a series of images produced by Albrecht Dürer and his disciple Matthias Gerung.[42] In plate eleven of his *Apocalypse*, Dürer places side by side among the worshippers of the dragon of Revelation 17 a pope and a sultan, both joined in supplication or prayer (see fig. 1). Plate thirteen similarly shows a richly dressed sultan mediating between the Whore of Babylon on her dragon and a crowd of European townspeople. In the foreground of a woodcut by Gerung, Catholic and Islamic armies clash, but this war only reveals how similar the two enemies are: the pope rides a lion-headed beast, opposite a devilish figure on an identical beast, riding beside the sultan. Monsters or devils appear in the ranks of both armies, and above each army floats the book of false laws for which it fights, one labeled "Decret," and the other, "Alcoran." In the clouds above, Christ preaches to an angelic host that has turned its back on both of these infidel armies (see fig. 2).[43]

This polemic shaped the central texts of the English Reformation. Perhaps the most readily available English text on Islam appears in the 1570 *Actes and Monumentes*, in which John Foxe enters into what seems to be a long digression from his history of martyrs: forty-five folio pages discussing the "Turkes storye" and "Prophecies concerning the Turkes and Antichrist."[44] Foxe's Turkish history ends with a "prayer agaynst the Turkes," but this prayer turns out to be only in part what it promises:

Renewe in thys thy Church agayne, the decayed fayth of thy sonne Iesus, which may plentifully bring forth in vs, not leaues onely, but fruites of Christian life: And forgeue our wretched Idolatrie, and blinde phantasies past, wherwith we haue prouoked manyfolde wayes, thy deserued indignation. . . . Miserably we haue walked hetherto, like sonnes not of Sara, but of Agar, and therfore these Turkishe Agarens haue risen vp against vs.[45]

This is not a prayer for protection against the Turks, but a prayer for reform. By the end, the Christians as well as the Turks are "Agarens,"

Fig. 1: Sultan and Pope worship the seven-headed beast from Revelation: Albrecht Dürer, *Apokalypse*, plate 11. Reproduced by permission of the Germanisches Nationalmuseum, Nürnberg.

Fig. 2: The Pope and Turk go to war. Woodcut by Matthias Gerung, reproduced from *The German Single-Leaf Woodcut*, 1550–1600, by permission of Abaris Books.

Fig. 3: A Protestant crusade: *Newes from Flanders* (London, 1600).
Reproduced from STC 11029 by permission of The British Library.

Fig. 4: The eagle of all empires, from Theodor Bibliander, *De fatis monarchiae somnium vaticinum Esdrae prophetae* (Basel, 1553). Reproduced by permission of The Beinecke Rare Book and Manuscript Library, Yale University.

descendents of Hagar rather than Sara. The corruption of proper doctrine threatens to obliterate any sense of the difference between Christian and infidel.

Foxe imagines a secret Islamicization of Christendom, so that when he writes of the Turks he writes also of Christian weakness, discord, and sin. "For though the Turke semeth to bee farre of," he warns, "yet do wee nourishe within our owne breastes at home, that may soone cause vs to feele his cruell hand" (2G5v). Foxe arges not only that Islam is a punishment for Christian sins, but also that the rise of the Turks is a divine punishment for the consolidation of Catholic doctrine:

> after the decree of Transubstantiation was enacted in the Councell of *Laterane* by Pope *Innoce[n]t* the iij. the yeare of our Lord .1215. not long after, about the yeare of our Lord .1260. was styred vp the power and armes of the *Oguzians*, and of *Orthogules* father of *Ottomannus*: Who about the yeare of our Lord .1294. began first to vexe the Christians about *Pontus* and *Bithynia*.[46]

A marginal note draws the lesson succinctly: "The tyme of Transubstantiation. The tyme of the Turkes" (2K5v). Foxe uses this Turkish history to interpret a series of scriptural and other prophecies, which he claims can be clarified by a historical analysis that recognizes in the pope the true Antichrist, but in the Turks a punishment for being seduced by Antichrist. Moreover, he places his Turkish history between the story of Julius II and that of the Henrician Reformation. Even structurally, the history of Islam appears to prove Foxe's thesis: papal violence provokes Turkish violence, and the solution to both lies in the continuing process of reform.

Foxe's discussion of Islam is localized in one section of his enormous book; John Bale, on the other hand, constantly glances at Islam in the course of his reading of Revelation.[47] For Bale, the supposed complicity of Islam and Catholicism suggested not only a historicized reading of prophetic scripture but also a way of reimagining Christian identity by reimagining the literary forms in which that identity could be narrated. Bale's rhetoric repeatedly hints that the reformation of religion also demands a refashioning of literature. It was Bale, I want to suggest, who had the most direct impact on Spenser's rewriting of romance in *The Faerie Queene*.

Spenser's apocalypticism has often been traced to *The Image of bothe Churches*, in which Bale reads the two women of Revelation—the "meke spouse of the lambe without spot" and the "rose coloured whore"—as figures of true and false faith. But although Spenserians have generally recognized Bale's women behind Spenser's Una and Duessa, no one has acknowledged the multiple forms of false faith Bale actually recognizes. Bale turns his opposition of Christ and Antichrist into an allegory of the multiple forms of apostasy, and a history that extends from scripture until the present day (d8r–e2v). "Rome the mother of all whordome," he writes, "had subiect vnto her the .vij. clymates or vniuersal partes of the worlde"; and now, though many heads have grown from that Roman Antichrist, the body is still the same: "I do take it for one vniuersal Antichrist . . . . comprehending in hym so well Mahomete as the Pope, so well yᵉ ragyng tyraunt as the still hypocryte, & all that wickedli worketh are of thesame body" (g5v–g6r). Islam and Catholicism are the dual inheritors of the legacy of Rome, splitting between them the world once ruled by a single empire—as an illustration included by Theodor Bibliander in his interpretation of Esdras depicts the three heads of the papacy, Byzantium, and Islam growing out of the body of the Roman empire (fig. 4).[48]

This recognition of a double Antichrist permits Bale to redraw the line between the faithful and the faithless. A Protestant exposition of scripture must assert that not all who profess to be Christians really are; in effect, the distinction between infidel and faithful is recapitulated within Christendom. The visible and apparent Christian church is a lie concealing the secret, almost invisible history of the true church. In this way Protestants can claim to be the small congregation of the elect, while Catholics are grouped among the outcasts and infidels, and revealed as a kind of Turks in disguise.

According to Bale, both Catholicism and Islam foster a scrupulous observance of outward signs of faith but a secret adherence to the devil. The fact that the rituals differ is of no consequence: all ritual represents the same violation, the same refusal to recognize faith alone as the path to salvation, and thus the same abjuration of Christ, scripture, and salvation altogether. "The pope in hys churche hath ceremonyes wythout nombre," Bale warns, and "Mahomete in his church is plentuouse also in holye obseruations."[49] Both attempt to seduce the faithful with glorious appearances, so that "a man seynge them . . . wolde thynke nothynge too be more pure, honest, godly, innocent, cleane, holy, & angelyck, than are theyr tradicions" (2H8v).

This profusion of outward observances conceals an inward emptiness. On the one hand, Bale emphasizes the multiplicity of ceremonies, and on the other hand he asserts that all of these external forms

must be recognized as aspects of the same departure from true doctrine. Bale writes of the "Popishe ceremonies without nombre,"
which in fact he tries to number, or at least to suggest in their almost
infinite variety: "None ende is there of theyr babiling prayers, theyr
portases, bedes, temples, aulters songes, houres, belles, Images, or-
ganes, orname*n*tes, Jewels, lyghtes, oylynges, shauinges, religio*n*s, dis-
gisinges[,] diuersite of feastes, co*n*strayned vowes, fastinges,
processions, & pratlinges" (B4v). But this overwhelming multiplicity
of evils is reduced to a single turning away from the doctrine of faith,
an apostasy that is the same wherever it occurs:

> The same abhominacions mayntaine they the worlde ouer, that
> the pope mayntayneth at Rome, & Mahomete in Barbary, of
> [or?] Turkye. Yea, the same supersticions and sorceryes, the
> same execrable tradicions and beggeryes. The same ceremonies
> haue they, . . . the same vnccions, the same orders, and the
> same masses.
>
> (i3v)

The difference of Christian and infidel gives place to the difference
of inward religious faith from outward irreligious ritual.

This hidden resemblance between Islam and Catholicism requires
a new conception of what it means to be Christian, and this in turn
requires a new kind of narrative. In his commentary on chapter
eleven Bale writes that "the beast of the bottomlesse pitte" is "the
pope with his bishoppes . . . in Europa, Mahomete with his dottinge
dousepers in Affrica, and so forth in Asia and India, all beastlye,
carnall, and wicked" (b7v). Elsewhere Bale compares "mytered Ma-
hometes" and Catholic prelates to "Mahoundes in a play."[50] "Mahound"—a corruption of the French "Mahon," itself a corruption
of "Muhammad"—was, of course, the idol of the Saracens in romance and in romance-inflected mystery plays like the Digby *Mary
Magdalen*. The word "dousepers" Bale also extracts from romance:
it is a Middle English corruption of the French "douze pers" or
twelve peers, Charlemagne's crusading knights. When Bale imagines
the "dousepers" of "Mahomete," and when he calls Catholic priests
"Mahounds," he collapses the terms of difference vital to romance.[51]
Bale expresses the secret Catholic complicity with "the Saracens"
through a fracturing of romance: this, his rhetoric suggests, is the
necessary literary consequence of the pope's resemblance to Muhammad. English reformers like Roger Ascham repeatedly voiced their

antipathy to romance as not only a frivolous but also a Catholic literary form, the favorite form of a time "whan Papistrie, as a standyng poole, couered and ouerflowed all England."[52] Ascham thought romance licentious, but for Bale, the problem of romance is rather that it is deceptive, like ceremonial religion itself: its terms of inclusion and exclusion reflect the appearance rather than the reality of religious faith, and it reposes itself too comfortably in the supposedly absolute difference of the Saracen. Tellingly, the medieval literary form that Bale sought to adapt to Protestant ends was the religious drama, not the romance, despite his evident familiarity with romance, and despite the drama's own borrowings from romance. Bale left a real problem for any author seeking to revitalize romance narrative for Protestant England. I want to suggest that we can see Spenser responding to this apparent impasse in the Saracen episodes of *The Faerie Queene*, and especially in the book most indebted to Bale's apocalyptic vision, the book of Holiness.

★

The Saracens play a larger role in Book I of *The Faerie Queene* than they do in any other book. Three Saracen brothers appear in that book, named, from oldest to youngest, Sansfoy, Sansloy, and Sansioy, without faith, without law, and without joy.[53] These Saracens share a genealogy with Duessa and Night: Night is the mother of Deceit and the grandmother of Duessa, and the Saracens are "nephews" of Night, whose family is engaged in a struggle with the children of Day, ruled by Jove.[54] The antithesis that drives Book I, between Una and Duessa, the true and the false church, is linked to the struggle of Day and Night, male gods and female demons, Christians and Saracens.

Duessa is repeatedly associated with her Saracen relatives. She enters the poem in Sansfoy's company, and although she later claims to have been his captive, at the time Redcross first sees them they are engaged in "mirth and wanton play" (I.ii.14). After Sansioy discovers Redcross and Duessa in the House of Pride and recognizes Redcross as his brother's killer, Duessa slips at night into the Saracen's room, addressing him as "deare *Sans ioy*, next dearest to *Sans foy*." "To thy secret faith I flye," she promises; "where euer yet I be, my secrete aid/Shall follow you" (I.iv.45; 51). When the two men fight in the next canto, she calls out, "Thine the shield, and I, and all" (I.v.11).

Comically, or perhaps pathetically, Redcross believes the words are directed to him, a misunderstanding made all the more ironic when the words intended for Sansioy revive Redcross out of his "swowning dreame" to strike a blow in the next stanza that brings the Saracen to his knees—at which point Duessa intervenes and saves him (I.v.12).

Duessa, the figure of duplicity—both deception and doubleness—links Catholicism to the Saracens. Even the scriptural allusions that cluster around her suggest a complicity with oriental imperialism: she is "clad in scarlot red," and wears "A *Persian* mitre." Her red dress identifies her as the Whore of Babylon from Revelation, and her mitre links her with Babylon and Rome. Protestants frequently asserted that Rome was the new Babylon.[55] But when Spenser brings this double-faced figure into a romance that includes real Saracens, he underscores the problem of recognition that Duessa poses. How can the Christian knight resist these many-faced infidels, when he cannot see the secret faith that unites them?

When he fights the Saracens, "the Redcross knight"—who carries and is named for the cross of the crusades—falls into unbelief himself. He kills the "faithlesse Sarazin" Sansfoy only to take his place as Duessa's lover.[56] As Foxe puts it, "We warre agaynst the *Turke* with our workes, masses, traditions, and ceremonies: but we fight not against him with Christ."[57] Redcross's failure to recognize Duessa's duplicity prevents active struggle against the enemies of the faith, and leads the crusader to play the infidel.

This collapse of crusader and infidel is emphasized when Redcross fights Sansfoy. Both are "fell and furious," and both merge without difference in a stanza-long simile that compares them to "two rams stird with ambitious pride" (I.ii.15–16). Two stanzas later, when one of them strikes the other, it is difficult to tell which has struck and which been struck. "Vpon his crest/With rigour so outrageous he smitt," Spenser writes, and only in the following stanza does it become clear which "he" is Sansfoy and which Redcross. Even syntactically, crusader and infidel can be told apart only with difficulty. Spenser suggests the same collapse of behavior and motivation when Redcross fights Sansioy, grammatically joining the combatants as dual subjects of the same sentence: they both desire "To be aueng'd each on his enimy." Vengeance and pride are the common emotional matrix of Redcross and his enemies.[58]

Redcross's failure to understand the significance of his own armor similarly suggests the extent to which he comes to share Saracen values. That armor is, as Spenser points out in the *Letter to Ralegh*, the "whole armour of God" from Ephesians, the armor not of the chivalric knight but of the Christian warrior.[59] But after defeating

Sansfoy, Redcross takes "The *Sarazins* shield, signe of the con-
queroure" (I.ii.20) and carries it into the House of Pride, where he
encounters another knight armed with a "heathenish shield," Sansioy, who recognizes him because he holds Sansfoy's shield "re-
nuerst" (I.iv.38; 41). When he takes up Sansfoy's shield, Redcross
shows himself committed to a code of knightly prowess whose signs
are legible to the Saracens.

Undertaking war against the Saracens only brings the crusader
closer to the infidel, and emphasizes the conjunction of opposites
inevitable in the confusion of a fight. In the ecclesiastical allegory of
Book I, this is surely to be read as a point about the crusades themselves. If the sin that provoked the rise of the Ottoman empire was
the promulgation of transubstantiation in 1215, that act marked the
high point of a period of increasing papal power associated by Protestants with the same figures who first preached the crusade. Bale
argued that the popes had used the crusades to occupy the secular
princes abroad while they consolidated their own power at home,
and in this he linked the reforms instituted by Gregory VII with the
crusades preached by his successor, "Turban" II.[60] The joke on Urban's name was repeated by Samuel Purchas, Thomas Fuller,
and—with a variation—by that expert parodist of godly rhetoric, Falstaff.[61]

Wars of faith turn out to be wars of faithlessness, fought by enemies
who cannot be distinguished. This idea is powerfully suggested in
Canto iii, when Una meets someone she thinks is Redcross, though
it is in fact a disguised Archimago (I.ii.11; I.iii.26). Una now accompanies a false knight, just as Redcross accompanies Duessa. Both pairs
immediately encounter Saracens: Redcross meets Sansfoy and Duessa
as soon as he has parted from Una, and in Canto iii Una and Archimago meet an enraged Sansloy, whose looks threaten "cruell re-
uenge" for the death of his brother in the previous canto (I.iii.33).
Sansloy mistakes Archimago for Redcross, attacks him, unseats him,
and then dismounts to finish him off (I.iii.35). But what he discovers
when he removes his opponent's helmet is not what he expected:

> Why *Archimago*, luckless syre,
> What doe I see? What hard mishap is this,
> That hath thee hither brought to taste mine yre?
> Or thine the fault, or mine the error is,
> In stead of foe to wound my friend amis?
>
> (I.iii.39)

Sansloy's recognition of Archimago emblematizes the multiple

forms of faithlessness that threaten Redcross and Una, and the complicity of their open and hidden enemies. The moment also underscores a suggestion made earlier in the canto, in the story of Abessa
and Kirkrapine. That story has notoriously frustrated critics because it
suggests the collusion of two groups usually understood to be radically
opposed, in English religious politics. Abessa, whose name recalls the
abbeys dissolved by Henry VIII and whose mother spends her time
counting beads and praying to the Virgin (I.iii.13), turns out to be
the lover of Kirkrapine, whose habits suggest puritan iconoclasm and
opposition to clerical vestments: he is "wont to robbe Churches of
their ornaments," to "disrobe" the "holy Saints of their rich vestments" and "the Priests of their habiliments" (I.iii.17). Puritan iconoclasm is oddly joined to Catholic devotion. I want to suggest that,
seen in conjunction with the story of the second half of the canto, this
odd couple, too, makes sense. In its conviction that the destruction of
images is a holy work, iconoclasm paradoxically becomes a version
of idolatry, an over-investment in objects. Puritan, Catholic, and
Saracen mirror each other, and the canto as a whole evokes a vision
of the many enemies of the true faith whose apparent conflicts conceal
their secret faith to each other.[62]

The complicity of these many enemies prevents any direct resistance against them. Religious faith in Spenser's poem is a difficult
notion, an inner truth always endangered by error and misrecogni-
tion, and as a result heroic action becomes problematic if not impossible. Redcross's own misguided fights suggest the limits of a crusading
ethos, which depends on a human claim to be able to do God's
work, a claim that in Book I of *The Faerie Queene* is always suspect.
Redcross's investment in his own chivalric power first aligns him
with the Saracens, then leaves him vulnerable to another Saracen
figure: Orgoglio, whose name derives from the last word of the *Orlando Furioso*, where the king of Algiers is described as "sì altiera al
mondo e sì orgogliosa."[63] Human, knightly action produces not
strength but a Saracenical pride.[64]

Even the fight with the dragon ends with Una praising God and
thanking "her faithful knight, / That had atchieu'd so great a conquest
by his might" (I.xi.55). Whose might does she mean? The ambiguity,
as Hamilton suggests, blurs the line between human and divine power
and renders uncertain the value of human labor. "Might" is at other
points associated more with the figures of faithlessness, with the
"matchlesse might" of Orgoglio (I.vii.10), or with the Souldan, that
"mighty man" (V.viii.18). As in the case of the disguised Archimago,
we are left with a problem of recognition: we must distinguish
worldly might in its debased forms from a power that mediates the

divine, and only when we are certain of this distinction can we be certain of the status of our own work. But how can we know?

At the end of Book I, we are returned to the problem of its beginning—how to distinguish false from true faith—except that now this problem has been extended to a scrutiny of our own actions and motives. Can the faithful actively resist faithlessness? The distinguishing mark of Spenser's Saracens is their elevation of worldly might over all else; but does it follow that the true believer must withdraw into the confines of an inner faith, accepting a political quietism whose only narratives are the narratives of conversion and martyrdom? Redcross seems to suggest as much when he vows to give up fighting altogether: "bloud can noght but sin, and wars but sorrowes yield," Contemplation assures him, and Redcross promises "shortly" to return "in Pilgrims poore estate."[65] But it is unclear when exactly he proposes to do this. When Una's father suggests that they "deuize of ease and euerlasting rest," Redcross answers that he is bound "to returne to that great Faerie Queene,/And her to serue six yeares in warlike wize,/Gainst that proud Paynim king, that workes her teene" (I.x.18). How do we take this? Is Redcross repeating the mistakes of the first cantos, or is the Christian warrior facing his obligation to continue a struggle that is both active and spiritual?

Redcross believes that he will fight a holy war after all, and Spenser seems to corroborate this just before the fight with the dragon, in the passage with which I began. There he invokes his muse, but asks her to come "gently," not with "that mighty rage" that "harts of great Heroës doest enrage" (I.xi.5–6). Spenser lays aside that higher vein until he will sing of Briton fields dyed with Saracen blood in the war between the Faery Queen and Paynim king; for now, he will sing "this man of God his godly armes" (7). It may seem peculiar to think of a "gentle" poetry as being appropriate for Revelation, but the point seems to be that the fight with the dragon is a spiritual struggle, not an epic and historical one. Yet it seems equally clear that this spiritual struggle is in some way the prologue for a later war which will reconcile the demands of chivalry and holiness, epic and apocalypse. At least, this is what Redcross thinks.

But when we get to the episode that seems to fulfill this promise, Redcross is nowhere to be seen. As James Nohrnberg has observed, while Book I promises a "full-dress treatment" of the defeat of the Armada, "when we come to the legend of justice, the subject has been abbreviated to an episode in the historical allegory."[66] The apparent disjunction forces us to think about the place of the war with Spain in the long narrative of British history, on the one hand, and

in the even longer trajectory of prophetic history, on the other; that
is, to think about how faith translates into politics.

Between Books I and V, Spenser suggests the place of the Fairy
Queen's victory over the Paynim king in the history of the "British"
Tudors, as described by Merlin in Book III. The British princes, he
reveals, will be displaced by the pagan Saxons, but they will return
under a virgin queen descended from the knights of chastity and
justice, to restore the true faith to their kingdom. This narrative of
exile and return is bracketed by two wars against pagan enemies, first
the war against the Saxons, and then the war "ouer the *Belgicke* shore"
against "the great Castle," that is, Philip of Castile.[67] The defeat of
Philip in the guise of the Souldan promises to resolve the long struggle for England.

Merlin also emphasizes the apocalyptic significance of this final
victory with the last words of his prophecy, "But yet the end is not,"
words that echo but also defer Revelation's promise that "the time
is at hand."[68] What is promised in the fight with the Paynim king is
the resolution of both the historical and the scriptural allegory.[69] In
Book V this plan remains unfulfilled. Apocalypse, like crusade, orients
us toward an ending, but it defers that ending to a place and time
beyond earthly experience. Spenser's treatment of history similarly
refuses resolution, as the episodes that follow the fight with the Souldan progressively frustrate the sense of an ending. The Spanish Armada is defeated, the Queen of Scots executed, and yet the faithful
must still struggle against unbelief and injustice in the Netherlands,
France, and Ireland. The narrative multiplies the scenes of engagement demanded by a faith that wants to exercise itself temporally
and politically, and it leaves that struggle famously incomplete, ending with Artegall recalled to court before he can complete Ireland's
"reformation." Spenser takes seriously the hope for a political world
transformed by faith, but refuses to let himself or his readers believe
that this desired and deferred moment is now at hand.[70]

Finally, and most famously, the projected structure of the poem
with its cycle of virtues itself collapses into the incomplete Book VII,
extant in only two cantos whose subject is, appropriately enough,
Mutabilitie's claim to govern the universe. The "tedious trauell" of
romance (VI.0.1)—both travail and travel—increasingly generates its
own resistance, in the desirable but dangerous hope of rest. Although
Redcross refuses the hope of "euerlasting rest," Spenser's poem ends
looking forward to the time "when no more *Change* shall be,/But
stedfast rest of all things firmely stayd/Vpon the pillours of Eternity."[71] The final line both evokes and frustrates this desire, calling
on a "Sabbaoth God" who may be the God of the Sabbath, of rest

after the labor of creation, but may also be the God of Hosts who, in Paul's paraphrase of Isaiah, will save a small remnant, but will make "a short word . . . on earth."[72] The poem ends invoking and deferring ending, acknowledging the necessity of continued labor while longing for the moment when the ongoing struggle of the faithful will finally be cut short by God's short word.

Spenser's romance suggests the secret complicities that frustrate heroic action, but while romance conventionally presses toward clarification, toward a realignment of self and other, Spenser defers that promise. No earthly authority successfully resolves the problem of duplicity and serves—like Tasso's Godfrey—to guarantee the union of human effort and divine will. We never arrive at Gloriana's court, never see Elizabeth's apotheosis into the Faery Queen or Arthur's arrival on the throne.[73] In this absence, the society of the faithful—the *respublica Christiana*, Christendom—must be imagined in new terms. In Book V, a godly England almost emerges to replace Christendom as the earthly, political embodiment of the true faith. But in the end we are left with the possibility that the true Christendom may manifest itself only in the community of the elect, a community that will not gather until the end of time.

In other words, there may be no such thing as a godly politics, no such thing as either Catholic Christendom or the Protestant elect nation.[74] The possibility of crusade—which unites political action and divine ends, the church militant and the military nation—can be sustained for Spenser only as a deferred promise, like the promise of apocalyptic scripture itself. Spenser evokes the desire for endings implicit in crusade narrative, but he also frustrates that desire, suggesting that Protestant faith may best express itself not in closed and end-directed forms like Tasso's but in an open-ended wandering. In this, Spenser may finally approach something like Bale's sense of the inadequacy of romance for telling the story of the Protestant faith. For Bale, this skepticism ultimately seems to include all narrative: as he writes, Revelation is "no storye . . . [but] a misterye." The events it depicts are not elements of a narrative but expressions of symbolic relations that are beyond narrative, just as its subject is finally the end of history, time, and narrative, in the kingdom of heaven (i6v–i7r). Spenser is more willing than Bale to play with the narrative possibilities of romance, and to imagine a fusion of romance and Revelation, but he seems suspicious of the effort to bring his romance to the close it itself at times imagines. His effort to rewrite romance for a fractured Christendom ends questioning romance's capacity to imagine a world transformed by faith.

SUNY at Stony Brook

Notes

For their generosity, knowledge, and encouragement, I would like to thank Anne Lake Prescott, David Scott Kastan, Jean Howard, and James Shapiro.

1. *The Faerie Queene*, ed. A. C. Hamilton (New York: Longman, 1977), I.xi.7.

2. *The Spenser Encyclopedia*, ed. A. C. Hamilton (Toronto: University of Toronto Press, 1990). There is, however, an entry for "Paynims." One exception to the almost universal silence on this subject is a brief article by Mark Heberle, "Pagans and Saracens in Spenser's *The Faerie Queene*," in *Comparative Literature East and West: Traditions and Trends: Selected Conference Papers*, ed. Cornelia Moore and Raymond Moody (Honolulu: University of Hawaii Press, 1989), 81–7. See also Frank Kermode, "*The Faerie Queene*, I and V," in *Essential Articles for the Study of Edmund Spenser*, ed. A. C. Hamilton (Hamden, CT: Archon, 1972), 277–8, and John E. Hankins, *Source and Meaning in Spenser's Allegory* (Oxford: Clarendon, 1971), 207–27.

3. See Emrys Jones, "'Othello,' 'Lepanto' and the Cyprus Wars," *Shakespeare Survey* 21 (1968): 47–52, and David C. McPherson, *Shakespeare, Jonson, and the Myth of Venice* (Newark: University of Delaware Press, 1990), 75–81. Selim II is reported as saying that the loss at Lepanto was like the trimming of a beard, but the loss of Cyprus was like the loss of an arm; see Folger MS V.a.381, f. 183: "The Turk said yt Selim had cutt of an arme of ye Christians, (yt was by taking Cyprus) & they had but shavd his beard (meaning ye battaile wch he lost in ye gulph of Lepanto)." This part of the MS apparently postdates James's reign, but the saying was often quoted. On the Habsburg-Ottoman struggle for control of the Mediterranean, see Fernand Braudel, *The Mediterranean and the Mediterranean World in the Age of Philip II*, trans. Sîan Reynolds (Berkeley: University of California Press, 1995), 2: 904–1244; for a concise summary of the growth of the empire, see Halil Inalcik, *The Ottoman Empire: The Classical Age 1300–1600* (New York: Praeger, 1973).

4. On medieval and early modern apocalypticism, see Richard Baukham, *Tudor Apocalypse: Sixteenth Century Apocalypticism, Millenarianism and the English Reformation* (Appleford: Sutton Courtenay, 1978); Paul Christianson, *Reformers and Babylon: English Apocalyptic Visions from the Reformation to the Eve of the Civil War* (Toronto: University of Toronto Press, 1978); Richard Emmerson and Ronald Herzman, *The Apocalyptic Imagination in Medieval Literature* (Philadelphia: University of Pennsylvania Press, 1992), esp. chap. 1; Katharine Firth, *The Apocalyptic Tradition in Reformation Britain 1530–1645* (Oxford: Oxford University Press, 1979); C. A. Patrides and Joseph Wittreich, eds., *The Apocalypse in English Renaissance Thought and Literature* (Ithaca: Cornell University Press, 1984); and Esther Richey, *The Politics of Revelation in the English Renaissance* (Columbia: University of Missouri Press, 1998).

5. Kenneth Setton broke new ground on the persistence of crusade in the 16th century in volumes three and four of his *The Papacy and the Levant, 1204–1571*, 4 vols. (Philadelphia: American Philosophical Society, 1976–84). See also Norman Housley, *The Later Crusades, 1274–1580: From Lyons to Alcazar* (Oxford: Oxford University Press, 1992); Jonathan Riley-Smith, *The Crusades: A Short History* (London: Athlone, 1987), chaps. 9 and 10; Christopher Tyerman, *England and the Crusades*

1095–1588 (Chicago: University of Chicago Press, 1988), and *The Invention of the Crusades* (London: Macmillan, 1998), chap. 3.

6.   Ganelon wears "Alexandrian silk"—the same material as Marsile's tent—under his "cloak of sable furs," the costume of Charlemagne's other nobles: see *The Song of Roland*, trans. Patricia Terry (New York: Macmillan, 1992), laisses 31 and 35; I'm grateful to Jim Cain for calling my attention too this detail. For Saladin, see Boccaccio, *The Decameron*, trans. G. H. McWilliam (London: Penguin, 1995), 1.3 and 10.9.

7.   For discussions of Islam, the Turks, and early modern England, see especially Samuel Chew, *The Crescent and the Rose: Islam and England during the Renaissance* (New York: Oxford University Press, 1937); Nabil Matar, *Islam in Britain 1558–1685* (Cambridge: Cambridge University Press, 1998), and *Turks, Moors, and Englishman in the Age of Discovery* (New York: Columbia University Press, 1999); Patricia Parker, "Preposterous Conversions: Turning Turk, and its 'Pauline' Rerighting," *The Journal for Early Modern Cultural Studies* 2.1 (Spring/Summer 2002): 1–34; Daniel Vitkus, "Turning Turk in Othello: The Conversion and Damnation of the Moor," *Shakespeare Quarterly* 48 (1997): 145–76, and Vitkus, ed., *Three Turk Plays from Early Modern England* (New York: Columbia University Press, 2000), introduction.

8.   Recent discussions of Reformation thought have begun to include sections on the reformers and their various cultural "others," chiefly Turks and Jews; but such material tends to be presented to seem secondary to the "real" history of the Reformation, an embarrassing by-product, or part of a history of tolerance, instead of an effort to come to terms with the problems of reform and schism themselves. See Carter Lindberg, *The European Reformations* (Oxford: Blackwell, 1996), 366–71, and Richard Marius, *Martin Luther* (Cambridge: Belknap, 1999), 372–80.

9.   Andrew King convincingly argues for the importance of Middle English romance to Spenser's effort to imagine English nationhood. But—as Robert Warm argues—English romances also looked to a sense of England's place in a troubled Christendom. See Warm, "Identity, Narrative and Participation: Defining a Context for the Middle English Charlemagne Romances," in Rosalind Field, ed., *Tradition and Transformation in Medieval Romance* (Cambridge: Brewer, 1999), 87–100, and Andrew King, The Faerie Queene *and Middle English Romance: Studies in the Poetics of a Mode* (Oxford: Clarendon, 2000).

10.   On the word "Saracen" and its cognates, see *OED*; Paul Bancourt, *Les Musulmans dans les Chansons de geste du cycle du roi*, 2 vols. (Aix-en-Provence: Université de Provence, 1982), esp. 1: 2–29, 113–14; W. W. Comfort, "The Literary Role of the Saracens in the French Epic," *PMLA* 60 (1940): 628–59; Norman Daniel, *Heroes and Saracens: An Interpretation of the* Chansons de geste (Edinburgh: Edinburgh University Press, 1984), 25–6, 107–116, 131, and 140–41; C. Meredith-Jones, "The conventional Saracen of the songs of geste," *Speculum* 17 (1942): 201–25; and Metlitzki, 117–219.

11.   I emphasize the monstrous and antichristian Saracen because that representation is crucial for Spenser; but the medieval Saracen is a more complex figure. See Bancourt on the comic Saracens of the "second generation" of the *chansons*, 1: 83; on conversion and marriage plots, see Sarah Kay, *The* Chansons de geste *in the Age of Romance: Political Fictions* (Oxford: Clarendon, 1995), chaps. one and six.

12. See *OED*, "Mahound." Muhammad's name also supplied Middle English with the word "mawmet," or idol, with the bizarre result that in Trevisa's translation of Ranulph Higden's story of the life of Muhammad, the Islamic prophet is said to have abandoned "mawmetrie" for monotheism; see Metlitzki, 205–7. Norman Daniel argues that Islam was widely believed to "[enjoy] a direct continuity with the pagans of the ancient world." See Daniel, *Saracens*, 131, 140–41, and Bancourt. A similar association of modern Muslims and pagan antiquity is revealed by the common conflation of "Turci" with "Teucri," Turks with Trojans, those other Anatolian empire-builders. See Robert Schwoebel, *The Shadow of the Crescent: The Renaissance Image of the Turk 1453–1517* (Nieuwkoop: B. de Graaf, 1967), 70–71, 148–49, 188–89, and Terence Spencer, "Turks and Trojans in the Renaissance," *Modern Language Review* 47 (1952): 330–32.

13. Ariosto's poem concludes when the converted Saracen hero Ruggiero finally kills Rodomonte the king of Algiers: "Downe to the lake, where damned ghosts do lie,/Sunke his disdainfull soule, now cold as Ise,/Blaspheming as it went, and cursing lowd,/That was on earth so loftie and so proud." (Harington, *Orlando Fvrioso in English Heroical Verse* (London, 1591), 46.123). See *Orlando Furioso*, ed. Lanfranco Caretti (Milan: Riccardo Ricciardi, 1954), 46.140.

14. The late Middle English romances already reveal a renewed anxiety about Islamic power in the wake of the fall of Constantinople to the Turks: see Helen Cooper, "Romance after 1400," in *The Cambridge History of Medieval English Literature*, ed. David Wallace (Cambridge: Cambridge University Press, 1999), 698–99 and 712.

15. See James Nohrnberg, *The Analogy of* The Faerie Queene (Princeton: Princeton University Press, 1976), 5–22, and Patricia Parker, *Inescapable Romance: Studies in the Poetics of a Mode* (Princeton: Princeton University Press, 1979).

16. See Fairfax's translation, *Godfrey of Bulloigne: A Critical Edition*, ed. Kathleen Lea and T. M. Gang (Oxford: Clarendon, 1981), 8.58.3–4; Tasso: he was "nacque in riva del Tronto e fu nudrito/ne le risse civil e di sdegno," *Poesie*, ed. Francesco Flora (Milan: Riccardo Ricciardi, 1952). Also see David Quint, *Epic and Empire: Politics and Generic Form from Virgil to Milton* (Princeton: Princeton University Press, 1993), 214–16 and 219–20.

17. Fairfax and Tasso, 8.6–25, and 8.43, esp. 8.43.1, where Tasso calls the messenger "il tedesco." Fairfax renders the word as "Dane," whether inadvertently or to suppress the allegory. I quote this passage from *Jerusalem Delivered*, trans. Ralph Nash (Detroit: Wayne State, 1987); Tasso: "che genti sì amiche e valorose/breve ora ha tolte e posa terra assorte."

18. The Lutheran Diets repeatedly postponed grants of military aid to the emperor until the resolution of religious questions, thereby forcing a reluctant Charles V to offer them concessions in return for money and soldiers. See Kenneth Setton, "Lutheranism and the Turkish Peril," *Balkan Studies* 3 (1962): 133–68; Dorothy Vaughan, *Europe and the Turk: A Pattern of Alliances, 1350–1700* (1954; reprint, New York: AMS, 1976); and especially Stephen Fischer-Galati, *Ottoman Imperialism and German Protestantism, 1521–1555* (Cambridge, MA: Harvard University Press, 1959).

19. See for example the encounter between Arthur and Pyrochles and Cymochles, in II.viii; in this, Spenser was perfectly in line with certain conventions of medieval

poetry. See Metlitzki, 177–92, on "The Converted Saracen" and "The Defeated Sultan."

20. I do not mean to assert that Arthur represents divine grace in any consistent way; as Darryl Gless argues, Arthur is "associated with" grace, but is not to be understood always as a figure for grace, or a representation of Christ; see *Interpretation and Theology in Spenser* (Cambridge: Cambridge University Press, 1994), 190.

21. V.ii.6, V.ii.9, and V.ii.10. For Neff's argument, see *The Works of Edmund Spenser: A Variorum Edition*, vol. 5, ed. Ray Heffner (Baltimore: Johns Hopkins University Press, 1936), 345–47. For an argument linking Pollente to Antwerp via the giant Druon, and thus to Spanish rule in the Low Countries, see Anne Prescott's article on "Burgundy" in *The Spenser Encyclopedia*.

22. As the argument announces. But in the canto itself it is only Arthur who fights the Souldan, while Artegall is confined to action against his lady and her household.

23. In this battle, moreover, Arthur for the first time "actively cooperates with grace," as Hamilton notes, deliberately drawing off the shield's veil, which in Book I fell off "by chaunce." See Hamilton, gloss to V.viii.37, lines 6–9; see also I.viii.19.

24. The figure of the sultan as both powerful enemy and beneficial lord was conventional in romances and related texts like *Mandeville's Travels*. Mandeville claims that the sultan of Egypt "would have married me richly with a great prince's daughter and given me many great lordships, so that I would have forsaken my belief and turned to theirs; but I would not." See *Mandeville's Travels*, ed. Malcolm Letts, 2 vols. (London: Hakluyt Society, 1953), 1: 25. The claim became standard in travel narratives—see, for example, Edward Webbe's *The rare and most wonderfull things* (London, 1590), C3v.

25. The Souldan's horses run away with him like "the firie-mouthed steeds, which drew/The Sunnes bright wayne to *Phaetons* decay" (V.viii.40). See also V.viii.28, 37, 40–41; René Graziani, "Philip II's *impresa* and Spenser's Souldan," *Journal of the Warburg and Courtauld Institutes* 27 (1964): 322–24; Nohrnberg, 396–421; and Jane Aptekar, *Icons of Justice: Iconography and Thematic Imagery in Book V of* The Faerie Queene (New York: Columbia University Press, 1969), 82–83 and 218–19.

26. Edward Daunce, *A Briefe Discovrse of the Spanish State* (London, 1590), E3r. See also Celio Curione, *A Notable Historie of the Saracens*, trans. Thomas Newton (London, 1575), L2v: "the number of *Saracens* dayly encreased in Spaine, in so much that the Spanyardes then changed not onely their religion and maners, but corrupted their language, and the names of their Cyties, Townes, Hilles, Ryuers, and all other places were likewise altered."

27. "The Moors and Barbarians, breaking over out of Africa, did finally possess all Spain, or the most part thereof, and did tread, under their heathenish feet, whatever little they found yet there standing. The which, though afterward they were beaten out by Ferdinando of Aragon and Elizabeth his wife, yet they were not so cleansed, but that through the marriages which they had made, and mixture with the people of the land, during their long continuance there, they had left no pure drop of Spanish blood." *A View of the State of Ireland*, ed. Andrew Hadfield and Willy Maley (Oxford: Blackwell, 1997), 50. See also David Read, *Temperate Conquests: Spenser and the Spanish New World* (Detroit: Wayne State University Press, 2000), 57–58.

28. For the story of "Roderick" or Roderigo, the king who lost Spain to the Moors by raping the daughter of his strongest baron and thereby turning the man

against him, see Curione, *A Notable Historie*, J4r—L2v; William Rowley, *A Tragedy Called All's Lost by Lvst* (London, 1633); and a text attributed to Ralegh, *The Life and Death of Mahomet* (London, 1637), 35–91.

29.   See Tyerman, *England and the Crusades*. For Elizabeth's efforts to establish an Anglo-Ottoman alliance against the Spanish in the 1580s, see Edwin Pears, "The Spanish Armada and the Ottoman Porte," *EHR* 8 (1893): 439–66.

30.   Compare Huntington MS EL 6162, which, in the course of a discussion of the revenues and military strength of Spain, suddenly intrudes two paragraphs of which the first recounts "The kinge of Spayne his style," and the second, "A trewe Coppie of the great Turk his style." The proverbial hypebole of Ottoman official letters (see chapter two) is collapsed with that of Spanish diplomacy, as Philip II is collapsed with his frequent opponent, Selim II. See also *Newes from Flanders* (London 1600), which illustrates a victory over Spanish forces with a woodcut of a Saracen army (fig. 3).

31.   See Daniel, *Islam*, 126–28, citing Alan of Lille, Guibert of Nogent, Gerald of Wales, Ranulf Higden, and Matthew Paris. For Dante, see *Inferno*, trans. Charles Singleton (Princeton: Princeton University Press, 1973), 28.22–27; see also *Purgatorio* 32.130–35, for what has since the early commentators been read as an allegory of Islam: see Singleton's commentary on these lines, and Edward Moore, "The Apocalyptic Vision," in *Studies in Dante. Third Series* (Oxford: Clarendon, 1903), 178–220.

32.   This point was first made by Eduard Doutté, "Mahomet cardinal," *Mémoires de la Société d'Agriculture, Commerce, Sciences, et Arts de la Marne*, 2nd ser., 1:2 (1898–99): 233–43. See also the C-text of *Piers Plowman*: "Men fyndeth that Makamede was a man ycrystned,/And a cardinal of court a gret clerk with-alle,/And porsuede to be pope pryns of holychurche," *The Vision of William Concerning Piers the Plowman*, ed. Walter W. Skeat, 2 vols. (Oxford: Oxford University Press, 1886), C: 18.165–67. On Sergius/ Bahîra, see Daniel, *Islam*, 104–12, and Metlitzki, 200–207.

33.   28.35; qtd. from Giorgio Petrocchi, ed., *La Commedia*, vol. 2 (Verona: Arnoldo Mondadori, 1975). See Edward Said, *Orientalism* (New York: Vintage, 1979), 68–70.

34.   Qtd. from *Selections from English Wycliffite Writings*, ed. Anne Hudson (Cambridge: Cambridge University Press, 1978), 107. I have expanded thorn into "th." See also Herbert B. Workman, *John Wyclif, A Study of the English Medieval Church*, 2 vols. (Oxford: Clarendon, 1926), 1: 336, Appendix E: "Wyclif also seems to have dipped into the Qur'an in the Latin translation made in 1153 by the order of Peter, Abbot of Cluny. See the remarkable reference in *Ver. Scrip.* [*De Veritate Scripturae*]."

35.   The B-text of *Piers Plowman* makes a similar argument, about the wealth of the monastic orders: after telling the story of "Makometh" the apostate who wanted to be pope, and how he "the Sarasenses so bigiled," Langland turns his attention closer to home, to talk about "How Englissh clerkes a coluer feden that Coueityse hatte,/And ben manered after Makometh that no man vseth treuth," and wishes that the monks would return to the simplicity of their original institutions. See B: 15.407–20. There seems to be reason to believe that knowledge of Islam may have played a role in the spread of heretical ideas. At least, Carlo Ginzburg suggests that the miller Menocchio may have read the Qur'an. See *The Cheese and the Worms: The Cosmos of a Sixteenth-Century Miller*, trans. by John and Anne Tedeschi (Baltimore: Johns Hopkins University Press, 1992), 101 and 107–08.

36. *A dialoge of comfort against tribulacion* (London, 1553 and 1573); see *The Complete Works of St. Thomas More*, vol. 12, ed. Louis Martz and Frank Manley (New Haven: Yale University Press, 1976), cxx–cxxxv, esp. cxxxiii: "More equates Protestant and Turk, heretic and infidel." In his book against Henry VIII, Luther imagined a debate between a Turk and a Catholic in which the Turk argued that to substitute tradition for the word of God is to Islamicize. More excerpted passages from this text, commenting, "What a Christian heart, that approves nothing but what the Turk approves along with you." See Luther, *Contra Henricvm Regem Angliae* (Wittenberg, 1522), in *D. Martin Luthers Werke: Kritische Gesammtausgabe*, vol. 10/2 (Weimar: Böhlau, 1907), 193. Subsequent references to the Weimar edition will be abbreviated "WA." For More, see *The Complete Works*, vol. 5, ed. John Headley (New Haven: Yale University Press, 1969), 227.

37. See Hartmut Bobzin, *Der Koran im Zeitalter der Reformation* (Beirut: Franz Steiner, 1995); Carl Göllner, ed., *Tvrcica: Die europäischen Türkendrucke des XVI. Jahrhunderts*, 3 vols. (Berlin: Valentin Körner, 1961–78), 3: 171–215; Michael Heath, *Crusading Commonplaces: La Noue, Lucinge and Rhetoric against the Turks* (Geneva: Droz, 1986); Manfred Köhler, *Melanchthon und der Islam* (Leipzig: Leopold Klotz, 1938); Jacques Pannier, "Calvin et les Turcs," *Revue Historique* 180 (1937): 268–86; and Victor Segesvary, *L'Islam et la Réforme*, 2nd ed. (San Francisco: International Scholars, 1998).

38. This claim was among the positions for which Luther was condemned by the papacy in 1520. The thesis reads "Papa no vult nec potest remittere ullas poenas praeter eas, quas vel suo vel Cannonum arbitrio imposuit"; in the course of discussing this assertion, Luther writes: "Licet plurimi nunc et iidem magni in ecclesia nihil aliud somnient quam bella adversus Turcam, scilicet non contra iniquitates, sed contra virgam iniquitatis bellaturi deoque repugnaturi, qui per eam virgam sese visitare dicit iniquitates nostras, eo quod nos non visitamus eas." *Resolutiones disputationum de indulgentiarum virtute* (Wittenberg, 1518), WA 1: 534–35. Luther was condemned in the bull *Exsurge Domine*, on 15 June 1520; see Hubert Jedin, *Geschichte des Konzils von Trient*, 4 vols. (Freiburg: Herder, 1949–75), 1: 142–58.

39. Two years later he called the popes "hos Romanos Turcissimos Turcas"; see the *Assertio omnivm articvlorvm M. Lutheri, per Bullam Leonis, X* (Wittenberg, 1520), WA 7: 141. Such rhetoric was heightened during the Turkish siege of Vienna in 1529, when both Luther and Melanchthon argued that the current crisis was evidence for the necessity of reform. See Philipp Melanchthon and Justus Jonas, *Das siebend Capitel Danielis* (Wittenberg, 1529); Luther, *Vom Kriege wider die Türken* (Wittenberg, 1529), WA 30/2: 81–148, and *Eine Heerpredigt widder den Türcken* (Wittenberg, 1529), WA 30/2: 149–97. See Bobzin, 13–156; J.W. Bohnstedt, *The Infidel Scourge of God: The Turkish Menace as seen by German Pamphleteers of the Reformation Era* (Philadelphia: The American Philosophical Society, 1968); Harvey Buchanan, "Luther and the Turks," *Archiv für Reformationsgeschichte* 47:1 (1956): 145–60; George Forrel, "Luther and the War against the Turks," *Church History* 14 (1945): 256–71; Heath, 13–25; Setton, "Lutheranism"; and Günther Vogler, "Luthers Geschichtsauffassung im Spiegel seines Türkenbildes," in *450 Jahre Reformation*, ed. Leo Stern and Max Steinmetz (Berlin: Deutscher Verlag der Wissenschaften, 1967), 118–27.

40.   WA 30/2: 141–42: "[D]er Bapst [ist] nicht viel frumer und sihet dem Mahometh aus der massen ehnlich, denn er lobet auch mit dem munde die Euangelia und
ganze heilige schrifft, Aber er helt, das viel stück drjnnen und eben die selbigen, so
die Turcken und der Mahometh zu schweer und ummüglich achten . . . [Er regieret]
auch nicht mit dem Euangelio odder Gottes wort, sondern hat auch ein new gesetz
und einen Alkoran gemacht nemlich sein Decretal, Und treibt dasselbige mit dem
Bann, gleich wie der Turcke seinen Alkoran mit dem Schwerd."
41.   WA Tisch-Rede 1: 135 and 3: 158–59. On the wall of Luther's study in Wittenberg was inscribed the prophecy that "in the year 1600 all Germany will be laid
waste by the Turks." See Vogler, 119. The idea apparently derived from Johannes
Hilten's prophecies; Hugh Goughe noted in the dedicatory epistle to his The Ofspring
of the house of Ottomanno (London, [1570?]) that "one Hiltenius by prophesyinge
hathe foretolde vs, [the Turk] shall haue dominion both in Italie and Germanie," A4r.
42.   Luther and Melanchthon sponsored the publication of books on Islam. Luther
wrote a preface for the Libellvs de ritv et moribvs Tvrcorvm (Wittenberg, 1530), WA
30/2: 207–09, and he translated the Confutatio Alcorani of Ricoldo da Montecroce
as the Verlegung des Alcoran Bruder Richardi (Wittenberg, 1542), WA 53: 261–396.
Melanchthon wrote prefaces for Paolo Giovio's Turcicarum rerum commentarius and
for the De origine imperii Turcorum, a volume including the narrative of the captive
Bartholomaeus Georgievicz. See Karl G. Bretschneider, ed., Philippi Melanthonis Opera quae supersunt omnia, 26 vols., Corpus Reformatorum (Braunschweig:
Schwetschke, 1834–60), 3: 440 and 9: 1026–27. (Future references to this edition
will be abbreviated "CR"). Foxe cites Melanchthon's edition of the De origine,
2L1r. Luther and Melanchthon provided letters for Theodor Bibliander's Machvmetis
saracenorvm principis, eivs'qve svccessorvm vitœ, ac doctrina, ipse'qve Alcoran (Basel, 1543),
which prints the "Cluniac corpus," a body of texts on Islam collected for Peter the
Venerable in the twelfth century. See James Kritzeck, Peter the Venerable and Islam
(Princeton: Princeton University Press, 1964). On Bibliander, see Bobzin, 158–275.
Luther interceded on behalf of the project when the Council of Basel refused to
allow the book to be sold.
43.   The reformers developed these polemical comparisons into a detailed historical
vision. Melanchthon traces the rise of the Turks to the emergence of the doctrine
of transubstantiation: "Ac uide quomodo congrauant tempora. Decretum de transub-
stantione, ut uocant, quod confirmauit horribilem ειδλομαν ιαμ, factum est anno
à natali Christi 1215. Innocentio tertio Pontifice. Statim secuta sunt auspicia regni
Othomanici, anno à natali Christi 1250. Mox igitur post confirmationem idolo-
maniæ, Regnum alibi exoriri cepit, & proferre arma uersus occidentem ad has
Ecclesiæ labes puniendas." See In Danielem prophetam commentarius (Wittenberg,
1543), qtd. from Omnivm opervm reverendi viri Philippi Melanthonis, ed. Kaspar Peucer,
vol. 2 (Wittenberg, 1562), 2Q2r. (See also CR 13: 823–980). Much of Melanchthon's text was redacted in George Joye's The Exposicio[n] of Daniell (London, 1545).
Joye translates the above passage from Melanchthon directly, P8v. As he later writes
in the margin, "Transubstanciacion and Othoman began together" (N3r).
44.   Foxe, Actes and Monumentes (London, 1570), vol. two, 2G4r - 2L2v.
45.   Foxe, 2L2v. Vitkus, "Turning Turk," quotes a prayer for the defense of Malta;
Roslyn Knutson, "Elizabethan Documents, Captivity Narratives, and the Market

for Foreign History Plays," *English Literary Renaissance* 26 (1996): 75–110, assembles evidence about prayers for Christian and particularly English captives in the Mediterranean.

46.   2K5v. This passage clearly recalls the passage from Melanchthon quoted earlier. The differences are perhaps accounted for by Foxe's reading in Turkish history: although Foxe cites as the source for this passage the historian Laonicus Chalcondylas, he seems nevertheless to be translating Melanchthon.

47.   *The Image of bothe Churches* (London, 1548?), A2v. Bale cites three books on Islam: William of Tripoli's *Tractatus de statu Saracenorum et de Mahomete pseudopropheta et eorum lege et fide*, a work not printed until the late 19th century but owned by Bale in MS, according to Honor McCusker, "Books and Manuscripts Formerly in the Possession of John Bale," *The Library*, 4th ser., 16 (1935–36); extracts of Turkish history from Johannes Cuspinian's history of the emperors, published as *De Tvrcarvm origine, religione, ac immanissima eorum in Christianos tyrannide* (Antwerp, 1541); and the *Ad nominis christiani socios consultatio, Qua nam ratione Turcarum dira potentia repelli possit ac debeat a populo Christiano* (Basel, 1542), by Theodor Bibliander, on which see Rudolf Pfister, "Das Türkenbüchlein Theodor Biblianders," *Theologische Zeitschrift* 9 (1953): 438–54, and the English translation, *A godly consultation vnto the brethren of the christen religyon* (Basel [Antwerp], 1542).

48.   See *De fatis monarchiae Romanae somnium Vaticinum Esdrae prophetae* (Basel, 1553). Gog and Magog Bale similarly reveals as "the Romysh Pope & Mahomete, with their blasphemouse and wicked generacions," whose beginnings were "basse," but who have grown "so high by theyr fayned simplicite & simulate holynesse, y^t they became the ij. chefe Monarkes of the earthe, and so in processe ruled the vniuersall worlde" (2H7v-8r). Islam and Catholicism are "subtyle satellites of antichrist which are the cruell members of Sathan" (A4r), and "the .ii. hornes or beastly kingdomes of the great Antechrist or whole body of the deuell" (2H8r). Instead of a single form of evil there is a multiplicity of evils that nevertheless work in harmony, a unity that holds at the apex of the structure even if the structure itself seems fractured.

49.   B4v. Bale in fact embarks on a point by point comparison of Islam and Catholicism. Both are monotheistic, both commend Christ, both accept the Hebrew and the Greek scriptures, but neither is truly Christian: as the Muslims deny the divinity of Christ, so the Catholics refuse to recognize him as "a ful sauer" (2H8v-2I1r). In 1597, William Reynolds and William Gifford argued that Protestantism is Islam in another form; see *Calvino-Turcismus* (Antwerp, 1597 and 1603) and, for other examples of the same argument, Guillaume Postel's *Alcorani seu legis Mahometi et Evangelistarum co[n]cordiæ Liber* (Paris, 1543), and the book attributed to Jacques Du Perron and published in England as *Lvthers Alcoran* (n.p., 1642). In 1599, Matthew Sutcliffe offered a systematic refutation of Reynolds and Gifford, asserting that Turks and Catholics both base their faith on false miracles, both substitute their own heretical traditions for scripture, both resist the translation of their scriptures, and both foster monasticism. See *De Tvrcopapismo* (London, 1599 and 1604), and, for other parallels, ¶*The Alcaron of the Barefote Friers* ([London, 1550]), and, citing this book, Stephen Bateman, *The Doome Warning all men to the Iudgemente* (London, 1581), 2E4r. See also Peter Milward, *Religious Controversies of the Elizabethan Age: A Survey of Printed Sources* (London: Scolar, 1977), 145–47.

50. g1v, h1r, and i3r; commentary on chapter thirteen. Despite the reference to "Mahoundes in a play," no extant mystery play has a member of the Islamic pantheon appear onstage, and Chew, at least, doubts that any such play ever existed (395). Bale may be confusing the dramatic Herods and Pilates with the god they worshipped; but compare Skelton's almost identical comment, quoted earlier.

51. E.g., "The Sowdone," lines 240–41: "The kinge of Fraunce I shal the bringe/ And the xij dosipers alle in fere."

52. Ascham, ed. Wright, 230–31; *The Scholemaster* (London, 1570), I3r-v. The passage seems to be a revision of a passage in Ascham's *Toxophilus* (London, 1545), a1r.

53. We are told the order of the birth in I.ii.25, at Sansloy's death. See Hamilton's gloss, and the *Spenser Encyclopedia* entry on the three brothers.

54. I.iii.38 and I.v.22. Compare II.iv.41: Pyrochles and Cymochles, who worship Mahound and Termagant, are also Duessa's relatives.

55. I.ii.13. For the Whore, see Revelation 17.4 and gloss, Geneva edition (London, 1560): she is "araied in purple & skarlat, & guilded with golde, & precious stones, and pearles," and the gloss clarifies that "This woman is the Antichrist, that is, the Pope with ye whole bodie of his filthie creatures." After 1599 the Geneva text began to be published with Franciscus Junius's commentary, which asserts roughly the same point, although in more words. The seven-headed monster Orgoglio gives Duessa to ride in Canto seven was deciphered by Protestant exegetes as figuring the papacy's claim to Rome's imperial legacy: see Junius's gloss to Revelation 11.7: "That beast is the Romane Empire, made long agoe of ciuill, Ecclesiasticall." Luther famously wrote in his commentary on Isaiah that "Rome is the true Babylon" (qtd. Nohrnberg, 238).

56. I.ii.12. The red cross was the symbol not only of St. George but also of the Knights Templar; on this basis Gregory Wilkin has even argued that Redcross represents the Templars: see "Spenser's Rehabilitation of the Templars," *Spenser Studies* 11 (1990): 89–100. St. George himself was apparently of Cappadocian origins, and seems to have become popular in England around the time of the crusades (see the entry in *The Spenser Encyclopedia*). Harold Weatherby argued that Spenser's St. George immigrated from the east much more recently; see "The True St. George," *ELR* 17 (1987): 122–41. For an argument that the legacy of St. George is contested between east and west in *The Faerie Queene*, see Lisa Jardine and Jerry Brotton, *Global Interests: Renaissance Art between East and West* (Ithaca: Cornell University Press, 2000), 13–23.

57. 2G4v. I do not mean to conflate Spenser with Foxe: I have already quoted Foxe's assertion, in the same passage, that "He that bringeth S. George or S. Denise, as patrons, to the fielde to fight agaynst the *Turke*, leaueth Christ (no doubt) at home." Spenser was perfectly willing to use a Catholic saint to allegorize Protestant theology.

58. I.iv.43. See Gless, 94, on their mutual desire for revenge.

59. Paul clearly asserts that this armor is metaphorical: "we wrestle not against flesh and blood." He then goes on to write that "we wrestle not against flesh and blood, but against principalities, against powers, *and* against the worldlie gouernours, *the princes* of the darkenes of this worlde, against spiritual wickednesses, *which are in*

the hie places." (Ephesians 6:11–12, qtd. from the 1560 edition of the Geneva text.) The distinction is not only between physical and spiritual combat, but also between combat and political resistance. Some English Protestants were willing to take Paul's armor in a double sense, literal and spiritual. In 1579, Geoffrey Gates exhorted England to war against Spain, adducing Paul as one of his authorities: what makes us strong in wars, Gates writes, glossing Ephesians, is "heauenly contemplation, and a righteous hearte"—"adding unto these matters the iron armour, the sword, the speare, the shield, and the horse, the corslet." See *The Defence of Militarie profeβion* (London, 1579), G1v.

60.   *The Pageant of Popes* (London, 1574), L6v.

61.   See *Purchas his Pilgrimes* (Reprint, New York: AMS, 1965), 8: 25: "Urban the second (the second Turban)," and Fuller, *The Historie of the Holy Warre* (Cambridge, 1639), C4v: "Urbane the second (whom Cardinall Benno called Turbane for troubling the whole world)." Falstaff borrows from this rhetoric when he compares his deeds at Shrewsbury to those of "Turk Gregory": see *1 Henry IV*, ed. A.R. Humphreys (New York: Arden, 1966), V.iii.46. The Gregory cited here is almost certainly Gregory VII; see Bale, *Pageant*, L2r-L3r.

62.   This is the logic of Luther's resistance to the "false brethren" among the Protestants, that is, to those who like Karlstadt or Zwingli thought Luther had failed to go far enough in his thinking about the Eucharist or in his iconoclasm: as Luther argued repeatedly, and especially in his 1531 lectures on Galatians, ceremonies do not matter. Neither their presence nor their absence can be central to our understanding of religious identity. In this sense, Zwinglians and Catholics both commit the same error, of attributing too much significance to the mass. See Mark U. Edwards, Jr., *Luther and the False Brethren* (Stanford: Stanford University Press, 1975).

63.   1.7.7. See *Orlando Furioso*, ed. Caretti, 46.140. Geoffrey of Monmouth's Arthur also fights a giant with a Saracen past: the giant of Mont St. Michel. See Geraldine Heng, "Cannibalism, the First Crusade, and the Genesis of Medieval Romance," *Differences* 10 (1998), 116–24. Orgoglio is the brother of Disdain and therefore also of Mutabilitie, all children of Titan. Disdain, in Book VI, is described like a Saracen. See VI.vii.41–43, VII.vi.2, and VII.vi.26–27.

64.   In the House of Holiness Redcross begins a spiritual convalescence whose many emphasize the tremendous work spiritual healing requires, and the helplessness of the individual knight to perform this work. At the last stage of his recovery, Redcross is brought to a hospital where he begins to learn what it means to act as a Christian, and even how a Christian can oppose the Saracens, from a bead-man whose office is "captiues to redeeme with price of bras, / From Turkes and Sarazins" (I.x.40). This is the only time in the poem that the Turks are mentioned, and the choice of that word suggests the pressure of contemporary experience. But the placement of this episode in the full narrative of convalescence suggests how dependant this human labor is on prevenient grace. Moreover, "redeeming" captives—an activity compared to Christ's harrowing of hell—is far from the chivalric action Redcross had hoped to accomplish.

65.   I.x.60 and 64. For a penetrating discussion of Spenser's use of pilgrimage allegory, see Anne Prescott, "Spenser's Chivalric Restoration: From Bateman's *Travayled Pylgrime* to the Redcrosse Knight," *Studies in Philology* 86 (1989): 166–97.

Pilgrimage and crusade are linked as "good works," by the more technical requirements of a Catholic theology of the remission of sins, and by their common emphasis
on the distinctive status of Palestine as "the holy land."

66.   Nohrnberg, 77. A. Kent Hieatt suggests that "the allegorically rendered victo-
ries of Arthur over the Armada and the Spanish in Antwerp . . . may have been
Spenser's cobbled together substitute for a sequel which he had given up." See "The
Projected Continuation of *The Faerie Queene*: Rome Delivered?" *Spenser Studies* 8
(1987), 186, and the exchange between Hieatt and Thomas P. Roche, Jr., 335–47.

67.   III.iii.49. Hamilton notes that Philip II's arms contain a castle.

68.   Revelation 22:10, qtd. from Geneva text of 1560; III.iii.50. At the end of
Book I, we discover along with Redcross that he is himself a Saxon: "thou springst
from ancient race / Of *Saxon* kings," Contemplation tells him (I.x.65). This interestingly complicates the historical narrative. Hamilton quotes Joanne Craig, suggesting
that this is simply a crack in the façade of the British myth: "'Spenser briefly discards
the fashionable notion that he and his contemporaries were the descendants of
Geoffrey's legendary Britons.'" But as I have argued elsewhere, there was an ongoing
controversy over England's Anglo-Saxon origins whose primary fault-line was religion, and I suspect that Spenser must have been aware of this. See my "John Foxe
and the Anglo-Saxons," in *John Foxe and His World*, ed. Christopher Highley and
John N. King (Burlington: Ashgate, 2002), 54–72. I think we are meant to experience a sense of paradox here, in being told that a descendant of the pagan Saxons
has become the knight of holiness, and are meant to recognize the limits of any
concept of "national" election. See below.

69.   Critics who rely on the *Letter to Ralegh* as evidence of Spenser's original plan
for his work have suggested that the war promised in Books I and III would have
been the subject of the unwritten twelfth or twenty-fourth book; A. Kent Hieatt
has extended this idea by arguing, on the basis of II.x.49, that Spenser's initial plan
would have culminated in Arthur's conquest of Rome, itself a crucial part of the
Arthurian material in Geoffrey of Monmouth and Malory. In order to make this
assertion, Hieatt insists that the Saracens referred to at I.xi.7 are in fact the pagan
Saxons, prefiguring the Catholic "pagans," and that the Saracens themselves have
no place in this historical scheme: see "The Projected Continuation," n. 2. But I
think this is to reduce a multivalent allegory to the literal conflict with Catholicism,
and to overlook the way Spenser writes that conflict into the romance narrative
of crusade.

70.   See generally Cantos x-xii, and especially V.xii.27: "ere he could reforme it
thoroughly, / He through occasion called was away, / To Faerie Court, that of necessity / His course of Iustice he was forst to stay." On the apocalypticism of Book V
see Kenneth Borris, *Spenser's Poetics of Prophecy in* The Faerie Queene *V* (Victoria:
University of Victoria Press, 1991) and Richard Mallette, *Spenser and the Discourses
of Reformation England* (Lincoln: University of Nebraska Press, 1997), chap. 5. See
also Gless, chap. 6, and Tobias Gregory, "Shadowing Intervention: On the Politics
of *The Faerie Queene* Book 5 Cantos 10–12," *ELH* 67:2 (2000): 365–97. This sense
of incompleteness extends into Book VI, on which see Harry Berger, "A Secret
Discipline: *The Faerie Queene*, Book VI," in *Revisionary Play: Studies in the Spenserian
Dynamics* (Berkeley: University of California Press, 1988), 219; Joseph Wittreich,

Visionary Poetics: Milton's Tradition and his Legacy (San Marino: Huntington Library, 1979), 62; and Borris, 10–11 and 59–68.

71.   VII.viii.2. These lines draw on the paradox already articulated by Nature in her verdict, VII.vii.58–59: all things change, but "by their change their being doe dilate." Dilation and change are rearticulated as the essential expression of being. This idea suggests the narrative dilations of romance, which on the one hand express the nature of things, but on the other hand generate a constantly deferred desire for ending, for that time when all things will have reached their fulfillment.

72.   The word "Sabaoth" appears twice in the Bishop's Bible, but in the Geneva text is both times rendered as "hostes." See Romans 9:28–29: "For he finisheth the worde, and maketh it shorte in ryghteousnesse: for a shorte worde wyll the Lorde make on earth. And as Esaias sayde before. Except the lorde of Sabaoth had left vs seede, we had ben made as Sodoma, and had ben lykned to Gomortha." See also James 5:4: "Beholde the hyre of labourers which haue reaped downe your fieldes, whiche hyre is of you kept backe by fraude, cryeth: and the cryes of them which haue reaped, are entred into the eares of the Lorde (of) Sabaoth." Both passages are quoted from the 1568 edition of the Bishop's Bible. See Nohrnberg, 83.

73.   Some efforts to interpret the politics of *The Faerie Queene* seem to me to have put too much weight behind the identification of Gloriana or Britomart or Mercilla with Elizabeth: Spenser's allegory never works by one-to-one correspondences, but rather through suggestions that cannot be taken as stable certainties. The important point seems to me to center on the problem of fulfillment: Elizabeth promises to be Gloriana as England promises to be like its idealization in Faeryland, but the deferral of that promise suggests critique as much as praise. A similar strategy may inform Spenser's tendency to praise figures who have fallen into disfavor at court.

74.   For the "elect nation" thesis, see William Haller, *The Elect Nation: The Meaning and Relevance of Foxe's Book of Martyrs* (New York: Harper & Row, 1963). This reading has been contested on the grounds that it misses Foxe's internationalist commitments, and that it oversimplifies the forms of English Protestant nationalism. See esp. Patrick Collinson, "Biblical Rhetoric: The English Nation and National Sentiment in the Prophetic Mode," in Claire McEachern and Debora Shuger, eds., *Religion and Culture in Renaissance England* (Cambridge: Cambridge University Press, 1997).

ANDREW ESCOBEDO

Despair and the Proportion of the Self

This article is the first of two linked essays about despair in
Protestant literature and especially in *The Faerie Queene*. Our
overall thesis is that despair functions simultaneously as a transparent manifestation of God's dispensation and as a kind of joint
or pivot between paradoxes inherent in Protestant Christianity,
especially regarding the relationship between the self and the
world and between body and soul. This first article interprets
early Protestant discourse about despair in Kierkegaardian terms,
as an oscillation between excessive finitude (the concretizing
reduction of self to worldliness) and excessive infinitude (the
imaginary abstraction of self from world). Kierkegaard gives us
an alternative to the common sequential description of despair
(in both sixteenth-century literature and twentieth-century
commentary) as a phase in a spiritual progress that moves (ideally) from pride to despair to repentance to salvation, in which
the meaning of despair becomes clear retrospectively at the end
of the sequence. The clarity of this description comes at the
cost of a certain oversimplification, ignoring the paradoxical
manner in which Christians experience despair, unlike the sins
of wrath, lechery, avarice, or fear, as both a reminder of and
abandonment by God. Taking despair as the repeated and nearly
inevitable disproportion of self to world, I argue that the fate
of Malbecco—to transform from literary type to allegorical
sign—reveals the danger of willful reduction. Conversely, I see
Redcrosse's experience on the mount of Contemplation, with
its striking echoes of the Despair episode in Canto ix, as an
illustration of the risk of the abstraction of self from world, a
risk that grows rather than recedes at the moment of spiritual
vision. Book I especially is framed by Redcrosse's initial designation as "too solemn sad" (i.2.8) and Una's mourning

(xii.41.9) when Redcrosse departs at the end. Between these two moments of sorrow, Spenser uses despair as a recurring sign of the slippage within a system trying to coordinate divine wrath and divine grace.

*I*N JOHN SKELTON'S *MAGNIFICENCE*, the eponymous main character sins against God's laws and keeps company with allegorical characters like Liberty, Crafty Conveyance, Cloaked Collusion, and Courtly Abusion, rioting in vice until he realizes the peril to his immortal soul—realizes too late, it seems, because the figure of Despair comes to him and prevents him from seeking God's forgiveness. Then, in a plot sequence familiar to readers of *The Faerie Queene*, Skelton's Despair offers Magnificence a dagger in order to kill himself, which the miserable man raises over his head, preparing to thrust it into his heart, when suddenly the figure Good Hope enters on stage, snatching the dagger from Magnificence's hand and assuring him, "Sir, your physician is the grace of God. . . . "[1] Good Hope explains that Magnificence's moment of despair was a dangerous sin, calling it "a great misadventure, thy maker to displease" (line 2341). Yet he also reveals that God gives man "[a]ffliction and trouble to prove his patience" (line 2371), and describes despair as "a wondrous fall" (lines 2341, 2375). "Wondrous" here hints at the other significance of despair, namely the experience that brings Magnificence to moral awareness, God's corrective rod that prepares the sinner for repentance. Thus, although Skelton's Despair is infernal, crying out "Hell burneth! Where shall I me hide?" (line 2324) when Good Hope saves Magnificence—and in this respect he anticipates Spenser's Despair, who is a "man of Hell"—he is nonetheless also part of the machinery of Grace, loosening the shell of hardened sin that keeps Magnificence in moral oblivion.

The ambiguous, dual identity of the Despair figure—at once salvation and damnation—is brought home forcefully by comparing Spenser and Skelton to other narratives featuring the pride-despair-salvation sequence. Richard Wever's *Lusty Iuventus* similarly represents a sinful youth reveling with all the wrong allegories, who, when confronted with the magnitude of his sin, exclaims "Alas alas what have I wrought and done?/Here in this place I will fall down desperate,/To ask for mercy now I know it is too late."[2] As we might expect, a salvation figure—Wever calls his "Good Council"—rescues the youth by chastising his "desperation" and urging him to "remember [God's] merciful promises and comfort thyself in him" (line 1029). Yet, in this play, the figure that brings on this "desperation" is not Despair but rather Good Council himself, who initially threatens that the youth's "blasphemy/Shall never be pardoned nor forgiven,/In this world, nor in the world to come" (lines 1010–13). If Good Council sounds here rather like Spenser's man of Hell or Skelton's Hell-burning villain, it is because despair conceptually oscillates between irremediable sin and moral awareness. Similarly, Nathaniel Woodes's 1581 allegorical *Conflict of Conscience* presents a despair figure named Horror whom Woodes calibrates to stand precisely at the point of intersection between Godly reminder and Satanic betrayal. Woodes dramatizes the famous despair and eventual suicide of Francis Spira, the Italian lawyer who recanted Calvinism to protect his family from punishment, a reprobate whose prolonged spiritual suffering drew both sympathy and condemnation from Protestant commentators throughout the sixteenth and seventeenth centuries.[3] When Horror initially confronts Spira (or Philologus, as Woodes calls him in the play), he suggests a charitable dimension of his role: "to correct impenitents, of God I am assigned."[4] But he then tells Philologus that God "will no longer in thy soul and spirit make abode:/But with the Graces, which he gave to thee, now is he gone . . . The peace of Conscience faded is, in stead whereof I bring/ The Spirit of Satan, blasphemy, confusion and cursing . . . deadly desperation" (lines 1979–84). We cannot with confidence place Woodes's Horror in either heaven or hell; he is both a Godly corrector and God's hated enemy; he reveals the truth about Spira's spiritual condition and removes all hope of God's Grace, removes it so effectively that the Spira-character falls into a suicidal despair.

This article is the first of two linked essays about despair in Protestant literature and especially in *The Faerie Queene*. I have offered the foregoing examples as a means of working toward our overall thesis: that despair functions simultaneously as a transparent manifestation of God's dispensation and as a kind of joint or pivot between paradoxes inherent in Protestant Christianity. On the one hand, despair clarifies Godly necessity: it brings spiritual crisis to a head, it exposes the misery of Godlessness, it reveals the emptiness of pride. On the other hand, despair erects conceptual impasses for Protestant theology: Is it a first step toward salvation, or the trapdoor to damnation? Does it result from excessive inward contemplation or from worldliness? Is it a medical or spiritual condition? Does it necessitate or make irrelevant godly exhortation? In our view, *The Faerie Queene* carries out one of the most complex investigations of this concept in the sixteenth century. Book I especially is framed by Redcrosse's initial designation as "too solemn sad" (i.2.8) and Una's mourning (xii.41.9) when Redcrosse departs at the end. Between these two moments of sorrow, Spenser uses despair as a recurring sign of the slippage within a system trying to coordinate divine wrath and divine grace.

The problematic qualities of despair were not limited to Protestantism, as the example of Skelton suggests. Yet Reformation theology did in fact exacerbate these qualities by demanding both a personal relationship to God and an acknowledgment of human unworthiness before the Law. For Luther, the recourse to an insufficient self makes despair inevitable, even necessary for salvation, while still remaining a grave sin. Susan Snyder has eloquently summed up the Protestant intensification of despair: "Where Augustine and Bernard warn the Christian, 'You may despair,' Luther thunders, 'You must!' "[5] Such an attitude helps to make sense of Robert Burton's otherwise somewhat surprising claim, despite his insistence elsewhere on the spiritual danger of the Roman faith, that Catholics are *unable* to despair as Protestants do:

> I see no reason at all why a papist at any time should despair, or be troubled for his sins; for let him be never so dissolute a caitiff, so notorious a villain, so monstrous a sinner, out of that treasury of indulgences and merits of which the Pope is dispensator he may have free pardon and plenary remission of all his sins.[6]

Despair emerges here momentarily as a sign of Protestant authenticity, the freedom from idolatrous distractions and the commitment to rigorous self-scrutiny. Indeed, Spenser himself appears to hint at this authenticity with the figure of Archimago, whom he allows to imitate Redcrosse almost perfectly (Truth herself cannot tell the difference), even describing the enchanter's appearance—"[f]ull jolly knight he seemed" (I.ii.11.7)—as an exact echo of our first vision of the knight of holiness (I.i.1.8). The primary difference is that Archimago lacks the melancholy of Redcrosse, who is, as the narrator informs us, "too solemne sad" (I.i.2.8). The unholy simulator can copy the cheer of holiness but not its despair. And whatever the traditional links between hope and fear, Spenser goes out of his way to reveal the spiritual anxiety that underlies Speranza's identity: "Not all so chearefull seemed she of sight,/As was her sister; whether dread did dwell,/Or anguish in her hart, is hard to tell" (I.x.14.3–5).

Yet whatever its role in authentic Protestant devotion, despair remained a difficult problem for Reformation theology. The emphasis on predestination, as it became prevalent in the English Church, offers a good example of such difficulty. Despite the commentators' frequent assurance that the doctrine ought not to create anxiety about salvation, predestination does appear to have contributed to the concern about hopelessness.[7] Luther and Calvin both warned their readers against immoderately brooding on the tricky issue of election.[8] Although the authors of the Thirty-nine Articles found the doctrine "full of sweet, pleasant, and unspeakable comfort," and although commentators managed to carve out a limited role for free will within the larger context of election, the authors of consolation tracts nonetheless felt themselves repeatedly obliged to warn their readers not to despair over the limited number of Christians whom God had chosen to save—as Matthew 20:16 warned, "many are called, but few are chosen." William Willymat's *Physic to Cure the Most Dangerous Disease of Desperation* (1604) acknowledges that the doctrine of Predestination causes many Christians "to fear, and to tremble, to stagger, and to doubt, whether they may think themselves to be in the number of those few that shall be saved, yea or no, and so are drawn into despair . . . . "[9] Robert Burton likewise identifies predestination as a danger for those who dwell obsessively on God's specific plans for them: "God's eternal decree of predestination, absolute reprobation, and such fatal tables, they form to their own ruin, and impinge upon this rock of despair."[10] Willymat and Burton, as with dozens of other writers of consolatory tracts about despair and melancholy, combat spiritual fear with a mixture of admonition and comfort: do not try to fathom the mysteries of God; despair about election will in fact guarantee damnation; even the elect have erroneously believed they were reprobate; God's mercy exceeds his wrath; and others. We might suppose that the sheer number of these comforts about predestination suggests the commentators' confidence that the doctrine need not lead to despair. Yet this proliferation of tracts also suggests the opposite: the commentators fear that predestination may create an insurmountable barrier to faith.

Was despair a sin? Yes and no. Medieval commentators relied on Paul's distinction between "godly sorrow" and "worldly sorrow" (2 Cor. 7:10) to designate a recognition of one's sins (leading to repentance and salvation) over against disbelief in God's mercy (leading to despair and death), although they sometimes acknowledged the difficulty of telling the difference.[11] Protestant commentators often refined this distinction into a contrast between the human inability to effect salvation and God's capacity to do so. That is, you should despair of yourself, but not of God's mercy. Willymat identified two kinds of despair: "the one a wicked kind of desperation of God's promises, power, goodness, and mercy towards sinners . . . the other an holy desperation of a man's own power in the obtaining of eternal life. . . . "[12] The preacher Edward Reynolds likewise distinguished between a form of despair that is "regular and allowable, I mean that which in matter of importance drives us out of ourselves, or any presumption and opinion of our own sufficiently" and that which "riseth out of a groundless unbelief of the Power, or distrust of the Goodness, of a superior Agent (especially in those things which depend upon the Will and Omnipotency of God). . . . "[13] We might expect that the distinction between holy and wicked sadness would clear up the ambiguity of despair in Protestant discourse—the elect feel a salutary despair of themselves while the reprobate experience a damning despair of God's forgiveness. Yet in fact the distinction rarely remains very clear, since so many famous saints themselves despaired of divine mercy as well as of their own power. William Perkins speaks of "holy desperation, which is when a man is wholly out of all hope ever to attain salvation by any strength or goodness of his own" and lists Paul, Daniel, and Ezra among the biblical possessors of this form of godly despondency.[14] Yet when he comes to David, whom other commentators regularly place in the earlier list of holy despair, Perkins includes him among those who "despair of God's mercy for a time . . . a dangerous sin" (378). That is, the wicked form of despair itself splits into two kinds, damning and temporary. Burton, while observing that "some kind of despair be not amiss, when, saith Sanchius, we despair of our own means," in fact makes his primary distinction between two forms of sinful despair: "final is incurable, which befalleth reprobates; temporal is a rejection of hope and comfort for a time, which may befall the best of God's children. . . . This ebbs and flows with hope and fear; it is a grievous sin howsoever. . . . "[15] Hence, the Protestant emphasis on human unworthiness sometimes blurred rather than maintained the useful medieval distinction between the "godly sorrow" of the believer and the "worldly sorrow" of the faithless. Despair emerges as a normative aspect of spiritual life precisely because it is part of the mechanism that may lead you to repentance—a necessary, dangerous sin that risks damnation.

In this essay I wish to examine the problematic of this slippage via the question of the proportion, or disproportion, of self to world. The sinner's relation to the world emerges from the necessary incommensurability between the sinner's obduracy and the extension of grace, between the human soul and the calculus of divine wrath and mercy. English preachers regularly discuss despair as a failure to fit oneself into this calculus: Robert Parsons observes that "[t]here be two things whereby sinners do stand in danger: the one in hoping too much (which is presumption); the other in hoping too little, which is desperation."[16] Such a Scylla-and-Charybdis description of vice, of course, seeks to encourage the reader to find an ideal mean between hope and fear. Nearly all commentators, however, recognize the elusiveness of such an ideal. Perkins, despite his insistence on the power of faith, acknowledges "what a wonderful hard thing it is at the same instant when a man is touched for his sins, then to apply God's mercy to himself."[17] Similarly, while Spenser suggests the authenticity of despair, at the same time he also hints at its inclination to slide into extremes—Redcrosse is, after all, "*too* solemne sad." Skelton also points to this sense of unbalance or disproportion in his depiction of Magnificence's despair: "I am weary of the world," he moans, "for unkindness me slayeth" (line 2283). A few lines later Despair responds with a terrible reciprocity: "The world waxeth weary of thee; thou livest too long" (line 2308). Beyond the idea that Magnificence pays the price for his worldliness, Skelton suggests the mutual alienation between man and world that calls for Magnificence's destruction.

Søren Kierkegaard's redaction of Protestant despair in *The Sickness Unto Death* focuses precisely on this issue of disproportion. To put it very briefly, Kierkegaard argues that despair arises out of a misrelation between ourselves and the world. God's distance from us, forcing us into a relation with worldly finitude, is Kierkegaard's version of the Fall, giving rise to human despair:

In the composite of the eternal and the temporal, man is a relation, in this relation itself and relating itself to itself. God made man a relation; to be a human being is to be a relation. But a relation which, by the very fact that God, as it were, releases it from his hand, or the same moment God, as it were, releases it, is itself, relates itself to itself—this relation can become in the same moment a misrelation. To despair is this misrelation taking place.[18]

God's "release" of the human being from his hand causes the self to emerge as a mediation between time and eternity, between the limited and boundless, creating the possibility of imbalance between the two poles. Despair manifests itself on the one hand as a *reduction* of self to world—what Kierkegaard calls an excessive "finitude" (33)—wherein we identify ourselves only with the material things before us and with an self-defeating understanding of the ways of the world. Conversely, despair may emerge as an *abstraction* of self from world—what Kierkegaard calls excessive "infinitude" (30)—wherein the "fantastic" power of the imagination overlooks the necessary limitations on human life. This second is a tricky misrelation to understand—should not abstracting from the world lead one closer to God? No, in the sense that this abstraction makes us forget that the world is the limiting condition of our current existence.[19] The self must struggle to find a mean between reduction and abstraction, as Spenser imagines despairing lovers "languishing twixt hope and feare" (III.vi.13.9). With both misrelations, Kierkegaard claims that the self fails to return to itself (30), reminiscent of Hooker's assertion that "men . . . are through the extremity of grief many times in judgment so confounded, that they find not themselves in themselves."[20]

Despite the risk of anachronism, I want to apply to Spenser's poem the Kierkegaardian notion of the disproportioned reduction to and abstraction from the world. It is important to remember that Kierkegaard writes not only as a post-Hegelian but also as a late-Protestant redactor of Scripture. He began to work on *The Sickness Unto Death* while reading medieval commentary on *acedia* and *tristitia*.[21] When describing the human attempt to fathom Christ's sacrifice, he quotes Luther's conclusion that God "cannot do otherwise" (126).[22] Many aspects of Kierkegaard's account of despair—possibility and necessity, a sinfulness both culpable yet existential, conscious and unconscious despair—derive from early Protestant interpretations of the phenomenon. On the other hand, Kierkegaard's distance from the Tudors allows him (and us) a perspective on Renaissance commentary that makes explicit part of the problematic of despair that remains only implicit in much sixteenth-century Protestant writing. Perhaps most important, his account give us an alternative to the common sequential description of despair (in both sixteenth-century literature and twentieth-century commentary) as a phase in a spiritual progress that moves (ideally) from pride to despair to repentance to salvation, in which the meaning of despair becomes clear retrospectively at the end of the sequence. In such an interpretive frame, for instance, we know with certainty that Spira's despair, despite the Italian's painful and seemingly sincere effort to repent, was of a reprobate nature because he failed to overcome it at the end of his life, yet the clarity of this description comes at the cost of a certain reductiveness, ignoring the paradoxical manner in which Christians experience despair—unlike the sins of wrath, lechery, avarice, or fear—as both a reminder of and abandonment by God. Skelton's Despair, Wever's

Good Hope, and Woodes's Horror are not only preinterpreted moments in a sequence but also placeholder figures whose indeterminacy signifies the difficulty of knowing one's relation to God's divine scheme. Indeed, Perkins himself, though he elsewhere relies on the elect/reprobate distinction, insists on the indeterminate status of Spira's despair:

> they are much overseen that write of him as a damned creature. For first, who can tell whether he despaired finally or no? Secondly, in the very midst of his desperation, he complaineth of the hardness of his heart, which made him that he could not pray: no doubt then he felt his hardness of heart: and the feeling of corruption in the heart is by some contrary grace, so that we may conveniently think that he was not quite bereft of all goodness, though he never felt it then, nor showed it to the beholders.[23]

The very sign that bespeaks reprobate despair—hardness of heart—may in fact signal salvation. The *present* moment of spiritual struggle, despite its interpolation into a narrative sequence, may finally remain inscrutable to outside observers. As Spenser notes of Speranza, "whether dread did dwell,/Or anguish in her hart, is hard to tell" (I.x.14.4–5). Kierkegaard's account emphasizes this ambiguous, extranarrative quality of despair, insisting that self-alienation is not part of a sequence but rather emerges as a condition of human existence: "[despair] is always the present tense . . . in every actual moment of despair the person in despair bears all the past as a present in possibility" (17).

The Kierkegaardian model of disproportion, wherein the self finds it difficult to achieve relation to worldliness neither too reductive nor too abstracted, illuminates much in Spenser's subtle investigation of Christian despair. The idea of a reduction of self to world, for example, allows us to see a dimension in Spenser's account of Malbecco's fate beyond the observation that a worldly, jealous man receives his just desert in the loss of his home and possessions. Spenser does, of course, draw details of Malbecco's story from Ariosto's Sospetto and Ovid's Daedalion and Aesacus; indeed, Spenser probably saw in Daedalion's suicidal refusal of solace—he hears his brother's words of comfort "quam cautes murmura ponti accipit"[24] —an example of the despairing sinner hardened against consolation. Yet his depiction of Malbecco is highly original in its presentation of mental anguish and rather shocking in its tonal shift from humorous fabliau (where jealousy traditionally resides) to the terrors of spiritual death. After Spenser's unusually casual and amused account of Hellenore's ménage with her new Satyr companions (III.x.44–52), we learn that Malbecco flees the scene, eventually hurling himself off a cliff, "desperate" and "fore-damned" (x.56.8). Following several stanzas in which Malbecco transforms into the figure of "Gelosy" itself, Spenser tells us that, like the character Despair who assaults Redcrosse (I.ix), "[y]et can he never die, but dying lives,/And doth himselfe with sorrow new sustaine,/That death and life attonce unto him gives" (x.60.1–3). By insisting on such metaphysical intensity, Spenser discloses the problem of despair as much as he does the problem of jealousy.

There are traditional links between the two ideas—especially, as Thomas Roche has noted,[25] the Petrarchan movement from jealousy to doubt to sorrow to despair—but Spenser seems to make the connection here in terms of the living death that both jealousy and despair impose. Malbecco's living death results from an obsession with worldliness. Spenser has already associated the cuckold's impulse to covet worldly things with death: Trompart refers to Malbecco's hiding place for his gold as "your treasure's grave" (x.42.8) and the narrator speaks of his treasure as "entombed" (x.54.2). After Malbecco discovers the theft of the money he concealed in the ground, he goes mad and appears as a spirit recently escaped "[f]rom Limbo lake" (x.54.6). If earth equals death, then we should expect Malbecco's attempted suicide at the cliff. His final fate, however, is not death but rather a terrible form of ontological reduction, what Kierkegaard calls a loss of "possibility" that makes Grace accessible.[26] Spenser signals Malbecco's isolation from heavenly mercy by actually burying him in the earth, within a dismal "cave":

> Into the same he creepes, and thenceforth there
> Resolv'd to build his balefull mansion,
> In drery darkenes, and continual feare
> Of that rocks fall, which ever and anon
> Threates with huge ruine him to fall upon,
> That he dare never sleepe, but that one eye
> Still ope he keepes for that occasion. . . .
>
> (x.58.1–7)

Here we see the terrifying link between worldliness and despair, pushed to the point of Kierkegaardian intensity. The earth has become both the condition of Malbecco's existence and the promise of his destruction. His watchful anticipation of the future "occasion" in fact becomes faintly ironic when we consider that he has no *occasio* before him, no possibility of preparing himself for grace. Malbecco's earlier self-consumption into an "aery Spright" (x.57.4)—Spenser's deliberate revision of his Ovidian models[27]—is not a renunciation of worldliness but rather the sign of his despairing disproportion with the world. He no longer belongs either on earth or heaven, just as he possesses neither life nor death.

Again, his fate is that of reduction: from castle to cave, from narrative agent to icon of vice, and from character to allegorical sign. We ought to pause over this last, since it invokes Gordon Teskey's description of allegory as a metaphysical reduction, a process whereby allegory must "capture the substantiality of beings and raise it to the conception plane."[28] The allegory does indeed seem to consume and reduce Malbecco in the way it does to few other characters, resulting in a physical transformation: "his substance was consum'd to nought" (57.3), he grows "crooked clawes" (57.8), and, unlike any other figure in the poem, he actually takes on a new name that designates his new essence: "Gelosy" (60.9). Paul Alpers has shrewdly raised the question of whether Malbecco does in fact transform rather than simply "remaining" what he already, really was.[29] Yet, regarding the issue of despair, I want to stress Spenser's choice to remind us that the transformed Malbecco "[f]orgot he was a man . . . " (x.60.9). With this phrase Spenser, at the very end of the episode, calls our attention to Malbecco's lost humanity. Indeed, as Louise Gilbert Freeman notes, Spenser has described Malbecco's tribulations with "real empathy,"[30] and this final reminder makes him more than simply a cautionary tale against reprobate despair. He is reprobate, of course, and his despair of God's mercy condemns him to "deathes eternall dart" (x.59.9). Yet his dual identity as hopeless Gelosy and former man reveals the manner in which Malbecco reiterates the despair episode of I.ix, merging the damnable qualities of the figure of Despair with the spiritual vulnerability of Redcrosse. As a "man," Malbecco signals the human susceptibility to worldly reduction, because we are all "worldlings." Yet, in describing Malbecco's reduction as a forgetting of his humanity, Spenser suggests that the human in us can, and ought to, find a proportioned, nonreductive relation to the world that allows for the possibility of grace.

Redcrosse suffers to some degree from the opposite problem—he is too eager to escape from the world. The other form of misrelation

Kierkegaard identifies—abstraction of self from world—must be applied with caution to Spenser, given the poet's repeated denigration of worldliness in contrast to spirituality. This denigration is especially apparent in the episode on Contemplation's mount, which concludes with the narrator's observation that "[s]o darke are earthly thinges compard to things divine" (I.x.67.9). Commentary on this episode has often emphasized the Aristotelian definition of contemplation as the highest intellectual faculty that most perfectly prepares men for action in the world.[31] But commentary has less commonly called attention to the Protestant view that contemplation could, in a variety of ways, lead to an immoderate despondency about earthly life. In the *Hymn of Heavenly Beauty*, Spenser himself implies that the "perfect speculation" on God's being demands a revised estimation of earthly things: "Mount up aloft through heavenly contemplation,/From this darke world, whose damps the soule do blynd."[32] Spenser ends the *Hymn* by urging his soul to avoid those worldly objects that ultimately cause only sadness: "Ah Ceasse to gaze on matter of thy grief" (42.7). The Dutch physician Levinus Lemnius makes a similar point, noting that "a contemplative life, or speculative science" ought to teach the Christian "that in this life there is no felicity, that this world is nothing else but a perilous pilgrimage, a maze of misery, a surging sea of sorrows and troubles, a continual conflict, a wretched warfare, a gulf of griefs, a huge heap of iniquities, and a waste wilderness full of vanities and vexation of the spirit, and that there is no profit under the sun."[33] Commentators also sometimes associated contemplation with abstract musing about heaven and election. Burton does advocate meditating on "God himself" with "spiritual eyes of contemplation"—a vision that will make us realize that "[a]ll those other beauties fail, vary, are subject to corruption, to loathing. . . ."[34] Yet he also goes on to criticize those who, out of "curiosity, needless speculation, contemplation, solicitude," "trouble and puzzle themselves about those questions of grace, free will, perseverance, God's secrets" (III:399). We might be inclined to assume that the hermit Contemplation, who meditates strictly on "God and goodness" (I.x.46.9), would be free of Burton's trouble and puzzle. Yet the "highest Mount" (x.53.1) to which the hermit leads Redcrosse invokes the issues of divine judgment (Stanza 53) and divine mercy (Stanza 54), and the revelation of his destiny leads the knight to question (Stanza 62) how he has merited membership with God's "chosen people" (57.4). The entire episode in fact implicitly raises questions that Luther and Calvin would prefer most Christians not to think about too deeply.

As with Spenser's Speranza, Contemplation offers Redcrosse a form of aspiration that entails a certain degree of desperation. Spenser himself suggests the link between Contemplation's abstraction from the world and the presence of despair by drawing a parallel between Despair's argument in Canto ix—"life must life, and bloud must bloud repay" (43.6)—and Contemplation's argument in Canto x: "bloud can nought but sin, & wars but sorrowes yield" (60.9). Redcrosse seems to remain in despair even after Una has Calvinistically assured him of his election in Canto ix: he still wishes in the House of Holiness to "end his wretched dayes" (x.21.8) and continues "disdeining life, desiring leave to die" (x.22.8). This death wish continues after the knight's meeting with Contemplation, during his fight with the dragon (xi.28.1–6). These persistent suicidal tendencies mark Redcrosse's hopelessness as wicked rather than salutary, the temporary "despair of God's mercy for a time . . . a dangerous sin," as Perkins puts it.[35] His wish for death in these moments constitutes an abstraction of self from the world that is significantly continuous with the abstraction that occurs on Contemplation's mount. That is to say, Redcrosse's continued despair does not represent only a necessary phase in a sequence whose conclusion will determine that despair's meaning, but also signals the extent to which Redcrosse remains unable to find an appropriate relation to a world that he recognizes as sinful but from which he cannot simply depart. The abstraction from the world that Contemplation offers carries its own perils, in this case Redcrosse's inability to find the proper proportion between his wish for heaven and his earthly commitments. After the hermit tells him of his fate, Redcrosse first expresses his wish to retain worldly love and chivalry, and then expresses his wish to never again revisit to the "fruitlesse" (x.63.2) joys of the world. He returns from the mount "dazed" (x.67.6) by the disparity between earth and heaven, and chooses, at the end of Book I, to continue his worldly chivalry despite Contemplation's instructions to give up the "suit of earthly conquest" (x.60.7) after helping Una. These vacillations between world and heaven in fact recall Kierkegaard's sense of the cost of abstraction: "willing . . . does not become proportionally as concrete as it is abstract . . . [failing] to carry out the infinitely small part of the work that can be accomplished this very day, this very hour, this very moment" (32).

My point in calling attention to these continuities is not to say that Despair and Contemplation are simply the same—after all, Despair promises death, while Contemplation promises Sainthood—but to suggest that both figures emerge from the same problematic of finding a proper relation to worldly existence. Redcrosse's experiences in the House of Holiness do not end up providing an Aristotelian balance between abstract thought and worldly action, but rather reveal how difficult it is to remain on earth after you have seen heaven. Carol V. Kaske, while noting the parallels between the Faerie capital and the New Jerusalem, observes that "the centrality of fame renders Cleopolis irreconcilable with Christianity."[36] Indeed, the episode does not so much place heaven and earth in proper proportion as reveal the fragmentation between them, a fragmentation that fuels the despair of both Hellenore's cuckolded husband and Una's uncertain guardian. In their most profound moments of self-definition, Malbecco sees the walls of his cave while Redcrosse sees the expanse of the New Jerusalem—what two visions could be more different? Yet both visions produce a sense of dislocation and sadness, a sadness that for Redcrosse culminates in Cantos ix and x, but that also runs throughout the entirety of Book I, from the knight's initial sadness to his encounters with joylessness and faithlessness to his wish to die during his encounter with the dragon. It is a sadness born out of the disproportion between self and world that Protestantism did not create but exacerbated by making Grace at once more personally immediate and implacably invisible, a divine obscurity that causes despair when, as Calvin observed, "miserable man endeavors to force his way into the secret recesses of Divine wisdom. . . . "[37] Grace is like the Pole Star that Spenser describes shortly before Redcrosse is to abandon Una in Canto ii, which "firm is fixt, and sendeth light from farre/To all, that in the wide deepe wandering arre" (I.ii.1.4–5). The rhetoric of simultaneous proximity and distance between God and the world is an analogy, in *The Faerie Queene*, for the disproportion between the world and a self trembling "twixt hope and fear."

Ohio University

NOTES

1. *Magnyfycence*, line 2349, in *John Skelton: The Complete English Poems*, ed. John Scattergood (New York: Penguin, 1983).
2. Lines 1013–15. *An Enterlude Called Lusty Iuventus*, ed. Helen Scarborough Thomas (New York: Garland, 1982).
3. For a discussion of the treatment of Spira's despair in Protestant accounts, see John Stachniewski, *The Persecutory Imagination: English Puritanism and the Literature of Religious Despair* (Oxford: Clarendon Press, 1991), 37–38.
4. Lines 1969. *The Conflict of Conscience*, ed. Herbert Davis (Oxford: Malone Society Reprints, 1952).

5.   Snyder, "The Left Hand of God: Despair in Medieval and Renaissance Tradition," *Studies in the Renaissance* 12 (1965): 25.

6.   Burton, *The Anatomy of Melancholy*, ed. Holbrook Jackson (New York: E.P. Dutton, 1932), III:403.

7.   The comments that follow in this paragraph owe much to the study by Stachniewski, even though we suspect he may underestimate the forms of consolation available even under a strictly Calvinist dispensation.

8.   Luther insisted that those imprudent persons "inquiring to no purpose whether they are among the elect . . . cannot help bringing disaster on themselves, either by failure or by running needless risks." (*Preface to Romans*, in *Martin Luther: Selections From His Writings*, ed. John Dillenberger [Garden City, NY: Anchor Books, 1961], 32.) Calvin likewise admonished that "[t]he discussion of predestination—a subject of itself rather intricate—is made very perplexed, and therefore dangerous, by human curiosity, which no barriers can restrain from wandering into forbidden labyrinths. . . . " (*Institutes of the Christian Religion*, 2 vols., trans. John Allen [Philadelphia: The Westminster Press, 1936], II:172.)

9.   Willymat, *Physic to Cure the Most Dangerous Disease of Desperation* (London, 1604), 19. Quotations are from the 1605 reprint.

10.   Burton, III: 419.

11.   On the medieval treatment of the dual nature of *tristitia*, see Snyder, 20–23.

12.   Willymat, 3.

13.   Reynolds, *A Treatise of the Passions and Faculties of the Soul of Man* (London, 1640), 236–37.

14.   Perkins, *The Works of that Famous and Worthy Minister of Christ in the University of Cambridge, Mr. William Perkins. The First Volume: Newly Corrected . . .* , 2 vols. (London, 1626), 365.

15.   Burton, III:394.

16.   Parsons, *A Booke of Christian exercise apperteining to Resolution . . .* (Oxford, 1585), 306–07.

17.   Perkins, 362.

18.   Kierkegaard, *The Sickness Unto Death: A Christian Psychological Exposition for Upbuilding and Awakening*, ed. and trans. Howard V. Hong and Edna H. Hong (Princeton: Princeton University Press, 1980) 143–44. *The Sickness Unto Death* (1849) follows upon the earlier *Concept of Anxiety* (1844), moving beyond the preliminary psychological examination of anxiety in the face of freedom and sin. In *Sickness*, Kierkegaard comes to the spiritual dimension of despair: as anxiety is related to the ethical, despair is related to the religious and eternal.

19.   Kierkegaard links these imbalances with an analogous set of disproportions. The reduction of self to world corresponds to a lack of "possibility" (37), making it harder for the self to imagine divine mercy. The abstraction of self from world corresponds to a lack of "necessity" (35), tempting the self to forego the discipline required for divine mercy.

20.   Hooker, *Sermon on the Certainty and Perpetuity of Faith in the Elect*; included in *Ecclesiastical Polity*, 4 vols. (New York: E.P. Dutton & Co., 1907), 6.

21.   See Kierkegaard's comments in his journal for this period: *Søren Kierkegaard's Journals and Papers*, 7 vols., ed. and trans. Howard V. Hong and Edna H. Hong (Bloomington: Indiana University Press, 1967–78), I:739–40.

22. Kierkegaard takes this phrase from Luther's concluding reply at the Diet of Worms.

23. Perkins, 378.

24. *Metamorphoses* 11:330–31; "as the crags hear the murmurs of the sea" (Loeb translation).

25. See "The Menace of Despair and Arthur's Vision, *Faerie Queene* I.9," *Spenser Studies* IV: 71–92.

26. Kierkegaard, 37–40.

27. Daedalion and Aesacus both transform into birds after they hurl themselves off cliffs (*Metamorphoses* 11.339–45 and 784–795). In both cases, their transformations result from the merciful intervention of the gods.

28. Teskey, *Allegory and Violence* (Ithaca: Cornell University Press, 1996), 18. See also Louise Gilbert Freeman's excellent account of *allegoresis* in this episode: "The Metamorphosis of Malbecco: Allegorical Violence and Ovidian Change," *Studies in Philology* 47:3 (Summer 2000): 308–330.

29. Alpers, *The Poetry of the "Faerie Queene"* (Columbia: University of Missouri Press, 1982), 389.

30. Freeman, 319.

31. E.g., see John Bernard's entry on "Contemplation" in *The Spenser Encyclopedia* (Toronto: University of Toronto Press, 1990), 190.

32. *Hymn of Heavenly Beauty*, 20.3–4; *The Yale Edition of the Shorter Poems of Edmund Spenser*, ed. William A. Oram et al. (New Haven: Yale University Press, 1989).

33. Lemnius, *The Sanctuary of Salvation*, trans. Hugh Kinder (London, 1592), ¶5v, ¶6r.

34. Burton, III:313, 315.

35. Perkins, 378.

36. Kaske, *Spenser and Biblical Poetics* (Ithaca: Cornell University Press, 1999), 93.

37. Calvin, II:221.

BETH QUITSLUND

Despair and the Composition of the Self

This essay argues that in the Despair and House of Holiness episodes of *Faerie Queene* I Spenser exploits the overlap of medical and devotional discourses to find "fit medcine" for Redcrosse's grief. The idea that despair or a "wounded" conscience requires healing appears in English Calvinist writing on both a metaphorical and literal level: through the idea of "curing" the soul of both sin and desperate guilt, and by addressing grief as a product of melancholy, a bodily disorder. Writers within a generally Calvinist framework took advantage of medical rhetoric and the ambiguous relationship between physical and spiritual concerns to understand and enable their own therapeutic interventions in what was, strictly speaking, a preordained transaction between God and the individual soul. Although the existence of despair, as a sin, is predicated on a distinction between the effects of a crazed body and eternal (predestined) soul, the practical treatment of despair in both Protestant exhortation and physic binds together body and soul and redefines their interactions. Spenserian allegory, which externalizes the inner self in much the same way that medicine and medical rhetoric do, thus provides a particularly effective mode for depicting despair as susceptible to methodical reparation.

*W*HEN BRITOMART ENCOUNTERS the desolate and sobbing Scudamour in Canto xi of Book III, her pity moves her to administer "fit medcine to his grief." While Scudamour beats his head against the ground, then, Britomart comforts him thus:

> Ah gentle knight, whose deepe conceiued griefe
> Well seemes t'exceede the powre of patience,
> Yet if that heauenly grace some good reliefe
> You send, submit you to high prouidence,

And euer in your noble hart prepense,
That all the sorrow in the world is lesse,
Then vertues might, and values confidence,
For who nill bide the burden of distresse,
Must not here thinke to liue: for life is wretchednesse.
Therefore, faire Sir, do comfort to you take . . .

                          (III.xi.13–15)[1]

However strange the idea of taking comfort from, among other things, inevitable wretchedness, Britomart's counsel is at least orthodox. Her admonitions—to find patience through grace, to submit to God's will, to remember that goodness overwhelms the most terrible sorrow, and to understand that no one is free of trial—sound like typical advice from an Elizabethan or Jacobean Protestant divine. As preachers never tired of repeating, the idea of predestination ("high prouidence") and inscrutable "heauenly" grace made English Calvinism "a most comfortable doctrine." Although Britomart's sage counsel may seem bathetic in response to what looks very much like a temper tantrum, in fact Scudamour is here a close parody of a despairing sinner who feels deserted by God, questions God's providential justice, proclaims his own unworthiness, brings himself near death by the violence of his grief, denies that any human action can help him, and wishes to die (III.xi.9–12, 16–17).

Calvinism, as Escobedo shows in the preceding essay, requires a difficult and sometimes impossible psychological task from the believer: careful self-scrutiny for evidence of assurance or reprobation, and awareness of one's inability to affect what he finds.[2] Calvin's own writing has little to recommend in the way of consolation for believers adrift in doubt. Internal conviction of assurance signals election, and the lack of such conviction signals a lack of regeneration or even reprobation; at the same time, Calvin and Calvinists admitted that even the reprobate could feel a mistaken sense of assurance, so that the subsequent experience of despair could then itself become a sign of reprobation for anyone.[3] What seems necessary in a system privileging spiritual self-evaluation to the exclusion of visible signs of grace is a convincingly objective comfort to ameliorate doubt and encourage faith.

The prodigious collection of consolatory treatises and sermons penned in the late sixteenth and seventeenth centuries testifies to the concern Calvinist ministers felt for conscience-stricken believers. Comfort for those in danger of despair varies depending on the theological and psychological preferences of the comforter, but there is plenty of common ground. Most argue that a well-wrung conscience is itself a hopeful sign, since it shows that the sufferer feels the degradation of his sins. Writers also seek to normalize suffering as a condition of the elect, either because God exercises the faith of the elect through trial, or because depravity will break out even in the elect; at the same time, many writers verge on Christian stoicism in contending, like Britomart, that the world itself is nothing but sorrow. But in addition to these rather passive comforts, consolatory tracts also urge a number of more direct actions on those in danger of despair, and of these, few are rigorously consistent with the logic of double predestination or the carefully maintained Calvinist dogma that the elect feel their own assurance. Many consolations, in fact, at least imply that individual men have the option of choosing faith, as the 1628 retitling of William Willymat's *Physic to Cure the Most Dangerous Disease of Desperation* (1604) suggests: *The anchor of faith. Upon which, a Christian may repose in all manner of temptations. Especially in that great and dangerous gulf of desperation. Wherein so many over-whelmed with the weight and burthen of their sin, and not resisting themselves by the hand of faith, upon the promises and invitations of Christ, have with Cain and Judas most fearfully fallen and shipwrackt themselves, to the utter confusion both of body and soul for ever.*[4] Arguing that in the "all who believe" of John 3:16 "is included every particular believing person," Willymat contends that "here God excludeth none from his promise, unless through their unbelief and despair, they exclude their own selves" (91). The more moderate version of this position is Perkins's in *A Dialogue of the State of a Christian Man*, in which the wise Eusebius counsels anyone tempted by despair that since the Lord can lift them up, "Go no further then downward, but lift up thy heart together with thine eye, and seek unto the Lord. . . . "[5] Strictly speaking, the Lord only raises up whom he chooses, and to seek God sincerely is an effect, rather than cause of faith; but no divine with any psychological insight (or, perhaps as importantly, compassion) would attempt to comfort a Christian in pain by observing that if he were *really* elect, he would eventually feel better. Britomart, confronting Scudamour's despair, herself follows the lead of these well-intentioned ministers. What gets that doleful knight up off the ground, finally, is not the promise of grace alone (which, she seems to argue, would allow submission to Providence, God's agency), but the suggestion that he himself can employ potent "vertue" and martial "value"—his renewed hope, that, with Britomart's valiant help, can do something about his situation.

Doing something about despair in both *The Faerie Queene* at large and in Spenser's culture resembles Britomart's intervention in another

way: spiritual rescue missions are frequently and effectively figured
as "fit medcine." The idea that despair or a "wounded" conscience
requires healing works itself out in English Calvinist discourse on
both a metaphorical and literal level. I would like to suggest that
writers operating within a generally Calvinist framework took advantage of medical rhetoric and the ambiguous relationship between
physical and spiritual concerns to understand and enable their own
interventions in what was, strictly speaking, a preordained transaction
between God and the individual soul. Although the existence of
despair, as a sin, is predicated on a distinction between the effects of
a crazed body and eternal (predestined) soul, the practical treatment
of despair in both Protestant exhortation and physic binds together
body and soul and redefines their interactions. If, for Kierkegaard,
an imbalance or opposition between "finitude" and "infinitude"
characterizes despair, it is also true that despair marks a junction
between the body and spirit for a number of Reformed writers.

Medical analogies pervade treatises on afflicted consciences. To
the suggestive title of Willymat's *Physic* we can add John Abernathy's
A Christian and Heavenly Treatise Containing Physic for the Soul (1615),
Samuel Ward's *Balm from Gilead to Recover Conscience* (published 1628,
preached 1616), Henry Denne's *A conference between a sick man and a
minister, showing the nature of presumption, despair and the true living faith*
(1643), and many others. When Kierkegaard reasons that "Everything
essentially Christian must have in its presentation a resemblance to
the way a physician speaks at the sickbed," he writes as a direct
descendent of Reformation comforters.[6] Though the Reformers
themselves inherit the trope of Christ as physician from the New
Testament and its medieval and patristic uses, the language of illness
and wounding becomes newly prominent and insistent in the Protestant discourse on conscience.

Calvinist treatises use medical terminology to describe two different but closely related sets of wounds or diseases: the sickness of sin,
and the disease of a wounded conscience itself. For both of these
illnesses divines cast themselves as (meta)physicians, ministering to
the ravages of sin and the consciousness of sin in overlapping ways.
The "physic" they offered was thus both guidance in repentance and
reassurance that the sinner's penitence was adequate for God's mercy.
These tracts often suggested steps to repentance that were both painful
and extremely active, like Richard Greenham's proposed course of
treatment:

[I]t is far safer before incarnative and healing medicines, to use
corrosive and mundifying waters, without which though some

sores may seem to close and skin up apace, yet they prove worse, and being rotten still at the core; they have above a thin skin, and underneath dead flesh. In like manner, we would cloak, we would hide and cover our sins, as it were with a curtain: but it is more sound Chirurgery to prick and pierce our consciences with the burning iron of the Law, and to cleanse the wound of the soul by sharp threatenings, least that a skin pulled over the conscience for a while, we leave the rotten corruption uncured underneath. . . . [7]

If the surgical removal and cauterization of sin is part of the cure for an afflicted conscience, though, so is a promise of ultimate mercy: "when men proceed in this cure, they must remember . . . to labour that the afflicted may be persuaded that their sins are pardonable, and their sores curable. . . . "[8] Perkins's Eusebius echoes Greenham, urging the application of "the Gospel a more gentle plaister, which suppled and swaged the wounds of my conscience, and brought me health" after the "corrosives" of the Law (382). These "Chiurgeries" and "plaisters" are God's own literal prescriptions, but they are wielded by the minister's human agency as if they were the ordinary instruments of medicine—as if, in fact, they depended on well-established natural causes rather than on the deep mystery of grace and predestination. The metaphor of medicine is thus a rhetorical device that itself does some of the work of comfort, placing despair into a discursive framework centered on conventional and mechanical healing.

But, as we shall see, the idea of a medical ministry is not restricted to metaphors in the writings of good Calvinists. The body also enters the Renaissance discussion of despair through medical literature on melancholy. Melancholy, besides being the most fashionable psychological disorder of the late sixteenth century,[9] is in addition the most extreme instance of the interdependence of mind and body, in which either an excess of the humor itself or the corruption of other humors into a more pernicious form of melancholy produced extravagant and varied effects on the sufferer: "heaviness, sorrow, sadness, fear, and dread of mishap to come, carefulness, thought, desperation and distrust, that is to say, clean out of hope of any better fortune,"[10] wild delusions, physical wasting, skin discoloration, hair loss, and halitosis, to name only a few of the more commonly listed effects. The Dutch Protestant Levinus Lemnius explains that melancholic psychological disorder arises from an obstructed spleen, "[f]or the fulsome vapours (which as it were out of a dampish Marsh or stinking Camarine,) strike upward, do annoy the Brain with grievous and odious fumes" (fol. 142ᵛ). Although all commentators on melancholy agree that anxiety and other psychological stresses could cause melancholy, its treatment remained a combination of behavioral and medicinal therapies, designed to relax the mind but also to reverse the deadly physical processes that sustained the disease. Through purgation, drugs, and surgery, that is, the physician strives to restore normal hope to those suffering from "desperation and distrust."

On the one hand, the spiritual sin of despair is not, physicians and ministers incessantly repeat, related to the physical disorder of melancholy. On the other, many orthodox writers seem incapable of fully separating them. If Perkins carefully explains why those who "are of opinion that this sorrow for sin is nothing else but a melancholic passion" are far mistaken, and that "physic" cures melancholy but not godly sorrow, he also concedes that "it must be acknowledged they may both concur together . . . " (365). Furthermore, not only does despair "weaken the body, and consume it more then any sickness," Perkins goes so far as to declare that repentance (the salve for wounded consciences) is a sovereign means of restoring physical temperance as well: "It turns the sadness of melancholy to godly sorrow, choler to good zeal, softness of nature to meekness of spirit, madness and lightness to Christian mirth; it reforms every man according to his natural constitution, not abolishing it, but redressing the fault of it."[11] Despair, that is, causes the same physical effects as melancholy, while repentance, despair's cure, alleviates melancholic humors.[12] Greenham, likewise, repeatedly asserts that no physic can cure an afflicted conscience, but also describes the inevitable depravity of mankind in terms indistinguishable from the symptoms of melancholy:

> For the godly shall not be so freed from sin, but that they shall be assaulted with evil motions, suspicions, delusions, vain fantasies and imaginations[,] for the body of sin shall never by from us so long as we live. For the scum thereof is almost continually boiling and walloping in us, foaming out . . . filthy froth and stinking savour into our minds, that it is not only detestable to the mind regenerate and renewed by the spirit of God, but also it would make abashed the very natural man, to look into so loathsome a sty of sin, and sink hole of iniquity.[13]

We might recall, here, Lemnius's description of the spleen as a "stinking Camarine" emitting "fulsome vapours" to addle the mind. In allowing the "bodie of sinne" to concoct fantastic delusions, Greenham demolishes the primary distinction between melancholy and a troubled conscience—that melancholics are victims of crazed imaginations, whereas the desperate respond to God's very real wrath.[14] While melancholy and despair are the products of sometimes opposite epistemologies, then, they make up to some degree one discourse in late sixteenth-century England.

Devotional writers' hints at a bodily role in producing spiritual confusion become fully, if inconsistently, explicit in English treatises on melancholy. At the extreme, Burton, who omnivorously digests psychological experiences into forms of melancholy, categorizes despair sometimes as a species of what he calls "religious melancholy," and other times as its unfortunate spiritual result.[15] Though he regards despair as a judgment of God, and in places refers its sole cure to prayer and repentance,[16] he does not allow theological inconsistency to prevent him from seeing the soul as seriously endangered by physical disorder. Timothy Bright, as a somewhat more consistent Calvinist, is much more anxious to separate melancholy from despair as "of diverse nature, never to be coupled in one fellowship."[17] Nor, Bright contends, can the body effect change in the soul. Where melancholy seems to influence the soul, it merely distorts the various senses through which the soul perceives the world; where the senses are sound, they "like a true looking glass representeth the countenance to the eye, in all points as nature" (77). At the same time, Bright frames his treatise on melancholy as comfort for a friend who feels himself deprived of God's grace. Bright suggests that though the action of this friend's bile is not the cause of his spiritual desperation, his physical melancholy is likely to have brought him into the contemplative frame of mind that brings on despair, and that the depression of his spirits arising from his illness is a serious impediment to his accepting spiritual consolation.[18] Even Calvin, when he concedes that the elect may experience some doubt in the midst of their assurance, ascribes this weakness not only to the initial ignorance of the newly converted soul, but also to the fallible capacities of the human body:

For as one shut up in a prison, where from a narrow opening he receives the rays of the sun indirectly and in a manner divided, though deprived of a full view of the sun, has no doubt of the source from which the light comes, and is benefited by

it; so believers, while bound with the fetters of an earthly body,
though surrounded on all sides with much obscurity, are so far
illumined by any slender light which beams upon them and
displays the divine mercy as to feel secure.[19]

Constrained and "surrounded . . . with much obscurity," the soul
can only with difficulty feel God's mercy. Despite an explicit and
anxious claim that the body cannot itself damn the soul, in these
writings the diseases of the frail flesh nevertheless also *do* both mimic
and encourage despair.

Although tracts on despair certainly include more Calvin than Ga-
len, then, it would be a mistake to miss the way in which the body
returns as a site of therapy. Offering a superabundance of external
means to alleviate a melancholic's torments, medical diagnosis can
soften the sometimes cold comfort of Calvinist spiritual advice, making the body a backdoor entrance to the soul. As the despairing Spira
says in Gribaldi's account, he was smitten "not with any affliction
or infirmity of the body (which he right gladly would have acknowledged for the chastisement and correction of sin, and would not
utterly have cast away hope and trust)."[20] While he cannot accept
the medical interpretation for himself, it is the only consolation that
he admits could have any effect. In linking despair to physical therapy,
medical discourse seems to function much the way medieval penance
did. The difference between penance and the medical cure of melancholy is that penance works on the soul through the body, whereas
medical discourse displaces the disease from the soul onto the body:
operating on what seems to be a sick soul through the body may
remove the physical defects which work as a funhouse mirror (rather
than the "true looking glass" of rational senses) by which the soul
sees and is seen. Once conceding the participation of the body in
spiritual grief, medical means become an obvious and even necessary
salve for despair. Greenham concedes that when "the mind is ap-
palled" for unknown reasons, natural causes may be contributing to
the disease, and therefore "I would never have the Physicians counsel
severed, nor the Ministers labour neglected; because the soul and
body dwelling together, it is convenient, that as the soul should
be cured by the word, by prayer, by fasting, by threatening, or by
comforting; so the body also should be brought into some tempera-
ture, by Physic, by purging, by diet, by restoring, by music, and by
such like means . . . "(245–46). If a true Christian at times has difficulty in apprehending his regeneration, says Bright,

much less can a body overcharged with melancholy, and drowned in that dark dungeon see the comfortable beams of his daystar, and brightness of the cheerful Sun of God['s] aboundant mercy, and a mind whose actions are hindered by means thereof, whereby it neither conceiveth nor judgeth sincerely and uprightly as the case requireth. . . . .

(233)

When the elect may find God's light refracted to a dim beam by their normal mortal capacities, could not the dungeon become entirely black when humoral imbalances overwhelm their faculties? And might medical means therefore make spiritual comfort possible?

We probably should not be surprised at the close association between medical discourse and spiritual consolation. In an era when ordained ministers were also frequently practicing physicians and medical doctors wrote popular moral and devotional manuals, a strict separation would seem strange.[21] The work of Gail Kern Paster and Michael Schoenfeldt has demonstrated ways that the physical body and the regulation of its humors contributed to the Renaissance sense of self, and I am particularly indebted to Schoenfeldt's instructive emphasis on the ethical significance of a porous, frequently-purged body for Spenser and his readers.[22] As Schoenfeldt convincingly argues, psychological and moral temperance in Book II of *The Faerie Queene* is the result of a dietary and medical discipline that balances what goes into and out of the body. Fittingly, then, the moral center of Book II is the Castle of Alma, an elaborate allegory of the digesting and thinking body, ruled by the gracious and healthy soul herself. Spenser's depiction of the positive aspects of dietary control helps us to see that a medical malady, such as melancholy, even as it presents a danger to the believer, also offers physical and behavioral means to address despair through the body. The temple in Book I which corresponds to Alma's Castle is, naturally enough, the House of Holiness, where Redcrosse goes to recover from his spiritual combat with Despair, and these sites are in a sense inverted images of each other. Alma needs Arthur, a figure of God's grace, to defend the body from the assault of the melancholic Maleager;[23] Redcrosse finds his spiritual cure through physical purgation in the medicalized regime of the House of Holiness.

In his descriptions of despair in *The Faerie Queene*, Spenser consistently superimposes medical terminology onto Calvinist theory. His allegorical structure here rests on the intrusion of medicine into the theology of despair and consolation, but also fuses the two modes more completely and seamlessly than his prose models do. Bright's presumably regenerate but desperately melancholy friend is perhaps closest in spirit to Redcrosse. Harold Skulsky has noted that the darkness of Orgoglio's dungeon seems to exceed what Calvin, with his insistence on some "slender light" of assurance, allows the elect to experience;[24] the dungeon of "balefull darkenesse" (I.viii.38) that we find the knight in, I'd like to suggest, is the one Bright describes, the "body overcharged with melancholy" and thus blinded to God's mercy. Such a body, unlike the one Calvin imagines, is an appropriate object for therapy, in which the afflicted sinner and his minis-ters—both medical and spiritual—can intervene in the narrative of despair. Medicine, like allegory, externalizes and renders tangible the inward self.

Like Britomart and like sixteenth-century theological comforters, Una exhorts Redcrosse to faith in prying him out of Despair's cave. Redcrosse is a "fraile, feeble, fleshly wight" who has no place judging God's capacities; Despair's thoughts are "diuelish," and moreover, she asks, "In heauenly mercies hast thou not a part?" (I.ix.53). Fortu-nately for the knight, Una is in an allegorical position to assure him of his election. Without Una's status as a kind of metaphysical certainty, though, the weak spot of her argument is the one that Spira fell through: an opposing mental conviction of reprobation. The psycho-logical difficulty of assurance reasserts itself as Redcrosse stubbornly continues to despair into the next canto.[25] As Escobedo notes above, Faith and Hope between them expound God's word so colorfully that "he desired to end his wretched dayes" (x.21.8). The talking cure, even when it includes manifest proofs of God's power and hope of his mercy, is not wholly revivifying.

For a more effective therapy, Redcrosse descends into yet another dungeon and submits to the ministrations of Patience and his posse of allegorical assistants, soon finding himself, in a relatively orthodox Calvinist manner, washed clean and ready for the charity that is the fruit of holiness:[26] Patience "gan apply reliefe/Of salues and med'-cines, which had passing priefe,/And thereto added words of won-drous might . . . " (x.24.4–6). These have some positive effect, but further and more dramatic treatment follows, for

> . . . the cause and root of all his ill,
> Inward corruption, and infected sin,
> Not purg'd not heald, behind remained still,
> And festring sore did rankle yet within,

Close creeping twixt the marrow and the skin.
Which to extirp, he laid him priuily
Downe in a darkesome lowly place farre in,
Whereas he meant his corrosiues to apply,
And with streight diet tame his stubborne malady.

In ashes and sackcloth he did array
His daintie corse, proud humors to abate,
And dieted with fasting euery day,
The swelling of his wounds to mitigate,
And made him pray both earely and eke late:
Amendment readie still at hand did wayt,
To pluck it out with pincers firie whot,
That soone in him was left no one corrupted iot.

And bitter *Penance* with an yron whip,
Was wont him once to disple euery day:
And sharpe *Remorse* his hart did pricke and nip,
That drops of bloud thence like a well did play;
And sad *Repentance* vsed to embay
His bodie in salt water smarting sore,
The filthy blots of sinne to wash away.
So in short space they did to health restore
The man that would not liue, but earst lay at deathes dore.

(x.25–28)

What has struck so many readers is the extravagant physicality of Redcrosse's penitential process and its apparent echoes of bodily Catholic penance.[27] The language that Spenser uses, though, is primarily medical, and poised precisely between the difficult physical process of purging recalcitrant melancholy and the medical rhetoric of treatises on conscience. The more relevant connections between the bodily allegory and the spiritual sense would seem, then, to be already in use by Protestants. When Caelia's "goodly counsell" proves insufficient, she sends not for a priest but for a doctor. As most medical manuals advise in cases of severe melancholy, the first measures are "salues," external "med'cines," and "diet" to "tame his stubborne malady." These failing to remove the complaint, other means of physic—"corrosiues," fasting, hot pinchers, bleeding, and a salt bath—must follow. If the disease or the remedies seem too violent for medical treatment, a look at the literature on melancholy quickly dispels that impression. Redcrosse's "[i]nward corruption and infected sin," which "festring sore . . . close creeping twixt the marrow and the skin" looks rather disgustingly like "adust" or "unnatural melancholy"—a disorder originating in "putrifaction" which will "corrupt and degenerate" healthy humors "into a quality wholly repugnant."[28] Stubborn melancholy nearly always requires purgation, sometimes draining the water from the surcharged "varices" beneath the skin, often through vomiting and "downward" purgatives, other times with burning clysters, bleeding, or, most popularly, opening the hemorrhoids.[29] For "head melancholy" (which seems closest to Redcrosse's symptoms), Burton goes so far as to suggest the application of hot irons or trepanning to expel the accumulated noxious spirits from the brain. While iron whips aren't a common way of ridding the body of excess blood and decayed bile, their effect is not much different from that of more ordinary phlebotomical instruments.

At the same time, Redcrosse's treatment also sounds strikingly like Greenham's prescription for curing consciences, using "corrosive and mundifying waters" and "Chiurgery to prick and pierce our consciences with the burning iron of the Law, and to cleanse the wound of the soul by sharp threatenings," lest "the rotten corruption" of sin remain. The language of purgation comes to Spenser, that is, both through medical discussions of melancholy and through the orthodox metaphorical structure of religious consolation, just as the "superfluous flesh" extirpated by Amendment is as much the metaphysical Pauline "flesh" as it is the literal humoral body that yields its excesses to medical purgatives.[30] Where the cure for melancholy doesn't correspond to Spenser's allegorical necessity, moreover, he drops it—a good physician would never allow a melancholy patient to lie anorectic in a dungeon. Curiously, though, from a spiritual perspective, the salves of Patience *precede* the corrosives in Spenser's account; either Patience is a bad comforter who (in Perkins's and Greenham's terms) applies the Gospel before the Law, or a good physician who tries conservative remedies first. In fact, the received ideas of melancholy and those of religious despair are consistently intertwined in *The Faerie Queene* and especially in Book I. Looking backward from the Despair episode, Donald Beecher points to Redcrosse's persistent joylessness and asserts that his "character could be perceived, in the Tudor context, in no other way than as a product of melancholy."[31] As many readers have noticed, other figures involved in Redcrosse's despair seem classically melancholic: Orgoglio because he appears as a manifestation of Redcrosse's torpor, Sir Terwin as a pitiable example of love melancholy, Sir Trevisan's extreme fear, like a stereotypical melancholic in "That of him selfe he seemd to be afrayd," and the figure of Despair himself with his mirror image in the solitary and ragged hermit Contemplation. As Paul Alpers notes, even Malbecco's metaphysical transformation in Book III is accompanied by the very specific physical conditions of melancholy.[32] Since the melancholy humor is thick and obstructive (the "dregs" of the blood), one might add to the list that Redcrosse's courage is "cruddled" when his blood (otherwise perplexingly) *cools* during his dalliance with Duessa, as Una's blood also curdles when Redcrosse takes the dagger from Despair; or that Fidelia's "heauenly documents . . . Of God, of grace, of justice, of free will" are notorious causes of physical melancholy as well as spiritual despair; one might even speculate on Orgoglio as a species of hypochondriac or "windy melancholy," since the flatulence of that disorder was known to cause lust by inflating the genitals.[33]

Rather than separating the spiritual and the physical aspects of despair, Spenser's allegory fuses them in such a way that they are simultaneous expressions of the same problem, the difficult experience of the Christian believer as a "fraile, feeble, fleshly wight." While Beecher argues that in mixing melancholy with despair Spenser follows "the logic of popular thought," which incorporates "a composite sequence of contradictory ideological parts" (115), I would contend that the desperate self Spenser composes is a deliberate answer to the potentially paralyzing double bind of assurance and predestination. Such a fusion, with its emphasis on the believer's own actions, produces some theological oddities (in the confusion of Redcrosse's repentant tears with Christ's blood as a purifying bath, for instance), but it may be a useful and ultimately comfortable description of the experience of spiritual doubt. Such a conclusion suggests something along the lines of Harold Skulsky's contention that the Book of Holiness functions as a kind of conduct manual guiding the doubtful Christian away from self-defeating contemplation and toward godly action.[34] If so, this conduct manual is also a book of physic. By engrafting medicine onto doctrine, Spenser joins the medical and religious commentators who both metaphorically and literally imagine replacing the search for internal certainty of election with regeneration as an externally visible therapeutic goal—even when the end of Spenser's narrative of Holiness is, like God's larger narrative, already determined.

Ohio University

NOTES

I have silently expanded contractions and modernized the spelling of all primary sources except *The Faerie Queene.*

1. All quotations of *The Faerie Queene* are from A.C. Hamilton, ed. (London: Longman, 1977).

2. This problem is exhaustively, if tendentiously, explored by John Strachniewski in the first chapter of *The Persecutory Imagination: English Puritanism and the Literature of Religious Despair* (Oxford: Clarendon Press, 1991).

3. John Calvin, *Institutes of the Christian Religion*, Henry Beveridge, ed., 2 vols. (Grand Rapids, MI: Eerdmans, 1989 this ed.), II:243. This is the problem that Harold Skulsky examines in "Spenser's Despair Episode," *Modern Philology* 78:3 (February 1981), 237–42. "The notorious truth," he writes, "is that the result of insisting on assurance was to create a scandal for believers by making a duty out of impossibility" (235).

4. London, 1628. All quotations from Willymat's text are from the 1605 reprint.

5. *The Works of That Famous and Worthy Minister of Christ in the University of Cambridge, Mr. William Perkins. First Volume: Newly Corrected . . .* (London, 1626), 383.

6. *The Sickness Unto Death*, trans. Howard V. Hong and Edna H. Hong (Princeton: Princeton University Press, 1980), 5.

7. *The Works of the Reverend and Faithful Servant of Jesus Christ, M. Richard Greenham*, ed. Henry Holland, 2nd ed. (London, 1599), 235.

8. "Epistle Dedicatorie," in Greenham, 214. Henry Holland, the volume's editor, here digests Greenham's precepts.

9. For sociological data on melancholy in the early seventeenth century, see Michael MacDonald, *Mystical Bedlam: Madness, Anxiety, and Healing in Seventeenth-Century England* (Cambridge: Cambridge University Press, 1981; reprinted 1988),150–60; the classic study of the literary and theoretical popularity of melancholy in the late sixteenth century is Lawrence Babb's *The Elizabethan Malady: A Study of Melancholia in English Literature from 1580 to 1642* (East Lansing, MI: Michigan State College Press, 1951).

10. Levinus Lemnius, *The Touchstone of Complexions*, trans. Thomas Newton (London, 1576), fol. 141[v].

11. Perkins, *Works*, 455–56.

12. The idea that despair is physically visible in bodily disorders is something of a commonplace; for example, see also Robert Bolton, *Instructions for a Right Comforting Afflicted Consciences* (London, 1631), 90.

13. Greenham, 259; for the failure of physic to cure the soul, see 8, 227, 245.

14. See Perkins, *Works*, 365; Timothy Bright, *A Treatise of Melancholy* (London, 1586), 188; 187–191 *passim*; and Robert Burton, *The Anatomy of Despair* (1638; London: Dent, 1932), III:396, who cites both (although he then characteristically wavers by immediately claiming that melancholy can be "a sufficient cause of this terror of conscience").

15. Burton, III:395–98.

16. Burton, III:413. He also specifically recommends to those in distress over their consciences the works of Perkins, Greenham, Abernathy, Bolton, and Bright, among others (III:409).

17. Bright, 190.

18. Bright, 196–97.

19. Calvin, I:486.

20. Matteo Gribaldi, *A Notable and Marvellous Epistle of the Famous Doctor, Mathew Gribalde . . . Concerning the Terrible Judgment of God*, (London, 1550),

21. On the overlap between the clerical and medical professions in sixteenth- and seventeenth-century England, see MacDonald, 7–9. It's worth making the point again that the two greatest chroniclers of melancholy, Timothy Bright and Robert Burton, were, respectively, a physician who later took orders and clergyman who devoted his life's work to medical theorizing and research.

22. Gail Kern Paster, *The Body Embarrassed: Drama and Disciplines of Shame in Early Modern Europe* (Ithaca: Cornell University Press, 1993); Michael C. Schoenfeldt, *Bodies and Selves in Early Modern England: Physiology and Inwardness in Spenser, Shakespeare, Herbert, and Milton* (Cambridge: Cambridge University Press, 1999), esp. 1–73.

23. On Maleager's melancholy, see Schoenfeldt, 51. His physical description is also quite similar to that of Redcrosse upon emerging from Orgoglio's dungeon and to Despair himself.

24. Skulsky, 235.

25. Skulsky reaches a similar conclusion, in that he argues against Redcrosse's assurance here (234). I would qualify his point by noting that the psychological context (in which Redcrosse is an ordinary Christian listening to what he thinks is an ordinary damsel in distress) is at least momentarily suspended in favor of metaphysics: Redcrosse responds to Una's appeal by picking himself up and leaving Despair. The usual expectation in treatises on despair is that a believer who thinks himself bereft of grace will endlessly argue the point, as Scudamour does in III.ix. Perkins even reprints, as a model of consolation, a dialogue by Theodore Beza that *ends* in Perkins's edition with the sufferer's obstinate skepticism; Perkins, *Works*, 114–116.

26. For this sequence, see Calvin, I:508–31.

27. The relationship of Redcrosse's punishments during his repentance to Calvin's "mortification of the flesh" is complicated, in part because Calvin is himself cagey about when such mortification is literally bodily pain and when it is metaphorical. There are "certain external exercises which we employ in private," but "mortifying the flesh" also and primarily refers to the necessity to "renounce our former nature" after being "smitten with the sword of the Spirit and annihilated" (I:522, 515).

28. Bright, 2, 3.

29. See Lemnius, fol. 153[r]; both Burton and Bright also repeatedly recommend this treatment.

30. See note 28 above. The Pauline opposition between "flesh" and "spirit" is largely irrelevant to the relationship of literal body to soul, although it encourages the tendency to metaphorize regeneration as a medical procedure. Theologically, for orthodox Protestants, the "flesh" is the naturally depraved part of the soul (present in the mind, will, and affections), whereas the body is a necessary and complementary part of the compound nature of mankind; see Perkins, *Works*, 469 and Calvin, I:518.

Yet in the *Institutes*, as in English Calvinist consolations and homiletics, "flesh" occasionally oscillates between this metaphorical status and the literal body (a gross, humiliating, and disabling home for the spirit). The latter appears primarily in descriptions of the ignorance and uncertainty which even the elect share, and suggestively brings the body into play as either a co-conspirator in the soul's guilty despair *or* as an extenuating circumstance.

31. "Spenser's Redcrosse Knight: Despair and the Elizabethan Malady," *Renaissance and Reformation*, n.s. XI:1 (1987), 114–15.

32. *The Poetry of the Faerie Queene* (Columbia, MO: University of Missouri Press, 1982), 224–25.

33. Lemnius, fol. 149ᵛ; Burton, I:413.

34. Skulsky, 241–42.

TY BUCKMAN

"Just Time Expired": Succession Anxieties and the Wandering Suitor in Spenser's *Faerie Queene*

This study proposes competing contexts for the interpretation of Arthur's errantry in *The Faerie Queene*. In the latter half of Elizabeth's reign, as it became increasingly apparent to her anxious subjects that she would not marry and hence would not provide a Tudor heir, it also became illegal to discuss the succession question publicly. At about the same time, Spenser was at work on a poem to be dedicated to Elizabeth that he hoped would take its place among the great achievements of Virgil, Ariosto, and Tasso in a generic tradition that had dynastic praise of the poet's patron as one of its distinguishing features. Faced with the paradox of celebrating a timeless dynasty in a poem dedicated to an aging Virgin Queen, Spenser brilliantly introduced the courtship of Arthur and Gloriana. The prospect of their union forestalls the succession question—and the end of his poem—indefinitely, even as Arthur's absurd inability to find his paramour becomes symptomatic of Spenser's failure to reconcile a vaulting mythopoesis with a keen sensitivity to the political reception of his work.

IN BOOK III OF *The Faerie Queene*, Britomart and her nurse seek out Merlin, hoping to learn from the magician where and how to find the man she has glimpsed in her father's enchanted mirror. Merlin more than obliges them, not only providing advice on locating Britomart's beloved, but recounting as well the chronicle of her illustrious descendants. Beginning with Artegall, Britomart's unwitting betrothed, Merlin ambles through the succession of Briton and Saxon dynasties on his way to the triumphant restoration of Briton rule in

107

the Tudors: "So shall the Briton bloud their crowne againe reclame" (III.iii.48)[1].His prophecy ends with a description of Elizabeth's reign and a mysterious, wordless fit:

> Then shall a royall virgin raine, which shall
> Stretch her white rod ouer the Belgicke shore,
> And the great Castle smite so sore with all,
> That it shall make him shake, and shortly learne to fall.
>
> But yet the end is not. There Merlin stayd,
> As ouercomen of the spirites powre,
> Or other ghastly spectacle dismayd,
> That secretly he saw, yet note discoure:
> Which suddein fit, and halfe extatick stoure
> When the two fearefull women saw, they grew
> Greatly confused in behauioure;
> At last the fury past, to former hew
> Hee turnd againe, and chearefull looks (as earst) did shew.
>
> (49–50)[2]

Merlin's fit has engendered much critical commentary; indeed, its obscurity seems intended to do so. Among those who have remarked the sanguine character of the passage is A. C. Hamilton, who reads Merlin's trance as "a vision of England's domination over Europe."[3] Hamilton arrives at this interpretation by extending the sense of the previous stanza—the smiting and fall of "the great Castle"—into the lines describing Merlin's fit. They are separated, however, by the phrase from Christ's portentous admonition in Matthew, which refers not to victory but to the war, faction, and pestilence of the apocalypse.[4] Joseph Wittreich notes the New Testament allusion but argues that it is, by virtue of its context, "an utterance that would dampen apocalyptic fervor and quiet millennial expectations."[5] Thomas Bulger also sees nothing ominous in Merlin's silence, observing blandly: "As the open-ended conclusion to Merlin's vision suggests, Elizabeth is currently in the process of influencing British history. . . . "[6] In a similar vein is Howard Dobin's Bakhtinian reading of the passage: " 'But yet the end is not.' That line captures the inconclusiveness of prophecy just as it undoes the totality of epic form," to which he later adds, "[n]either Merlin, Spenser, nor the reader can see beyond the Queen's death."[7]

While Dobin is right, I think, to connect Merlin's silence with the Queen's death, he stops short of identifying the particular anxieties that the prospect of her death would have evoked for Spenser's early readers. Not so Richard McCabe: "Doubtless the queen was intended to ponder it deeply: only she held the key to succession, only she could envisage the future towards which Spenser gestures."[8] What Merlin sees in the post-Elizabethan future, then, may not be Albion triumphant but an unsettled succession leading to political chaos and civil war. Spenser, of course, remains guarded and ambiguous in this passage, careful to avoid the risks of actual prophecy. The text suggests that Merlin's fit might simply constitute part of the prophetic experience—a kind of vatic power-surge[9]—or he might have seen something dismaying: "That secretly he saw, yet note discoure." Perhaps Merlin is by some "ghastly spectacle dismayd" precisely because England's uncertain future held out this possibility as well. When Spenser wrote these stanzas in the late 1580s, it was not necessary to resort to prophecy to foresee that the century-long Tudor dynasty would die with the aging Elizabeth: "the end" was indeed at hand. The instability that resulted from her decision not to marry, and not to attempt to provide an heir, was compounded by her steadfast refusal to name a successor or even allow the issue to be discussed openly. In a sense, then, Spenser's Merlin is speechless as he glances at the future *by royal decree*.[10]

In the sections that follow, I will outline both the succession problems that necessarily plagued Elizabeth as an unmarried monarch and Spenser's generic imperative to celebrate his patron's dynastic ambitions, showing how these two forces collide in the person of Arthur, suitor to a Faery Queen whom he can glimpse in a dream but never find. A source of acute political anxiety in England in the 1580s and 1590s, the succession dilemma casts a long shadow over *The Faerie Queene*, threatening the endurance of the fictional Fairyland no less than the historical survival of the Pax Elizabethana.

I.

During the first half of Elizabeth's reign, the question of the royal succession was closely bound up with the prospect of the queen's marriage.[11] When Elizabeth came to the throne as a young woman of twenty-five, her subjects assumed that she would follow her sister's example and choose a consort. Various suitors had been proposed for her long before she had reached the throne, but marriage negotiations got under way in earnest immediately after she became queen.[12] It eventually became apparent to her privy council and others at court that the queen was not eager to select a husband. As her reluctance became more widely known (she admitted as much on several public occasions) and the queen grew older, the question of who would succeed her became more pressing.[13]

During the contentious parliament of 1566, Elizabeth had sparked a furious debate when she instructed the members not to discuss the succession. The House of Commons chafed at this infringement on their traditional rights and Elizabeth was forced to back down.[14] By 1581, however, the mood in parliament had changed. "An Act againste sedicious Wordes and Rumours uttered againste the Queenes most excellent majestie" began as a revision of the harsh Marian statute under which John Stubbs had lost his right hand two years before for warning the queen against making a French marriage.[15] The proposal to revise the law was apparently brought to the House of Lords by a council representative and underwent days of heated debate in both houses before emerging in its final form. The "Statute of Silence," as it came to be known, declared that "any one who shall set forth by express wordes, deeds or writings, who shall raigne as King or Queen of this Realme after her Highnesse Decease . . . every such offence shal be felonie . . . every offender shall suffer the payns of death and forfeyte . . . without benefit of Cleargie."[16]

In direct reversal of its use under Mary Tudor, Protestants conceived the revision of the bill as a means of limiting Catholic political influence, but in its final version it censored Protestant expression no less than Catholic. The law made discussion or speculation about the queen's successor a punishable offense, and it marked a turning point in the public treatment of the issue. After 1581, there would be no more vociferous calls in parliament for Elizabeth to name a successor, nor was the succession a topic of public debate. But anxiety about the succession remained, and was even encouraged by the government on occasion as a means of solidifying Elizabeth's political position. The anonymous author of *Leicester's Commonwealth*, for example, describes a speech by Sir Christopher Hatton at the pardoning of a man who had fired a pistol toward Elizabeth and hit one of her boatsmen:

And in that oration he declared and described very effectually what inestimable damage had ensued to the realm if her Majesty by that or any other means should have been taken from us.

He set forth most lively before the eyes of all men what division, what dissension, what bloodshed had ensued, and what fatal dangers were most certain to fall upon us whensoever that doleful day should happen, wherein no man should be sure of his life, of his goods, of his wife, of his children; no man certain whither to fly, whom to follow, or where to seek repose and protection.[17]

Hatton's account of the uncertainty that would plague the body politic upon Elizabeth's demise reflects an anxiety closer to home: courtiers like him who depended for their livelihood on the favor of the monarch stood to lose most. The young courtier Robert Carey shared Hatton's disquietude. His memoirs include this reflection on Elizabeth's sickness near the end of her life: "I, hearing that neither the physicians, nor none about her, could persuade her to take any course for her safety, feared her death would soon after ensue. I could not but think in what a wretched estate I should be left, most of my livelihood depending on her life."[18]

Spenser would not have escaped his contemporaries' anxiety over the question of the succession; it was, as we have seen, a political concern throughout his adult life.[19] Spenser's various government positions in Ireland and the pension he presumably hoped for (and was later granted) from the queen represented a considerable material interest in the continuation of her reign. As an English colonist and landholder in Munster, he was also particularly vulnerable to political uncertainty in London and to the changes in foreign policy that could result from a change in regime.[20] Thus *The Faerie Queene* contains several passages, especially in the "Briton moniments" section, that demonstrate an awareness on Spenser's part of the dangerous implications of the death of a childless monarch.[21]

To suggest, however, that he therefore regarded the succession with anxiety seems at first glance to contradict the public record. Spenser was, after all, a principal if freelance architect of the Virgin Queen myth that drew attention away from the need for an heir. In fact, Spenser's portrayal of the queen as a beautiful and ageless goddess squares neatly with what soon became the government's official line on royal representations.[22] In the same year that James took offense at Spenser's portrayal of Duessa—in July 1596–the Privy Council empowered the queen's "Serjeant Painter" to confiscate and destroy any unauthorized and unseemly portraits of Elizabeth, and to restrict the production of royal portraits to those he approved. Roy Strong has argued that this resulted from "a policy of deliberate rejuvenation," one that "may not have reflected vanity so much as a genuine fear of the dangers inherent in dwelling on the physical mortality of the sovereign while the succession was unsettled."[23] We might see in the fervor with which some subjects embraced this image of their queen a compensation for or a fleeing from the political insecurity inherent in the death of an unmarried queen. The project of immortalizing Elizabeth—whether by associating her with the classical Astraea or the Catholic Virgin Mary—can thus be seen, in part, as an attempt to avoid the question of the succession altogether.

When we recall that the Virgin Queen myth began to be propagated in earnest about the time that the Alençon negotiations were breaking down in the early 1580s, the logic behind its Protestant sponsorship becomes clearer. To Sidney, Leicester, and others of their circle, the duke's unsettling courtship pressed home the point that the rule of an unmarried Protestant queen was greatly to be preferred over the prospect of another Catholic king.[24] Of course, this constituted a "solution" only so long as Elizabeth occupied the throne. A better alternative, but one which was no longer practicable after 1580, would have been for Elizabeth to marry a husband with impeccable English and Protestant credentials, who would not only free the country of its residual Papist elements and provide leadership in the struggle against the Catholic forces in the Low Countries, but would also father a child and ensure the continuance of the Tudor line. For a patriotic Protestant, such a man would be Elizabeth's ideal suitor.

II.

The political forces that conspired to discourage Spenser from venturing a detailed prophetic look beyond Elizabeth's reign were considerable. Not only did the "Statute of Silence" make any treatment of the succession subject to censorship, Elizabeth's well-known sensitivity to the topic meant that offending authors faced the added threat of royal displeasure. In crafting his *Faerie Queene*, however, Spenser found that political expediency ran directly counter to the generic tradition in which he determined to place his poem. In his *Letter to Ralegh*, Spenser writes:

I haue followed all the antique Poets historicall, first Homere, who in the Persons of Agamemnon and Vlysses hath ensampled a good gouernour and a vertuous man, the one in his Ilias, the other in his Odysseis: then Virgil, whose like intention was to doe in the person of Aeneas: after him Ariosto comprised them both in his Orlando: and lately Tasso disseuered them againe. . . . [25]

Spenser's immediate topic—the moralization of the epic hero—should not distract from the fact of the list itself: he places his poem, and more specifically his depiction of Arthur, in an unbroken epic tradition that starts with Homer and continues through Tasso, Spenser's Italian contemporary. Of course, Spenser does not claim to be imitating slavishly his epic precursors, nor will his poem permit such an interpretation. Instead, as he acknowledges in his *Letter*, he wants *The Faerie Queene* to be seen as participating in the tradition in a larger, structural sense, as carrying the essential generic markings of the epic poem as he understands them.[26]

The dynastic theme is one of those characteristic features. Weaving the contemporary into the past as a means of flattering a patron was one of Virgil's bequests to the genre, and the esteem afforded its inventor in the Renaissance would have ensured its generic survival even if it had not proven so useful a tool for soliciting and repaying patronage. The form that this flattery took was in keeping with the ambitious scope of the epic poem, and it was given such a prominent place in the poetic efforts of Virgil and his later disciples that it has come to be regarded by some critics as the defining characteristic of a distinct literary category: "dynastic epic." The subgenre is distinguished by a common theme: "the rise of imperium, the noble house, race, or nation to which the poet professes allegiance."[27]

The dynastic theme in its Virgilian manifestation consists of two closely related strands. The first involves the protagonist's pursuit of his destined spouse (the founding of the dynasty by an original dynast), the second the celebration of their progeny (its providential continuity). Both are part of the poem's fundamental orientation toward history: an expectant, prophetic celebration of the reader's present in the creation of a quasi-historical past. Thus the *Aeneid* looks forward to the founding of Rome, the martial glory of the Roman people, and a lasting peace to follow.[28] In one sense, Virgil proves a deficient propagandist for his patron, for he often seems to celebrate with greater energy the invincibility of Rome as an idea or a *volk* rather than the particular fate of Augustus. But this is a distinction largely foreign to the poem, for Virgil acknowledges no difference between the future of Rome and the endurance of Augustus' line, and in the end his glorification of Rome fosters for the ascendant regime a myth of cosmic intentionality and permanence—the appropriate Spenserian term would be *immutability*—that serves his patron well.

Virgil constructs the founding myth of the *Aeneid* on its protagonist's marriageability.[29] This is why Aeneas' passion for Dido must be replaced by his dutiful pursuit of Lavinia; at one level she is his dynastic intended and in their anticipated marriage lies the future glory of the Italians, at another the destiny of his people must be shown to outweigh even the force of his own desires. Thus when Mercury rebukes Aeneas, he appeals to Aeneas' future and the Roman reader's present:

> quid struis? aut qua spe Libycis teris otia terris?
> si te nulla movet tantarum gloria rerum
> nec super ipse tua moliris laude laborem,
> Ascanium surgentum et spes heredis Iuli
> respice, cui regnum Italiae Romanaque tellus
> debentur.
>
> (4.271–76)

("What plannest thou? or in what hope dost thou waste idle hours in Libyan lands? If the glory of such a fortune stirs thee not, and for thine own fame's sake thou shoulderest not the burden, have regard for growing Ascanius and the promise of Iülus thy heir, to whom the kingdom of Italy and the Roman land are due.")[30]

Aeneas' frequently interrupted voyage, his war for control of Latium, and his personal battle with Turnus all make up his "courtship" of Lavinia. She is his destination, his link to the future, and the prospect of their marriage provides a vector along which the action of the poem proceeds.

Virgil, however, makes the achievement of this goal a foregone conclusion for the reader by virtue of the second part of his dynastic project, the celebration of Aeneas' progeny. In Book 6 of the *Aeneid*, Aeneas enlists the help of the Sibyl to visit his father, Anchises, in the underworld. Virgil uses the occasion to tie the poem more closely to Roman history and to Rome's future glory. At one point, Anchises invites his son:

Nunc age, Dardaniam prolem quae deinde sequatur
gloria, qui maneant Itala de gente nepotes,
inlustris animas nostrumque in nomen ituras
expediam dictis et te tua fata docebo.

(6: 756–59)[31]

("Come now, what glory shall hereafter attend the Dardan line,
what children of Italian stock await thee, souls illustrious and
heirs of our name—this will I set forth, and teach thee thy
destiny.")

A parade of descendants follows. Surprisingly, however, the chronology culminates not in a paean to Augustus but a lament for the early death of his adopted heir Marcellus.[32] Thus, Aeneas' look at the future suggests at its closing not dynastic triumph, but the fragility of human design.

This somber note is struck again by Virgil's Italian successor, Lodovico Ariosto. Taking up Boiardo's unfinished *Orlando Innamorato* at the end of the fifteenth century, Ariosto followed his predecessor's lead by blending into his sequel both epic and romance conventions. One part of the Virgilian inheritance that he made eager use of was the dynastic praise of his patrons, the powerful Este family of his native Ferrara. Like Virgil, he presents a dynastic pair as the ancestors of his patrons, but he gives the convention an Ariostan twist: in the *Furioso*, it is the genetrix of the future dynasty that must pursue her husband. Still, the structural implications of the dynastic theme are essentially the same for Ariosto, as Bradamante and Ruggiero's anticipated union brings together the disparate story lines of the poem. Thus, early in the poem Bradamante is shown a parade of her illustrious descendants at Merlin's tomb, which closes with this stanza:

Francesco, il terzo; Alfonsi gli altri dui
ambi son detti. Or, come io dissi prima,
s'ho da mostrarti ogni tuo ramo, il cui
valor la stirpe sua tanto sublima,
bisognerà che si rischiari e abbui
più volte prima il ciel, ch'io te li esprima:
e sarà tempo ormai, quando ti piaccia,
ch'io dia licenzia all'ombre, e ch'io mi taccia.

(3.59)

("Francesco, the third; Alphonso the other two both are named. But, as I said before, if I were to show you each of your branches—by whose virtue the race is so greatly exalted—the sky would lighten and darken many times before I could declare them all. It is time now, with your permission, that I release the shades and hold my peace.")[33]

Ariosto's tribute to his patrons concludes with an image of Estean proliferation, of Francises and Alfonsos multiplying and subduing the earth. Later in the poem the disguised enchantress Melissa offers Ruggiero the same promise, in a scene that recalls Mercury's rebuke of Aeneas:

Se non ti muovon le tue proprie laudi,
e l'opre escelse a chi t'ha il cielo eletto,
la tua successïon perché defraudi
del ben che mille volte io t'ho predetto?
deh, perché il ventre eternamente claudi,
dove il ciel vuol che sia per te concetto
la glorïosa e soprumana prole
ch'esser de' al mondo più chiara che 'l sole? (7.60)

("Even if you are not moved by thoughts of your own renown and the high deeds which heaven has ordained for you, why deprive your descendants of the good that a thousand times I have foretold to you? Alas, why seal eternally the womb where heaven wills that you conceive an illustrious and godlike progeny that will shine more brightly than the sun?")

Ruggiero is called to act on behalf of his endless line of glorious heirs. His future encompasses the reader's past, but because the Este line was not in obvious danger of extinction at the time of Ariosto's writing, it also looks forward to the reader's future and thus becomes, vague though it is, actual prophecy.

Perhaps the best evidence for the dynastic theme's status as essential to the genre is to be found in Torquato Tasso's *Gerusalemme Liberata*, where it receives a merely perfunctory presentation. Tasso consistently chooses to give the moral precedence over the historical in his poem, which accounts for his decision to refer in his appended allegory neither to contemporary personages nor events. Still, he will not allow himself to pass over the epic requirement that he celebrate the dynastic pretensions of his patrons, and so he casts Rinaldo and Armida, the crusader errant and the sorceress, as the unlikely progenitors of the Estean line.

In the seventeenth canto of the *Liberata*, Rinaldo arrives in Palestine and the wiseman of Ascalon, a wizard or *magus*, shows him the progression of his ancestors as depicted on an elaborate shield. The scene is based on the extended description of Aeneas' shield in the eighth book of the *Aeneid* (and Achilles' before it), but Tasso substitutes for Virgil's celebration of the Roman future a celebration of the Estean past.[34] The wiseman concludes his presentation by assuring Rinaldo of the endurance of his line:

Taciti se ne gian per l'aria nera,
quando al garzon si volge il veglio e dice:
—Veduto hai tu de la tua stirpe altera
i rami e la vetusta alta radice;
e se ben ella da l'età primiera
stata è fertil d'eroi madre e felice,
non è né fia di partorir mai stanca,
ché per vecchiezza in lei virtù non manca.

(17.86)[35]

("They were proceeding in silence through the black night air
when the old man turns to the youth, and says: 'You have seen
the branches of your noble family tree, and its deep and venerable root; and though it has been from the earliest age the fecund
and fortunate mother of heroes, it is not nor ever will be weary
of bearing fruit, for its vigor will never be lacking in it by reason
of old age.' ")

Even for Tasso, who is more committed to a non-historical program of moral and religious didacticism than Spenser, the promise of dynastic continuity is the bridge that connects the past and future of his poem with the reader's present.

What Spenser found in the epic tradition was the marriage of a sweeping vision of providential history with the fate of a particular dynasty, of which the poet's patron was invariably the current scion. But while each of the works we have considered purports to be concerned with the dynasty's forebears, the focus does not remain on the past, for the celebration of the founding of the dynasty leads inevitably to the celebration of its continuance. And in this regard Spenser found himself in a unique position, attempting to craft dynastic praise for a Virgin Queen.

III.

It has been my intention thus far to evoke two contexts to aid our interpretation of the courtship of Arthur and Gloriana. The first concerns the political uncertainty that resulted from the undecided succession, the second the generic precedents for celebrating the dynastic ambitions of an epic poet's patrons. Because these two considerations stood at cross purposes, the Elizabethan epic poet was left in an awkward position: there was no Tudor future for the poet to hail, nor was there a consensus as to who should fill the void that would necessarily follow the reign of a virgin queen. Spenser had a choice, then, between two alternatives: drawing attention to the succession and the risks attendant upon it, or reinterpreting epic convention to fit his political circumstances. In true Spenserian fashion, he chose both.

Spenser realized that the best solution to the succession problem also satisfied the requirements of generic precedent. He divided the dynastic project into two parts, one belonging to Britomart and Artegall, the other to Arthur and Gloriana. The former pair function as founding dynasts after the examples of Aeneas and Lavinia, Ruggiero and Bradamante, Rinaldo and Armida. The courtship of the latter pair, Arthur and Gloriana, not only holds out the possibility of a fruitful marriage and a peaceful succession, it stands in place of the celebration of an endless Tudor dynasty. In this way, *Arthur's search for Gloriana becomes the succession dilemma in narrative form.* If he can find her, the dynastic future is assured in the marriage of England's greatest king to her greatest queen. Of course, Spenser's compromise led him into a considerable degree of bad faith at the level of the poem's historical allegory—Elizabeth had long since abandoned thoughts of marriage—but it allowed him to avoid a future that was legally unutterable and politically unthinkable, a future without the Virgin Queen.

It is in the ninth canto of Book I that the reader learns the details of Arthur's encounter with the Faery Queen—the first phase of their courtship—and the circumstances are almost wholly conventional.[36]

The scene opens with a standard romance motif, the request to the victorious but unknown knight to tell his story (I.ix.2).[37] At Una's prompting, the knight explains that as a young man he despised Love and mocked his devotees. He managed to ward off Cupid's arrows, he explains, until one day when he lay down to sleep after frolicking and riding in the woods: "Me seemed, by my side a royall Mayd/ Her daintie limbes full softly down did lay" (13). He then describes what followed:

> Most goodly glee and louely blandishment
> She to me made, and bad me loue her deare,
> For dearely sure her loue was to me bent,
> As when iust time expired should appeare.
> But whether dreames delude, or true it were,
> Was neuer hart so rauisht with delight,
> Ne liuing man like words did euer heare,
> As she to me deliuered all that night;
> And at her parting said, She Queene of Faeries hight.
>
> (14)

At one level, Arthur's encounter encodes an elaborate compliment to Elizabeth, emphasizing the beauty and transcendence of the Faery Queen and presenting her as the single obsession of the poem's most virtuous knight.[38] However, even a cursory consideration of the stanza above confronts the reader with a puzzling inconsistency: Elizabeth's apparent proxy treats Arthur with an openness that ill befits a maiden queen. Not only is there no mention of the queen's celebrated virginity, but Arthur reveals that he was "ravisht with delight" by the "royall Mayd" at his side—language which suggests consummation rather than chastity.[39]

How are we to interpret this seeming contradiction in the presentation of the queen? C. S. Lewis and others have argued that the scene betrays a submerged neoplatonism, whereby the knight is ravished by the idea of glory rather than Gloriana herself.[40] I submit, rather, that the place to start is with Spenser's distinction in the *Letter to Ralegh* between the queen's two persons, one "a most royall Queene or Empresse, the other . . . a most vertuous and beautifull Lady."[41] The former he associates with the Faery Queen, the latter with Belphoebe. Belphoebe's virginity is not simply one aspect of her identity, it is presented as her defining characteristic—hence the repeated comparisons with Diana.[42] In her private role as a "Lady," Spenser grants the queen the freedom to choose an unmarried life, and even defends her choice against a frustrated Timias. However, in her official capacity as queen she labors under different expectations, which may help to explain why Spenser places the Queen of Faeries in the comparatively amorous fairy mistress tradition, rather than one more in keeping with the expected behavior of an unmarried monarch.[43]

Other aspects of the scene warrant further attention. If we look closely at the first four verses, the rudiments of a troth-plighting ceremony or a secret marriage pact can be identified: the exchange of vows ("and bad me loue her deare,/For dearely sure her loue was to me bent"), the expectation of a later public declaration ("As when iust time expired should appeare"), and the consummation ("Was neuer hart so rauisht with delight"). The vow that Arthur makes after he awakes, "neuer . . . to rest, till her I find" (I.ix.15), would thus be his pledge not to break troth, and the nine months that he has sought his beloved in vain would suggest the gestation period of the Faery Queen's long awaited heir.

Whether or not, however, we take Arthur's first meeting with the queen to be a nuptial ceremony is ultimately less important than the recognition of the context in which it occurs. In the midst of re-counting his vision, Arthur confesses that he is unable to determine "whether dreames delude, or true it were," and therefore whether the favor he received from his beloved is real or imagined. That the relationship between Arthur and Gloriana commences *within Arthur's dream* is not accidental; by so doing Spenser abstracts the events one remove from the narrative, diminishing the impression that he is questioning the wisdom of the queen's matrimonial choices in the 1560s and 1570s or otherwise flagging in his dedication to the cause of the Virgin Queen. In effect, the poet hides behind Arthur's doubt much as he will behind Merlin's speechlessness in Book III.

When Arthur awakes, he encounters a truly masterful sign: "nought but pressed gras, where she had lyen" (I.ix.15).[44] The inden-tation left by her fairy body confirms the reality of the queen's physi-cal presence in Arthur's vision even as it signals her subsequent absence. In fact, the pressed grass that Arthur finds is the closest the poem comes to picturing the Faery Queen, and this is made more intriguing when we observe that this singular near-appearance takes place in an erotically charged context. All of this points to the degree to which the poem not only glorifies the queen, but also fetishizes her presence.

The Faery Queen is too closely linked with Elizabeth and too seldom involved in the action of the poem for this scene not to reflect in some way upon Spenser's sovereign. The allegorical effect of the passage is to imagine a queen willing to yield her virginity for the sake of her dynastic destiny. As a result, the fierce independence and the inapproachability that Spenser will ascribe to Belphoebe in Books III and IV are noticeably absent from the depiction of Arthur's beloved in Book I, who pledges her love to her ideal suitor without hesitation, and will even go so far as to play Angelica to Arthur's Rinaldo.

If Arthur's dream encounter with the Faery Queen is the poet's flirtation with rewriting Elizabeth's personal history, then Arthur's subsequent search for her is evidence for the corrective power of the historically actual. The second phase of their courtship commences in the poem's second stanza, where the poet refers to: "fairest Tanaquill, / Whom that most noble Briton Prince so long / Sought through the world, and suffered so much ill, / That I must rue his vndeserued wrong" (I.Pr.2). From the very beginning of *The Faerie Queene*, Arthur and Gloriana are at once inseparable and irreconcilable, joined in the mind of the narrator but not in the action of his poem. In fact, the arc of Arthur's fruitless quest stretches from this stanza in the Proem to Book I through Book VI and presumably beyond, until Arthur's dream of the Faery Queen is a distant memory for both him and the reader.[45]

Arthur's formal introduction into the poem is matched only by Belphoebe's in its length and detail, although the narrator dwells upon the arms and armor of the former and the physical beauty of the latter. We are told of Arthur, "from top to toe no place appeared bare" (I.vii.29), and to illustrate the point, the narrator describes his belt, sword, sheath, helmet, crest, and shield with meticulous iconographical detail. The description of the knight ends abruptly with the following observation:

It Merlin was, which whylome did excell
All liuing wightes in might of magicke spell:
Both shield, and sword, and armour all he wrought
For this young Prince, when first to armes he fell;
·But when he dyde, the Faerie Queene it brought
To Faerie lond, where yet it may be seene, if sought.

(36)

The reference to Arthur's death is strangely placed at the end of an account of his invincible weaponry and impregnable armor. However, in one sense, mentioning Arthur's demise even before he enters

the narrative is very Arthurian. It can be read as a concretization of
the impending doom that hangs over Arthur and his kingdom in
Malory, or the haunting sense of preordained loss in some chivalric
fictions going back to the *Song of Roland* itself. More relevant to the
present study, though, is the presence of the Faery Queen in these
lines. If the earlier quotation from the poem's second stanza marked
the beginning of Arthur's quest, this stanza prematurely heralds its
end. For in addition to Arthur's death, we learn by implication that
he will not die in Faery Land, that the Faery Queen will outlive him,
and that she will collect his shield, sword, and armor and bring them
to her kingdom.[46]

By way of contrast, this passage can be interestingly juxtaposed
with one in Book II, where Arthur intervenes to prevent Pyrochles
and Cymochles from stripping the arms from the unconscious Guyon.
Here, Pyrochles argues that spoiling a knight of his accoutrements is
the prerogative of the victor:

> Yet since no way is left to wreake my spight,
> I will him reaue of armes, the victors hire,
> And of that shield, more worthy of good knight;
> For why should a dead dog be deckt in armour bright?
>
> (2.8.15).

Pyrochles' ranting casts a strange light on the Faery Queen's appropriation of her suitor's belongings, leaving the sense that Arthur is twice
vanquished by the queen, once in the loss of his freedom after his
amorous vision, and again in death when she carries away his arms
and armor.

Even though the poem announces Arthur's eventual demise in
Book I, Spenser has many appointments for Arthur to keep before
he is allowed to expire somewhere beyond the horizon of Book VI.
Book I has him defeating Orgoglio and exposing Duessa, before
departing "on his way/To seeke his loue" (I.ix.20). He then appears
in Book II to rescue Guyon in the passage quoted above, and accompanies him on his way to the house of Alma. En route, Arthur asks
Guyon about the beautiful woman portrayed on his shield, and learns
that Guyon has the good fortune of being a servant of the Faery
Queen (II.ix.4). Arthur then inquires about joining her service and
concludes with a resounding declaration:

> Certes (then said the Prince) I God auow,

That sith I armes and knighthood first did plight,
My whole desire hath beene, and yet is now,
To serue that Queene with all my powre and might.

. . .

Yet no where can her find, such happinesse
Heauen doth to me enuy, and fortune fauourlesse.

(7)[47]

Arthur's errantry assumes a deflationary character as the poem progresses. His inability to locate the Faery Queen despite his passionate
determination becomes almost comical in a poem whose main characters all hail from her court. Guyon tells Arthur to "constant keep
the way" in his search for Gloriana, but regrets that his own quest
prevents him from leading him there (presumably Una and Redcrosse
pled the same excuse). And in Book III Arthur meets Florimell's
dwarf, who arrives out of breath after his journey "From Faery court"
(III.v.4) but is too preoccupied with locating his mistress to point
out the correct path to the errant stranger. In these and similar encounters later, Arthur meets and assists characters newly arrived from
Gloriana's court, but their knowledge is somehow unable to bring
him any closer to his destination.

Arthur's various duties in Books IV and V have little direct bearing
on his courtship of Gloriana; indeed at times he seems to have forgotten his quest. In Canto vii of Book IV, for example, Arthur is on
his way "through the wandring wood," "Seeking aduentures, where
he mote heare tell," when he happens upon his squire (42). But a
few cantos later, after arranging the marriage of Poeana and Placidas,
he recalls his purpose: "Him selfe, whose minde did trauell as with
chylde,/Of his old loue, conceau'd in secret brest,/Resolued to pursue his former quest" (ix.17). Spenser's highly unusual figure has
reversed the gender roles of the knight's dream encounter, so that *he*
has "conceav'd"" and is "with chylde." The simile also plays on the
earlier passage's use of the phrase, "As when iust time expired should
appeare" and "nine months," all to suggest that Arthur is bearing the
burden of their encounter in a manner that biology will not allow.[48]
If we take the implication a step further, we might say that Arthur
is carrying the genetic future with him, it being impossible for Elizabeth in her role of Virgin Queen. Ultimately, however, this line of
interpretation ends in Elizabeth as a descendant of herself—less a
comment on the queen's narcissism than on the poet's inability
wholly to harmonize contradictory yet counterpointed epideictic
strategies.

In Book I Arthur recalls his vision of the Faery Queen; in Book
II he asks Guyon how to find her; Book III shows him wishing
Gloriana were Florimell. The second installment continues the pattern: Arthur is pictured wandering in Book IV before resolving to
pursue his "old love"; in Book V his courtship is mentioned only
as "his former iourney," and in Book VI, it is "his first quest."
Arthur's fatigue may reflect the poet's own growing political disillu-
sionment, or it may have a more particular historical reference: the
pattern generally follows the history of Elizabeth's actual courtships,
which began in the 1560s with great expectation, but then trailed
off into flattering but ultimately meaningless diplomatic games.

The courtship of Arthur and Gloriana has structural implications
in excess of its relatively minor place in the narrative of *The Faerie
Queene*. In the works we considered in the previous section, especially the *Aeneid* and *Orlando Furioso*, the dynastic theme provides a
larger context for the individual episodes, imbuing the poems with
a sense of unity. In *The Faerie Queene*, this function falls to Arthur—and by extension to his quest for Gloriana. Arthur is bound
up closely with the problem of unifying the poem, as his appearances
in each book not only help that book's protagonist demonstrate the
virtue in question, but also weave together the poem's disparate parts
into a whole—at least at the conceptual level.[49] This is the Arthur of
the *Letter to Ralegh,* in which Spenser states, "So in the person of
Prince Arthur I sette forth magnificence in particular, which vertue
for that (according to Aristotle and the rest) it is the perfection of all
the rest, and conteineth in it them all. . . . "[50] Leaving aside Spenser's
vexing reference to Aristotle, we may remark the dual nature of
Arthur's narrative function: he is both behind and within the poem,
embodying the sum of all virtues even as he is shown manifesting
them individually.

We cannot long consider Arthur as a unifying structural principle
without encountering the mistress he himself could not find, for
Arthur is not the only figure to be both within and without the
poem; he shares this distinction with the Faery Queen.[51] Both characters figure in the narrative incidentally—Arthur more than the Faery Queen to be sure—but primarily inhabit the vast structure
implied by the poem and of which the reader is only permitted
glimpses.[52] To the extent that this structure depends upon their courtship, or rather, to the extent that the poem bases its teleology on the
anticipated union of Arthur and Gloriana, it is already historically
compromised. For Spenser has pursued contradictory strategies in
representing Elizabeth in his poem, praising the queen's virginity on

one hand, while positing her ideal suitor on the other. The fundamental contradiction begins to appear, I think, in Arthur's absurd
inability to make his way to Faery Court. He is condemned to wan-
der the periphery of Gloriana's kingdom because to draw too close
would have an effect on the Virgin Queen myth analogous to Calidore's incautious approach to the dancing graces on Mount Acidale:
"But soone as he appeared to their vew,/They vanisht all away out
of his sight" (VI.x.18).[53]

Spenser faced a difficult task in molding a dynastic form to the
political needs of a virgin queen. Caught between generic precedent
and historical fact, his situation betrays deep anxieties within Elizabethan society, anxieties about venturing into an uncertain political
future without an heir to the throne or a clearly-favored claimant.
Spenser's response to this anxiety is to advance the courtship of Arthur and Gloriana. As a political solution, it is no solution at all,
consisting of equal parts wish-fulfillment and escapist recourse to
nostalgia. As a narrative device, however, the romance of Arthur and
Gloriana is brilliant, imposing a semblance of structural unity on the
disparate parts of the poem and providing the poem's moral allegory
with a single, all-encompassing exemplar. It has the further advantage
of retrospectivity, refocusing the reader's attention on a glorious past
rather than a painfully contingent future. Only one problem remains:
Arthur and Gloriana cannot marry. Spenser gives his poem a telos it
can never reach, a goal that can be approached only asymptotically.
In a sense, Arthur's and Gloriana's infinitely deferred union becomes
a structural metaphor for Spenser's unfinished and unfinishable *Faerie
Queene*. But even more suggestively, its fleeting presence calls attention to the dream of continuity and stability in a mutable world, to
the Tudor heir that Elizabeth—and her sister before her—never delivered.

Wittenburg University

NOTES

Thanks to James Nohrnberg, J. Daniel Kinney, and Scott Lucas, who read and
commented helpfully on earlier versions of this essay.

1. All quotations from *The Faerie Queene* are from A. C. Hamilton's edition, *The
Faerie Queene* (London: Longman, 1977), and are cited parenthetically.

2. I am grateful to Anne Prescott for suggesting to me two apt resonances for
this passage. The first, quoted in another context below, is Anchises' lachrymose

description of his ill-fated heir Marcellus in *Aeneid* Book 6. The second is the encomiastic prophecy for then Princess Elizabeth put into the mouth of Thomas Cranmer at the end of *The Famous History of the Life of King Henry the Eighth:*

> Let me speak, sir.
> For heaven now bids me; and the words I utter
> Let none think flattery; for they'll find 'em truth.
> This royal infant—heaven still move about her!—
> Though in her cradle, yet now promises
> Upon this land a thousand thousand blessings,
> Which time shall bring to ripeness (V.iv.14–20, *The Riverside Shakespeare,*
> ed. G. Blakemore Evans, et al. (Boston: Houghton Mifflin, 1974)).

Elizabeth's reign had ended a decade or so before these lines were written, rendering it an anodyne subject for literary prophecy.

3. Ibid. III.iii.50 n.

4. The context of Christ's phrase bears this out: "And ye shal heare of warres, and rumors of warres: se that ye be not troubled: for all these things must come to passe, *but the end is not yet*. For nacion shal rise against nacion, and realme against realme: & there shalbe pestilence, and famine, and earthquakes in divers places. All these are but the beginning of sorowes." (Matthew 24: 6–8, emphasis added); quoted from *The Geneva Bible: A Facsimile of the 1560 Edition*, introduction by Lloyd E. Berry (Madison: University of Wisconsin Press, 1969).

5. *Spenser Encyclopedia*, ed. A. C. Hamilton (Toronto: University of Toronto Press, 1990) s. v. "prophecies." Wittreich's reading of the phrase's meaning in *Matthew* is correct and astutely noted. It seems likely, however, that any dampening effect of the phrase would be outweighed by its jarring evocation of the apocalyptic theme in general.

6. Thomas Bulger, *The Historical Changes and Exchanges as Depicted by Spenser in* The Faerie Queene (Lewiston, New York: Mellen, 1993) 103.

7. Howard Dobin, *Merlin's Disciples: Prophecy, Poetry, and Power in Renaissance England* (Stanford: Stanford University Press, 1990) 152.

8. Richard McCabe, *The Pillars of Eternity: Time and Providence in* The Faerie Queene (Dublin: Irish Academic Press, 1989) 193.

9. This is close to Richard McCabe's reading: "As he peers beyond Elizabeth, Merlin reaches the limits of rational interpretation and may go no further. He begins to experience visions his mind cannot yet encompass" (Ibid., 49).

10. This is true in two senses. First, because to speak about Elizabeth's successor was forbidden; second, because the practice of "prophesying" (the term had many meanings) was suspect. Compare Carole Levin's assessment: "Another period of even more intense belief in prophecy, however, was the late 1580s and 1590s. With the fears brought on by an uncertain succession, there was more and more interest in the reassurance of prophecy." *"The Heart and Stomach of a King": Elizabeth I and the Politics of Sex and Power* (Philadelphia: University of Pennsylvania Press, 1994) 100. On Elizabeth's opposition to "prophesying" by her clergy, see Patrick Collinson, *The Elizabethan Puritan Movement* (Berkeley: University of California Press, 1967)

168–76; and Paul E. McLane, *Spenser's Shepheardes Calendar: A Study in Elizabethan Allegory* (Notre Dame, Indiana: University of Notre Dame Press, 1961) 140–57.

11.   My overview of this aspect of Elizabeth's life draws upon Mortimer Levine's *The Early Elizabethan Succession Question, 1558–1568* (Stanford: Stanford University Press, 1966); J. E. Neale, *Queen Elizabeth I*, (London: Jonathan Cape, 1934); Carole Levin, *The Heart and Stomach of a King: Elizabeth I and the Politics of Sex and Power* (Philadelphia: University of Pennsylvania Press, 1994); and Susan Frye, *Elizabeth I: The Competition for Representation* (New York: Oxford University Press, 1993).

12.   For example, Henry VIII sent Bishop Gardiner to negotiate a marriage between the young Elizabeth and Charles V's son Philip (the same Philip who later married Elizabeth's sister). See Maria Perry, *The Word of a Prince: A Life of Elizabeth I from Contemporary Documents* (Woodbridge, England: Boydell Press, 1990) 34.

13.   On February 10, 1558, Elizabeth informed the House of Commons in a speech: "And in the end this shall be for me sufficient, that a marble stone shall declare that a queen having reigned such a time, lived and died a virgin." And in a passage from a 1566 speech quoted below, Elizabeth states: "I sent them answer by my council I would marry although of my own disposition I was not inclined thereto." *The Public Speaking of Queen Elizabeth: Selections from Her Official Addresses*, ed. George P. Rice, Jr. (New York: Columbia University Press, 1951) 116, 78.

14.   On this imbroglio, see Norman Jones, *The Birth of the Elizabethan Age: England in the 1560s* (Oxford: Blackwell, 1993) 148–50.

15.   On the Alençon courtship, see *Discoverie of a Gaping Gulf: With Letters and Other Relevant Documents*, ed. Lloyd E. Berry (Charlottesville: University Press of Virginia for Folger Shakespeare Library, 1968).

16.   The text of the statute is found in *The Statutes of the Realm* (London, 1819) 23 Eliz. c. 2. (659–61). On the parliamentary history of this act, see Neale, *Elizabeth I and Her Parliaments: 1559–1581*, 393–99. In addition to a general ban on speculating about the succession, the law singled out certain occult practices associated with discerning the future: "setting or erecting of any Figure or Figures, or by casting of Nativities, or by calculacion, or by any Prophecieng Witchcrafte Cunjuracions or other lyke unlawfull Meanes whatsoever . . . " On the effect of the law, see John H. Pollen, *Mary Queen of Scots and the Babington Plot* (Edinburgh: Scottish Historical Society, 1922) xiii–xiv.

17.   *Leicester's Commonwealth: The Copy of a Letter Written by a Master of Art of Cambridge (1584) and Related Documents*, ed. D. C. Peck (Athens, Ohio: Ohio University Press, 1985) 140. Hatton's rhetoric should be read in the context of other, contrasting developments. In the 1580s, for example, the longing for a certain succession seemed to mix with a fatigue for women's rule to produce rumors of the secret survival of Edward VI. See Levin, *"The Heart and Stomach of a King,"* 99–101.

18.   F. H. Mares, ed. *The Memoirs of Robert Carey* (Oxford: Clarendon Press, 1972) 58. Of course, the fate of the crown remained uncertain for an extraordinary length of time; it was not until after Essex's death in February 1601 that Robert Cecil began corresponding secretly with James about preparations for the new monarchy. Ironically, Robert Carey was one of the first courtiers to ride to Scotland to share the news of Elizabeth's death and begin cultivating the favor of the new monarch.

19.   "Spenser grew up in the atmosphere created by the uncertain succession. During his most formative years he saw the fall of Mary Stuart in Scotland, her flight

into England, and the ensuing discord that followed her like a handmaid. His patron Leicester was closely linked with the problem of Mary Stuart and the succession through the possibility of a marriage with either Elizabeth or Mary," says Kerby Neill, "The Faerie Queene and the Mary Stuart Controversy," quoted in *The Works of Edmund Spenser: A Variorum Edition*, eds. Edwin Greenlaw, Charles Osgood, Frederick Padelford, and Ray Heffner, 10 vols. (Baltimore: Johns Hopkins University Press, 1932–49) 5: 320.

20.   Although these events took place after the first six books of *The Faerie Queene* had appeared and could not, therefore, have influenced his shaping of the poem, it is illuminating to note that if James VI had succeeded Elizabeth while Spenser was still alive, the poet could have expected his pension to be replaced by a prison term for the unflattering rendering of the Scottish King's mother in Book V. Robert Bowes wrote to Burghley from Edinburgh on November 12, 1596: "The King hath conceaued great offence against Edmund Spencer publishing in prynte in the second part of the Fairy Queene and ix*th* chapter some dishonorable effects (as the k. demeth thereof) against himself and his mother deceassed." And he continues, "he still desyreth that Edward Spencer for his faulte, may be dewly tryed & punished." Quoted in Frederic Carpenter, *A Reference Guide to Edmund Spenser* (Chicago: University of Chicago Press, 1923) 41–42.

21.   The chronicle records several relevant examples of "the greedy thirst of royall crowne,/That knowes no kinred, nor regardes no right" (II.x.35). Of England's first Christian king, Lucius, Arthur reads:

> This good king shortly without issew dide,
> Whereof great trouble in the kingdome grew,
> That did her selfe in sundry parts diuide,
> And with her powre her owne selfe ouerthrew. (2.10.54);

and of Maximinian: "Who dying left none heire them to withstand, /But that they ouerran all parts with easie hand" (2.10.61). Compare Matilde's lament prior to adopting the bear-baby in Book 6:

> For th'heauens enuying our prosperitie,
> Haue not vouchsaft to graunt vnto vs twaine
> The gladfull blessing of posteritie,
> Which we might see after our selues remaine
> In th'heritage of our vnhappie paine:
> So that for want of heires it to defend,
> All is in time like to returne againe
> To that foule feend, who dayly doth attend
> To leape into the same after our liues end (VI.iv.31).

22.   See, for example, *Faerie Queene* 1.Pr.4, 2.9.4, 6.10.28.

23.   Roy Strong, *Gloriana: The Portraits of Queen Elizabeth I* (New York: Thames and Hudson, 1987) 20. Strong goes so far as to date this shift in representational strategy: "sometime about 1594 a government decision was taken that the official

image of the Queen in her final years was to be of a legendary beauty, ageless and unfading" (20).

24.   On this choice, see Ty Buckman, "The Perils of Marriage Counselling: John Stubbs, Philip Sidney, and the Virgin Queen," *Renaissance Papers 1995* (Raleigh, North Carolina, 1995) 125–41.

25.   Hamilton, *The Faerie Queene*, 737. I quote this passage to demonstrate Spenser's self-conscious placement of his poem in a tradition; whether that tradition is properly termed "epic" is a debate unto itself. This said, I will use the term as shorthand to refer to whatever generic hybrid Spenser's list of romances and epics represents.

26.   On Spenser's use of these works as models, see A. Kent Hieatt, "The Passing of Arthur in Malory, Spenser, and Shakespeare: The Avoidance of Closure," in *The Passing of Arthur: New Essays in Arthurian Tradition*, eds. Christopher Baswell and William Sharpe (New York: Garland, 1988) 173–192, especially 179–180.

27.   Andrew Fichter, *Poets Historical: Dynastic Epic in the Renaissance* (New Haven: Yale University Press, 1982) 1. Fichter's work, though in pursuit of a thesis largely unrelated to mine, has nevertheless proven helpful to me in formulating this section.

28.   See Jupiter's pronouncement in *Aeneid* 1.257–96, which includes the lines, "his ego nec metas rerum nec tempora pono;/imperium sine fine dedi" (1.278–79; see n. 29). ("For these I set neither bounds nor periods of empire; dominion without end have I bestowed.")

29.   An idea that Virgil borrowed from Homer. Odysseus' dalliance with Calypso is an allegory of his loss of concern for his homeland—his season as a lotus-eater, as it were—just as his return to Penelope signals the restoration of Ithaka.

30.   Virgil's Latin text and its English translation are quoted from H. R. Fairclough's edition: *Virgil*, 2 vols. (Cambridge, Massachusetts: Harvard University Press, 1916).

31.   Compare also 6.679–83 and 6.716–18.

32.   O gnate, ingentem luctum ne quaere tuorum.
　　　ostendent terris hunc tantum fata, nec ultra
　　　esse sinent. nimium vobis Romana propago
　　　visa potens, superi, propria haec si dona fuissent. (6: 868–71)

("O my son, ask not of the vast sorrow of thy people. Him the fates shall but show to earth, nor longer suffer him to stay. Too mighty, O gods, ye deemed the Roman stock would be, were these gifts lasting.")

33.   Lodovico Ariosto, *Orlando Furioso*, ed. Dino Provenzal (Milan: Rizzoli Editore, 1955). I cite this edition of the poem parenthetically by book and stanza number. Translations of Ariosto are my own.

34.   Presumably because Aristotle's praise of verisimilitude prevented Tasso from such *maraviglie* as parades of future descendants and ecstatic visions (see Fichter, *Poets Historical*, 112–26). Thus, where Aeneas and Ruggiero were chastened to duty by visions of the future, Rinaldo's instruction comes from the example of the past:

　　　Vedrai de gli avi il divulgato onore,
　　　lunge precorso in loco erto e solingo;
　　　tu dietro anco riman', lento cursore,

per questo de la gloria illustre arringo.
Su su, te stesso incita: al tuo valore
si sferza e spron quel ch'io colà dipingo.
Così diceva; e l cavalier affisse
lo sguardo là, mentre colui sì disse.

(17.65; see n. 34)

(" 'You will see the far-spread honor of your forebears, first heralded far off
in a hard and lonely region; you are still left behind, a slow runner in these
noble lists for glory. Up up, arouse yourself, let that which I depict there
be whip and spur to your valor.' So he spoke, and the knight there fixed
his gaze, while thus he was speaking.")

An alternative explanation for Tasso's backward-looking stance is his own lateness
in the tradition of the heroic poem.

35.   Tasso's poem is quoted from Torquato Tasso, *Gerusalemme Liberata*, eds. Clau-
dio Varese and Guido Arbizzoni (Milan: Mursia, 1983). The translation is Ralph
Nash's: Torquato Tasso, *Jerusalem Delivered: An English Prose Version*, trans. and ed.
Ralph Nash (Detroit: Wayne State University Press, 1987).

36.   On Arthur's vision, see Sheila Cavanagh, *Wanton Eyes and Chaste Desires:
Female Sexuality in the* Faerie Queene (Bloomington: Indiana University Press, 1994)
14–16; David Lee Miller, *The Poem's Two Bodies: The Poetics of the 1590* Faerie
Queene (Princeton: Princeton University Press, 1988) 120–63, Elizabeth Bellamy,
Translations of Power: Narcissism and the Unconscious in Epic History (Ithaca: Cornell
University Press, 1992) 212–21.

37.   Arthur's lengthy response to Una's question shows him to be in the earliest
stages of acquiring self-knowledge. He explains at the outset of the passage that his
lineage and his father's identity "from me are hidden yit" (I.ix.3), and he is in love
with a woman whom he has encountered only as a nocturnal vision. A verbal clue
links these two uncertainties. Merlin reassured him, Arthur tells Una and Redcrosse,
"That I was sonne and heire vnto a king, / As time in her iust terme the truth to
light should bring" (I.ix.5). Later, the Queene of Faeries offers, "For dearely sure
her loue was to me bent, / As when iust time expired should appeare" (I.ix.14). In
both cases he is promised a future revelation, but the delayed knowledge suggests
that who Arthur is and whom he loves are somehow related "through that fatall
deep foresight"—that is, by his destiny.

38.   This is the sense that Spenser gives the passage in the *Letter to Ralegh*, where
Arthur was "to haue seene in a dream or vision the Faery Queen, with whose
excellent beauty rauished, he awaking resolued to seeke her out, and so being by
Merlin armed, and by Timon throughly instructed, he went to seeke her forth in
Faerye land." (Hamilton, *The Faerie Queene*, 737).

39.   Arthur's description of his nocturnal encounter with the Queene of Faeries
recalls Redcrosse's similar experience at Archimago's home, when the wizard "made
him dreame of loues and lustfull play, / That nigh his manly hart did melt away"
(I.i.47).

40.   *Studies in Medieval and Renaissance Literature*, ed. Walter Hooper (Cambridge:
Cambridge University Press, 1966) 158–59.

41.   Hamilton, *The Faerie Queene*, 737.

42.   Strangely, in the scene that Arthur describes, it is *Arthur* who most resembles Belphoebe, "raunging the forest wide on courser free" (I.ix.12), "for-wearied with my sports" (13), comfortable enough in the woods to make "The verdant gras my couch" (13). The connection leads one to imagine an improved configuration in which Arthur courts Belphoebe and Timias the more-willing Faerie Queene. Spenser, however, cleverly avoids this possibility by placing the couples on different narrative axes, so that when Arthur meets the forlorn Timias, for example, in Book IV, he reads "B E L P H E B E" carved on the trees, "Yet who was that Belphebe, he ne wist" (IV.vii.46).

43.   Compare the narrator's prayer to Cupid at the beginning of Book IV: "From her high spirit chase imperious feare,/And vse of awfull Maiestie remoue:/.../ Sprinckle her heart, and haughtie courage soften,/That she may hearke to loue, and reade this lesson often." (IV.Pr.5). On the fairy mistress tradition, see *The Works of Edmund Spenser*, 1: 267–68.

44.   On Spenser's handling of this scene, see Sheila Cavanagh, " 'Beauties Chace': Arthur and Women in *The Faerie Queene*," in *The Passing of Arthur: New Essays in Arthurian Tradition*, ed. Christopher Baswell and William Sharpe (New York: Garland Publishing, 1988) 207–218; especially 212–13.

45.   For a survey of these appearances, see Sherry L. Reames, "Prince Arthur and Spenser's Changing Design," in *Eterne in Mutabilitie: The Unity of* The Faerie Queene, ed. Kenneth J. Atchity (Hamden, Connecticut: Archon Books, 1972) 180–206.

46.   The manipulation of time in this stanza is quite complex. It begins with the narrative past and Merlin's manufacture of Arthur's weapons and armor, and then jumps immediately to his death in the narrative future and the Faerie Queene recovering his armor. Finally, it closes with a glance at the reader's present and the suggestion that the items in question may "yet" be seen.

47.   Compare Arthur's vow here with his earlier one at I.ix.15, and both with Redcrosse's at I.xii.18.

48.   *Faerie Queene* I.ix.14–15.

49.   W. L. Renwick observes, "The Faerie Queene treats of many actions of many men, but there is an attempt to give it unity by interweaving with these actions the single epic action of the single epic hero, Prince Arthur's search for Gloriana." *Edmund Spenser: An Essay on Renaissance Poetry* (London: E. Arnold, 1933) 50.

50.   Hamilton, *The Faerie Queene*, 737. In a sense, Arthur's relationship to the various heroes and their respective virtues is a symbiotic one. Only after an adventure has been undertaken can Arthur appear and assist the hero in his time of trial; only after a virtue has been introduced can Arthur represent its perfection.

51.   Compare, for example, the following compliment from the Proem to Book VI: "Right so from you all goodly vertues well/Into the rest, which round about you ring" (VI.Pr.7).

52.   To this structure belong, for example, Spenser's plans for a twelve or even twenty-four book work, the origin of the various quests at the court of the Faerie Queen, the distinction between Fairyland and England, and the relationship between the historical present and the mythic past. On Spenser's spectacular intentions, see James Nohrnberg, *The Analogy of* The Faerie Queene (Princeton: Princeton

University Press, 1976) 35–42; C. S. Lewis, *Spenser's Images of Life*, ed. Alastair Fowler (Cambridge: Cambridge University Press, 1967) 137–40; *The Works of Edmund Spenser*, 1: 314–62.

53.   Compare James Nohrnberg's observation that "Arthur and Gloriana belong to the poem's framework, and partly express the poem's theory. In a way, they 'looke vnto the end of that which shulde be abolished,' namely the poem itself. *As symbols of its limits*, the royal pair should be assimilated to not only the poem's 'end,' but also the poet's . . . " (Ibid., 55, emphasis added). Also compare Sherry Reames's contention, "Even if Arthur was not meant to have a specific counterpart in real life, Spenser could not allow him to win Gloriana unless Queen Elizabeth actually married . . . Without the concurrence of historical events, therefore, Spenser could not allow Arthur even to approach the Faerie Queene" ("Prince Arthur and Spenser's Changing Design," 186).

JUDITH H. ANDERSON

Busirane's Place: *The House of Rhetoric*

The first two rooms in the House of Busirane indicate that it consists of rhetorical "places" familiar both to Britomart and to Spenser's readers. Thomas Roche has glossed Busirane as *abuse* or the archaic *abusion* (deceit, deception, delusion), to which I would add *abusio*, a Renaissance term for catachresis, a wrenched or extravagant use of metaphor, for in Book III's House of Rhetoric, *abusio* reigns, or "ranes," supreme. Britomart cannot destroy Busirane without killing what Amoret is, the cultural object par excellence. This may be why the poem has such trouble with the figure of Amoret after Book III and why, though Busirane's art works vanish, he must survive, bound by the very chain, or, according to traditional iconography, the rhetorical art, that he has abused. In Book III, Busirane abuses figuration outrageously, fantasizing that metaphor is the same as reality; feigning and faining rape. His real legacy, however, is the reading that believes him.

O VER THE LAST THREE or four decades, the House of Busirane has variously been seen as Busirane's projection, as Amoret's, as Scudamour's, as Britomart's, and without regard for the niceties of mediating characters, as the narrator's. For this reason, I'll begin with the flat declaration that the House of Busirane, like the House of Holiness, the Bower of Bliss, The Gardens of Adonis, the Temple of Venus, or any other such place in *The Faerie Queene*, is a cultural site. Representation of this site is finally the poet's, as are all the figures within it, though by now it goes almost without saying that the poet's control of the site, his agency with respect to it, is mediated, limited, and compromised by his own position in language and history. Moreover, like other cultural sites in *The Faerie Queene*, the House of Busirane has a special pertinence to the figures within it, especially to Britomart, the major figure in Book III, even as the

House of Pride and the House of Holiness, for example, have special pertinence to Redcrosse but without being solely attributable to him.[1]

Britomart arrives at the House of Busirane by chasing a Chaucerian allusion, namely, Ollyphant, the destructive fantasy that leads her to Scudamour, whose shield clearly identifies him as "*Cupids* man" (III.xi.7, IV.x.54). Five cantos earlier in Book III, a heavenly Venus loses control of a wayward Cupid and descends to earth to seek him, only to find Diana. After a temporary reconciliation with Diana to search for Cupid, Venus separates from Diana again, taking with her instead of Cupid the twin she names Amoret. The name she chooses "in her litle loues stead" makes it clear that *Amor(etta)*—feminized love, hence beloved or love object—compensates and consoles her for Cupid's absence (III.vi.28). When Britomart finds Cupid's man Scudamour, then, a composite Venus-Diana might finally be said to have found Cupid. Symbolically, this seems a promising development, but the representative of Cupid Britomart finds has been disabled by Busirane, who has abducted, and in this sense has ravished, Scudamour's beloved or, as it turns out, the very possibility of Scudamour's actualizing his love. More pointedly, the Enchanter has "penned," or through his art confined, the Amor(et) principle—"*Venus* mayd," who is the necessary complement of Cupid's man (III.xi.10, IV.x.54).

Although in recent years the enchanted House of Busirane has most often been discussed in Petrarchan terms, this site is surely no less classical and specifically Ovidian. It is also more broadly medieval than simply Petrarchan, and of course it is more exactly the composite of these forms in sixteenth-century guise. Once Britomart enters this enchanted site, the first room she finds seems to signal the inevitability of her arrival there. The tapestries on its walls share both their Ovidian source in the *Metamorphoses* and their sense of erotic compulsion with a number of Britomart's earliest experiences, for example, her beholding the tapestry in the House of Malecasta that depicts the love of Venus for the boy Adonis and the discovery of her passion for Artegall to Glauce in terms that evoke specific comparison with the loves of Myrrha, Byblis, Pasiphaë, and Narcissus (III.1.34–38, ii.41, 44). While Britomart's arrival in Busirane's "vtmost rowme" isn't exactly a homecoming, it is a familiar "place" or "house" in the rhetorical sense both to her and to Spenser's readers (III.xi.27). The *Metamorphoses* was a standard text in Elizabethan schools, excerpted for beginners and read in its entirety later on. It was memorized, its rhetoric extensively imitated, and its cultural message imbibed. Lynn Enterline has suggested how a figure like Ovid's suffering Hecuba could become "a 'mirror' or 'example'"—to which

I'd add, a "place"—"for pupils to imitate," ostensibly to develop their own styles but inevitably with further "social, imaginary, and personal" impact. Both Shakespeare's Lucrece and his Hamlet, she notes, use Ovid's Hecuba as just such a mirror "in and through which to understand and to express what they claim to be their 'own' emotions."[2]

The specific Ovidian passage on which the tapestries in the House of Busirane draw is the ecphrasis of Arachne's art in her ill-fated weaving contest with Pallas Athena. Immediately, there are ironies and crossings of gender in this situation, whose many complications discussion more gradually unlayers. When Britomart initially encounters Busirane's enchantments, she asks Scudamour in dismay, "What monstrous enmity prouoke we heare,/Foolhardy as th'Earthes children, the which made/Battell against the Gods? So we a God inuade" (III.xi.22). Then boldly invading this god, the female knight gazes at a tapestry that pointedly recalls the one woven by Ovid's Arachne, a woman bold—perhaps too bold?—in protesting the violent excesses of the gods' passions but also one whose protest is depicted sympathetically in many readers' eyes by the classical male poet.[3] The tapestries Britomart views similarly show more than one sign of satiric protest: for example, in Mars's undignified "shreek" (rhyming with "eek") of passion, "With womanish teares, and with vnwarlike smarts," or in the sequence of Neptune's undying love only for Bisaltis in the alexandrine of one stanza—"Ne ought but deare *Bisaltis* ay could make him glad"—followed immediately in the next stanza by the laconic statement "He loued eke *Iphimedia* deare,/And *Aeolus* faire daughter *Arne* hight" (III.xi.41–42, 44).

But the cross-dressed knight Britomart finds her tapestry of female protest within the chambers of a male enchanter, who, like herself, is also the creation of a male poet. We might well stop at this point to ask, with Susanne Wofford, whose tapestry this is and through whose eyes we see, or more properly, "rede" it.[4] Arachne's, Ovid's, his narrator's, Britomart's, Busirane's, Spenser's, his narrator's, the interpretive tradition's, or our own? Going beyond the possibilities Wofford endorses, it would appear difficult to exclude any of these, and the ecphrasis of the tapestry itself explicitly invites them in describing Jove's rape of Leda, breaking into apostrophe in the manner of Ovid to do so:

> O wondrous skill, and sweet wit of the man,
> That her in daffadillies sleeping made,
> From scorching heat her daintie limbes to shade:

Whiles the proud Bird ruffing his fethers wyde,
And brushing his faire brest, did her inuade;
She slept, yet twixt her eyelids closely spyde,
How towards her he rusht, and smiled at his pryde.

(III.xi.32)

Considerable ambiguity of reference marks this much-discussed stanza. Is the skilled and sweet witted man in the first line Busirane, the narrator, or Spenser himself? This time, the lines cited have no direct parallel in Ovid, hence no parallel in Arachne's tapestry, and they therefore belong to the three possibilities enumerated. But are we to forget that Britomart is our gazer and that these lines could also have something to do with her vision or her response to Arachne's?[5] In whose opinion is the man "sweet witted"? And what do the last two lines of the stanza mean: "She slept, yet twixt her eyelids closely spyde,/How towards her he rusht, and smiled at his pryde"? Leda sleeps, like Verdant in the Bower of Bliss, and yet, also to an extent like him, between her eyelids she seems to see—to spy—the swan rushing toward her. Is she awake or in a trance or in a daydream? Each of these possibilities would imply a different kind and degree of agency. The simple adverb "closely" could indicate that her eyes are indeed shut ("closely twixt") or that she spies with close attention an object close to her ("closely spyde"). The word "spy" itself carries an insistent association with stealth or closeness—intense, secretive observation. The final clause of the line, as Katharine Eggert has noted, is also ambiguous: does Leda smile in anticipation of rapture or does the swan smile in anticipation of ravishment?[6] And is the smile one of Jovian arrogance, of pure pleasure, his, hers, or theirs; or is it an ironic smile, a self-reflexive, deflating, Ovidian possibility that the availability of female perspectives enforces?

Another passage, even more frequently remarked, expresses ambiguity of reference as well. The walls of the Enchanter's House are clothed with arras,

Wouen with gold and silke so close and nere,
That the rich metall lurked pruily,
As faining to be hid from enuious eye;
Yet here, and there, and euery where vnwares
It shewd it selfe, and shone vnwillingly;
Like a discolourd snake, whose hidden snares
Through the greene gras his long bright burnisht backe declares.

(III.xi.28)

This time the inwoven threads of metal have an explicit precedent in

Ovid, although it proves as striking in its difference as in its similarity: "There, too, they [Pallas and Arachne] weave in pliant threads of gold, and trace in the weft some ancient tale" (illic et lentum filis inmittitur aurum/et vetus in tela deducitur argumentum.).[7] In Ovid's version, the gold thread, belonging to Arachne and Pallas alike, lacks the last six lines of Spenserian description, which call attention—indeed, demand heightened attention—to the serpentine filaments. Rather than betraying the presence of art, they shout it by comparison to Ovid's text, unwilling as they may be, or rather, feign to be so. The participial pun "faining" as easily supports an exhibitionist impulse as it denies it, since the pun means either pretending or desiring: "As faining to be hid." The alternative of merely pretending to hide from but actually enticing the "enuious eye" would relate the serpentine threads to the gold grapes in Acrasia's Bower, which enfold themselves among the leaves "As lurking from the vew of couetous guest"—as if lurking but actually seducing (II.xii.55).

But art in the House of Busirane is not finally the same as in the Bower, where "The art, which all that wrought, appeared in no place" (II.xii.58).[8] Here, not unlike the rhetorical device *occupatio*, the sonneteer's topos of inarticulateness, or the elaborate *declamatio* uttered in full chase by Ovid's Apollo, art may want or pretend to hide but instead it displays itself, unwillingly or not. Like the pun "faining," the word "unwillingly," which specifically refers to shining, or conspicuousness—"It shewd it selfe, and shone vnwillingly"—again evokes the oscillating play of visual and interpretive perspectives. Moreover, it does so "vnwares," which is precisely the ambiguous way Malecasta sneaks up on Britomart and the way Busirane's knife wounds her and the knowing and not knowing way that Leda, in all her ambiguity, awaits the rush of the swan. This is an acute, incredibly telling way of realizing the combination of cultural exposure and innocence, knowing and not-knowing, that characterizes Britomart's condition and observation, as indeed her reading of Ovid. Once more, Britomart does not cause this place, whose meaning at once precedes and exceeds her role in it, but this place of rhetorical culture bears a special pertinence to her condition and quest. Again as with Leda, she is mirrored to an extent in the object or site.

Before leaving the tapestries, I want to glance at some other relevant passages in which Spenser explicitly uses or more elusively recalls Ovid's tale of Arachne. I would speak of a genealogy of these uses, if questions of dating did not dissuade me from attempting it. In addition to the tapestries in the House of Busirane, Spenser uses Arachne's weaving contest with Pallas at length in "Muiopotmos." In this poem, Arachne's metamorphosis to a spider is the consequence of her "poysonous rancor" rather than of the spiteful temper of the goddess, as in Ovid (344). Thus Arachne is merely too bold an over-reacher, rather than a courageous, if willful, exposer of divine predation. There is little here of the complication of an empathetic female observer's perspective, and the erotic depredations of the gods are reduced to the single instance of Jove and Europa, celebrated, according to Leonard Barkan, as "an intense orgasmic sea-triumph" (204). But one stanza describing Arachne's son, the spider Aragnoll, finds a curious refraction (or vice versa) in the Bower of Bliss. In it, the narrator describes the amazingly subtle net that Aragnoll spins to catch the joyous butterfly. This is "networke" so cunning and curious that neither damsel nor weaver, nor other skilled craftsmen dare compare their work to it, nor even, as the narrator continues,

> . . . doo I thinke, that that same subtil gin,
> The which the *Lemnian* God framde craftilie,
> *Mars* sleeping with his wife to compasse in,
> That all the Gods with common mockerie
> Might laugh at them, and scorne their shamefull sin,
> Was like to this.
>
> (368–74)

For a moment, Aragnoll, Arachne's malicious descendent, has a disconcerting resemblance to the Palmer in the Bower of Bliss, who captures Acrasia and Verdant in his "subtile net"—a latter day "*Lemnian* God," or Vulcan, netting his Venus and Mars. But another artist in the Bower, Acrasia herself, is also associated disconcertingly with Arachne's web-work, for she is "arayd, or rather disarayd,/All in a vele of silke and siluer thin . . . More subtile web *Arachne* can not spin,/Nor the fine nets, which oft we wouen see,/Of scorched deaw, do not in th'aire more lightly flee" (II.xii.77, 81). Artists both, Acrasia and the Palmer are also opposites, but their oppositional status gets a bit blurry.[9] Arachne is also found in the Cave of Mammon, where her presence is associated with the fetishized eroticism of gold, on which, witness Marinell and Malbecco in Book III and in Book II Mammon himself, auto-erotically feeding his eye and "couetous desire" on the "masse of coyne" in his lap (II.vii.4).[10] Entering the "house" of Mammon, Guyon first sees a vault from which "the ragged breaches hong,"

Embost with massy gold of glorious gift,

And with rich metall loaded euery rift,

. . . .

And ouer them *Arachne* high did lift
Her cunning web, and spread her subtile net.

(II.vii.28)

Perhaps it is not irrelevant to eroticism or, for that matter, to poetry
in the broader, Renaissance sense of eroticism that in a letter to
Shelley, Keats used the second of these lines as a metaphor for the
poet's art.[11] The wicked Mammon's House is a rhetorical "place,"
too, and in fact a biblical "place" (not to mention a parable), and it
is also one insistently relevant to debate about the poet's craft—his
seductive, "sensefull words"—and the value of his calling (VI.ix.26).
Like Keats, Shakespeare and Milton remembered this House, the one
for its verbal riches and the other for its moral worth, and Spenser's
poet-figure in the October Eclogue, the shepherd Cuddie, has both
words and wealth in mind when he dismisses poetry for its lack of
"gayne" (10):

So praysen babes the Peacoks spotted traine,
And wondren at bright *Argus* blazing eye:
But who rewards him [the poet] ere the more for thy?
Or feedes him once the fuller by a graine?

(31–34)[12]

Not surprisingly, the poet also likens himself more than once in
the *Amoretti* to a spider weaving courtship's web of words and bonds
(XXIII, LXXI). Such weaving invokes an echo chamber of Ovidian
ironies, including the courting poet's awareness of her awareness of
the game he is playing, an awareness he shows more openly elsewhere
in the sequence and memorably in sonnets XVIII ("But when I
pleade, she bids me play my part") and LIIII: "Of this worlds Theatre
in which we stay,/My loue lyke the Spectator ydly sits/beholding
me that all the pageants play." Aside from the obvious fact that Ovid's
tale of Arachne engraved itself on Spenser's memory, these various
occurrences of it in his work all bear on art and the role of the artist,
and all occur in sinister or "daungerous," eroticized contexts—even
in "Muiopotmos," when we recognize the full resonance of Clarion's
"riotous excesse" amid "the pleasures of that Paradise" (168,186).
Taken together, they reinforce both the sense of multiple awarenesses

playing over Arachne's tale and the correlative presence of Spenser's ambivalence toward it and personal engagement with it, despite any number of mediating figures, that we also find in the multifaceted rendering of Arachne's tapestry in the House of Busirane.

Britomart passes next from the tapestries to a Mammonic room overlaid with pure gold, in which the "monstrous formes" of false love are depicted, and on whose glittering walls hang the trophies of love's wars and conquests (xi.51–52). There she witnesses the procession of Cupid's masquers, figures that stage the very process of a false love, hardly distinguishable at moments from a true one. Ambiguity of origin characterizes the creations of this room, as before the tapestries described. As Hamilton conveniently summarizes, the masquers draw directly on the conventions of the medieval courts of love and of Renaissance triumphs, not least Petrarch's own, as well as on those of the Renaissance masque.[13] Again, these figures are hardly Britomart's creation, although they have special relevance to her condition and quest, as they do to Amoret's and Scudamour's, and to many another character's in Book III. The very fact, long recognized, that they can be read from either a male or a female point of view indicates their basically cultural, rather than exclusively personal, status. Their formal artificiality also proclaims their radical constructedness. Unlike the insidious art forms in Acrasia's Bower, they make no claims on nature. On reflection, who would want such mirrors of passion as these?

Their relation to Busirane is worth pursuing, however. Cupid's masquers are too close for comfort to the kind of form Malbecco becomes at the end of canto x, one that "Is woxen so deform'd, that he has quight/Forgot he was a man, and *Gealosie* is hight" (60). Malbecco's metamorphosis into a "passion . . . in the mind" introduces the first canto in which the House of Busirane figures centrally, and, in effect, it prepares for the masquers, whose humanity, like Malbecco's, has vanished. Like the fixed and fixated emblem "Gealosie," the masquers are impostors of the living and every bit as artificial, as "personified," hence metaphorized, as the "carkasse dead" of the False Florimell (III.viii.7, xi.1). Even though the masquers are in a procession—a kind of dead march—each pair in itself is a frozen stage of courtship, removed from the necessarily narrative process of allegory.[14] I am willing to call this Busirane's art and to consider the "inner roome" from which it emanates his as well. Years since, Thomas Roche glossed Busirane as *abuse* in the sixteenth-century senses of "imposture, ill-usage, delusion" or as the archaic *abusion*, meaning a "perversion of the truth, deceit, deception, imposture" and, in the words of Book II, implying "fond . . . illusions" (xi.11.

vs. 8–9.)[15] To these meanings I would add *abusio*, the familiar Renaissance word for catachresis, a wrenching of metaphor or an extravagant use of it, in any case, a violent (mis)use of language, of which the masquers' dead likenesses strike me as being a prime exhibit.[16] In this place, this house of rhetoric, *abusio* would appear to reign, or "rane," supreme.

With Britomart, I am finally led to the third chamber of the House of Busirane, where its patron, the figure or at least the first figure behind the curtains, Busirane himself, primarily represents the radical constructedness of the entire place. As I have earlier noted, this artfull place simply doesn't make the same claims as Acrasia's Bower about its nearness to or indistinguishability from nature. This is art in capital letters, and alarmingly, Amoret's life in some sense depends on Busirane. Thus "the Lady [Amoret], which by him stood bound, / Dernely vnto her [Britomart] called to abstaine, / From doing him to dy" (xii.34). Once in Busirane's clutches at least, Amoret recognizes herself, and is recognized, as his creation, pleading for his life in order to preserve her own. Her identity as love, which is her life, depends on loving. She is, after all, "*Venus* mayd" (Venus made?) and the complement of "*Cupids* man," as she is described by Scudamour in Book IV (x.54). The adverb "dernely," which conveys the tone or manner in which Amoret calls on Britomart to spare Busirane's life, means "secretly" or "privately, confidentially;" it also carries the sense "inwardly." *Dernely* is a strange but suggestive word in context, one that in the past often has been too casually glossed in the derived senses "dismally" or "direly." More significantly, it intimates a special appeal or relationship, perhaps something understood between the two women. Yet *derne* means also "dark" and like "secret" in the sense "done in the dark" often has associations with craft, deceit, or evil.[17]

Conceivably, if disturbingly, it could further connect Amoret with her captor, at least while in his power. By way of association, the "dark secret life" that destroys Blake's rose comes to mind.

Clearly, however, Britomart cannot destroy Busirane without destroying what Amoret is, the cultural subject par excellence. This may be the reason the poem has so much and such interesting trouble with the figure of Amoret after Book III, and it might also be the reason that, while Busirane's art works may vanish, he must survive, bound by the very chain, or, in terms of traditional iconography, by the rhetorical art, that he has abused.[18] Without him there is only a vacuum, and this vacuum might also have something to do with the fact that Spenser's own *Amoretti*, written and published between Book III and its sequel, cannot wholly escape but indeed must use and try to reshape the available conventions of erotic discourse. The furnishings of Busirane's rooms may indeed vanish, but this is hardly the last we see of their kind in Spenser's poetry.

Busirane also represents a fantasy and, perhaps, additionally a culture of rape, as others have argued without qualification, but it should be noted as well that he is not successful. His fantasy remains exactly that, and Amoret remains a virgin: "Die had she leuer with Enchanters knife,/Then to be false in loue, profest a virgine wife" (IV.i.6). If it were otherwise, Busirane's whole significance as a peculiarly rhetorical form of abuse, an art with the power in actuality to arrest love, would be lost and with it the real cultural critique of the Book. Busirane abuses figuration and the perception based on it to feign that metaphor is the same as reality, that it IS absolutely rather than is and is not, as Paul Ricoeur would gloss this figure of perverse predication—"perverse" (from *pervetere*), "turned away, around, about"; "athwart," hence "tropic."[19] It is Busirane who *feigns* (and fains) rape. And his legacy is the reading that believes him.

Britomart herself is wounded, although not deeply, by Busirane and is therefore vulnerable to him. Her heart is also pierced and her hair stood on end by his bloody verses, even while, her threatening sword above him, she controls him.[20] At one point in the description of his disenchanting verses—a rhetorical spell, which, like all spells, must be unbound—a truly ambiguous pronoun occurs, (con)fusing Britomart with Amoret. With "threatfull hand" unslackened, Britomart waits "[un]dismayd" (or un-dismaided) by the quaking of this House and undeterred by "daungers dout," a phrase offering to reassume the familiar form of an actual pair of the masquers earlier seen (cf. xii.10–11, 37); thus she "abode," occupying and inhabiting this "place,"

> . . . to weet what end would come of all.
> At last that mightie chaine, which round about
> Her tender waste was wound, adowne gan fall,
> And that great brasen pillour broke in peeces small.
>
> (III.xii.37)

The ambiguous referent of the pronoun "her" signals Britomart's *involvement*—literally her enwrapping, winding (Latin *involvere*) —in Busirane's "mightie chaine," in the toils (and coils) of his rhetoric, thus invoking the familiar iconographic identification of rhetoric with spellbound enchainment that I have earlier referenced. Arguably, the first seven lines in the next stanza also encompass Britomart and Amoret, although my own awareness of the situation described makes me think such a reading unlikely. Be that as it may, what is significant about this momentary identification of Britomart with Amoret is that it comes only with Amoret's freeing at Britomart's hand. It implicates Britomart in Amoret's predicament, and she could hardly not be, but again, like Britomart's superficial wounding, in doing so it more tellingly exhibits the superiority *and* intimacy of her *deme*, or dark, secret power.

★

But let us suppose that the stanza of whose identification with Britomart I am skeptical, does indeed continue the identification of Britomart with Amoret, since this stanza offers the best evidence for the actual raping of Amoret and, in Susan Frye's argument, of Britomart as well:

> The cruell steele, which thrild her dying hart,
> Fell softly forth, as of his own accord,
> And the wyde wound, which lately did dispart
> Her bleeding brest, and riuen bowels gor'd,
> Was closed vp, as it had not bene bor'd,
> And euery part to safety full sound,
> As she were neuer hurt, was soone restor'd:
> Tho when she felt herself to be vnbound,
> And perfect hole, prostrate she fell vnto the ground.
>
> (III.xii.38)

The crucial words occur in the lines: "Her bleeding breast, and riuen bowels gor'd,/Was closed vp, as it [the wound] had not been bor'd." While these lines are about as transgressively suggestive as *The Faerie Queene* gets, I would reject a reading that swallows catachresis whole, actualizing the radical metaphors present here. The meaning of the lines depends heavily on that of the words "bowels" and "as" in them. Contrary to the popular twentieth-century understanding of *bowels* exclusively as "guts," in the sixteenth century this word commonly referred to "the seat of the tender and sympathetic emotions" or the "heart, centre," and in Spenser's writing it frequently, though

not always, carries the latter meaning, as is also true of English translations of the Bible in this period.[21] Doublets, such as "bleeding brest"
and "riuen bowels" in the first of the crucial lines quoted above, are
rife in Spenser, and the prominence in canto xii of Amoret's transfixed
heart would appear to favor the archaic meanings I have cited. In
fact, use of the singular verb "was," as well as a singular pronoun, for
the dual subjects "brest" and "bowels," though not the grammatical
offense in Spenser's time that it is in ours, enforces identification of
them as a single unit.

The other word, *as*, in the phrase "as it had not bene bor'd,"could
be read "as if," but it need not be. This word can also mean "inas-
much as" or "since," and that is what I take it to mean here: "inas-
much as it had not been bored."[22] Of course I would not reject the
other possible reading out of hand, either, although in context I may
find it a stretch—"far-fet" and, indeed, an *abusio*. Metaphor, after all,
even abusive, catachrestic metaphor, *is*, as well as is not. But the
possibility of the counter-factual reading "as if," like the former possibility of reading *bowels* as "guts," hence "belly"or reproductive or-
gans, would only return us to the multiple perspectives of the
participants in this canto—here specifically those of Amoret, Britomart, Busirane, the sometimes unreliable narrator, and Spenser himself. The pun on "whole" in the final line of the stanza is equally
undisturbed by the reading I have advanced or by the one that
chooses Busirane's literalizing perspective on it: Amoret, representative object of love, is rendered "whole and wanting," at once perfect,
or completed, for the passion of Cupid's man and both lacking and
desiring him. Freely now, her responses, like Britomart's, are holistic
in every sense of the hopeful or disheartening pun, as the reader will
have it.

We hear or half hear what I would call submerged or, more graphi-
cally, *(im)possible* puns of the sort just addressed even when prolonged
attention to syntax indicates that they are far-fetched and grammatically irrational. They are plentiful in the literature of the period, in
Shakespeare and Donne for obvious instances, and notably in Spenser
as well.[23] Studying the mental processes by which we select and com-
prehend words, the linguist Jean Aitchison has found evidence to
support the viability of such puns: readers or listeners "briefly activate
both meanings of a homonym, even in cases where one of them is
inappropriate"; indeed, according to one model, "A whole army of
words, it seems, marches up for consideration each time a word
begins."[24] Whatever the precise workings of our mental circuitry, a
third Spenserian example is ready to hand slightly earlier in Britomart's confrontation with Busirane, and it raises similar issues of

reading, thus contributing to this significant interpretive pattern.
When Busirane's knife wounds Britomart, "Exceeding wroth there-
with the virgin grew, / Albe the wound were nothing deepe imprest"
(xii.33). In an examination of Spenser's puns on the word "nothing,"
Eggert has suggested that *nothing* here might be a noun and therefore
a sexual pun, the familiar Shakespearean equivalent of "hole," or
"vagina, genitalia": in this reading, "nothing [is] deepe imprest."[25]
Once again, though surely prematurely, Britomart is presumed to
have been raped. But, as Eggert has agreed, the concessive "Albe"
(meaning albeit, although) preceding "nothing" syntactically negates
such a pun and indicates instead that "nothing" is an adverb—that
is, "nothing [or, not at all] deepe imprest," with the result that Britomart is far from having been violated except in a superficial sense.
Once the grammatical reading dominates, the (im)possible pun spec-
trally present serves to insinuate a more threatening potential in the
situation—one submerged and unrealized—and it may intimate as
well the precariousness of Britomart's control at this early stage, a
control that she maintains increasingly. Once again, the abusive reading is finally meaningful only as an expression of the threat and indeed
of the projected fantasy of Busirane. The (im)possible pun would
nominalize the word "nothing," insisting on its literal sense "no
thing"; this is the sense that negates the male member, or "thing,"
in a common Elizabethan sense of the word *thing*, while also invoking
it, and thus motivates the sexual pun. In this way, the "abusive"
reader deconstructs the more abstractive adverb to find the material
root that makes it a noun and a metaphor. Shades once again of that
notorious debate between Derrida and Ricoeur about the viability
of dead metaphors.

★

Earlier, I suggested that Amoret is the cultural subject par excellence
and that this may be why the poem has such trouble with her figure
after Book III. This possibility could throw light on the oddities of
her role in Book IV, and briefly I would pursue it. With others, I
have tended to view Amoret largely as an idealized figure in IV, one
who has to be abandoned in the face of an ever-more nearly en-
croaching reality. While I'm not prepared to renounce this view, I
would like to explore another one, which can perhaps be reconciled
with it in the play of idealized and temporal perspectives that characterizes this book. Amoret, as Petrarchan love object, is something of

an embarrassment to Britomart as they ride along together, sharing one horse and one saddle. If I allow myself a distracting thought about horses and passions, the imagistic possibilities are comic, as well as significant. What is Britomart to do with the bundle of predictable assumptions and expectations called Amoret that she has won in the House of Rhetoric? Her grumpiness itself is a qualification of her triumph, and it signals her discomfort: for an awkward moment, the darker memory of Redcrosse's Pyrrhic victory over Sans Foy, his trophies Duessa and the shield of Faithlessness, may even come to mind. But Redcrosse doesn't have, or at least doesn't grasp, a clue regarding the irony into which he is sinking, whereas Britomart seems at least partly aware of a problem. Britomart "maske[s] her wounded mind" from Amoret, who is in one sense the unfolded Venerian aspect of her own double identity, but whether Britomart's is the love-wound of Artegall's image or the result of a scarring realization in the House of Busirane or the superimposition of the one on the other is left us to ponder, while Amoret's emotions are manipulated "Through fine abusion of that Briton mayd" (IV.i.vii). Exploratory but surely cruel, Britomart's abusive playing with and upon Amoret's responses at once suggests curiosity and resentment—an openness to experience and a resistance to the stock-in-trade of conventional womanhood, to something of what Shakespeare's Angelo calls "the destined livery" of woman. It does not go without notice, of course, that a measure of Busirane's own abusive masking has rubbed off on Britomart, his victorious enchainer, who is in this sense the apparent heiress of his art, as well as of Amoret, its ultimate object.[26]

The addition of a real male, the unnamed knight whom Britomart claims for herself on entering the nameless castle in Canto i, seems subsequently to allow her to assume her female identity and to achieve rapport with Amoret, who becomes her emotional intimate and bedfellow. But when the next morning Amoret and Britomart become an autonomous twosome again in an exteriorized and less private landscape, they are not long on that horse together before Blandamour challenges Britomart for possession of Amoret. Now occurs the strange stanza that I've discussed at length elsewhere in which perspectives oscillate between Britomart's and Blandamour's, and between chivalric and erotic, outer and inner, and narrative and lyric values (i.36).[27] The only point needed here, however, is that Amoret just does not fit smoothly or easily into Britomart's story (or vice versa); or perhaps the point is that a form whose content accommodates them both is persistently elusive and insistently problematical. Not entirely unlike the disappearing Fool in *King Lear*,

Amoret has to be vaporized into symbolism, incorporated into and consumed by Britomart, or else to be separated from her to follow out the narrative logic of her own figure, "*Venus* mayd"—Petrarchan object, fixated and predictable form. From the vantage point of Amoret's figure, both her form and its content, it makes sense that she should unwittingly stray from Britomart's side straight into Lust's predatory arms and become the hot potato (unless it's the tar baby) that Timias finds. It makes even more sense that she should have to withdraw from Britomart's company before Britomart can truly find and achieve "accord"—heartfelt harmony—with Artegall. Poor Amoret finally disappears from the story as an unregenerate regression in the memory of Scudamour, "*Cupids* man." Although freed from the immediate threat of Busirane, her figure is never truly reformed; instead, it is idealized in the poet's complaint in canto viii—stellified and transfigured and thus removed from the process of life—much as is Belphoebe's "ensample dead" in Book III.[28] In this ironic sense, the twinship of Amoret and Belphoebe is realized and thus fulfilled. To Britomart belong the actual possibilities, such as they might prove, of the living. But as we know, this, with the *Amoretti* as well, is another story.

Indiana University

NOTES

1.   References to Spenser's poetry are to the Variorum edition: *The Works of Edmund Spenser*, ed. Edwin Greenlaw et al., 11 vols. (Baltimore: Johns Hopkins University Press, 1932–57). *The Faerie Queene* is in vols. 1–6, "Muiopotmos" and the *Amoretti* in vol. 8. Subsequent reference is parenthetical.

2.   *The Rhetoric of the Body from Ovid to Shakespeare* (Cambridge: Cambridge University Press, 2000), 19, 25–26. Also Jonathan Bate, *Shakespeare and Ovid* (Oxford: Oxford University Press, 1993), 19–22, 28.

3.   For example, see Leonard Barkan, *The Gods Made Flesh: Metamorphosis and the Pursuit of Paganism* (New Haven: Yale University Press, 1986), 2–5; and Ann Rosalind Jones and Peter Stallybrass, *Renaissance Clothing and the Materials of Memory* (Cambridge: Cambridge University Press, 2000), chap. 4, esp. 89–97.

4.   Wofford, remarking the frequent puns on *read* (or "rede") in III.xi and xii, focuses attention especially on Britomart's gazing. Our arguments share ground in distinguishing between Busirane's literalist perspective and Britomart's healthier responses: "Gendering Allegory: Spenser's Bold Reader and the Emergence of Character in *The Faerie Queene* III," *Criticism*, 30 (1988), 1–21. William Oram's remarks on the House of Busirane are current, succinct, and much to the point: "Spenserian Paralysis," *Studies in English Literature*, 41 (2001), 60.

5.   Of particular interest in this regard is Jones and Stallybrass, chap.6, which treats women's use of mythological sources in their needlework and their utilization of such work for protest, at times, as in the instance of Mary Stuart, whose needleworks were even introduced as evidence by prosecutors at her trial. Or for a witty case in point, see *Amoretti* LXXI:

> I joy to see how in your drawen work,
>   Your selfe vnto the Bee ye doe compare;
>   and me vnto the Spyder that doth lurke
>   in close awayt to catch her vnaware.

6.   Katherine Eggert, "Spenser's Ravishment: Rape and Rapture in *The Faerie Queene*," *Representations*, 70 (2000), 11–12.

7.   Ovid, *Metamorphoses*, trans. Frank Justus Miller, 2nd. ed., 2 vols. (1921; rpt. London: Heinemann, 1966), 1:292–93.

8.   For a useful, but on this point a differing, comparison of Bower and House, see Sarah Annes Brown, *The Metamorphoses of Ovid: From Chaucer to Ted Hughes* (New York: St. Martin's Press, 1999), 41–46, 50–56.

9.   The Palmer is elsewhere in Book II an artist, a spinner of myth, as I have argued long since in "The Knight and the Palmer in *The Faerie Queene*, Book II," *Modern Language Quarterly*, 31 (1970), 162–65.

10.   Witness also Ben Jonson's *Volpone*, and see note 11, below.

11.   Keats writes, "*an artist* must serve Mammon—he must have 'self concentration' selfishness perhaps." He continues, "you might . . . be more of an artist, and 'load every rift' of your subject with ore": From *The Letters of John Keats*, ed. Hyder Edward Rollins (Cambridge, MA: Harvard University Press, 1958), 2:322–23; cited by Paul J. Alpers in *The Poetry of "The Faerie Queene"* (Princeton: Princeton University Press, 1967), 264. Provocative, too, in connection with a broader eroticism than a post-Freudian one (if not necessarily one swift on the heels of regicide and dictatorship) is Debra Kuller Shuger's claim that "The identification of the erotic with sexuality" and the privileged "location of erotic desire in the genitals . . . emerged sometime after 1650." "Sexual desire," she later adds, is "an inflection of erotic longing, not its origin or essence": *The Renaissance Bible: Scholarship, Sacrifice, and Subjectivity* (Berkeley: University of California Press, 1994), 178.

12.   On Shakespeare, see Harold F. Brooks, "*Richard III*: Antecedents of Clarence's Dream," *Shakespeare Studies*, 32 (1979), 148–50. Milton refers to the House of Mammon in *Areopagitica* in *Complete Prose Works*, ed. Ernest Sirluck (New Haven: Yale University Press, 1959), 2:516.

13.   A. C. Hamilton, ed., *The Faerie Queene*, by Edmund Spenser (London: Longman, 1977), 413.

14.   I disagree with the general tendency in recent criticism to reduce allegory to abstraction and then to oppose it to narrative, not recognizing that allegory is itself a narrative mode. See, for example, my reviews of otherwise admirable books by Gordon Teskey and Sayre Greenfield: the first in *Arthuriana*, 7 (1997), 21–24, and the second in the *Spenser Newsletter*, 30 (1999), 1–4.

15.   *The Kindly Flame: A Study of the Third and Fourth Books of Spenser's "Faerie Queene"* (Princeton: Princeton University Press, 1964), 82.

16.   Richard A. Lanham cites as an instance of the catachrestic wrenching of language Hamlet's resolving, "I will speak daggers to her." Another instance of extravagant (and implicitly emblematic) metaphor, he suggests, might be "when a weeping woman's eyes become Niagra Falls." Lanham's handbook is primarily based on Renaissance and classical terms and usage: *A Handlist of Rhetorical Terms* (Berkeley: University of California Press, 1968), 21.

17.   *OED*, s.v. *Deme, adv.*; *Dem, a.* and *sb.*, 1–2, 5–6; *MED*, s.v., *Demeli(che), adv.*, a–d. The spelling of the adverbial form in Spenser's text conceivably suggests familiarity with the medieval usage; the contextualized meaning does so more definitively. The exception, published since the writing of this essay, is A. C. Hamilton's new edition of *The Faerie Queene* (Harlow, England: Longman, 2001), 404n: Hamilton still offers "earnestly or dismally" but now prefers "secretly" most likely but rationalizes it on the grounds that Amoret does not want Busirane to hear her plea. This gloss, while moving in the right direction, perhaps oversimplifies what is at stake here. Busirane himself, after all, could tell Britomart about his power over Amoret in order to save his neck, or at least he could if he actually grasped its extent. In any event, Hamilton's explanation would not preclude my less innocent reading. My argument would also lend a more knowing or even more sinister cast to Lauren Silberman's view of Amoret as "the lady who says yes": *Transforming Desire: Erotic Knowledge in Books III and IV of "The Faerie Queene"* (Berkeley: University of California Press, 1995), 63.

18.   Rhetoric is often associated with a chain. Alciati's popular emblem book, for example, depicts Hercules, representative of eloquence, whose art is rhetoric, "as an old man, trailing after him a crowd of people fastened by the ears with chains issuing from his mouth." The description is Jean Bodin's in his *Six Books of the Commonwealth*, cited with further bibliographical references, by Jane Aptekar, *Icons of Justice: Iconography and Thematic Imagery in Book V of "The Faerie Queene"* (New York: Columbia University Press, 1969), 229–30, note 18.

19.   "The Metaphorical Process," in *On Metaphor*, ed. Sheldon Sacks (Chicago: University of Chicago Press, 1979), 151. Also Ricoeur's *The Rule of Metaphor: Multidisciplinary Studies of the Creation of Meaning in Language*, trans. Robert Czerny, with Kathleen McLaughlin and John Costello (Toronto: University of Toronto Press, 1977), 248, 254–56. I derive the suggestive term "perverse predication" from Jonathan Hillman's "deviant predication," derived in turn from Ricoeur.

20.   For a radically different reading of this scene (or place), see Susan Frye, *Elizabeth I: The Competition for Representation* (Oxford: Oxford University Press, 1993), 122–24, 129–30.

21.   *OED*, s.v., *Bowel, sb.*, 3–4, but also 1–2.

22.   *OED*, *As, adv. (conj.*, and *rel. pro.*), 18.

23.   E.g., see my discussion of the end of Donne's *Deaths Duel* in *Words That Matter: Linguistic Perception in Renaissance English* (Stanford: Stanford University Press, 1996), 227–29; and of *Hamlet* in "Translating Investments," *Texas Studies in Literature and Language*, 40 (1998), 251–52.

24.   Jean Aitchison, *Words in the Mind*, 2nd. ed. (Oxford: Blackwell, 1994), 215, 217, but all of chapters 17–18 should be consulted.

25.   Unpublished paper delivered July 7, 2001, at the International Spenser Society Conference in Cambridge, England, to which I refer with Katherine Eggert's kind permission.

26. See note 18, above.

27. See "Whatever Happened to Amoret? The Poet's role in Book IV of *The Faerie Queene*," *Criticism*, 13 (1971), 191.

28. *The Faerie Queene* III.v.51–52, 54; IV.viii.29–33. See my essay "'In liuing colours and right hew': The Queen of Spenser's Central Books," in *Critical Essays on Edmund Spenser*, ed. Mihoko Suzuki (New York: Simon & Schuster Macmillan, 1996), 171–76.

MARY R. BOWMAN

Distressing Irena: Gender, Conquest, and Justice in Book V of *The Faerie Queene*

Issues of gender are integral to the ethos of justice Artegall constructs in the early cantos of Book V, and to the political issues figured in the book's final cantos; consequently, gender provides a common thread connecting the frequently isolated segments of the book and an important tool for understanding how the female figure of Irena functions within the context of the book. In the early cantos, Artegall succeeds in acquiring the aura of a "righteous man" in part by subtly redefining the cases that are brought before him, a redefinition that entails the erasure of women as autonomous beings. The Radigund sequence joins this tendency to the violent propensities exhibited in the Giant episode. The reduction in female power accomplished in the last section of Book V is integrally related to the ethos of justice that is evident from the earliest episodes of the book, and both help in turn to naturalize an aggressive policy in Ireland; all three dimensions of the Book coalesce in the figure of Irena.

*I*T SEEMS THAT BOOK V of *The Faerie Queene* distresses almost everyone. For those who want to keep art and politics separate, the intrusion of topicality ruins it as poetry; those who have no objection to politics per se may find Spenser's politics oppressive; feminist readers find it an unwelcome retreat from the more woman-friendly Books III and IV; students first encountering the book find Artegall's methods of meting out justice disquieting.[1] From various perspectives readers can find cause to echo C. S. Lewis's famous denunciation: "Spenser was the instrument of a detestable policy in Ireland, and in his fifth book the wickedness he had shared begins to corrupt his imagination."[2]

It is no coincidence that the same text provokes distress in so many directions. For the features of the book that generate the most distress—gender politics, imperialism, poetic form, and the representation of justice itself—are complexly interrelated. However, as one critic has recently observed, the structure of Book V has been "replicated by a criticism that takes up Book 5 only in piecemeal fashion," and more work is needed to continue to "bridge the gap" between the different sections of the book.[3] Toward this end, I will draw together three strands in recent criticism—ethical, feminist, and historicist—to show how integral issues of gender are to the image of justice Artegall portrays and to the political issues figured in the book's final cantos. These themes ultimately coalesce in the inevitably female figure of Irena, the symbol of peace and a damsel in distress.

The First Four Cantos: The Invisible Woman

Critics who have recently focused on the concept of justice that is explored in Book V give us a picture of justice that is at best imperfect, at worst autocratic: a book not so much about justice in the abstract but as about "the gap between justice in its ideal form and actual political experience."[4] This view forms the main theme of Thomas Bulger's recent book-length exploration of history in *The Faerie Queene*, in which he argues that "the legend of justice portrays human society as being frequently out of touch with natural law, thus making the realization of history's mythic potential considerably more difficult."[5] While an ideal of justice may be discerned in the poem, particularly in the adventures of Arthur, Artegall's experiences more frequently illustrate the way in which "the historical present all too frequently frustrates rather than fulfills the ultimate ends of *The Faerie Queene's* historical fiction": "Though they serve other functions as well, Arthur's actions in the poem symbolize the divinely-ordained path of historical being. Artegall's tribulations at the end of Book V, on the other hand, illustrate the frustration of an individual's efforts to follow this path, due to his own shortcomings and to forces beyond his control."[6]

In the most important recent analysis of Book V from a philosophical perspective, Elizabeth Fowler has explored the "irreconcilable" approaches of political and ethical philosophy as they play out in the second half of *The Faerie Queene*, "in which grounds for dominion derived on the one hand from ethics and on the other from political philosophy seem to come into conflict, resulting in the eventual disruption of the structure of the poem itself."[7] Ethical philosophy locates virtue within individual characters, an approach for which personification allegory is well suited. But "personification effects a multiple displacement of the agency of consent,"[8] a dynamic that Fowler explores in detail in two episodes, Scudamour's removal of Amoret from the Temple of Venus and Artegall's encounter with the egalitarian giant, both of which end in violence:

> According to Scudamour and Artegall, the proper test of dominion lies not in the subject's voluntary consent, but in the virtue of the suitor, the ruler, the judge, the lord. If the *dominus* is virtuous, they argue, dominion is just. This doctrine of virtue, this particular ethics, is set in conflict throughout the second half of *The Faerie Queene* with a political philosophy that emphasizes consent, mutuality, and social bonds. . . . Both episodes end in tears as their particular brands of heroic ethos transform the conversation into brute force, dissolving rather than forging bonds, and revealing the limitations of these rights theories when measured against the goals of political philosophy.[9]

We emerge with a decidedly unidealistic view of the ethical approach to justice which is embodied in Artegall: "Thus by degrees Artegall's ethics becomes a defense of a particular self-serving political arrangement, though it claims to be merely an obedience to a universal divine order."[10]

What such readings have not yet attended to is the role that women, or more precisely, the status accorded to them by Artegall, plays in creating Artegall's ethos. Fowler's choice of the Giant episode calls attention to the use that such an ethos makes of force to compel compliance with his judgments. Another early episode, of Pollente and Munera, is similarly violent. But the surrounding episodes also work to mystify Artegall's status as judge without his resorting to as high a level of violence. In fact, he repeatedly offers his services as arbiter as a more effective alternative to physical battle: He suggests to Sanglier and the squire that he might "all further quarrel end," to avoid the "ill" that may result from "ordele, or . . . blooddy fight" (V.i.25), and he tells Amidas and Bracidas, "Certes your strife were easie to accord,/Would ye remit it to some righteous man" (V.iv.16).[11] Examining these nonviolent judgments made by Artegall in the early cantos will reveal an important feature of the way Artegall creates his own ethos. He succeeds in acquiring the aura of a "righteous man" in part by subtly redefining the cases that are brought before him, a redefinition that entails the erasure of women as autonomous beings.

The first case Artegall encounters is that of Sir Sanglier. This knight is accused of having taken a squire's lady by force and of killing his own lady, charges he flatly denies. In an obvious imitation of Solomon's famous judgment about the living and dead babies in I Kings 3:16–27, Artegall decrees that each man should get half of each woman. Only the squire, who cannot bear to see his lady harmed, dissents, thereby proving the truth of his claim. The successful imitation of Solomon would seem designed to demonstrate that Artegall, too, has "an understanding heart to judge [God's] people, that [he] may discern between good and bad"[12] and that he has learned well of Astrea "the skill of deeming wrong and right" (V.i.8). But this claim to Solomonic wisdom requires a dispute properly analogous to Solomon's—to whom does the lady truly belong?—whereas the situation that first confronts Artegall is a murder: he sees the dead woman and asks the squire "who had that Dame so fouly dight" (V.i.14). To fit Artegall into the role of Solomon, the homicide investigation quickly modulates into a case of disputed ownership of property. The squire has described the abduction of the living woman as a crime against himself more than against her—reporting that Sanglier "Fro me reft mine away" (V.i.17)—and the other men follow suit. When Sanglier is confronted, his response suggests that he has been accused both of murder and of taking the squire's lady, whom he labels as a "good," as property: "For neither he did shed that Ladies bloud,/Nor tooke away his loue, but his owne proper good" (V.i.23). The Solomonic resolution of the case focuses on determining who should rightfully possess the living lady. Although Sanglier's punishment is to carry the dead woman's head "to tell abrode [his] shame" (V.i.28), Artegall does not even make a show of ascertaining his guilt or innocence of the murder; the squire's proof of "ownership" of the living women is tacitly assumed to corroborate his entire version of the story. The abduction of one woman is viewed as a crime not against her, but against her squire, and the other woman's murder, initially the central focus, becomes secondary at best. In short, a woman is reduced from a person who has been wronged to a piece of property that has been wrongfully taken, a sleight of hand necessary in order to transform the case from that of a crime calling for punishment under law to a situation calling for the justiciar's ability to divine and reveal the truth and restore property to its rightful owner.[13] The episode privileges wisdom—the virtue of Solomon—as the essential quality of justice, but doing so requires both objectifying women and redefining the nature of the situation originally presented.

In thus recasting his case to match Solomon's, and thereby claiming Solomon's wisdom, Artegall glosses over other differences between his case and Solomon's, differences which, when highlighted, further call attention to the way in which Artegall's approach effaces the autonomy and agency of the women involved. The "object" in dispute in the Old Testament story is a baby, whereas the lady in Spenser's story is an adult, capable of being a participant in the resolution of the dispute. The squire, in narrating the events, acknowledges the subjectivities of both women:

> He, whether mine seem'd fayrer in his eye,
> Or that he wexed weary of his owne,
> Would change with me; but I did it denye;
> So did the Ladies both, as may be knowne.
>
> (V.i.17)

He also recalls the actions of the dead woman, and appears to regard her murder as a significant part of the knight's crimes:

> she follow'd fast,
> And on him catching hold, gan loud to crie
> Not so to leaue her, nor away to cast,
> But rather of his hand besought to die.
> With that his sword he drew all wrathfully,
> And at one stroke cropt off her head with scorne,
> In that same place, whereas it now doth lie.
> So he my loue away with him hath borne,
> And left me here, both his and mine to mourn.
>
> (V.i.18)

But when Artegall comes to decide the case, the living woman is given no say in her own disposition. (As if to underscore the point, even Guyon's horse, in Canto iii of this book, is able by his behavior and by the distinctive mark in his mouth to play some part in identifying his true owner—but here the unnamed woman is permitted no agency at all in her own disposition.)[14] And though she is the only other living witness to the episode, she is not even asked to give her version of what happened. Talus does make a point of bringing her back with the knight:

> Thence he him lad,
> Bound like a beast appointed to the stall:
> The sight whereof the Lady sore adrad,
> And fain'd to fly for feare of being thrall;
> But he her quickly stayd, and forst to wend withall.

(V.i.22)

Yet it is evident that she is retained not as a material witness but as the piece of property in dispute; perhaps her fears of thralldom were not unfounded. Although some glimmer of recognition of women's autonomy endures in the squire's report, it is quickly lost.[15] Already the nature of the justiciar's task has become slippery, the basis of his judgments unclear—and the effacement of women's personhood a precondition to his mystification as "wise."

A similar, though more complex, slippage is at work in the dispute between Amidas and Bracidas. This episode further problematizes Artegall's role, and again the status of women is integrally connected to the construction of that role. Bracidas claims ownership of the chest of treasure that has washed up on his island; Amidas contests his claim, although he too has benefitted from the actions of the sea, which has eroded much of Bracidas's island and enlarged his own. Artegall decrees that each brother rightly possesses whatever the sea has washed onto his shore: "what the sea vnto you sent, your own should seeme" (V.iv.17/18).

Though this has, even recently, been called a "simple dispute over property,"[16] as in the Sanglier episode there are competing notions of the nature of the case; here, there is a lack of agreement about just what property losses are relevant. Bracidas clearly views the treasure as a fair compensation for the losses he has already incurred—and in his reckoning, the loss of land is paralleled by the loss of Philtera:

> And though my land he first did winne away,
> And then my loue (though now it little skill,)
> Yet my good lucke he shall not likewise pray;
> But I will it defend, whilst euer that I may.

(V.iv.14)

Amidas acknowledges the changes in the islands, but insists that it is only possession of the chest which is in dispute:

Full true it is, what so about our land
My brother here declared hath to you:
But not for it this ods twixt vs doth stand,
But for this threasure throwne vppon his strand.

(V.iv.15)

On the other hand, Artegall treats the transfer of land from Bracidas's island to Amidas's as legally identical to the transfer of the treasure in the opposite direction (both are "what the sea vnto [them] sent"). Following Artegall, many critics have read the episode as illustrating the principle of equity, largely in the light of Bracidas's loss of land.[17] For many readers, it does "feel" right for Bracidas to have the treasure in the light of his loss of land. While the loss of Philtera, which Bracidas describes as a loss entirely parallel to his loss of land, does not factor into Artegall's decision, it may add subliminally to the sense that some kind of compensation is appropriate.

Similarly contested and unclear is the legal authority or principle under which Artegall's judgment is made. Attempts to apply English law to the situation have required the equity reading, for the letter of the law denies Bracidas's claim: Herbert Nelson, in an early study of the law regarding the ownership of flotsam and wreck, contended that

> it is clear that from early times down through the time of Spenser efforts, not always successful, were made to return the wrecked property to the owner if he could prove ownership within a year and a day. By the statutes of the realm, then, Bracidas had no claim to the chest of treasure, being entitled only to payment for his labor in recovering the flotsam.[18]

Following this argument, awarding the treasure to Bracidas is an act of equity rather than strict observance of the law. Thus Maurice Evans, for example, argued that "Amidas is legally entitled to both the land and the coffer," and that therefore Artegall's judgment, which seems more just, is an application of equity, "that part of justice designed to preserve the spirit against the tyranny of the letter and to ensure that the detailed application does not violate the larger principles of justice."[19]

An alternate reading is possible when the case is viewed in the context of Irish, rather than English, law. Roland M. Smith has argued for this approach and concluded that under Irish law Bracidas *does* have a claim to ownership, because that law awards ownership to anyone who goes out to sea to retrieve flotsam. He contends that "here we have the law which applies to Bracidas, who has done Lucy the 'great fauour' of risking his life to rescue her," citing stanza 12 in support of this argument[20]:

> Where I by chaunce then wandring on the shore,
> Did her espy, and through my good endeauor
> From dreadfull mouth of death, which threatned sore
> Her to haue swallow'd vp, did helpe to saue her.[21]

In so arguing, Smith equates rescuing *Lucy* with recovering the *treasure*, demonstrating the ease with which critics may fall into the equation of women with property that Bracidas introduces.[22]

In the light of such arguments, it is interesting that Artegall appears instead to be appealing to a different law or principle, citing the authority of the sea to distribute possessions:

> For what the mighty Sea hath once possest,
> And plucked quite from all possessors hand,
> Whether by rage of waues, that neuer rest,
> Or else by wracke, that wretches hath distrest,
> He may dispose by his imperiall might,
> As thing at random left, to whom he list.
>
> (V.iv.19)

In so doing, he applies the same principle that Cymodoce appeals to in Canto xii of Book IV, whose legalistic language and approach make it function as a transition to Book V. Cymodoce, determined to free Florimell from Proteus's control in order to free her son Marinell from love-sickness, goes over Proteus's head to Neptune, who as sovereign of the seas lays claim to Florimell "by high prerogat-iue" (IV.xii.31). Though this episode has been read as also illustrating equity at work,[23] Cymodoce explicitly claims that Proteus's posses-sion violates the letter of the law as well as the spirit of justice upheld by equity: Florimell "nor his, nor his in equitie." Applying the prin-ciple of equity to the Florimell episode is problematic because of the status of Neptune as lord of the seas. If, as Knight states, "equitable jurisdiction is specifically invoked today when property is lost at sea and becomes either the property of the finder at sea (salvage) or that of the sovereign of the land on which it comes to rest (windfall),"[24] the allegorical figure of the sea's sovereign produces competing claims: Proteus found Florimell at sea, and so under English equity could claim ownership of her as salvage, but because Neptune rules the sea, he can claim Florimell as windfall because she is in his domain. In effect, there is no such thing as salvage in Faeryland, where the sea itself has a sovereign.

In justifying his disposition of the chest of treasure, Artegall talks as if he were appealing to this "high prerogatiue" of Neptune's, referring to the sea as an entity with will and agency ("He may dispose by his imperiall might . . . to whom he list"). However, the "mighty Sea" is not here treated as a figure to whom one could, like Cymodoce, appeal; the actions of a literal sea are *cited* as if they were the equitable decisions of a wise and just monarch, and this application of the principle yields a judgment in favor of Bracidas, the opposite of what a literal application of English law would do. In effect, Artegall imposes his own sense of what is equitable, attributing that judgment to a sea whose status—literal, allegorical, or mythical—is ambiguous.

In short, although Artegall's judgment does seem fair (I know of no critic who has been troubled by it, as so many have been by the treatment of the Giant), it is nevertheless difficult to identify any clear justification for it, whether in English law or in the principles of equity, or even in the allegorical "law" which Artegall and Cymodoce cite. Although it seems fair, the judgment is as arbitrary and dependent upon Artegall's uncontested authority as any other decision in the first four cantos of the book.[25]

Like so much of the early cantos of the book, then, this episode both mystifies the authority of Artegall as wise dispenser of justice and frustrates attempts to identify the basis of that authority. And like the Sanglier episode, though in a more subtle way, the Amidas and Bracidas episode links this lack of juridical precision with an elision of women's agency and a tendency to treat women as property (a tendency we have already seen in Bracidas's statement of his claim, and in Smith's attempt to justify it under Irish law). Though Bracidas believes he deserves the treasure in compensation for his losses, he reports that he gained possession of the treasure not through recovering it himself but as a gift from Lucy, who, after all, found it first at sea:

She then in recompence of that great fauour,
Which I on her bestowed, bestowed on me

The portion of that good, which Fortune gaue her.

(V.iv.12)

The question of Lucy's right to the treasure, or of Bracidas's right to claim it as a gift from her, goes unremarked in both the text and the criticism, although it is a sound argument under the legal principles cited by Knight and laws regarding property ownership in marriage.[26] Indeed, it is Philtera's right that Amidas cites in support of his claim to the treasure, "Which well I proue, as shall appeare by triall,/To be this maides, with whom I fastned hand" (V.iv.15). Yet women's status as owners of property, though clearly relevant to the facts of the case, is never directly addressed and figures not at all in the resolution, although doing so would make the law much clearer. If this episode indeed marks a transition to the theme of equity, the omission is all the more remarkable in the light of Constance Jordan's claim that the principle of equity was used by *women* to circumvent legal restrictions on their rights: "it was in chancery and the other courts of equity that women could press for rights to own and manage their own property."[27] In Artegall's court, however, those rights can easily be effaced, and women's status as owners of property is quickly obscured by the pervasive tendency to view them *as* property.[28]

The Radigund Sequence: The Tyranny of Gender

Immediately after leaving Amidas and Bracidas, Artegall begins his extended encounter with Radigund, which will occupy the bulk of the central cantos of the book and hand him his first failure. Before it is over, this sequence will bring together the violent propensities exhibited in the Giant episode and Artegall's dependence for his success on the effacement of women's autonomy. Having seen how much Artegall's status as a wise and equitable dispenser of justice has relied on the erasure of women as autonomous agents, we can appreciate what a profound challenge Radigund represents. Upon encountering a woman whose agency is not so easily erased as that of the women he has met earlier, Artegall is at first unable to defeat her, and his ability to continue on his quest depends on both her violent demise and the reinstatement of a male-dominant order in the land she previously ruled. Where the elision of women's agency has failed, the same mentality that could not see violence against women in the Sanglier episode must now rely on violence against Radigund.

Not surprisingly, feminist criticism of Book V has focused primarily on this segment of the book. A recurrent theme in this body of criticism is that the second half of the poem, and Book V in particular, marks a dramatic reversal from the more woman-centered Books III and IV, a reversal that is most evident in these central cantos. Maureen Quilligan, for example, argues that with the appearance of the last three books and the accompanying change in Book III's ending, Spenser's program to foster cross-gender understanding is abandoned: "The 'Letter to Ralegh' was canceled. And the cancellation of the hermaphrodite image would also suggest that the gynandromorphic flexibility that Spenser had asked of his readers in Book III would be canceled as well."[29] A similar sense of change in the gendering of the poem's perspective is noted by Shirley Staton. Staton, who focusses on structural changes in the poem, argues that the narrative technique of Books III and IV functions, like the subject matter, to make them more amenable to women readers than the other books: "Contemporary readers of *The Faerie Queene* are no longer constrained to value only the heroic narratives of the first two books. Now they can appreciate also the ambiguous, relational realities structuring the romance genre of Books III and IV."[30] Like Quilligan, she regards the changed ending of Book III as a harbinger of change in the poem's gender focus, which becomes again male-centered. Her structural emphasis, however, causes her to locate the return to a masculine ethos not in Book IV but in Book V: "For me, the change in ending signals the poem's resumption in Book V (The Legend of Artegall, or Of Justice) of the masculine epic structures of Books I and II."[31]

Most recently, in an important article, Katherine Eggert has argued that Book V enacts a struggle to be free of both feminine authority and feminine narrative structure, exhibiting what she calls a nostalgia for the male world of Books I and II, where heroic action and closure were possible: "It is therefore Book 5's turn toward history, not romance, that carries the force of nostalgia: nostalgia for Guyon's antiromantic narrative thrust, which managed in its 'rigour pitilesse' to conquer the effeminacy induced by both a desiring queen and an arrested, uncloseable poetics."[32] In her reading, the Radigund sequence represents a kind of relapse. Artegall, whose heroic quest began when Astraea's influence was removed, now finds himself imprisoned by another powerful woman, who renders him effeminate and in whose presence the narrative structure becomes more like that of Books III and IV, less linear and more resistant to closure.[33] To extricate him, and the poem, from this predicament requires the violent outcome, which paves the way for the final cantos of the book: "If Book 4 conforms to the poetics of castration . . . Book 5 castrates the castrators, proposing a thoroughgoing revision of literary construction that ought for good and all to sever the poem from feminine influence. Feminine rule and feminine poetics are repealed in favor of the most straightforward mode that *The Faerie Queene* will ever assume, historical allegory."[34]

Eggert's emphasis on female authority is important, however, for as her own analysis shows, it is not all women who must be destroyed, but only the powerful. So the particular brand of misogyny we have here is not a desire to avoid or eradicate women altogether, but to recontain them in carefully defined roles, to render all women as much under men's control as the women in the early cantos. "Book 5 debunks the misogynist fallacy of *The Faerie Queene's* earlier scenes of seduction and wedlock: Artegall's recall [from Irena's island] reveals that heroic expeditions are delayed not in the private female world—not in the illicit bower or the sanctioned bridal chamber—but rather in the public world of political aspiration."[35] In Book VI, Spenser reveals a preference for a nameless, faceless woman safely removed from public action: "Queen Elizabeth's appearance . . . is a pointed non-appearance, as on the revelatory Mount Acidale Colin Clout eliminates Gloriana from his configuration of the graces' dance, replacing her instead with 'certes but a countrey lasse.'"[36]

Moreover, it is interesting to note how undermotivated any form of misogyny is within the surface level of the narrative. Although Radigund is a woman, it is only because of the way that Artegall reacts to her that her gender becomes an issue. Where before he showed a tendency not to see women at all, as persons, he is able to see Radigund, whom he cannot ignore as a person, only as a woman. Indeed, it is only this focus on her womanhood that enables Radigund to defeat him. Before meeting her face to face, Artegall has reason to see Radigund as an enemy of the cause of justice to which he is dedicated. The episode begins as Artegall comes upon Radigund's warriors about to hang a knight, rejoicing "like tyrants, mercilesse, . . . at his miserable case" (V.iv.22). Saved from this death, Terpine tells Artegall more about Radigund: how she uses military strength to put to death or to imprison men for no legitimate reason; rejected by a man "to whom she bore most feruent love" (V.iv.30), she changed "her loue to hatred manifold" and set about to punish all other men, unfairly, for the actions of one.[37] From a moral standpoint, there is no need to distinguish her actions from those of Pollente, for example. In spite of this, Artegall treats Radigund differently from other tyrants he has met. He permits her to retreat

into her city unpursued; then he accepts her challenge to single combat and even her conditions, which lie outside "the lawes of cheual-
rie" (as Britomart points out in refusing to honor the same
conditions, V.vii.28); and, finally, he throws away his sword in response to her beauty. Particularly in this last, and most fatal, action,
it is clear that he is responding to her not as an enemy of justice but
as a woman—responding, in fact, precisely as he responded earlier
to Britomart, thus revealing an inability to make distinctions between
women based on their character, as he is assumed to be able to do
among men.[38]

The opening of Canto viii emphasizes the decisive role played by
beauty in his capitulation:

Nought vnder heauen so strongly doth allure
The sence of man, and all his minde possesse,
As beauties louely baite, that doth procure
Great warriors oft their rigour to represse,
And mightly hands forget their manlinesse;
Drawne with the powre of an heart-robbing eye,
And wrapt in fetters of a golden tresse,
That can with melting pleasaunce mollifye
Their hardned hearts, enur'd to bloud and cruelty.

(V.viii.1)

Although this stanza seems to suggest that the debilitating influence
of beauty is irresistible, Artegall has previously shown the ability to
resist it when justice so demands, remaining resolute while Talus
kills Munera:

Thence he her drew
By the faire lockes, and fowly did array,
Withouten pitty of her goodly hew,
That *Artegall* him selfe her seemlesse plight did rew.
Yet for no pitty would he change the course
Of Iustice, which in *Talus* hand did lye;
Who rudely hayled her forth without remorse.

(V.ii.25–26)

When in an entirely analogous situation he does "chaunge the course/Of Iustice," therefore, he does so not because he cannot do otherwise, but because in some sense he has chosen to respond to Radigund as a man to a woman, not as the knight of Justice to a tyrant.

The narrator echoes Artegall's response to Radigund in his famous condemnation of her, reacting to her gender rather than her actions and ascribing to her gender the cruelty that, in a man, would be condemned directly: "such is the crueltie of womenkynd." He further locates her "crueltie" in her inversion of the male-dominant social order—one which Britomart will later make a point of reinstating—that is, for her refusal to accept the status accorded the ladies in the Sanglier and Amidas/Bracidas episodes:

> Such is the crueltie of womenkynd,
> When they haue shaken off the shamefast band,
> With which wise Nature did them strongly bynd,
> T'obay the heasts of mans well ruling hand,
> That then all rule and reason they withstand,
> To purchase a licentious libertie.
>
> (V.v.25)

The narrator takes this line of thought one step further than Artegall, however, recognizing that it could be understood as an attack on a legitimately powerful queen, such as Gloriana or Elizabeth, and rather awkwardly carving out the necessary exception:

> But vertuous women wisely vnderstand,
> That they were born to base humilitie,
> Vnlesse the heauens them lift to lawfull soueraintie.
>
> (V.v.25)

This stanza has sent many critics off to study, and locate Spenser within, the debate over the legitimacy of women rulers which went on through much of the sixteenth century, in response to the unusual situation of female monarchs in Scotland and England.[39] The most frequent conclusion among such critics is that Spenser articulates the basic Protestant "compromise" position holding that, while women as a group were not authorized to rule, there could be divinely appointed exceptions to this general prohibition. This is a position that many Protestant writers adopted following the accession of Elizabeth, rejecting the categorical denunciation of women's rule voiced in John Knox's *First Blast of the Trumpet Against the Monstrous Regiment of Women* (1558), without defending women's absolute right to rule.[40] The fact that Spenser raises the question of women's rule at this point in the poem is accounted for, when addressed, by associating it with equity: the "compromise" position turns on the idea of an *exception* from a general principle of male sovereignty that is logically parallel to the legal concept of equity.[41]

Placed in the context of the earlier episodes, however, the interest of this stanza is less in its explicit content or its conceptual connection to justice than in the rhetorical similarity between the woman ruler debate it evokes and the reactions to Radigund that give rise to it.[42] Just as the tyranny of Radigund inheres in her behavior, not her gender, the woman ruler debate was not exclusively about gender, though it clearly was shaped by and in turn endorsed a pervasive misogyny. Gender serves as substitute for other concerns. As Paula Louise Scalingi remarks, "it is notable that the participants in the great debate over gynecocracy were concerned with the religion, politics, and moral character of the ruler rather than with sex."[43] Thus, although attacks on the two Marys were articulated in terms of gender, it was not entirely because of the threat they represented to the gender hierarchy; few Catholics felt any need to object to Mary Tudor, but that does not mean that they would have accepted fundamental changes in the social order more than Protestants would. Rather, because these two Catholic monarchs happened also to be women, gender offered itself as easy grounds for denouncing them and, perhaps, as a rhetorical strategy to inspire agreement in male readers whom a strictly religious or political argument might not convince.

The woman ruler debate can thus be seen as an example of Karen Newman's thesis that "gender was a significant way of *figuring* social relations in early modern England" (xviii).[44] The debate *could* have taken a different form; attacks on the two Catholic queens could have been limited to the religious and political issues which primarily motivated them. And there were a few defenders of Elizabeth's legitimacy who distinguished between the motives of attack and defense and the gender terms in which they were cast.[45] But by and large, writings praising or condemning female monarchs were couched in terms of gender. As a result, defenders of Elizabeth were faced with a difficult rhetorical task: they had to argue against the sweeping denunciations of female rule, but few, whether Protestant or Catholic, were prepared to argue against traditional male dominance. The compromise position was the natural result of the way the debate had been constructed: arguments against female rule were allowed to stand, with Elizabeth elevated as a divinely appointed exception.

This rhetorical choice also created danger for those who adopted it. John Knox, especially, found himself in a difficult situation when the Protestant Elizabeth took the throne, and he tried unsuccessfully to worm his way out of it, much in the way Spenser's narrator feels the need to do. And this may be the real point of the stanza: it would have been safer for the narrator—and for Spenser—not to raise the issue at all, not to make her gender a *casus belli*, just as Artegall would have been better off not letting her beauty be the principal determinant of his reaction to her. The stanza is particularly dangerous if, as Christopher Highley has argued, Book V criticizes Elizabeth's dilatory policy in Ireland, and still more so if we accept Eggert's reading of Radigund in particular as embodying Spenser's genuine dislike of female rule.[46]

The Radigund sequence thus presents the other side of the coin minted in the early cantos. There, the real issues were obscured in part by effacing women as autonomous agents; here, issues are obscured with equal effectiveness by reducing women to nothing more or less than their gender. And doing so raises disturbing questions about the nature of the justiciar's authority. How do we distinguish female tyrants from divinely anointed exceptions? If Artegall cannot adhere to meaningful distinctions between Britomart and Radigund, how can his real-life counterparts presume to know an Elizabeth from a Mary? Or, for that matter, distinguish Elizabeth's womanish policies from those of her male counselors?[47]

The Final Cantos: Damsels in Distress

The obvious reference to the women ruler debates in the Radigund episode heralds the transparent topicality which characterizes the remainder of the book.[48] This topicality, which has largely contributed to the low critical esteem in which the book is held, is accompanied by a further curtailment of the space given to female figures. In other parts of the poem, female figures have exhibited the full range of complexity available to Spenserian representations, from Britomart, central and almost novelistically round, Duessa, always a dangerous Other but multifaceted in her signification; but in these last few cantos of Book V, the female figures are neither central nor complex. Radigund is dead, and Britomart, having killed her, promptly wanders out of the poem, not to return; Duessa is executed shortly thereafter. The female figures that remain typically do not represent types of human beings, or human characteristics, or even abstract qualities, but simply, and transparently, nations: Belge, Flourdelis, Irena.

The connection between gender and this new allegorical style has been effectively analyzed by Eggert. But as she reminds us, this is also the section of the book that has attracted the attention of historicist critics, particularly those with an interest in colonialism, for the heroic action attempted here, and not always achieved, is foreign policy, including the policy of Lord Grey in Ireland. Recent critical attention to Spenser's *A View of the Present State of Ireland*, and to Book V in light of the *View*, has tended to see Spenser as earnest in his call for a thorough-going program of subjugation and reformation in Ireland, and critical of Elizabeth's policies only in not being decisive enough.[49] As Eggert's treatment of the last part of Book V shows, the historical situation acquired a gendered dimension much in the way the Radigund episode does: it is Elizabeth's female power which is perceived as preventing male action. Christopher Highley, coming from a historicist direction, has reached conclusions remarkably similar to Eggert's, arguing that Book V, like much colonialist writing, expresses a yearning for a male homosocial community free of debilitating feminine influence, and here again the failure of such men as Lord Grey to complete the reformation of Ireland is attributable to the effeminate policies of Elizabeth. Similarly, many critics and historians have noted the way in which a readily available cultural misogyny informed the colonialist representation of the Irish, who are often depicted as having a feminized culture, their need for reformation evident in the unnaturalness of their social structure.[50] The Spenser of the *View* is no different in this regard: Clare Carroll, for example, argues that "*A View* represents the Irish as a feminized, culturally barbaric, and economically intractable society that must be subjected to complete cultural and economic destruction and reorganization by the English colonists."[51]

Such analysis has tended to concentrate on the *View*, with relatively little detailed analysis of how these connections play out in the allegory of the last segment of Book V. Highley does discuss the misogyny in these cantos, but focuses on acts of violence, such as the treatment of Munera: "The misogyny intrinsic to homosocial systems surfaces in Book Five—as elsewhere in the poem—in acts of violence against women."[52] As we have seen in the early cantos of Book V, however, it is often when violence is absent that the erasure of women is most easily accomplished.[53] It is my contention that the reduction in female power accomplished in the last section of Book V is integrally related to the ethos of justice that is evident from the earliest episodes of the book and that both help to naturalize an aggressive policy in Ireland, with all three dimensions of the book coming together in the figure of Irena.

Three figures in particular appear remarkably narrow both in their one-to-one correspondence to historical correlatives and in their agency within the text: Belge, Flourdelis, and Irena.[54] These female figures take the various political and religious events of Spenser's era and cast them in the familiar scenarios of romance. Every nation that requires English intervention is figured as a woman in need of male rescue. Belge is a widow "Wrapt in great dolours and in deadly feares" (V.x.6), deprived of her husband and unable to protect her children from Geryoneo, and therefore in need of Arthur's aid. Flourdelis is the familiar figure of a faithless woman, "Entyced" to betray the "faith she first did plight" by the "golden giftes and many a guilefull word" of Grantorto (V.xi.50), and eventually reunited with her knight through a combination of Artegall's military victory and his harsh rebuke. Irena is the classic damsel in distress: "a distressed Dame,/Whom a strong tyrant did vniustly thrall" (V.i.3), waiting helplessly for a "champion" who "will her cause in battailous array/ Against him iustifie" and save her from death (V.xi.40). They seem as passive as the women in the early cantos of the book, as nearly deprived of agency, and as they represent countries, might even be seen as extending to extreme literalness the tendency in the early cantos to view women as property: they are not persons, but real estate.

A number of critics have noted that the personification of Irena facilitates an argument for a violent approach to the "Irish problem" by paradoxically dehumanizing the Irish people. With it, McCabe notes, "he adroitly detaches 'Ireland' from the native Irish."[55]

Fowler argues that "ethnographic writing in the period can be seen as the project of making a coherent 'people' or culture out of populations that could not submit to conquest unless they could be conceived as politically unified wholes. . . . a personification such as the character Irena . . . is a figure for Ireland who can be rescued from the Irish—whose unification is imaginatively an already accomplished fact."[56] But these ends could be achieved by any personification, as indeed Fogarty has claimed for the *View*'s male figure of Irenius, who "may be regarded as the voice of the conquered land itself, which raises a plea for its own subjugation. Hence, his account of Irish affairs masks a further erasure on which the political vision of the *View* is grounded. By arrogating to himself the opinions of an entire people, Irenius inverts the rebelliousness symbolized by Ireland and turns it into submission."[57]

Though he uses the male Irenius in the *View*, Spenser makes his *Faerie Queene* voice of Ireland female. This choice may in part reflect the feminized nature of the Irish so prevalent in colonialist discourse; in this sense, the defeat of Radigund and the restoration of right gender order in her realm is the necessary precondition to successful conquest, and Irena as a woman who passively awaits rescue contrasts with both Radigund and the Irish. But this choice is also influenced by the gender dynamics of the early cantos of Book V. While a female symbol will not always or necessarily lead to the subjugation of the nation she symbolizes, replacing the Irish people with a female symbol within the context of Book V has an especially pronounced effect of depriving the Irish of autonomy, and of obscuring that deprivation. Irena functions even more completely than Irenius to turn Irish rebellion into submission; her femaleness naturalizes her dependence, her passivity, and the ease with which men such as Artegall assume the authority to determine her disposition without her consent.

In spite of the apparent similarity in their allegorical technique—the use of female figures for nations, the use of familiar romance motifs—the episodes in the Netherlands, France, and Ireland in fact have some differences worth exploring, for both the precise situations in the narrative and the historical situations they figure vary. Varying also is the degree and influence of the female figures' agency and autonomy, or to put it more pointedly in this geopolitical context, their sovereignty.

Sovereignty turns out to be an interesting question in the Belge episode. A widow could have a degree of legal autonomy not available to an unmarried woman, and that proves to be the case for Belge—though it is perhaps noteworthy that she displays a penchant for giving control of her property away to men. The choice of this particular scenario to figure the Netherlands leads to a subtle evasiveness on the question of sovereignty within that region.[58] When Geryoneo arrives, he does not claim a prior right to Belge's land. Rather, he is the consummate con man, "of her widowhood/Taking aduantage, and her yet fresh woes" (V.x.12). He gains her trust and offers her his "seruice"; she takes him for her "champion" and eventually yields control of her property to him:

> [S]he did at last commit
> All to his hands, and gaue him soueraine powre
> To doe, what euer he thought good or fit.
>
> (V.x.13)

Her act of *giving* Geryoneo "soueraine powre" suggests that he does

not own it at first, that it is her power to give. His power could
arguably be rendered illegitimate by his betrayal of her trust, and it
certainly ends when he is killed by Arthur; sovereignty then presumably reverts to Belge. Thus when she offers it to Arthur (V.xi.16),
she has, implicitly, the right to do so, and Arthur, had he accepted
it, would have become the legitimate sovereign.

At the historical level, of course, the question of sovereignty was
quite different. Philip II was the legitimate sovereign of the Netherlands, and Elizabeth was adamant in not questioning it. Arthur's refusal of Belge's offer represents Elizabeth's parallel refusal, but hers
was not motivated by any belief in the Netherlands' autonomy; in
fact, the appeal to her was bolstered by an argument that she already
had a legitimate claim, complete with "a family tree showing how
the provinces might be shown to have legally descended to the
Queen," an argument that reportedly sent Elizabeth into a fit of
rage.[59] The queen's position, and the traditional reading of Spenser's
episode, recognized Philip's sovereignty and justified English intervention as necessary only to protect his subjects from tyrannical rule.[60]
It lies beyond the scope of this article to pin down Spenser's views
on the question, and it would be taking things too far, I think, to
argue that Spenser was insisting on Netherlands autonomy and arguing for democracy. What is important to observe is the way Spenser's choice of figuration facilitates a degree of vagueness or
obfuscation of that question. Spenser doesn't clearly deny Philip's
sovereignty, but neither does he directly acknowledge it—not surprising perhaps for an English Protestant—and Belge's widowhood
makes this evasiveness possible.

There is no such obfuscation in the French episode, where the
narrative details fit their historical referents rather tidily and, significantly, Burbon is present to figure the sovereign power of that country, Henry of Navarre; asserting his right in the face of rebellious
subjects is the purpose of Artegall's/England's intervention. Flourdelis's volition is nevertheless of considerable significance to the episode, however; like Radigund's rule, hers is a female agency which
must be reformed.

Flourdelis's will is one of the two central problems in the episode
(along with Burbon's casting away his shield), just as the French
people's acceptance of Henry's succession was the central problem in
the civil war the episode allegorizes. Although Flourdelis has previously accepted Burbon's love—Spenser's text is not entirely explicit
on the nature of the promise—she has been lured away by the gifts
and blandishments of Grantorto:

But sure to me her faith she first did plight,
To be my loue, and take me for her Lord,
Till that a Tyrant, which *Grantorto* hight,
With golden giftes and many a guilefull word
Entyced her, to him for to accord.
O who may not with gifts and words be tempted?
Sith which she hath me euer since abhord,
And to my foe hath guilefully consented.

(V.xi.50)

The wilfulness of her betrayal is a matter of some uncertainty. Though Grantorto is blamed for his very active enticement and his "guilefull word[s]," it is Flourdelis who gets a stern talking-to from Artegall. At some moments Burbon seems inclined to make excuses for his beloved's behavior; for example, he expresses doubt about her willingness to abandon him: "Whether withheld from me by wrongfull might,/Or with her owne good will, I cannot read aright" (V.xi.49). But at other moments he blames her unequivocally. In the stanza quoted above he suggests that anyone might yield to such temptation ("O who may not . . . be tempted"), but in the next breath states that she "hath guilefully consented"; a line later he condemns her betrayal not as a general human failing but as an explicitly female fault: "Ay me, that euer guile in wemen was inuented." Even the narrator is noncommittal on Flourdelis's situation when Artegall arrives on the scene. Though Burbon is clearly in need of Artegall's assistance, "in daungerous distresse" much like Irena in Artegall's next adventure, Flourdelis is described as in much the same state, "all succourlesse,/Crying, and holding vp her wretched hands/ To him for aide" (V.xi.44)—and Spenser's characteristic ambiguous pronoun reference underscores the uncertainty of the scene: is she crying for Artegall's aid, or Burbon's? Her description after the defeat of the "rude rout" is richly ambivalent:

Her half dismayd they found in doubtfull plight,
As neither glad nor sorie for their sight
Yet wondrous faire she was, and richly clad
In roiall robes, and many Iewels dight,
But that those villens through their vsage bad
Them fouly rent, and shamefully defaced had.

(V.xi.60)

Flourdelis's own behavior suggests uncertainty or inconsistency.

When Burbon first approaches her, her reaction is emphatically negative: "she backstarting with disdainefull yre,/Bad him auaunt" (V.xi.61). After she is "rebuked and vpbrayded," she no longer resists his "clasping [her] twixt his armes" or his lifting her "Vpon his steede," but her attitude is a study in neutrality: he "bore her quite away, nor well nor ill apayd" (V.xi.64).

Historically, Flourdelis's uncertain or divided will no doubt reflects the divided will of the French people, but here at the end of the episode it also bears a striking resemblance to the wills of women in the early cantos of the book. Is she ambivalent at this point, still divided in her own will, or has her will been simply neutralized, stamped out entirely by the severity of Artegall's rebuke? Saying that she is neither pleased nor displeased is, after all, not quite the same as, and rather more inscrutable than, saying she is both pleased and displeased simultaneously. Given the fate that has met female volition and agency throughout the book, it is likely not coincidental that the female figure in the last three cantos who has the greatest impact on events has the most perverse (or perverted) will, or that Artegall acts to neutralize if not efface it. The romance scenario Spenser chose for this episode in European history allows Artegall to go about his business in his customary manner: ignoring or denying female will and viewing the situation as fundamentally about men.[61] Artegall acts not to save the "succourlesse" Flourdelis but to assist the dispossessed Burbon, at his own request (V.xi.57)—and that reluctantly—and once Burbon is restored to his right, Artegall restrains Talus and hurries on to save Irena, leaving Flourdelis in Burbon's sovereign male hands.

In the Irena episode, we find some notable similarities to the scene Artegall has just left: the woman helpless and in danger, the military power of Artegall and Talus which liberates her, even the same villain, Grantorto. But there are also significant differences. Here there is no Burbon, no one who has legitimate power over Irena; in this way Irena is more like Belge than Flourdelis, though she is not a widow. Most interestingly of all, Irena differs from both Belge and Flourdelis in what and how she signifies. As Eggert notes, Irena is unique in these last cantos in having two meanings, Ireland and Peace,[62] but upon close examination her significance is even less transparent than this simple dual formulation. Belge and Flourdelis represent political entities, nations and people; their monarchs and governors are represented by other figures. But Irena is neither the Irish people nor the land itself, for she herself is explicitly the sovereign ruler of her "saluage Iland" (V.xi.39), having been deprived of "Crowne"

(V.xi.38) by Grantorto, and she appeals to Gloriana as the "Patronesse" of "weake Princes" (V.i.4) for help in restoring her to her right. As McCabe has observed, "Irena's real identity becomes rather problematic": "Her role in the romance narrative is to beseech and obtain Gloriana's aid against the injustice of Grantorto. . . . But Spenser is committed to the view that there is no Irish sovereignty independent of the English crown. Consequently, . . . Irena, by a highly solipsistic inversion, proves to be a pseudonym of Gloriana."[63] So Irena is in a sense really Elizabeth, and her people must be either the New English planters or an English fantasy of the compliant Irish who will be liberated by Lord Grey's military success, for they rejoice at Artegall's defeat of Grantorto and restoration of Irena's rule:

Which when the people round about him saw,
They shouted all for ioy of his successe,
Glad to be quit from that proud Tyrants awe,
Which with strong powre did them long time oppresse.

(V.xii.24)

As Peace, Irena represents the ultimate rhetorical sleight of hand: she is peace as defined by the victor, a mystified idea of the peace that will come when the Irish people are fully deprived of autonomy, and those who don't quietly submit to this erasure have, like Radigund, had their agency violently obliterated.

Complicating the picture even further, Irena herself suffers a kind of erasure. In spite of her explicit sovereignty, Artegall does not leave things in her hands (as he did with Burbon) or offer her his service (as Arthur, and even Geryoneo, did with Belge). Instead, "hauing freed Irena from distress" (V.xii.27), he takes it upon himself to conduct her kingdom's business. Irena is as passive after Grantorto's death as she was in his prison; it is not she who is leading here, but Artegall, "Who streight her leading with meete maiestie . . . Did her . . . to her kingdomes seat restore agayne" (V.xii.25). (And just who possesses the "meete maiestie"?) He "sorely punishe[s]" those who had supported Grantorto; he works "day and night . . . to reforme that ragged common-weale"; and he sends Talus out to root out and punish "all hidden crimes" (V.xii.25–6). What might be appropriate to do for Belge, who lacks the ability or maybe the desire to conduct her country's affairs, or for Burbon, who claims a right to control Flourdelis and who asks for Artegall's aid, is startling to undertake here without Irena's request. Indeed, once led to her seat by Artegall, Irena never speaks, or acts, or is seen again.

The choice of a female Irena and her familiar female distress, then, enables a curious and complex slippage in this climactic episode. Artegall is acting according to his long-established habits: not seeing or not recognizing women's legitimate autonomy and rights, making no meaningful distinctions between queens and subjects or between good queens and tyrants. Indeed, he appears to regard Irena as much like Flourdelis, though without the dubious virtue: freed from the illegitimate control of Grantorto's thugs, they must both be restored to some legitimate male control; Flourdelis he restores to Burbon's arms, here he takes over himself. One wonders if he would have refused Belge's offer as readily as did Arthur.

This is dangerous territory. If Irena does represent Elizabeth's authority in Ireland, then it is Elizabeth's power that Artegall usurps. Does this reflect Spenser's misogynistic desire to do just that, or to see some man such as Lord Grey do so? Or does it express his belief that this is what Lord Grey or some of his predecessors did? And if so, does he record it with approval, or with disapproval, or Flourdelis-like, with neither? Or has Artegall, perhaps, now become a prophetic figure of Essex? Is it a warning or a wish?

I don't claim to have the answers to these questions; I'm inclined to think they can't be answered. However, we can become attentive to the way that Spenser's choice of allegorical material in these last few cantos creates a slipperiness that both raises such questions and makes them impossible to answer. These slippages are easy to miss when we have been conditioned by the preceding book not to recognize women's agency or (in spite of the narrator's protestations) their sovereignty, and to have issues of the greatest significance obscured by an overemphasis on the femaleness of female figures. It is easy for Artegall—or for the careless reader—to see Irena as a woman first and foremost and to fit her into the increasingly narrow range of what that category permits: not to see her as sovereign, but to lump her into the same category as Flourdelis and to gloss over their differences. Whatever she represents—Ireland, or Elizabeth, or Peace—the fact that it is figured female leaves it utterly within Artegall's control.

Conclusion: No Justice, No Peace

It is easy to emerge from reading recent criticism of Spenser's Book V and *View* with an image of works that are deeply grounded in both misogyny and racism. Spenser, we learn, was not so much the instrument as the advocate of a detestable policy. At the same time, there are reminders that the detestableness of that policy is a value of our own era, not Spenser's, and there are repeated urgings not to judge his view by our own: "To impose on the allegory a distaste for violence is both sentimental and anachronistic—especially against a foreign enemy, especially in a religious war"[64]; "Those who conceive the task of historians to consist in explaining, rather than judging, events in the past may find rather disturbing this exhortation to condemn the recommendations made by Edmund Spenser for Ireland in 1596."[65]

But the fact remains that as readers we do have our own values, which often are at odds with the values expressed in a poem, and students especially will feel the clash in encountering the poem for the first time. Anecdotes collected by Willy Maley powerfully illustrate the kind of emotion Spenser may provoke:

> Colin MacCabe expresses the predicament of the Irish reader faced with an epic whose author is deeply implicated in colonial violence: "I find it difficult to read *The Faerie Queene* without remembering that Spenser urged the most brutal policies in Grey's administration and wrote of his delight in seeing the Irish starve." . . . . Tom Healy tells of a seminar that reached a similar conclusion: "A student of mine . . . suggested it seemed peculiar to be reading a piece by an author commonly hailed as one of the great writers of the English Renaissance putting forward views which makes [sic] him a type of war criminal within a twentieth-century perspective." . . . Andrew Hadfield recounts an incident that can be juxtaposed with the responses of MacCabe and Healy: "At a conference I attended in 1985, entitled 'Spenser and Ireland', a student stood up at the end and thanked the speakers for helping her to appreciate that there may well have been some interest in studying a figure she had previously regarded only as the brutal butcher of her ancestors."[66]

In Wisconsin, where I teach, there are relatively few students of Irish descent who might react in precisely this way, but many will recognize with horror the similarity to the ethnic violence of other areas of the world.

To be sure, there is value in acquiring the knowledge base and the imaginative flexibility to understand political positions from a very different age. Recent scholarship helps to do this, and such an approach can and does have salutary effects: Cavanagh reports that in her course "typical resistance to book 5 gives way to a fresh appreciation of the political as well as the poetic implications of the poem."[67] But there is a risk here too: of suppressing the distress, of giving the impression that a student's initial reaction was wrong rather than incomplete, of seeming to preach a relativism more radical than we in fact practice, of leaving students with a Spenser who offers them nothing but a historical document laying out an alien ideology. My goal is to create a reading experience—for myself and for my students—in which understanding Spenser's thinking does not invalidate students' own values—or validate them for that matter—but creates a productive and energizing dialogue between them, in which difference becomes an opportunity to learn more about one's own beliefs as well as about another's: to reexamine, clarify, better understand, and even strengthen one's own without dismissing the other out of hand.

Artegall's progress within Book V and the book's placement within the poem as a whole allow for a reading experience that makes ideology a process rather than a product. Most readers of Book V come to it having previously read at least some of the earlier books, and where Books III and IV are available as context, the gender shift felt by feminist critics such as Quilligan and Staton shapes the experience of reading Book V and can be drawn upon as resource for analysis. While Book V exhibits a nostalgia for the more masculine world of Books I and II,[68] it is noteworthy that restoring male control and a linear plot requires a more radical simplification and a higher degree of violence than are characteristic of the earlier books. No one complains about transparency of I and II, for example. Duessa is significantly killed not in I but in V; and neither Duessa nor Acrasia is denounced in the explicitly misogynistic terms that are used for Radigund. The experience of III and IV has made reinstating a masculinist ideology more difficult for the poet and, I submit, less certain to persuade readers. This structure creates the possibility and the opportunity to make the experience of reading Book V a study in how gender, power, and empire are intertwined. It allows a reading—not of Spenser's intention necessarily, but of his poem—that neither rejects Spenser's politics nor adopts a radical relativism that disarms judgment. After all, a peace that violates one's own sense of justice is a distressing peace indeed.

University of Wisconsin—Stevens Point

NOTES

1. Student "disquiet" figures prominently in the two essays on teaching Book V published in *Approaches to Teaching Spenser's Faerie Queene*, ed. David Lee Miller and Alexander Dunlop (New York: MLA, 1994): Sheila T. Cavanagh's "'That Savage Land': Ireland in Spenser's Legend of Justice," 143–152, and Edwin Craun's "'Most Sacred Virtue She': Reading Book 5 alongside Aristotle and Thomas Aquinas on Justice," 153–161.

2. C. S. Lewis, *The Allegory of Love: A Study in Medieval Tradition* (Oxford: Oxford University Press, 1936), 349.

3. Katherine Eggert, "'Changing all that form of common weale': Genre and the Repeal of Queenship in *The Faerie Queene*, Book 5," *ELR* 26 (1996): 261.

4. Annabel Patterson, "The Egalitarian Giant: Representations of Justice in History/Literature," *Journal of British Studies* 31(1992): 105. For an earlier perspective on the gap between ideal and practical in Spenser's treatment of justice, see Sheila T. Cavanagh, "Ideal and Practical Justice: Artegall and Arthur in *Faerie Queene Five*," *Renaissance Papers* 1984: 19–28.

5. Thomas Francis Bulger, *The Historical Changes and Exchanges as Depicted by Spenser in* The Faerie Queene (Lewiston: Edwin Mellen, 1993), 146.

6. Bulger, *Historical Changes*, 18, 156. Cavanagh reads the pairing of Arthur and Artegall similarly in " 'Such Was Irena's Countenance': Ireland in Spenser's Prose and Poetry," *Texas Studies in Language and Literature* 28 (1986), 41–42.

7. Elizabeth Fowler, "The Failure of Moral Philosophy in the Work of Edmund Spenser," *Representations* 51 (Summer 1995): 47, 49.

8. Fowler, "The Failure of Moral Philosophy," 56.

9. Fowler, "The Failure of Moral Philosophy," 56, 60. Fowler goes on to argue that Artegall's behavior in this episode actually "violates received jurisprudence" (60); see pages 60–63. For a similar view of Artegall's handling of the giant, grounded in a more explicitly political analysis, see Patterson, "The Egalitarian Giant," esp. 110. Another analysis of the role that power plays in Book V's conception of Justice is offered by Clark Hulse in "Spenser, Bacon, and the Myth of Power," in *The Historical Renaissance: New Essays on Tudor and Stuart Literature and Culture*, ed. Heather Dubrow and Richard Strier (Chicago: University of Chicago Press, 1988), 315–46, esp. 323–26.

10. Fowler, "The Failure of Moral Philosophy," 64.

11. All quotations from *The Faerie Queene* are from the edition by A. C. Hamilton (London: Longman, 1977), with book, canto, and stanza numbers cited in the text.

12. I Kings 3:9, KJV.

13. We can usefully compare Artegall in this episode with Fowler's reading of Scudamour in the temple of Venus. In spite of a context "in which mutual consent, reciprocity, and mastery on the part of the woman as well as the man are praised fulsomely" (57), Scudamour insists on his right to claim Amoret by conquest, to take her by force: "Rather than requiring her voluntary consent, his action must be based upon his own worth" (57). The same dynamic that, in Scudamour's view, justifies a violent act against a woman here renders violence against women invisible, or redefines it as something else.

14.   She also contrasts remarkably with Doralice in Canto 27 of *Orlando furioso*, who is allowed to settle the dispute between Mandricardo and Rodomonte by choosing which she prefers.

15.   The conflation of women with property in this episode has sometimes been echoed, unexamined, by critics. Douglas A. Northrop, for example, equates women (metonymically referred to as "love") with property when he observes that all of Artegall's tests involve "the distribution of temporal goods—love in the episode of Sir Sanglier and the squire, money in the episode of Pollente, and, more generally, all the things of the world in his dispute with the Giant" ("Spenser's Defence of Elizabeth," *University of Toronto Quarterly* 38 [1968–9]: 290).

16.   Craun, "Most Sacred Virtue," 155.

17.   Herbert B. Nelson, for example, argued it this way: "By the law, . . . it made no difference that most of his island had washed away to increase the size of his brother's island, for according to both Roman law and English law, the land added gradually by accretion belonged to the owner of the adjacent land. . . . Bracidas had lost his land but had no legal right to damages; he had found a treasure chest equal in value to the land he had lost but was denied its possession by both common law and admiralty law. Obviously, the only way to secure justice was to ignore the law and apply the principles of equity" ("Amidas and Bracidas," *Modern Language Quarterly* 1 [1940]: 398–99).

18.   "Amidas and Bracidas," 395–96.

19.   Maurice Evans, *Spenser's Anatomy of Heroism: A Commentary on "The Faerie Queene"* (Cambridge: Cambridge University Press, 1970), 203.

20.   Roland M. Smith, "Spenser's Tale of the Two Sons of Milesio," *Modern Language Quarterly* 3 (1942): 557.

21.   Ultimately the argument fails, because stanza 11 makes it clear that although Bracidas does save Lucy from drowning, he does so only after she has been washed ashore: "After long tossing in the seas distrest,/Her weary barke at last vppon mine Isle did rest" (V.iv.11).

22.   Cf. the observation of W. Nicholas Knight that all of Artegall's decisions involve property disputes, an observation that requires viewing people as property: "all appeals, decisions, and quests deal with some form of property, even if it is 'my lady' or 'my son' " ("The Narrative Unity of Book V of *The Faerie Queene*: 'That Part of Justice Which Is Equity,' " *Review of English Studies* 21 [1970]: 274).

23.   Knight, "Narrative Unity," 268–69.

24.   "Narrative Unity," 269.

25.   Cf. Fowler's reading of his argument with the Giant, in which he "promotes equity not in its conventional English sense as an aspect of justice, but as the justification of his own power" ("Failure of Moral Philosophy," 64).

26.   On questions of women's right to own property and the transfer of ownership to husbands upon marriage, see Pearl Hogrefe, "Legal Rights of Tudor Women and their Circumvention by Men and Women," *Sixteenth Century Journal* 3 (1972): 97–105.

27.   Constance Jordan, *Renaissance Feminism: Literary Texts and Political Models* (Ithaca: Cornell University Press, 1990), 5.

28.   As I have read them here, the Sanglier and Amidas/Bracidas episodes exemplify one of the central claims of Lowell Gallagher's reading of Book V in *Medusa's*

Gaze: Casuistry and Conscience in the Renaissance (Stanford: Standford University Press, 1991). Here as elsewhere the text presents "competing claims to what is just or true and the ensuing resolution by an authoritative voice, whose 'doome' is accepted universally" (153); at the same time, it includes those details, such as Lucy's claim to the treasure, which must be omitted for the authoritative reading to work: by "[l]eaving a trail of narrative details that must be made meaningless, or superfluous, in order for the whole to 'work,' . . . the book thematizes its own blindness" (170). Though Gallagher's work came to my attention after my own reading was substantially worked out, there is a great deal of harmony between them; Gallagher, however, is not specifically concerned with gender issues.

29.   Maureen Quilligan, *Milton's Spenser: The Politics of Reading* (Ithaca: Cornell University Press, 1983), 203. Harry Berger, Jr., has contested some of Quilligan's reading of Book III, particularly in the Garden of Adonis, suggesting that it offers a "peculiarly male perspective of the narrative occasionally addressed to female readers to whose interests it is clearly sympathetic" ("Actaeon at the Hinder Gate: The Stag Party in Spenser's Garden of Adonis," in *Desire in the Renaissance: Psychoanalysis and Literature*, ed. Valeria Finucci and Regina Schwartz [Princeton: Princeton University Press, 1994], 109). However, accepting Berger's analysis still allows for a sense of change in the later books, for even that sympathy appears to have vanished.

30.   Shirley Staton, "Reading Spenser's *Faerie Queene*—In a Different Voice," in *Ambiguous Realities: Women in the Middle Ages and Renaissance*, ed. Carole Levin and Jeanine Watson (Detroit: Wayne State University Press, 1987), 146.

31.   "Reading Spenser's *Faerie Queene*," 158.

32.   Eggert, "Changing all that forme of common weale," 265.

33.   Eggert, "Changing all that forme of common weale," 274.

34.   Eggert, "Changing all that forme of common weale," 278.

35.   Eggert, "Changing all that forme of common weale," 285.

36.   Eggert, "Changing all that forme of common weale," 285.

37.   Susanne Woods argues for a more sympathetic view of Radigund in "Amazonian Tyranny." While I find the view of Radigund as "interesting victim" (55) compelling in some respects, it is not convincing as a defense of this particular course of action.

38.   For a discussion of the similarities between Artegall's encounters with the two women, see, e.g., Mary R. Bowman, " 'she there as Princess rained': Spenser's Figure of Elizabeth," *Renaissance Quarterly* 43 (1990): 511–12; Woods, "Spenser and the Problem of Women's Rule," *Huntington Library Quarterly* 48 (1985): 153 and T. K. Dunseath, *Spenser's Allegory of Justice in Book Five of "The Faerie Queene"* (Princeton: Princeton University Press, 1968), 132–33. Woods says that it is "not altogether clear why" these identical actions seem to carry different moral valences ("Amazonian Tyranny," 55). While it is true that, for the reader, blurring such moral distinctions is a large part of Book V's project, from Artegall's position the crimes of which Radigund is accused provide sufficient ground to respond to her beauty differently.

39.   For general studies of the controversy, see James E. Phillips, Jr., "The Background of Spenser's Attitude Toward Women Rulers," *Huntington Library Quarterly* 5 (1941–42): 5–32; Paula Louise Scalingi, "The Scepter or the Distaff: The Question

of Female Sovereignty, 1516–1607," *The Historian* 41 (1978–79): 59–75; and Jordan, "Woman's Rule in Sixteenth-Century British Political Thought," *Renaissance Quarterly* 40 (1987): 421–451. Studies of *FQ* V in this context include Kerby Neill, "*The Faerie Queene* and the Mary Stuart Controversy," *ELH* 2 (1935): 192–214; Phillips, "The Woman Ruler in Spenser's *Faerie Queene*," *Huntington Library Quarterly* 5 (1941–42): 211–234; Douglas A. Northrop, "Spenser's Defence of Elizabeth," *University of Toronto Quarterly* 38 (1968–9): 277–94; Pamela Joseph Benson, "Rule, Virginia: Protestant Theories of Female Regiment in *The Faerie Queene*," *ELR* 15 (1985): 277–92; and Susanne Woods, "Spenser and the Problem of Women's Rule."

40.   This reading is offered, for example, by Northrop (277), Phillips ("The Woman Ruler," 213), Neill (209), and Benson (279).

41.   For examples of this view, see Northrop 277–78 and Phillips, "Renaissance Concepts of Justice and the Structure of *The Faerie Queene*, Book V," in *Essential Articles for the Study of Edmund Spenser*, ed. A.C. Hamilton (Hamden, CT: Archon Books, 1972), 479.

42.   It is too brief and unsubtle a statement to add very much; as Neill puts it, "Spenser's attitude toward the entire problem is in no way original, but it is merely the poetic expression of the commonplace views of the Protestant English party" (209, n.64). It is a rather belated effort as well: although writings on the issue were published until even after Elizabeth's death, the most active period of debate was in the early years of the reign, long before *The Faerie Queene*.

43.   "The Scepter or the Distaff," 75.

44.   Karen Newman, *Fashioning Femininity and English Renaissance Drama* (Chicago: Chicago University Press, 1991), xviii. For an extended analysis of the relationship of gender and other social hierarchies, see Susan Dwyer Amussen, *An Ordered Society: Gender and Class in Early Modern England* (Oxford: Basil Blackwell, 1988).

45.   Aylmer, for example, pointed out that the problem with the Catholic queens was not their gender but their religion. See the discussion of his *An Harborowe for Faithfull and Trewe Subiectes* in Phillips, "The Background of Spenser's Attitude," 16.

46.   This is the argument of Highley's chapter 5, "'A softe kind of warre': Spenser and the Female Reformation of Ireland," in *Shakespeare, Spenser, and the Crisis in Ireland* (Cambridge: Cambridge University Press, 1997), 110–33.

47.   Eggert argues that criticism of England's incomplete commitment to the Low Countries was misplaced in this way: "Although Burleigh was partially if not primarily responsible for this policy, the Queen herself was blamed for womanish inconstancy and lack of will" ("Changing all that form of common weale," 283). Some historians disagree, however, insisting that Elizabeth was firmly in control of her own policy: as Charles Wilson puts it in *Queen Elizabeth and the Revolt of the Netherlands* (Berkeley: University of California Press, 1970), 123, "the Council might propose; the Queen disposed"; see also R. B. Wernham, *The Making of Elizabethan Foreign Policy, 1558–1603* (Berkeley: University of California Press, 1980), 4–5.

48.   The distaste for this aspect of the closing cantos of Book V has a long critical history, one too frequently rehearsed to need further discussion here. See for example Patterson, "The Egalitarian Giant," 103–04 and Eggert, "Changing all that form of common weale," 259–60. Eggert, 279–80, quotes critical commentary and also reviews the qualities of the poetry that give rise to it. Willy Maley is atypical in

taking exception to seeing these cantos as transparent, but he fails to provide a well-developed alternative to it ("To Weet to Work Irenaes Franchisement: Ireland in *The Faerie Queene*," *Irish University Review* 26 [1996]: 303–19).

49.   E.g., Walter S. H. Lim: "Spenser's conception of justice expressed in Book V can be read as a poeticization of the vision of justice given in *A View of the Present State of Ireland.* . . . While paying lip service to the laudable virtue of the Queene's [sic] mercy, he criticizes, for example, her half-hearted endorsement of actions that will effectively control the state of lawlessness in neighbouring Ireland. Therefore, the exercise of justice necessary for social stability and order is, for Spenser, central also to the project of English imperialism and colonialism. Spenser is the unabashed apologist for the use of force to order and consolidate England's *imperium*" ("Figuring Justice: Imperial Ideology and the Discourse of Colonialism in Book V of *The Faerie Queene* and *A View of the Present State of Ireland*," *Renaissance and Reformation* 19 [1995]: 46). Also see Richard McCabe, "The Fate of Irena: Spenser and Political Violence," in *Spenser and Ireland: An Interdisciplinary Perspective*, ed. Patricia Coughlan (Cork: Cork University Press, 1989), 109–35; Ciarán Brady, "The Road to the View: On the Decline of Reform Thought in Tudor Ireland," in *Spenser and Ireland*, 25–45; and Anne Fogarty, "The Colonization of Language: Narrative Strategy in *A View of the Present State of Ireland* and *The Faerie Queene*, Book VI," in *Spenser and Ireland*, 75–108. Clare Carroll has argued for a similarity between the procedure followed in conquering and reforming Radegone and the plan for conquest of Ireland in outlined in the *View*: "In fact, the actions which attend this change of 'common weale' correspond point for point with Spenser's reorganization of Irish society in the third part of *A View*" ("The Construction of Gender and the Cultural and Political Other in *The Faerie Queene* 5 and *A View of the Present State of Ireland*: The Critics, the Context, and the Case of Radigund," *Criticism* 32 [1990]:184). For a reading less convinced of Spenser's unequivocal zeal, see Patterson, "The Egalitarian Giant": "I am not suggesting that Spenser was opposed to the policy of Irish subjugation that the *View* as a whole promotes. . . . But it is a mistake to believe he was *comfortable* with this final solution or only inadvertently revelatory of the contradictions in the ideology of Justice that appear in both the Legend of Justice and the *View*" (124).

50.   For example, see William Palmer, "Gender, Violence, and Rebellion in Tudor and Early Stuart Ireland," *Sixteenth-Century Journal* 23 (1992): 699–712.

51.   Carroll, "The Construction of Gender," 163. Also see the extended discussion of gender and sexuality in the *View* in Cavanagh, " 'Licentious Barbarism': Spenser's View of the Irish and *The Faerie Queene*," *Irish University Review* 26 (1996): 268–80; see especially page 278.

52.   *Shakespeare, Spenser, and the Crisis in Ireland*, 126.

53.   And as a reader of an earlier draft of this article reminded me, Book V also features acts of violence against male figures, such as Malfont.

54.   Eggert has pointed out how limited in their sexual power are the female figures that appear after Radigund's demise ("Changing all that form of common weale," 279), but these three are notably powerless in other respects.

55.   "The Fate of Irena," 120.

56.   "The Failure of Moral Philosophy," 55.

57. "The Colonization of Language," 89.

58. It has, of course, long been known that Spenser did not invent the image of the widow Belge looking to England for help, which was used in pageants celebrating Leicester's arrival in the Low Countries, as demonstrated by Ivan L. Schultze, "Spenser's Belge Episode and the Pageants for Leicester in the Low Countries, 1585–86," *SP* 28 (1931): 235–40. On the other hand, it was Spenser's choice to use the image, and to give it narrative rather than iconic form.

59. Wilson, *Queen Elizabeth*, 35.

60. Northrop, "Spenser's Defence," 282.

61. Here, as in the Belge episode, it should be acknowledged that Spenser did not create the scenario. Anne Lake Prescott has recently revealed how much of Spenser's material was already part of Henry's iconography in "Foreign Policy in Fairyland: Henri IV and Spenser's Burbon," *Spenser Studies* 14 (2000): 189–214. Henry was routinely cast as a chivalric hero (see esp. 191), whose resumé included defeating Geryon (playing the role of Philip; see page 196), and his coronation was described as a marriage (194). Still, here as in the Netherlands, Spenser had to chose to make use of this imagery, and to give it narrative form.

62. "Changing all that form of common weale," 280.

63. "The Fate of Irena," 120–21.

64. Richard Mallette, "Book Five of The Faerie Queene: An Elizabethan Apocalypse," *Spenser Studies*, 11 (1990): 151.

65. Nicholas Canny, "Introduction: Spenser and Reform in Ireland," in *Spenser and Ireland*, ed. Coughlan, 14.

66. *Salvaging Spenser: Colonialism, Culture, and Identity* (New York: St. Martin's, 1997), 2–3.

67. "That Savage Land," 144.

68. Eggert, "Changing all that form of common weale," 265.

LIN KELSEY

Spenser, Ralegh, and the Language of Allegory

This paper suggests that the skill of Renaissance poets in writing "Under the foote," as Colin slyly puts it in "Colin Clouts Come Home Againe," has paradoxically been underestimated. An exploration of the use of continued metaphor (the formal rhetorical definition of "allegory") in both Colin's tale of Bregog and the Shepherd's "lamentable lay," long identified with Ralegh's "Ocean to Cynthia," finds a powerful metaphorical unity underlying the supposed incoherence of the "Ocean." But Ralegh's lyrical high road as Cynthia's impetuous Ocean is finally no match for Spenser's allegorical low road as a river that goes underground, hiding its course or discourse under multiple layers of meaning. Singing "Under the foote of *Mole*" —and under the recent censorship of his *Complaints* by Lord Burghley in 1591—Spenser/Colin demonstrates that he can sing what he pleases undetected under the poetic foot, offering a saucy Ovidian account of his dealings with Elizabeth's mighty statesman which is also a bold manifesto of his intention to sing on unimpeded. The poet is not only the wily Bregog but on a deeper, more truly "allegorical" level, the river Alpheus passing untainted under the sea to pursue his beloved Arethusa (virtue herself, as the ancients thought) to a distant island.

> SPENCER . . . is Master of what he treateth of; he can wield it as he pleaseth: And this he hath done soe cunningly, that if one heed him not with great attention, rare and wonderful conceptions will vnperceived slide by him that readeth his works, & he will thinke he hath mett with nothing but familiar and easy discourses. . . . those streames that steale away with least noyse are vsually deepest, and most dangerous to pass ouer.
> —Sir Kenelm Digby[1]

SPENSER'S ACCOUNT IN "Colin Clouts Come Home Againe" of the meeting in Ireland of Colin Clout and the Shepherd of the Ocean—aka Edmund Spenser and Sir Walter Ralegh—offers a revealing glimpse into a kind of allegorical speech that the two poets share there and of which Spenser in particular is the unrivaled "Master." The nature of this language shows a great deal about the ability of Renaissance poets to write "Under the foote," as Colin slyly puts it in this poem (l. 57),[2] with great facility—much greater and more entertaining facility, I would suggest, than we have as yet appreciated. Annabel Patterson has directed our attention to the political dimension of such "underness."[3] While it is true that skill in writing under the foot had acquired a special political value in the years of Elizabeth's reign, allowing things to be said that might otherwise have been unacceptable, we should not forget that such techniques overlapped in intriguing and important ways with the most ancient ideas about the hidden, sacred dimensions of the poet's, and especially the allegorist's, calling.

One of the paradoxical consequences of this skill in writing under the foot is that many poems—as I hope to show is the case here with both Colin's tale of Bregog and the Shepherd's "lamentable lay" (l. 164), usually identified by critics with Ralegh's "Ocean to Cynthia" —appear to have been underread and even misread metaphorically and thus underestimated both politically and poetically. Learning to read Spenser's allegory more clearly will reward us not simply with new appreciation of his way with words but with clues to historical and political questions we cannot otherwise hope to answer, such as how Spenser responded to the "calling in" of his volume of *Complaints* in 1591.

The historical background of the famous encounter described by Spenser in "Colin Clouts Come Home Againe" is well known.[4] Visiting his estates in Ireland in 1589, whether simply to stamp his claim (as he says) or to avoid some temporary royal disfavor related to the rise of Essex (as a contemporary letter writer suggests),[5] Ralegh became acquainted, or perhaps reacquainted, with Spenser, who held the neighboring lands of Kilcolman. This meeting, which resulted in Spenser's almost immediate return to England with Ralegh to present the first three books of the *Faerie Queene* to Elizabeth, is celebrated in Spenser's poem as an agreeable encounter between two shepherds on the banks of the river Mulla. In Colin's own account:

One day (quoth he) I sat, (as was my trade)
Under the foote of *Mole* that mountaine hore,
Keeping my sheepe amongst the cooly shade,
Of the greene alders by the *Mullaes* shore:
There a straunge shepheard chaunst to find me out,
Whether allured with my pipes delight,
Whose pleasing sound yshrilled far about,
Or thither led by chaunce, I know not right:
Whom when I asked from what place he came,
And how he hight, himselfe he did ycleepe,
The shepheard of the Ocean by name,
And said he came from the main-sea deepe.

                                        (ll. 56–67)

The conversation of the two shepherds is presented as a pastoral singing match in which each tells a tale of troubled love involving thwarted, indeed actively threatened and endangered, waters.[6] The delight the shepherds take in each other's song reflects the pleasure of two poets who discover that they speak the same language, to say nothing of sharing a fondness for cross-rhymed quatrains, the form of both "Colin Clout" and the "Ocean to Cynthia."[7] The situation is neatly emblematized by the fact that the two share a single pipe, passing it back and forth from lip to lip in a rather unhygienic intimacy not to be found in any pastoral model:[8]

And when he heard the musicke which I made,
He found himselfe full greatly pleasd at it:
Yet aemuling my pipe, he tooke in hond
My pipe before that aemuled of many,
And plaid theron; (for well that skill he cond)
Himselfe as skilfull in that art as any.
He pip'd, I sung; and when he sung, I piped,
By chaunge of turnes, each making other mery,
Neither envying other, nor envied,
So piped we, untill we both were weary.

                                        (ll. 70–79)

In this engaging picture of the two shepherd-poets "each making other mery"—making each other laugh with delight at a shared wit whose source remains unspoken—there is an element of secret relish that goes beyond a simple exchange of poems and suggests a new dimension in the sudden meeting of minds that made Ralegh take up Spenser's cause with such vigor.

In the exchange Colin sings of "my river *Bregogs*" love for the "shiny *Mulla*" (ll. 92–93), who is destined by her mountain-father Mole for a more prestigious match with the neighboring River Allo, or Broadwater. Bregog, Mulla, and Broadwater are of course real rivers, although ironically only the Bregog, whose name means "deceitful" in Gaelic, is presented under its true name. The tale is based on the curious behavior of the Bregog, which disappears from sight under its boulder-strewn bed in dry weather. In the poem this behavior becomes a "deceitfull traine" (l. 118) that allows Bregog to meet Mulla secretly underground:

> First into many parts his streame he shar'd,
> That whilest the one was watcht, the other might
> Passe unespide to meete her by the way;
> And then besides, those little streames so broken
> He under ground so closely did convay,
> That of their passage doth appeare no token,
> Till they into the *Mullaes* water slide.
> So secretly did he his love enjoy. . . .
>
> (ll. 138–45)

Detected in his ruse by the enraged father, Bregog is ostensibly silenced but undeterred in his devotion by the attempt of old Mole to destroy his course by filling the stream with stones rolled down from his mountainous heights—an image which, as we will see, reaches deep into Spenser's ideas of the vicissitudes of the poetic career.

Indeed, Spenser wastes no time in "Colin Clout" in establishing that the river's "course" and the poet's "discourse" are closely related. Cuddy's request to Colin to repeat the song he sang to the Shepherd of the Ocean "should it not thy readie course restraine" (l. 82) suggests not only an exemplary deference to the poet's judgment in ordering his own materials but a model of proper reluctance to impede the poetic "course." Cuddy's ingenuous remark prepares the way for the doubling language of Colin's account of how old Mole, having observed from on high "Which way his course the wanton *Bregog* bent"—to whom and to what end the lovelorn poet bends his hidden discourse—takes revenge by showering down huge rocks which punningly "spill" or destroy the river-poet's "water-courses" or water-discourses and (in perhaps another pun on hindering authorship) "encomber . . ./His passage" (ll. 135, 150–51).

Colin's song of the sufferings of Bregog is, he insists, "No leasing new, nor Grandams fable stale,/But auncient truth confirm'd with credence old" (ll. 102–03)—a formulation which, as we shall see, carefully establishes the tale's credentials as allegory in the ancient mode as described by Natalis Comes. The answering song of the Shepherd of the Ocean, who represents bigger and more tumultuous waters, is on the other hand "all a lamentable lay" to "*Cynthia* the Ladie of the sea," whose favor he has lost unjustly (ll. 164, 166). In contrast to Colin's apparent denial of any private, topical reference ("Nor of my love, nor of my losse . . ./I then did sing"; ll. 88–89), the historical allusion here is open. It has long been accepted that the Shepherd's lament is evoked either by the brief royal disfavor that may have brought Ralegh to Ireland in 1589 or, more likely, by the far more serious disgrace of 1592, when the queen discovered Ralegh's secret marriage to Elizabeth Throckmorton, one of her maids of honor. The second possibility, favored by most critics, is indeed persuasive, given the fact that "Colin Clout," although dated December 1591, was not published until 1595, and then with clear signs of revision.[9]

The sobriquet "shepheard of the Ocean" of course represents Spenser's twofold compliment to Ralegh, first as Elizabeth's favorite "Water," her famous nickname for him that plays on the element of Ralegh's great naval triumphs as well as on the name "Walter," commonly shortened to "Wat."[10] The second half of the compliment honors Ralegh as the author of the "Ocean to Cynthia," a work of which only the penultimate book and a fragment of a second and final book survive. The sorrowing lines of the two books, which fit Colin's description of the Shepherd's song as "all a lamentable lay," are written in a by now familiar idiom, constituting as they do eloquent testimony to the turning aside of a stream and the progressive drying up of a poetic voice.

Readers of Ralegh's poem, while often admiring its power, have usually focused on its incoherence, on the final inadequacy of its language to deal with the poet's experience, and on its failure to meet the metaphorical obligations of its title, which promises a speaking Ocean in this lament of the "Ocean to Cynthia."[11] It is true that there are only some five references to ocean or sea in over 500 lines, one of them concealed in a pun. But Ralegh's hidden hydrology is in fact in perfect accordance with Renaissance theories about the relationship of the ocean to the streams, a topic of some mystery in which the speculations of Aristotle, Seneca, and Pliny mingled freely with the word of the Bible as proclaimed in Ecclesiastes 1:7: "All the rivers run into the sea; yet the sea is not full; unto the place from whence the rivers come, thither they return again."[12]

The voice of the "Ocean to Cynthia" is indeed the voice of the Ocean, which well knows that for all its size and bluster, the ocean is not self-sufficient but depends on the constant infusion of fresh or "sweet" water to replenish its stores and dilute its saltness. This life-giving gift of moisture comes back in cyclical fashion to the rivers and springs themselves, as the fruits of Ralegh's triumphs at sea returned to the queen who encouraged and financed them. Hence the painful ordeal of the poem, in which the queen, that "springe of ioyes" that formerly provided the "small dropes of ioies" which "sweetned great worlds of woes," denies the ocean its crucial sustenance (ll. 347, 50).[13]

In the first surviving book, the mind of the poet is slowly turned before our eyes into an arid wasteland as Ralegh meditates at length on "The Idea . . . of a wasted minde" (l. 12). The process of dessica-tion is a long and agonizing one. "Lost in the mudd of thos hygh flowinge streames/Which through more fayrer feilds ther courses bend," the poet who once enjoyed a harvest of weighty sheaves is reduced to seeking "fair floures amidd the brinish sand" (ll. 17–18, 24), shrinking at last to a backwater no more visited by the "course" of the mighty river that is Elizabeth:

> Thos streames seeme standinge puddells which, before,
> Wee saw our bewties in, so weare they cleere.
> Bellphebes course is now obserude no more,
> That faire resemblance weareth out of date.
> Our Ocean seas are but tempestius waves
> And all things base that blessed wear of late. . . .
>
> (ll. 269–74)

No longer are there any "pleasinge streames fast to the ocean wen-dinge/The messengers sumetymes of my great woe" (ll. 33–34)—a glance back to former times when the sweet waters flowed quickly and copiously. The troubled Ocean perhaps alludes here also, as the "great woe" suggests, to the days when Elizabeth sent messages calling her courtier back from his ships and glory, in happier times because she could not spare his company, on the latest occasion in 1592 to consign him to the Tower. Such returns are a tribute to the irresistible force exerted by Cynthia, who is not only the stream that nurtures the Ocean but, as the moon, ruler of its tides: "When I was gonn shee sent her memory/More stronge then weare ten thowsand shipps of warr,/To call mee back" (ll. 63–65).

The debasement is progressive, until at last the Ocean's "tempestius waves," unheeded except as a source of unwelcome disturbance, dwindle into a "fallinge streame" whose poetic "murmeringe" or complaining has become a mere soporific:

> Thy lines ar now a murmeringe to her eares
> Like to a fallinge streame which passinge sloe
>
> Is wovnt to nurrishe sleap, and quietnes.
> So shall thy paynfull labors bee pervsde
> And draw on rest, which sumetyme had regard.
>
> (ll. 362–66)

The description of the falling career of this "fallinge streame,"[14] passing from boisterous waves to slow-flowing water to "mudd," parched ground, and finally "brinish" or salty sand (ll. 17, 24), would not have been lost on Spenser, the original author of the "faire resemblance" of the queen to Belphoebe. Such a resemblance was indeed sadly out of date for Ralegh, once constantly in the royal presence as Captain of the Guard, now in his disgrace barred from following his queen's "course" (both movement and discourse) as it winds through other channels. Spenser's image of the dry bed of the River Bregog choked with stones is a variant on this trope of the silencing of the voice of the poet and the loss of name that follows. As Bregog "Did lose his name" (l. 155) but not his determination to love on, so "Walter," for all his protestations of devotion, must inevitably cease to be the queen's "Water" as the aridity of the landscape increases.

"To seeke for moysture in th'Arabien sande/Is butt a losse of labor, and of rest," the poet of the "Ocean to Cynthia" at last concludes (ll. 478–79), contemplating the vast desert that is the final consequence of the "small rent" (l. 223) in the dam he had built to divert the flow of the queen's affections in his direction. The catastrophic bursting of this barrier is the beginning of the end, destroying the work of a lifetime in a moment. The angry royal stream turns its life-giving waters into other channels, leaving behind a scene of desolation:

Onn houre deverts, onn instant overthrowes
For which our liues, for which our fortunes thrale. . . .
. . . .
All is desolvde, our labors cume to nought,
Nor any marke therof ther douth indure;

No more then when small dropps of rayne do fall
Vppon the parched grounde by heat vp dried,
No coolinge moysture is perceude att all
Nor any shew or signe of weet douth byde.

                                          (ll. 231–32, 235–40)

The pastoral singing match in which these two water plaints are
exchanged is revealing not only for what it suggests about the fuller
historical truth behind the occasion (of which more shortly), but for
what it tells us about Spenser's poetic strategy, and particularly about
the crucial role played by language in Spenser's idea of himself as an
allegorist. The formal rhetorical definition of "allegory" as an extended or continued metaphor is of course long established. Cicero's
early formulation, interestingly enough, itself uses the metaphor of a
"stream" or stream-like flow to describe the phenomenon by which
allegory is sustained: "cum fluxerunt continuae plures tralationes, alia
plane fit oratio; itaque genus hoc Graeci appellant *allegorian*" ("When
there is a continuous stream of metaphors, a wholly different style of
speech is produced; consequently the Greeks call it . . . 'allegory'").[15]
The definition survives in Spenser's time in Puttenham's character-
ization (1589) of allegory as "a long and perpetuall Metaphore." The
fact that Puttenham also labels allegory "the Figure of false semblant"
or "dissimulation" may offer a new perspective on why an allegorist
might appropriately be named Bregog, or "deceitful."[16]
But while Ralegh gets high marks, in this sustained tale of what
he punningly calls his mind's "long deseas" or slow de-seaing (l.
421),[17] for the skillful deployment of a continued metaphor, the true
terms and extent of which have remained unrecognized in recent
comment, his real gift lies in the upper registers rather than the lower
registers inhabited by the true allegorist. Thus the juxtaposition of
the two tales becomes in effect something of a study in the difference
between the lyrical high road and the allegorical low road. Arriving
at the logical conclusion of his particular brand of high-flown water
language, Ralegh is almost literally left high and dry as the flow of
favor that gave life to his poetry dries up, until at last he "Writes in

the dust as onn that could no more" (l. 91). The full implication of
the curious identity between the "fallinge streame" of favor whose
diversion leaves the mill wheel "att stay" and the "fallinge streame"
of the poet's words is now apparent (ll. 84, 81, 363). To lose favor
is to lose voice, to subside from a flood into mere dust.

Just how far this sometimes voracious flood has fallen is underlined
by the language of a letter written at the height of Ralegh's influence
by Elizabeth herself to Hatton, her "Bell-wether." In it she reassures
the uneasy minister that "the beasts of the fields were so dear unto
her that she had bounded her banks so sure as no water or floods
could be able ever to overthrow them."[18] The witty expansion of
Elizabeth's nickname "Water" into "Ocean" suited both Ralegh's
ambitions, which were known to be boundless (the sea of Ecclesiastes, after all, is never "full"), and his style, which was both haughty
and "salt" in the Renaissance sense of stinging and pungent.[19] The
drying up of such a proud and essential body of water can only be
the result of a cataclysm in nature such as that produced by Phaeton's
disastrous flight in Ovid's *Metamorphoses*, where "et mare contrahitur
siccaeque est campus harenae,/quod modo pontus erat" ("even the
sea shrinks up, and what was but now a great, watery expanse is a
dry plain of sand"; II. 262–63).[20] Hence the effect of feverish incoherence and the sense of nature turned upside down and seasons out
of joint: we are witnessing the death throes of a mighty, almost
elemental force.

Spenser's Bregog, on the other hand, confronted with a dry spell
and with rocks hurled down by a vengeful mountain, simply goes
on about his business underground.[21] Unlike his rival the Allo or
Broadwater, whose Spenserian names suggest an impressively wide
but perhaps shallow (not to say self-important and superficial) body
of water where all is apparent at a glance — "broad" language is
open, blunt, and even vulgar talk (*OED* a. 6)—Bregog runs deep,
carefully hiding his "course" or discourse like a prudent courtier, or
perhaps more to the point, a good allegorist. In taking the low road,
the shrewd rural stream follows Colin's own pastoral strategy of using
a low posture as a safe vantage point. A stream flowing through
subterranean passages is a fitting metaphorical disguise for the voice
of a poet with a horror of both heaped up waters and heaped up
words. Not without reason does Colin's mock terror of the high
seas—"A world of waters heaped up on hie,/Rolling like mountaines
in wide wildernesse,/Horrible, hideous, roaring with hoarse crie"
(ll. 197–99) — recall Polyhymnia's distaste in "Teares of the Muses"
for "Heapes of huge words uphoorded hideously,/With horrid sound
though having little sence" (ll. 553–54).

Yet even as Spenser appears to be conceding the heights, he may be working beneath the surface of the tale to make a molehill out of a mountain. "Mole" is of course Spenser's invented name for the range of mountains overlooking Kilcolman, a name Renwick guessed to be "a back-formation from *Mulla*, perhaps with the Latin *moles* behind it."[22] The Latin *moles* may indeed be crucial to Spenser's meaning. In the dedicatory sonnet to Burghley belatedly added to the *Faerie Queene,* Spenser had discreetly played on Burghley's name—"burly" meant variously stately or imposing in appearance, massively built, or simply domineering (*OED* a. 1, 2, 3)—to characterize the minister as an Atlas-like mountain on whose shoulders the cares of state rested. A Latin *moles*, like an English "mole" (*OED* sb.[3]1, 2), is not only such a large, weighty mass, but specifically a "breakwater," a massive stone structure built out into the water to protect the inner harbor from waves, much as Elizabeth's minister shielded the queen from those who would trouble the political waters. In breaking Bregog's water, Mole is only doing his job.

If such veiled hints, which were of course much beloved of Elizabethan readers, managed to slip by, there were others. Mole's "watchfull ward" over his daughter (l. 136) could not but recall to such an audience Burghley's entrenched position as Master of the Court of Wards, as well as the belief in some quarters that he had amassed a huge fortune through such common practices as selling wards in marriage to the highest bidder, much as old father Mole attempts to do in disposing of his own daughter to the largest available stream.[23] Similarly, the tattling shepherd boy who reports Bregog's activities to the mountain would recall Burghley's reputation as the master of an extensive network of spies or "moles" groping in the dark for juicy political morsels (*OED* sb.[2]2).[24] In this context the later allusion to the nuzzling "Moldwarps nousling" at court (l. 763) may carry a special charge. The image of a squirming litter of baby moles eagerly nursing could suggest that Burghley/Mole nurtures a whole company of little recruits to espionage (perhaps even his own wards or nurslings), who suck blissfully away at their benefactor in a state of moral oblivion.

A further twist in the historical background of the dialogue of the two shepherd-poets seems to confirm that larger issues than the disappointment of a river in love are at stake. When Spenser dedicated "Colin Clout" to Ralegh in December 1591 he himself was back in Ireland under a cloud after a prudent retreat from London. His hasty return, it is now known from a contemporary letter, was almost certainly precipitated by the calling in by the authorities of "Mother Hubberds Tale," an allegorical beast fable published as part of his

Complaints shortly after the appearance of the *Faerie Queene* and containing material offensive to Burghley if not to the queen herself. As Sir Thomas Tresham puts it in the newly discovered letter of 19 March 1591, despite Spenser's success with the *Faerie Queene*, "nowe in medlinge with his apes tayle he is gott into Ireland, also in hazard to loose his forsayd annuall reward"—that is, his freshly awarded pension from the queen.[25]

This new tale of Bregog, I would suggest, uses the language of water to deliver a bold manifesto in the face of such censorship: no mountain can stop Bregog from flowing on and loving on, and by implication from writing on. Although Bregog's allegorical ways have apparently dried up his career and caused him to lose his good name, he will love on with fierce loyalty "so long/As water doth within his bancks appeare" (ll. 94–95). It is in this context that we can understand the strange note of defiance in Colin's later, parallel declaration that he will think and speak (and write) of his queen "So long as life my limbs doth hold together" (l. 629). So passionate is his assertion that it startles his audience with its intensity:

> Much was the whole assembly of those heards,
> Moov'd at his speech, so feelingly he spake:
> And stood awhile astonisht at his words. . . .
>
> (ll. 648–50)

The means of promulgation that Colin lists—inscriptions on trees, arrangements of stones, speaking trees, murmuring waters, baaing lambs, and (posthumously) singing shepherds' daughters (ll. 632–43)—quickly multiply beyond the ability of any censor to keep up, becoming a kind of rural underground press.

The tale of Bregog is thus written "Under the foote of *Mole*" (l. 57) in more than one sense. It is surely not unintentional that the phrase recalls the classic victor's stance with foot planted on the vanquished opponent. But while Burghley appears to be the victor, having in effect driven Spenser out of England over the affair of "Mother Hubberd," the double meaning suggests that in fact the poet has eluded the Mole-like "peer" by singing his song "Under the foote" — that is, by writing poetic feet in which the allegorical message is concealed under the apparent sense. To heighten the wit, Spenser hides his discourse in a tale about a river that stubbornly survives by hiding its course—a tale whose telling could nevertheless, Cuddy fears, "restraine" Colin's "readie course" (l. 82), that is, damage his career, perhaps by leading to further censorship.

The best proof of Spenser's success in writing under the foot has been the great reluctance of critics to identify the shifty Bregog with Spenser. Sam Meyer has suggested that the tale is simply the sad story of what happens when the hierarchy is breached, Thomas Edwards that Bregog shows "the impropriety of pursuing what's above your worth," Wyman Herendeen that the lovers provide a "narrative lesson" in the "attractive force of Concord." William Oram, Patrick Cheney, and others see in Bregog's disgrace a covert allusion to Ralegh's unwise marriage. Donald Cheney lets Bregog come closest to Spenser, although not the Spenser of 1591, by finding in the tale an image of the poet's own marriage of 1594 far from the queen's watchful gaze, achieved "at the cost of losing one's name." More recently, Sue Petitt Starke has firmly separated Spenser's fate from Bregog's, insisting that unlike the unfortunate river, the poet managed to avoid losing his identity.[26]

The real skill in writing under the foot lies in the ability to layer meaning so that continued metaphor can be read on deeper and deeper levels, reaching finally beyond self-interest into sacred philosophical and moral realms—something that Ralegh's wonderful poem, metaphorically ingenious as it is, fails to do.[27] In trying to reconstruct the kind of "allegory" contemporaries expected from or saw in Spenser, we might do worse than consult Sir John Harington, writing in the "Preface, or . . . Apologie" prefixed to his translation of Ariosto in 1591, apparently (since he elsewhere cites a passage) having read part or all of the first three books of the *Faerie Queene*. He calls special attention to the verbal skill by which ancient poets "wrapped as it were in their writing diuers and sundry meanings":

> First of all for the litterall sence (as it were the vtmost barke or ryne) they set downe in manner of an historie, the acts and notable exploits of some persons worthy memorie; then . . . as a second rine and somewhat more fine, as it were nearer to the pith and marrow, they place the Morall sence, profitable for the actiue life of man, approuing vertuous actions and condemning the contrarie. Manie times also vnder the selfesame words they comprehend some true vnderstanding of naturall Philosophie, or somtimes of politike gouernement, and now and then of diuinitie: and these same sences that comprehend so excellent knowledge we call the Allegorie. . . . Now let any man iudge if it be a matter of meane art or wit to containe in one historicall narration either true or fained, so many, so diuerse, and so deepe conceits. . . .

Harington goes on to explain that each of these levels has its own audience:

> For the weaker capacities will feed themselues with the pleasantnes of the historie and sweetnes of the verse, some that have stronger stomackes will as it were take a further taste of the Morall sence, [and] a third sort more high conceited then they, will digest the Allegorie. . . . [28]

This precise description of how allegory is expected to work in 1591 is the more worthy of our attention because it is closely echoed in the very next year by Abraham Fraunce, another writer with early and intimate knowledge of Spenser's work.[29] More important yet, we have Spenser's own testimony about his strategy. A clear outline of just such layering, I would submit, has already slid by us in Colin's account of how Bregog operates. The devious river divides its stream into a number of smaller streams, which it then "closely" conveys "under ground," so that "whilest the one was watcht, the other might/Passe unespide." Thus the wily river-author ensures that there will be "no token" of his most important "passage"—the one which allows him to slide into his beloved Mulla (ll. 139–44).

In intently watching Colin Clout, then, we may well be missing more than half the show. If on the first level Spenser has used the landscape of Kilcolman as the setting for a historical event lightly veiled in pastoral guise—Spenser's congenial meeting by the banks of the Mulla with his new patron Ralegh—we should be aware that we are observing an allegorist engaged in hiding his course or discourse further and further beneath this idyllic pastoral landscape. On a second level, Spenser offers what is now recognizable as an essentially Ovidian account of his dealings with a certain mighty figure in Elizabeth's court—and not incidentally demonstrates, both on this and on a third, yet deeper, more properly "allegorical" level, that he can sing whatever he pleases undetected "Under the foote," or as Harington suggests, correctly stressing the importance of multivalent language to the success of allegory, "vnder the selfesame words."

In the first two books of the *Faerie Queene* Spenser offers two versions of Ovidian transformation in the opposed plights of the sluggish nymph of Book I, who sits down in the middle of the race and is transformed into a sluggish spring as a punishment, and the cold nymph of Book II, who is changed into an equally cold and pure spring in answer to her prayer to Diana for protection from the advances of Faunus. In the tale of Bregog, we find just such a pairing of transformations for punishment and protection. In turning Burghley into a mountain, Spenser is simply spinning out the less complimentary implications of his outwardly flattering dedicatory sonnet to Burghley, in which he compared this mainstay of the English state to Atlas, portraying him as one

> . . . on whose mightie shoulders most doth rest
> The burdein of this kingdomes gouernement,
> As the wide compasse of the firmament,
> On *Atlas* mighty shoulders is vpstayd. . . .
>
> (Ded. Son. ii, ll. 3–6)

The repetition of "mightie shoulders"/ "mighty shoulders" underlines not only Burghley's weighty responsibilities but his sheer bulk—an emphasis possibly not entirely welcome to the recipient. "Burly" could suggest not only imposing but corpulent, large of body or trunk, or simply puffed up (*OED* a. 2, v. obs.[1]). In the Ovidian text that stands obliquely behind both the sonnet and the portrait of Mole (*Met.* IV.627–62), Atlas is presented as a figure "hominum cunctos ingenti corpore praestans" ("far surpassing all men in huge bulk of body"; l. 631). The looming Atlas is equally imposing in his wealth; in addition to holding vast flocks and herds, he is the nervous guardian of a golden tree bearing golden apples. This was an eminently suitable incarnation for Burghley, who as Lord Treasurer of England controlled the queen's largesse. Even more appropriately, Ovid's Atlas is turned into a mountain as a punishment for his inhospitable and stony-hearted treatment of Perseus, who has come as a visitor to his shores—a configuration of events that recalls Spenser/ Colin's visit to England in the poem.

Worried that Perseus is after his golden apples (although his guest in fact only wants to rest for the night before pursuing his journey), the physically imposing Atlas decides to push his visitor out of his kingdom. The "mightie shoulders" of the dedicatory sonnet may reappear in a subtle reenactment of this expulsion in "Colin Clout," where "gentle wit" finds itself forcibly "shouldred" out of court:

> Ne is there place for any gentle wit,
> Unlesse to please, it selfe it can applie:
> But shouldred is, or out of doore quite shit,

As base, or blunt, unmeet for melodie.

(ll. 707–10)

In Ovid's story the weaker Perseus saves himself by showing his host the head of Medusa, much perhaps as Spenser had shown Burghley the disturbing embrace of Amoret and Scudamore at the end of Book III of the 1590 *Faerie Queene*. At the sight of Medusa's head, Atlas is immediately turned to stone: "quantus erat, mons factus Atlas . . . ossa lapis fiunt" ("Straightway Atlas became a mountain huge . . . and his bones were changed to stones"; ll. 657, 660).

Although there is of course no comparable moment of transformation in Spenser's tale, there is some wonderful play with the Ovidian conventions for such occasions. The transformed mountain sheds not drops of water, like the perspiring and weeping nymphs of the *Faerie Queene*, but the boulders appropriate to his new form. The fact that these are called "mightie stones" (l. 150) suggests all over again that these are fragments of the "mightie" figure of the dedicatory sonnet, and perhaps even more specifically fragments dislodged by the frowning contractions of the "rugged forhead" of the opening lines of Book IV (1596). "Rugged" meant not only frowning but full of stones and rocks, austere or harsh, or even lacking in culture or refinement (*OED* a.¹3a-b, 2b, 6, 7). It is perhaps no accident that this burly brow looming over the text in a state of displeasure over the memory of the lovers' embrace at the end of the 1590 Book III (now of course erased in the 1596 edition) is reminiscent of the rock-hurling Mole looming censoriously over Bregog's invisible slide into Mulla. As in Ovid, the punishment is made to fit the crime. Through the transformation the very essence of Burghley's character as Spenser sees it, his cold and stony imperviousness to the melting feelings of love, is made manifest, just as the so-called "virtues" of the two nymphs are exposed in their respective transformations to sluggish and chilly waters.

Spenser's Ovidian act of turning the mountain-like Burghley into Mole and himself into a river that goes underground to escape Mole's persecutions is a complicated piece of wit which turns the ostensible reading of the tale upside down. A tale of the punishment of a river becomes the story of the punishment of a mountain; a tale of how a river's career was impeded becomes the story of how a river's career was inadvertently made stronger and more enduring. Bregog is by nature a river that likes to operate under the surface. By burying him further, Mole has only enhanced a strategy which has already proved successful. (Bregog had, after all, already slid into Mulla's waters before he was caught.) The implication is that Burghley—and Spenser's exile—has simply thrown the poet into the briar patch.

Yet it is the violent nature of Bregog's punishment, focusing our attention as it does on Mole's cruelty, which catches the eye, as no doubt Spenser intended it should. By transforming himself into a river to elude Mole, Spenser has already aligned himself with virtuous Ovidian nymphs who deserve protection rather than with those Ovidian figures whose transformation, like that of the stony-hearted Atlas, constitutes a punishment that fits the crime. The particular form of Bregog's intended punishment—death by stoning—has further implications both for Bregog's true nature and for the true nature of his so-called crime or "deceit" as we are meant to understand it.

In Renaissance iconography, to be stoned was to be either a martyred saint or a rebellious giant—a connection thrown into interesting relief by the fact that Giulio Romano's painting of the stoning of St. Stephen (ca. 1523) served as something of a preliminary study for the magnificent frescoes of his Sala dei Giganti at Mantua ten years or so later, with their powerful rendering of the moment at which the giants are buried beneath the stony ruins of their impious attempt to scale Jove's heavens.[30] To Mole, "sitting still on hie" like Jove (l. 132) in order to spy out and repel the social-climbing advances of an upstart river who hopes to marry above himself, Bregog's sin, like that of the giants, is one of sheer hubris. From Mole's lofty perspective, the sin is not only social but political. The giants' storming of Olympus, like the comparable rebellion of the Titans, which was often elided with the giants' act, was seen at this moment of history as emblematic of an intolerable challenge to established authority.[31]

The motif could, however, have something of a double edge. The Titans, unlike the more clearly wicked giants, have a point about Jove's usurpation of his powers, as Mutabilitie suggests in Book VII of the *Faerie Queene*. "Mother Hubberds Tale," the work that angered Burghley and led to the calling in of Spenser's *Complaints*, was in fact a veiled accusation that Elizabeth's minister was usurping royal powers, presented under the story of a fox and an ape who steal the crown, scepter, and even the skin of a sleeping lion. In casting Bregog as a rebel against Jove, Mole thus runs the risk of casting himself as a usurper if not a tyrant—an image that Spenser reinforces by the brutality of the treatment he has Mole mete out to Bregog. Mole's anxiety is not simply the comical anxiety of the tyrannous stage father but the more dangerous anxiety of the insecure despot who sees climbing rebels even in rivers that deliberately lower themselves and thieves under every riverbed. From Spenser's point of view, as we shall see, Bregog is most certainly not a sinner but a saint—a pursuer of virtue and a martyr in the cause of virtuous love.

The fact that Bregog has been compared to Alpheus only lightly and in passing[32] testifies to how well the identity of the poet as not simply the pastoral Colin but the wily Bregog and finally the sacred Alpheus has been hidden. Spenser has promised us a tale that was neither new lies nor old wives' tales but "auncient truth confirm'd with credence old" (l. 103). In using such language he closely echoes the formulation of Natalis Comes at the opening of his *Mythologia* (1567), where Comes describes how the sacred precepts of philosophy, imported from Egypt to Greece in the dress of fables, were misunderstood by the vulgar and finally dismissed as the tales of old women and lying poets:

> Deinde cum sequentibus temporibus res fuisset denudata . . .
> pauci fabulas, antiquum philosophiae domicilium, vt ita dicam,
> respexerunt: easque modo uanam theologiam stultorum homi-
> num, modo aniles nugas, futiliaque mendacium poetarum fig-
> menta fuisse crediderunt.

> (Thereafter when in later times these things were exposed . . .
> few [men] respected fables, the ancient home of philosophy, so
> to speak: and they believed them to be now the vain theology
> of foolish men, now tales of old women and worthless figments
> of lying poets).[33]

On the deepest level of the fable of Bregog, Spenser keeps his promise to give us ancient truth well tested by time and not coincidentally keeps his secret rendezvous with virtue. Although the tale of Alpheus is rendered vividly by Ovid in his *Metamorphoses* (V. 572–641), its origins and its meanings are far more ancient. Like the story of Bregog, the fable of Alpheus is on its plainest level an etiological tale which attempts to account for the strange behavior of a river—in the case of Alpheus, its curious habit of disappearing beneath ground, until finally it travels under the surface of the sea to emerge intact in the fountain of Arethusa on the island of Ortygia, or Sicily.

In his *Description of Greece* the traveler Pausanias (flor. AD 150) notes the river's amazing achievement: "Not even the Adriatic [can] check its flowing onwards, but passing through . . . so large and stormy a sea, it shows in Ortygia, before Syracuse, that it is the

Alpheius, and unites its water with Arethusa" (VIII.liv.3). Anticipat-
ing disbelief, Pausanias offers no less an authority than the Delphic
oracle:

> But that the Alpheius passes through the sea and mingles his
> waters with the spring at this place I cannot disbelieve, as I
> know that the god at Delphi confirms the story. For . . . he
> uttered this oracle:
>
> > An isle, Ortygia, lies on the misty ocean
> > Over against Trinacria, where the mouth of Alpheius
> > bubbles
> > Mingling with the springs of broad Arethusa.
>
> For this reason, therefore, because the water of the Alpheius
> mingles with the Arethusa, I am convinced that the legend arose
> of the river's love-affair.
>
> > > > > > > > > > (V.vii.3)[34]

In Alpheus's feat (as in Bregog's) the role of love is crucial, as Moschus
had suggested some three centuries earlier: "So it is that the spell of
that . . . sly and crafty teacher of troubles, Love, hath e'en taught a
river how to dive" (vi, ll. 7– 8).[35]

The specific aspect of this strange natural phenomenon which so
interested the ancients was the miraculous ability of Alpheus to keep
its identity and its name while passing through the tumultuous ocean.
Moschus notes not only its integrity but its secrecy: Alpheus "so
runneth [his course] that the two waters mingle not and the sea never
knows of the river's passing through" (ll. 4–6). The later Ammianus
Marcellinus (AD 330–95), praising the way in which the river Rhine
keeps itself intact in passing through Lake Constance, cites Alpheus
as the supreme example of such integrity:

> Hanc ergo paludem spumosis strependo verticibus amnis irrum-
> pens, et undarum quietem permeans pigram, mediam velut finali
> intersecat libramento, et tamquam elementum perenni discordia
> separatum, nec aucto nec imminuto agmine quod intulit, voca-
> bulo et viribus absolvitur integris. . . . quod, ni ita agi ipse doc-
> eret aspectus, nulla vi credebatur posse discerni. Sic Alpheus
> oriens in Arcadia, cupidine fontis Arethusae captus, scindens

Ionium mare, ut fabulae ferunt, ad usque amatae confinia pro-
ruit nymphae.

(Into this pool [Lake Constance], then, the river [Rhine] bursts
roaring with frothing eddies, and cleaving the sluggish quiet of
the waters, cuts through its midst as if with a boundary line.
And as if the element were divided by an everlasting discord,
without increasing or diminishing the volume which it carried
in, it emerges with name and force unchanged. . . . if one's very
sight did not prove it to be so, one would not believe it possible
for [the two waters] to be kept apart by any power. In the same
way the river Alpheus, rising in Arcadia and falling in love with
the fountain Arethusa, cleaves the Ionian Sea, as the myth tells
us, and hastens to the retreat of the beloved nymph.)[36]

Such natural hydraulic wonders came even more directly into
Spenser's life in the form of a passage from Jerome Turler's *The
Traveiler* (1575), a travel guide to Italy which Spenser presented to
his friend Gabriel Harvey in 1578. Harvey read and annotated the
book, giving us a glimpse into his private interests and perhaps those
of the friend who gave the gift. Book II, chapter 9 treats of "A Well
or Fowntaine in the Sea": "Ther ariseth out of the Sea a passing
running cleere, and sweet fowntayne of fresh water. . . . I suppose
the causes thereof are certen secret passages under the ground, which
conueie the water thyther from the shoare adioining, where it
breaketh foorth. . . . It yeeldeth foorth water so abundantly, that a
man may discerne the streame thereof a great way runninge along,
from the sea water. . . . "[37]
In the passage Harvey has underlined two phrases: "certen secret"
(in the phrase "certen secret passages") and "shoare adioining."
Whether or not the two friends had talked about the implications of
the behavior of this stream, Harvey's underlinings should lead us to
an important point. For anyone learned in ancient lore, the way in
which "certen secret passages" got Spenser from the "shoare adioining" to an island in the middle of the sea—the way in which Spenser's
allegorical writings got him to Ireland—made this tale of Alpheus a
perfect emblem of his career not only topographically but on a truly
"allegorical" third level which comprehends, in Harington's words,
"some true vnderstanding of naturall Philosophie . . . and now and
then of diuinitie."
The tale of Alpheus has always been especially fertile ground for
fable, Comes notes in Book VIII, chapter 21 of his *Mythologia*. In

explicating the story of Alpheus and Arethusa, he pauses to remind his readers that

> ... antique sub fabularum integumentis naturae arcane occultarunt, quodque per has ambages verborum naturam & vires elementorum ac rerum omnium explicabant, quae illis tantum errant manifesta, qui facti essent horum mysteriorum participes.

> (... the ancients hid the secrets of nature under the skin of fables, and through these obscure windings of words they explained the nature and force of the elements and all things, which were openly manifest to those who had been made participants in these mysteries.)

For some, Comes says, Alpheus stands for cleanness of both soul and body; hence the tradition of using only his sacred waters in certain ceremonies. Others, he continues, have seen in the fable the imperfect soul in pursuit of virtue: "Haec causa est cur Alpheus fingebatur sequi Arethusam, cum Alphos macula ut dictum est, sive imperfectio, & Arete virtus a Graecis nominetur" ("This is the reason why Alpheus is feigned to follow Arethusa, since Alpheo is made spotted, as it is said, and virtue is called Arete by the Greeks").[38]

In his gloss of the tale, Fulgentius (AD 467–532) combines the motifs of the stream that keeps itself pure and the flight after virtue, adding a copulation of river and fountain which recalls Bregog's slide into Mulla. More important still, Fulgentius's interpretation suggests the way in which this ostensibly shocking union should be read. To arrive whole and still sweetly fresh in Arethusa's embrace is to have successfully avoided contamination by the salty evil of the courtly world through which the Elizabethan poet in search of patronage must pass:

> When passing through the midst of the sea, [Alpheus] retains its freshness as it plunges into [Arethusa's] hollow. . . . For Alpheus is for the Greek aletiasfos, that is, the light of truth; while Arethusa is for areteisa, that is, equality of excellence. For what can the truth love but equity, or the light, but excellence? And it retains its freshness when passing through the sea because clear truth cannot by any mingling be polluted by the surrounding saltiness of evil ways.[39]

In his 1632 translation of Ovid's *Metamorphoses*, George Sandys made both the Ovidian text and this reading of the tale available to a wider English audience after Spenser's death. In his gloss, Sandys combines the readings of Comes and Fulgentius:

> By this fable . . . the ancients expressed the divine affection of the soule, and excellency of virtue. For as the matter seeks after her forme, as her proper and only good . . . even so is vertue pursued by the Soule. *Alpheus* which signifies blots or imperfections, is therefore said to follow *Arethusa*, which is by interpretation Virtue. But *Fulgentius* more fully, that *Alpheus* is the light of Truth, and *Arethusa* the excellency of equity, and what can truth more affect then equity; or light then excellency? *Alpheus* runs unmixt through the sea: because illustrious truth, although invironed with vices, can never be disseasoned with their bitternesse, but unpolluted falls into the bosome of *Arethusa*, or noble integrity.[40]

In Alpheus, then, Spenser may have found the perfect emblem for the career of an allegorical poet—one, moreover, which to all appearances remained essentially undeciphered in the years after his death. In reading the fable of Bregog on this most intimate and sacred level we may perhaps more clearly understand Spenser's own version of his exile. In leaving the English court he was by choice pursuing virtue to Ireland, almost miraculously preserving the integrity of his sweet waters while passing through both the physical ocean and the salty vices of the court he leaves behind. That Spenser could hide a tale about his own career so openly in a tale about a river that hides its course, combining the most sacred matter with a bold challenge to a powerful statesman, is testimony not only to his control of the subliminal depths of language but to his still largely unplumbed depths of wit and humor. In putting together the tale of Bregog, Spenser is clearly enjoying himself immensely. Our proper reaction is figured in the unexpected response of the shepherd Thestylis to Bregog's tragic story: "Now by my life this was a mery lay" (l. 157). Such a response deliberately directs us back to the moment at the start of the poem when two shepherds mysteriously, and no doubt irreverently, made each other "mery" (l. 77). If Thestylis's enigmatic observation that "Most wretched he that is and cannot tell" is true (l. 659), Spenser and Ralegh are clearly not among the wretched.

In 1589, when the two shepherds sang together, one had perhaps been "chased . . . from the Court" and "confined . . . into Ireland" temporarily by Essex, as a court gossip reported. By December 1591, the ostensible date of "Colin Clout," the other had most certainly "gott into Ireland," as Tresham puts it, more or less for good by angering Burghley and perhaps even the queen with a transparent fable of a fox, an ape, and a negligent lion. By 1595, when "Colin Clout" was finally published, Ralegh had both suffered the major disgrace of his marriage in 1592 and recovered his fortunes somewhat by his 1595 exploration of the Orinoco River. If Colin's tribute in the poem (presumably reflecting the situation in 1595) is not just wishful thinking, the Shepherd of the Ocean may have owed this recovery not only to the Orinoco but at least in part to the power of his "lamentable lay": "Full sweetly tempred is that *Muse* of his/ That can empierce a Princes mightie hart" (ll. 430–31). A wry contrast between a penetrable "mightie hart" and stony and unyielding "mightie shoulders" may lurk here.

The exchange of song between the two, then, is not confined to one occasion, or even one meeting, as Spenser seems to suggest when he ingenuously asserts in the dedication that "Colin Clout" is a *"simple pastoral . . . agreeing with the truth in circumstance and matter."* There is, as we have seen, nothing *"simple"* about the occasion of Spenser's pastoral, which stretches from the meeting of 1589 and an eventful visit of over a year in England to a declared composition date of December 1591 (back in Ireland) to intervening revision and a publication date of 1595. Thus the period of time encapsulated in "Colin Clout" extends over vicissitudes in both careers that might explain the strong bond the two seem to feel. It is perhaps worth noting that the happy scene by the Mulla is one of the few in Spenser's work in which the Blatant Beast is clearly absent: "Neither envying other, nor envied,/So piped we" (ll. 78–79).

In the context of Ralegh's known affinity for companion poems, it appears that he has found an ideal singing partner. In this ongoing dialogue or counterpoint of song it seems clear that on one level the two poets are conversing eloquently about the ups and downs of their careers and fortunes, perfectly in tune with Sidney's description of pastoral. Trading tales, Meliboeus-like, of life "vnder hard Lords" (a plight that Spenser almost literally exemplifies in Colin's account of plying his trade "Under the foote" of stony and vengeful Mole), the two poets skillfully hide these stories "vnder the prettie tales of Wolues and Sheepe," which "sometimes . . . can include the whole considerations of wrong dooing and patience."[41] On another level, the songs are about differing ideas about love, its power and its nature. The passion of Ralegh's Ocean, as stirring as it is, is finally no match for the depth, resourcefulness, and determination of love displayed by Spenser's Bregog–Alpheus.[42]

Spenser never again wrote quite as transparently as he had in "Mother Hubberd"—though King James might beg to differ. In place of the Aesopian animal fable, a populist form in which the message under the tale is meant to be widely understood, he turned even more fully, as was his inclination from the very start, to the more elitist form of allegory, with its pedigree extending back to ancient *fabulae* that hid philosophical, moral, and natural truths for the worthy few under their skins. In short, he went underground, escaping the forces of censorship by tunneling ever deeper under the foot. The results are always profound and often merry as well. Spenser's tongue was no doubt firmly in his cheek when in the dedication to "Colin Clout" he urged Ralegh—himself the author of the deceptively "simpell wordes" of "Ocean"—to protect him from those whose mouths are *alwaies wide open to carpe at and misconstrue my simple meaning.* It seems likely that only a select few penetrated the pastoral veil, and that those who did enjoyed the tale in discreet silence, until finally their numbers dwindled and Bregog's secret languished.

Yet it may not be entirely true that Spenser's deeper meaning remained undeciphered in the years after his death. In Phineas Fletcher's *Purple Island* (1633), that inveterate Spenserian launches a heartfelt attack on Lord Burghley which ends with Spenser's own words from the "Ruines of Time." Addressing the dead Colin, Fletcher mourns his fate in terms which may glance at the towering Atlas figure of Spenser's dedicatory sonnet and possibly even the looming shape of a mountain called Mole, a fatherly shape turned to stone by his own lack of generosity. Appropriately enough, Fletcher comforts Colin by predicting that the dead Burghley, entombed in a mountain, will sink like a rock:

> Yet shalt thou live, when thy great foe shall sink
> Beneath his mountain tombe, whose fame shall stink;
> And time his blacker name shall blurre with blackest ink.
> . . . . . .
> Let thy abused honour crie as long
> As there be quills to write, or eyes to reade:
> On his rank name let thine own votes be turn'd,
> *Oh may that man that hath the Muses scorn'd,*
> *Alive, nor dead, be ever of a Muse adorn'd!*

(I, sts. 20, 21)[43]

Fletcher's hatred of Burghley was spurred not only by the minister's shabby treatment of Spenser but (among other family slights) by Burghley's censorship of Fletcher's own father, Giles Fletcher the Elder (1549–1610/11), Spenser's contemporary and a fellow Cantabrigian, sometime ambassador to Russia. In 1591, the very same year in which Spenser's *Complaints* was called in, Giles Fletcher had published an eight-volume account of the government of Russia, far from flattering to that state, dedicated to the queen herself. The work was quickly suppressed by Burghley at the request of merchants worried about its effect on trade. An earlier project proposed by Giles, a history of the reign of Queen Elizabeth in Latin, also died at the hands of Burghley.[44]

There may be an even more piquant example of later ability to read "under" fellow writers. Spenser's influence on Milton, fruitfully explored in many books and articles, may take an especially interesting turn in Milton's "Lycidas." Offering an invocation to the fountain of Arethusa followed by an extended and passionate Spenserian denunciation of bad priests placed in the mouth of St. Peter, Milton breaks off to begin anew with an odd summons: "Return *Alpheus*, the dread voice is past,/That shrunk thy streams" (ll. 132–33).[45] There is, however, no legend that Alpheus's waters were ever diminished, either by a dread voice or by any other means. This happens only in Spenser's fable of Bregog, with its account of Mole's attempt to "spill" the "course" of the river that refused to abandon its fierce love for Mulla. "Dread" is moreover a quintessentially Spenserian word for the great; Elizabeth was his "dearest dred" (*FQ* I. Pr. 4.9), Burghley no doubt simply his "dred." It is possible that in Milton's words we have evidence that Bregog's disguise and Spenser's condemnation of a powerful censor had been penetrated by another fellow poet—and not just any poet, but one who, as David Norbrook has recently pointed out, was already in "Lycidas" covertly confronting Laud's censorship and the issues he himself would later address openly in the *Areopagitica*.[46]

As for the friendship of Spenser and Ralegh, there are ample signs that it was alive and well in 1596. In addition to the more open support of Ralegh's case presented by Spenser in the sad story of Timias's unjust sufferings at the hands of Belphoebe (another example of allegory's second layer, available to "stronger stomackes" able to taste the "Morrall sence," as Harington puts it), Spenser seems to have left behind a subtler tribute for digestion by the third group, the "more high conceited." In the midst of the river procession of Book IV (xi.21), we encounter the "Rich Oranochy," standing in for its recent discoverer Ralegh, marching along companionably in the same stanza with a triumphant "Alpheus still immaculate."

Yale University

NOTES

1. "A Discourse Concerning Edmund Spencer," B.L. MS Harleian 4153, written sometime before 1643. Quoted from *Spenser Allusions in the Sixteenth and Seventeenth Centuries,* ed. William Wells (Chapel Hill: University of North Carolina Press, 1972), 213. I have normalized "with" and "that."

2. The texts of Spenser's shorter poems are quoted from *The Yale Edition of the Shorter Poems of Edmund Spenser,* ed. William A. Oram et al. (New Haven and London: Yale University Press, 1989). The text of *The Faerie Queene* is quoted below from *Spenser: Poetical Works,* ed. J. C. Smith and E. de Selincourt (Oxford and New York: Oxford University Press, 1912).

3. See Annabel Patterson, *Censorship and Interpretation: The Conditions of Writing and Reading in Early Modern England* (Madison: University of Wisconsin Press, 1984), esp. 18–19 and chaps.1 and 2. On the Aesopian fable as a political genre, see further her *Fables of Power: Aesopian Writing and Political History* (Durham, NC: Duke University Press, 1991).

4. On the meeting and later relationship between Ralegh and Spenser see Katherine Koller, "Spenser and Ralegh," *ELH* 1 (1934): 37–60; James P. Bednarz, "Ralegh in Spenser's Historical Allegory," *Spenser Studies* 4 (1984): 46–69; and William A. Oram, "Elizabethan Fact and Spenserian Fiction," *Spenser Studies* 4 (1984): 33–47, and "Spenser's Raleghs," *SP* 87 (1990): 341–62. A symposium of four views on Spenser and Ralegh appeared in volume 15 of *Spenser Studies* (2001): William A. Oram, "What Did Spenser Really Think of Sir Walter Ralegh When He Published the First Installment of *The Faerie Queene*?," 165–74; Wayne Erickson, "Spenser Reads Ralegh's Poetry in(to) the 1590 *Faerie Queene,*" 175–84; Jerome S. Dees, "Colin Clout and The Shepherd of the Ocean," 185–96; and Michael Rudick, "Three Views on Ralegh and Spenser: A Comment," 197–203.

5. In a letter of 27 December 1589 to his cousin Sir George Carew, Ralegh declares, "For my retrait from the Court it was uppon good cause[,] to take order for my prize. If in Irlande they thincke that I am not worth the respectinge they shall mich deceave them sealvs" (quoted from the original at Lambeth Palace Library by Edward Edwards, *The Life of Sir Walter Ralegh,* 2 vols. [London, 1868], II: 41–42). Although "prize" could refer to naval booty, Ralegh may be using it "as a euphemism for his Irish seignory" (see Agnes Latham and Joyce Youings, eds., *The Letters of Sir Walter Ralegh* [Exeter: University of Exeter Press, 1999], 50–51, 379). Sir Francis Allen in a letter of August 1589 to Anthony Bacon offers a very different view of Ralegh's visit: "My Lord of Essex hath chased Mr. Ralegh from the Court, and hath confined him into Ireland" (quoted from the original at Lambeth by Edwards, I:119; see also J. H. Adamson and H. F. Folland, *The Shepherd of the Ocean* [Boston, MA: Gambit, 1969], 169).

6. The idea that a common vocabulary is at work here is supported by Donald Cheney's suggestion, in a rather different context, that "Colin's exchange of songs with the Shepherd of the Ocean provides a pair of contrasting myths which express erotic quests in watery terms" ("Spenser's Fortieth Birthday and Related Fictions," *Spenser Studies* 4 [1984]: 17).

7. The shared use of cross-rhymed quatrains, a favorite form for Ralegh, is noted by Koller: "Spenser was undoubtedly paying Ralegh a compliment in selecting this particular form and metre" ("Spenser and Ralegh," 45).

8. Although pipes are sometimes inherited, given as gifts, or won as prizes in the pastoral tradition, I have found no instance where a single pipe is shared in a singing match.

9. For a summary of the debate on the dating of the "lamentable lay" and a discussion of post-1591 revisions in "Colin Clout," see Sam Meyer, *An Interpretation of Edmund Spenser's* "Colin Clout" (Notre Dame, IN: Notre Dame University Press, 1969), 150–53. Pointing to the presence of increased enjambment (a characteristic of Spenser's later verse), Robert Ellrodt suggests that both the tale of Bregog and Colin's praise of love (ll. 835–94) may be later additions (*Neoplatonism in the Poetry of Spenser* [Geneva: Droz, 1960], 219–23).

10. On Elizabeth's nickname for Ralegh, see, e.g., Walter Oakeshott, *The Queen and the Poet* (New York: Barnes & Noble, 1961), 26. In Essex's poem "Muses no more but mazes be your names," he plays with his enemy's nickname, declaring that "filthy water makes unholsome broth"; of the queen's fondness for Ralegh, he exclaims, "But oh, no more, it is to much to thinke,/So pure a mouth should puddle water drinke" (quoted from Folger Library MS V.a.339, fol. 185 by Steven May, *The Elizabethan Courtier Poets: The Poems and Their Contexts* [Columbia: University of Missouri Press, 1991], 251).

11. Critics stressing the erratic nature of the poem's imagery include Philip Edwards, *Sir Walter Raleigh* (London: Longmans, Green, 1953), 96–126; Joyce Horner, "The Large Landscape: A Study of Certain Images in Ralegh," *EIC* 5.3 (July 1955): 197–213; Donald Davie, "A Reading of the Ocean's Love to Cynthia," in *Elizabethan Poetry* (New York: St. Martin's Press, 1960), 71–89; and Michael L. Johnson, "Some Problems of Unity in Sir Walter Ralegh's *The Ocean's Love to Cynthia*," *SEL* 14 (1974): 17–30. On the inadequacy of language, see Robert L. Stillman, "'Words cannot knytt': Language and Desire in Ralegh's *The Ocean to Cynthia*," *SEL* 27 (1987): 35–51; and Marion Campbell, "Inscribing Perfection: Sir Walter Ralegh and the Elizabethan Court," *ELR* 20 (1990): 233–53. For a recent view of such "form(lessness)" as politically strategic, see Anna Beer, "'Knowing shee cann renew': Sir Walter Ralegh in Praise of the Virgin Queen," *Criticism* 34.4 (Fall 1992): 497–515.

12. Quoted from the King James version. On the view that the rivers feed the sea, returning to their sources by an underground path, see, e.g., Aristotle, *Meteorologica* II.2 (354b); Seneca, *Quaestiones Naturales* III.iv–v; Pliny, *Natural History* II.lxvi.166; see also Lucretius, *De Rerum Natura* VI.608–38. A useful though somewhat disorganized gathering of classical, medieval, and Renaissance sources on this theory of the "reversed hydrologic cycle" is found in Yi-Fu Tuan, *The Hydrologic Cycle and the Wisdom of God: A Theme in Geoteleology* (Toronto: University of Toronto Press, 1968).

13. Ralegh's text is quoted from *The Poems of Sir Walter Ralegh*, ed. Agnes M. C. Latham (Cambridge, MA: Harvard University Press, 1951). See also the text and commentary of Michael Rudick, ed., *The Poems of Sir Walter Ralegh: A Historical Edition* (Tempe, AZ: Arizona Center for Medieval and Renaissance Studies and Renaissance English Text Society, 1999). The intriguing controversy over Ralegh's calligraphy (do we have the 11th and 12th books or the 21st and 22nd?) is not relevant here.

14. Cf. Ralegh's later use of the metaphor of a "falling stream" to describe a faltering career in his *History* (I.ii.5): "For this tide of man's life, after it once turneth and declineth, ever runneth with a perpetual ebb and falling stream, but never floweth again" (*The Works of Sir Walter Ralegh*, 8 vols. [Oxford, 1829], II: 60–61).

15. *Orator* xxvii.94; text and translation are quoted from the Loeb edition, tr. H. M. Hubbell (Cambridge, MA, and London: Harvard University Press and Heinemann, 1971); cf. Quintilian, *Institutio Oratoria* VIII.vi.44.

16. Puttenham is quoted from the facsimile reprint of Edward Arber's 1906 edition of *The Arte of English Poesie*, intro. Baxter Hathaway (Kent, OH: Kent State University Press, 1970), 196–97 (Bk. III, chap. xviii). See also *Institutio Oratoria* VIII.vi.57, where Quintilian emphasizes the ironic or other-saying powers of allegory: "Praeter haec usus est allegoriae, ut tristia dicamus mollioribus verbis urbanitatis gratia" ("Further, we may employ *allegory*, and disguise bitter taunts in gentle words by way of wit"). Quoted from the Loeb edition, tr. H. H. Butler, 4 vols. (London and New York: Heinemann and Putnam, 1921), III:333.

17. Rudick notes that "Oakeshott read this as 'disease,' Hannah as 'decease'" (*Poems of Sir Walter Ralegh*, 163). But the true nature of the pun is cleverer yet, suggesting not simply a long discomfort or sickness ("dis-ease" or "disease") or a prolonged dying ("decease") but, more specifically, a painful demotion from sea to arid desert ("de-seas").

18. Quoted by Oakeshott, *The Queen and the Poet*, 26.

19. On this sense of "salt" see *OED*, a¹5. Ralegh's choice of the Ocean as his persona is a characteristic piece of hubris. Most courtiers and poets saw themselves, more modestly, as rivers paying tribute to a royal sea. Cf. Spenser's compliment to the queen: "So from the Ocean all riuers spring,/And tribute backe repay as to their King./Right so from you all goodly vertues well/Into the rest, which round about you ring" (*FQ* VI, Pr. 7, ll. 4–7). Perhaps significantly, in urging the queen's support of Ralegh's venture in his poem "De Guiana" (1596), George Chapman adopts Ralegh's own metaphor: "Nor was there euer princelie Fount so long/Powr'd foorth a sea of Rule with so free course,/And such ascending Maiestie as you"; the queen, he goes on to say, should be "as a riuer from a mountaine running," increasing its empire as it goes (ll. 49–51, 56ff.; quoted from *The Poems of George Chapman,* ed. Phyllis Brooks Bartlett [1941; reprt. New York: Russell and Russell, 1962], 354).

20. The text and translation of the *Metamorphoses* are quoted here and below from the Loeb edition, tr. Frank Justus Miller, 3rd edn., rev. G. P. Goold, 2 vols. (Cambridge, MA, and London: Harvard University Press and Heinemann, 1977).

21. Spenser could not have been unaware of the contrast the determined and resourceful Bregog presented to Ovid's response to censorship, disgrace, and exile as described in *Ex Ponto* IV.ii.17–20: "ut limus venas excaecat inundans,/laesaque

suppresso fonte resistit aqua,/pectora sic mea sunt limo vitiata malorum,/et carmen vena pauperiore fluit" ("just as clogging silt jams channels and the outraged water halts in the choked fountain, so my mind has been injured by the silt of misfortune, and my verse flows with a scantier vein"). Text and translation are quoted from the Loeb edition, tr. Arthur Leslie Wheeler, 2nd edn., rev. G. P. Goold (Cambridge, and London: Harvard University Press and Heinemann, 1988).

22.   *Daphnaida and Other Poems*, ed. W. L. Renwick (London: Scholartis, 1929), 183. For a Latin use of *moles* as "breakwater," see Ovid, *Met.* XI.728–30.

23.   On Burghley and the Court of Wards, see Joel Hurstfield, *The Queen's Wards: Wardship and Marriage under Elizabeth I* (London: Cass, 1958), 181– 296. Conyers Read comments, "Upon the thorny question of Burghley's profits from the office, though commonly regarded by his contemporaries as the chief source of his wealth, the evidence is too scanty to justify any positive estimate" (*Lord Burghley and Queen Elizabeth* [New York: Knopf, 1961], 10). A more recent account of Burghley and his wardships is found in Mary Thomas Crane, *Framing Authority: Saying, Self, and Society in Sixteenth-Century England* (Princeton: Princeton University Press, 1993), 116–35.

24.   On Burghley as "the founding father of Elizabethan espionage," see Alan Haynes, *Invisible Power: The Elizabethan Secret Services, 1570–1603* (New York: St. Martin's, 1992), 16 and *passim*.

25.   See Richard S. Peterson, "Spurting Froth Upon Courtiers," *TLS* , no. 4911 (16 May 1997): 14–15; and "Laurel Crown and Ape's Tail: New Light on Spenser's Career from Sir Thomas Tresham," *Spenser Studies* 12 (1998): 1–35.

26.   See Meyer, *An Interpretation*, 5, 89, 181, 188; Thomas R. Edwards, *Imagination and Power: A Study of Poetry on Public Themes* (London: Chatto & Windus, 1971), 48–64; Wyman H. Herendeen, "Spenserian Specifics: Spenser's Appropriation of a Renaissance Topos," *M&H* , n.s. 10 (1981): 168–73; Oram, "Spenser's Raleghs," 161; Patrick Cheney, "Spenser's Pastorals: *The Shepheardes Calender* and *Colin Clouts Come Home Againe*," in *The Cambridge Companion to Spenser*, ed. Andrew Hadfield (Cambridge: Cambridge University Press, 2001), 99; Donald Cheney, "Spenser's Fortieth Birthday," 17– 18, 25; and Sue Petitt Starke, "Briton Knight or Irish Bard? Spenser's Pastoral Persona and the Epic Project in *A View* and *Colin Clouts*," *Spenser Studies* 12 (1998): 133–51. In a recent comment, Dees notes that "The standard interpretation of Colin's myth of Bregog and Mulla is that it allegorizes the effects of Ralegh's disastrous 1592 marriage," suggesting in addition that Spenser is making a connection between Bregog/Ralegh and the muddy streams of Ralegh's own poem ("Colin Clout," 195).

27.   On the practical nature of Ralegh's poetry as a bid for patronage see May, *Elizabethan Courtier Poets,* chap. 4, "Utilitarian Poetics: Gorges, Ralegh, and Essex," 102–39. For a lively debate on Spenser's own estimation of Ralegh's poetry vis-à-vis his own, see Oram, "What Did Spenser Really Think"; Erickson, "Spenser Reads"; and Rudick, "Three Views."

28.   *Orlando Furioso in English Heroical Verse* (London, 1591), "A Preface, or rather a Briefe Apologie of Poetrie, and of the Author and Translator," iiii [r-v]. Harington discusses *FQ* III.vii.53–60 on p. 373 of his annotated text.

29.   In Fraunce's *The Third Part of the Countesse of Pembrokes Yuychurch. Entitled Amintas Dale* (1592), the wise commentator Elpinus observes: "He that is but of a

meane conceit, hath a pleasant and plausible narration . . . set forth in most sweete and delightsome verse, to feede his rurall humor. They, whose capacitie is such, as that they can reach somewhat further than the external discourse and history, shall finde a morall sence included therein, extolling vertue, condemning vice, euery way profitable for the institution of a practicall and common wealth man. The rest, that are better borne and of a more noble spirit, shall meete with hidden mysteries of naturall, astrologicall, or diuine and metaphysicall philosophie, to entertaine their heauenly speculation" (quoted from the edition of Gerald Snare [Northridge: California State University, 1975], 9–10). A member of Sidney's circle, Fraunce had shown his familiarity with Spenser's work in his *Arcadian Rhetorike* (1588), quoting from Book II of the *Faerie Queene* (iv.35) two years before it was published.

30. On the history and interpretation of these works see Frederick Hartt, *Giulio Romano*, 2 vols. (New Haven: Yale University Press, 1958), I: 55–56, 152–58, and II: 337–47 (illustrated in figs. 95–99).

31. On Renaissance political interpretations of the giants' rebellion see Roger O. Iredale, "Giants and Tyrants in Book Five of *The Faerie Queene*," *RES* n.s. 17, no. 68 (1966): 373–81. For the fullest discussion of Spenser's use of giants and Titans, see Anne Lake Prescott in *The Spenser Encyclopedia*, ed. A. C. Hamilton et al. (Toronto, Buffalo, and London: University of Toronto Press, 1990), s.v. "giants," "Titans," who notes that Spenser sometimes merges the two rebellions, and "uses *Titan* and *giant* synonymously."

32. Alpheus and Arethusa are mentioned without comment by Renwick, ed., *Daphnaida and Other Poems*, 184; Roland M. Smith, "Spenser's Irish River Stories," *PMLA* 50 (1935): 1051; Herendeen, "Spenserian Specifics," 172–73; Donald Cheney, "Spenser's Fortieth Birthday," 18; and Shohachi Kukuda in *Spenser Encyclopedia*, s.v. "Bregog," "Mulla." Spenser would have found precedent for bringing together Burghley, Alpheus, and Arethusa in Ronsard's poem "Au Seigneur Cecille, Secretaire de la Royne d'Angleterre" (*Elegies, Mascarades et Bergerie* [Paris, 1565]; in *Oeuvres Complètes* , ed. Paul Laumonier, vol. 13 [Paris: Nizet, 1948], 159–70). Ronsard fancifully associates the etymology of "Cecil" with "Sicily," home not only of the two river lovers but of the restless giant Typhaeus, who lives on as a volcano, buried beneath the rocks for his rebellion.

33. Bk. I, chap. 1 (p. 1); the text of Comes is quoted here and below from the Venice edition of 1581. The translation is mine.

34. By contrast, Strabo, an unbeliever, insists that such a passage is impossible; see *Geography* VI.ii.4. The translation of Pausanias's text is quoted from the Loeb edition, tr. W. H. S. Jones and H. A. Ormerod , 5 vols. (London and New York: Heinemann and Putnam's, 1926–35), IV:167; II: 415.

35. The translation of Moschus is quoted from the Loeb edition: *The Greek Bucolic Poets*, tr. J. M. Edmonds, rev. edn. (London and New York: Heinemann and Putnam's, 1928), 461.

36. XV.iv.4–6. The text and translation of Ammianus Marcellinus are quoted from the Loeb edition, tr. John C. Rolfe, 3 vols. (Cambridge, MA, and London: Harvard University Press and Heinemann, 1963), I:126–29.

37. For text and underlinings see the facsimile edition of Harvey's copy of Turler's *Traveiler*, intro. Denver Ewing Baughan (Gainesville: University of Florida Press, 1951), 143–44.

38. Comes 1581, p. 603 (this chapter on Alpheus does not appear in the 1567 edition). Alpheus's bifurcated reputation as both pure and stained may be useful to Spenser, who notes the skill of some at court in "breeding [their enemy] some secret blot of shame" (l. 697). Though Bregog is ostensibly in disgrace, to the initiated the stain on his reputation may represent a *macula* that identifies him with the spotted Alpheus as a true pursuer of virtue. Cf. Sidney's mysterious impresa of a sheep marked with pitch, bearing the motto "macular modo noscar" ("I am spotted to be known"). On Sidney's impresa, preserved by Fraunce, see D. Coulman, "Spotted to be Known," *JWCI* 20 (1957): 179–80; Katherine Duncan-Jones, "Sidney's Personal Imprese," *JWCI* 33 (1970): 321–24, points out the importance to a nobleman of concealing the meaning of his impresa from the vulgar.

39. *Mythologies*, Bk. III, no. 12; quoted from *Fulgentius the Mythographer*, tr. Leslie George Whitbread (Columbus: Ohio State University Press, 1971), 98–99.

40. George Sandys, *Ovid's Metamorphosis Englished, Mythologized, and Represented in Figures*, ed. Karl K. Hulley and Stanley T. Vandersall (Lincoln: University of Nebraska Press, 1970), 261–62.

41. Sidney's famous description of pastoral in his *Apologie* is quoted from *Elizabethan Critical Essays*, ed. G. Gregory Smith, 2 vols. (London: Oxford University Press, 1904), I:175. The double use of "under" is noted by Patterson, *Censorship*, 28–29.

42. For another view of the differing positions of Ralegh and Spenser on the subject of love in the two poems, emphasizing neoplatonic ideas, see Dees, "Colin Clout," 185ff.

43. Quoted from *Giles and Phineas Fletcher: Poetical Works*, ed. Frederick S. Boas, 2 vols. (Cambridge: Cambridge University Press, 1908–09), II:16. Fletcher slightly misquotes Spenser's lines, which read: "O let the man, of whom the Muse is scorned,/Nor alive, nor dead be of the Muse adorned" ("Ruines of Time," ll. 454–55). The couplet closes a stanza on a repressive enemy of virtue long identified as Burghley.

44. On the part played by Burghley in the career of Giles Fletcher, see Abram Barnett Langdale, *Phineas Fletcher: Man of Letters, Science, and Divinity* (New York: Octagon, 1968), 11–36, 134; and *DNB*, s.v. Giles Fletcher. Tellingly, Phineas used the broken pipe, symbol of Colin's disappointed hopes, in his description of his own father's thwarted career (see Lin Kelsey and Richard S. Peterson, "Rereading Colin's Broken Pipe: Spenser and the Problem of Patronage," *Spenser Studies* 14 [2000]: 260 and nn. 48, 49).

45. Quoted from *Poems of Mr. John Milton: The 1645 Edition with Essays in Analysis by Cleanth Brooks and John Edward Hardy* (New York: Harcourt, Brace, 1951), 54. (Cf. Milton's "Arcades," ll. 30–31.) Brooks and Hardy suggest that the lines indicate that the dread voice "has shrunk the pastoral stream," requiring Milton to reestablish the pastoral mode (182), while Rosemond Tuve believes that the voice announces a final justice in which "even Alpheus' innocent streams shall indeed be forever shrunk" (*Images and Themes in Five Poems of Milton* [Cambridge, MA: Harvard University Press, 1957], 78). More recently, David Norbrook finds in the lines Milton's signal that a longer attack on the clergy "would have completely shrunk the pastoral streams, would have broken out of the genre of the pastoral elegy" (*Poetry and Politics in the English Renaissance* [London: Routledge & Kegan Paul, 1984], 277). For other

views of Arethusa and Alpheus in the poem see Merritt Y. Hughes's summary in his edition (*John Milton: Complete Poems and Major Prose* [Indianapolis, IN: Odyssey, 1957], 119). Stella P. Revard has lately seen in the pair a manifestation of Milton's theme of transformation and resurrection through a sea change (*Milton and the Tangles of Neaera's Hair* [Columbia: University of Missouri Press, 1997], 175–79).

46.   *Poetry and Politics,* 265–85. Norbrook suggests that the vehemence of the Spenserian passage is a direct reaction to the pressures of Laudian repression at the time: "In this climate of increasing dislike of censorship, the apparent digressiveness of the most explicitly polemical passage in the poem, St. Peter's attack on the clergy, takes on a particular significance" (277).

ALAN STEWART AND GARRETT A. SULLIVAN JR.

" 'Worme-eaten, and full of canker holes': Materializing Memory in *The Faerie Queene* and *Lingua*"

This essay looks again at a familiar site of memory, Eumnestes's chamber in Book II of *The Faerie Queene*. We argue that Spenser's mobilization of apparently commonplace metaphors of memory as written text hints at newly perceived stresses bearing on memory in the period. To pursue this, we examine a near-contemporary gloss on the Alma episode in Thomas Tomkis's play *Lingua* (c. 1604), the indebtedness of which to Spenser was long ago noted by M. P. Tilley. In *Lingua* the comically dysfunctional relationship of the forgetful old man Memory (Eumnestes) and his discontented page Anamnestes is exploited dramatically to parody common notions of memory retrieval, and to deplore the perceived detrimental effects on memory of the new antiquarian and critical vogues for worm-eaten manuscripts and indiscriminate print chronicles. Prompted by *Lingua* to reexamine Spenser's engagement with aspects of textual and social history, we provide a reading of Book II, Cantos ix-xii that uncovers some of the latent tensions in the poem's account of relations among memory, history, discipline, and heroic action.

*T*HIS ESSAY SEEKS TO LOOK AGAIN at that most familiar site of memory, Eumnestes's chamber in Book II of *The Faerie Queene*. In his description of memory's operations in the House of Alma, Spenser literalizes metaphors that figure memory as a written text: its raw materials are the "rolles," "old records," "books," and "long parchment scrolles" that Eumnestes turns to when performing his

215

basic functions.[1] These images are by no means novel to the Renaissance,[2] but the particular nature of their mobilization, both in Spenser's poem and in a dramatic gloss on the Alma episode, in the play *Lingua* (c. 1604), hints at newly perceived stresses bearing on memory in the period. At fifteen years' distance, *Lingua* is able to expand upon and diagnose some of the latent tensions in *The Faerie Queene*, which offers a normative if hitherto under-analysed account of the relations among memory, history, discipline and heroic action. *Lingua* produces those tensions as such; it functions as a rare contemporary critique of *The Faerie Queene* that reveals the nature of Spenser's purchase on, if not anxiety about, early modern social and textual forms organized around memory.

§

In Book II, Canto ix of *The Faerie Queene*, Sir Guyon and Prince Arthur visit the House of Temperance, where "sober Alma [the soul] dwell[s]" (II.ix.argument). Alma shows her guests around the castle, capping her tour with a visit to a turret, the head, in which they encounter "three honorable sages" (II.ix.47) who "counselled faire *Alma*, how to gouerne well" (II.ix.48): "The first of them [Phantases] could things to come foresee: / The next [who is unnamed] could of things present best aduize; / The third things past could keepe in memoree, / So that no time, nor reason could arize, / But that the same could one of these comprize" (II.ix.49). Memory, here named Eumnestes [Just Memory] lies in "th' hindmost roome of three" (II.ix.54). In this depiction, Spenser follows standard period physiological conceptions of memory. "The memorie called the Threasure of the mynde," writes Thomas Wilson typically, "lieth in the hynder parte [of the head], the whiche is made moste perfect by temperatnesse, and moderacion of qualitees in the brain."[3] Depending on which medical or philosophical authority you consulted, the brain was divided into three, four, or five ventricles, but all agreed that the memory was in the last and hindermost.[4]

While drawing on physiological literature Spenser imaginatively develops his depiction of memory as follows:

> That chamber seemed ruinous and old,
> > And therefore was remoued farre behind,
> > Yet were the wals, that did the same vphold,

Right firme and strong, though somewhat they declind.

(II.ix.55)

These lines establish a distinction between the external appearance of decay ("*seemed* ruinous and old") and the internal firmness and strength of memory. What is striking, though, is the final clause ("thought somewhat they declind"), which complicates the sentence's movement from "false" appearance to "true" reality. This clause typifies a pattern of qualification that slightly skews a description that could be taken to be an idealized or idealizing one. That internal strength presumably attests to the power of memory as a faculty, and while not apparent in his "feeble corse," the "liuely vigour" of his mind "recompenst him with a better scorse: / Weake body well is chang'd for minds redoubled force" (II.ix.55). However, this depiction of the chamber, echoed in the depiction of Eumnestes himself, is complicated by the fact that the chamber's ruin encompasses the raw materials of Eumnestes's operations:

His chamber all was hangd about with rolles,
And old records from auncient times deriu'd,
Some made in books, some in long parchment scrolles,
That were all worme-eaten, and full of canker holes.

(II.ix.57)

This description is immediately followed by the only image we have of Eumnestes's operation: "Amidst them all he on a chaire was set, / Tossing and turning them withouten end" (II.ix.58). Eumnestes's activity is difficult to recognize as reading. It takes the form of a physical "endlesse exercise" (II.ix.59), a continual "tossing and turning" of texts that are at best partly defaced and thus imperfectly legible.[5]

So what do we do with a depiction of Memory in which his actions are revealed as contingent upon perishable materials? The most influential answer to this question has been offered by Judith Anderson.[6] She locates true imperishable memory in Eumnestes's "immortall scrine," described by Spenser as follows:

This man of infinite remembrance was,
And things foregone through many ages held,
Which he recorded still, as they did pas,

Ne suffred them to perish through long eld,
As all things else, the which this world doth weld,
But laid them vp in his immortall scrine,
Where they for euer incorrupted dweld.

                                                        (II.ix.56)

"Scrine," as Anderson notes, sends us back to the proem of Book II,
in which *The Faerie Queene*, "this famous antique history," is the
"matter of iust memory," that is, punningly, the matter of Eumnestes.
"Records," she argues, "are permanent only in Faerie Land, which is
the only place Eumnestes's 'immortal scrine' remains, resides, dwells
incorrupted" (25). However, this view fails to contain a paradox.
Anderson notes that, "The content of Eumnestes's 'immortall scrine'
appears to be considerably purer than the books and scrolls, 'all
worme-eaten, and full of canker holes,' that hang about his walls.
These physically decrepit records are explicitly contrasted with the
disembodied purity and seeming transcendence of the content of
memory, which nevertheless derives from them. Well removed from
physical worms, the content of Eumnestes's scrine belongs to a figure
'of *infinite* remembrance' " (20–21). What is striking about Anderson's account is the disjunction it assumes between a specific picture
of memory's operations and an ideal representation of them as existing somehow beyond memory itself. Rather than focussing on
the contradiction between the chamber as "immortall scrine" and as
repository for "worme-eaten rolls," Anderson sees Alma's house,
Eumnestes's chamber and Eumnestes's scrine as "like so many Chi-
nese boxes" (21), but her reading requires that Eumnestes—himself
a scrine—must have a further, unseen scrine/memory. We contend
that while Spenser's depiction of memory gestures toward some invisible, transcendent scrine, it also directs us more immediately to a
series of specifically early modern concerns.

Spenser's emphasis on rolls, records, books and scrolls invites us
to consider memory in relation to early modern textual practices.
Period depictions of memory often represent it in terms of written
texts and those who transcribe or compose them. In the above description of "tossing and turning," memory is effectively bifurcated
between the old man and his papers, a division quite common in
writings of the late sixteenth century, as memory begins to be off-
loaded onto the material book. Mary Carruthers has persuasively argued that in classical and medieval accounts of memory, the physical
book often functioned as a mnemonic device for the book of memory: "books are themselves memorial cues and aids, and memory is

most like a book, a written page, or a wax tablet."[7] Over the course of the early modern period, the relationship is reversed: the book moves from being mnemonic to memory. This is especially true of commonplace books, through which, John Willis tells us, "[Y]ou will keep in mind things worthy [of] remembrance, better, safer, sooner, more certainly, profitably, and delightfully, then by that monstrous repetition, prescribed by some Authors in this Art of Memory, which nevertheless cannot be effected without long study, very great defatigation of the understanding & pernicious damage of the memorative faculty."[8] For Willis, keeping your thoughts in a commonplace book *is* keeping them "in mind."

If in Willis's model memory emerges as a particular relationship between subject and material text, period depictions of the operations of memory often represent them in terms of the relations between human subject and material object. In Pierre de la Primaudaye's *Second Part of the French Academie*, for example, Memory is described as "in place of a Notary and Secretary"—a humanization of Memory—"and as it were a register booke," an inanimate memory without a body.[9] Through the remainder of the discussion, Memory swings between being both "secretary and register"; it is "as it were . . . a roll or booke of accompt" (K8ᵛ), and a "secretary" at "the hindermost part of the braine" (Lʳ). Finally, de la Primaudaye expands his mixed metaphor:

> Therefore must the minde turne ouer all the leaues of his Booke or Register of Memorie, or at leastwise a great part thereof to finde them out, as if a Chauncellour or Secretary shoulde search all his Papers and Registers, and all his Rolles of Chauncery, vntill hee had found that which hee sought for. And wee see among our selues, what notes and obseruations wee vse, that they might bee as it were a memoriall booke vnto our memories.
>
> (L2ʳ⁻ᵛ)

While at the beginning of this passage "minde" would seem to describe the faculty of judgment—the occupant of the central ventricle of the brain, known for consulting memory in order to perform its stated function—by the end it becomes plain that it is memory that is both reading and being read. Specifically it is both a secretary *and* the register he uses—a "memoriall booke *vnto* our memories."

Just as the depiction of Eumnestes and his papers alludes to the textual materiality of early modern memory, so Spenser's description of his chamber evokes innovations in period architecture that also informed relations between texts and subjects. What is important here is the idea of the hindmost ventricle being a "roome" at the back of other rooms.[10] As Alice Friedman argues, sixteenth-century English societal changes were registered and reproduced "in architectural terms . . . by the creation of smaller and more private rooms in domestic structures of all types" and, within the larger country houses, by "an increasing attention to the provision of small offices and private cabinets," and many of them—like Eumnestes's chamber—were "associated with increased emphasis on record-keeping, education, and professionalism." Such "closets and chambers were tucked away in the four corners of the house and on the principal floors and formed the inner recesses of the suites."[11] Lena Cowen Orlin has produced ample evidence to argue convincingly that in reality the early modern closet was far from homogenous: "[it]s size, contents, activities, and practices were still fluid." Without disputing this, our suggestion here is that the closet did claim a very particular, fixed place in a widely-shared mindset, and that it is this *idea* of the closet as an "inmost room"[12] that was available to be exploited in figurative and literary works, and that is drawn on in Spenser's depiction of Eumnestes's chamber.

The significance of this "inmost room" was signalled by the ostentatious passage through outer (and thus less important) chambers by those who entered it: as Patricia Fumerton puts it, "one moved inward, but inwardness could be reached only after running a gauntlet of public outerness."[13] Richard Rambuss shows how Edward Wettenhall, in a more modest setting, sited his ideal prayer closet "within a suite of private chambers, so that 'my passage thereunto should be through two outer rooms, at least through one, the door or doors of which I might ever have shut, when I thither retired.' "[14] This architectural progression took on a clear ritualistic and political role when applied to the greatest houses. Thus Sir John Harington relates how, when ordered to come to King James's closet, he made his entrance through the presence-chamber (where he saw "the lordlie attendants, and bowede my knee to the Prince"), then waited "neare an houre" "in an outwarde chamber," before being led by a "specyal messenger" "up a passage, and so to a smale roome, where was good order of paper, inke, and pens, put on a boarde for the Prince's use." When the audience was over, Harington "withdrewe downe the passage, and out at the gate, amidst the manie varlets and lordlie servants who stoode arounde."[15] The progression to James's closet echoes Guyon and Arthur's passage to Alma's "inmost room," the closet of Memory. Once they had been granted entry to Alma's castle

(II.ix.17), the knights are brought to the "castle hall" (20) to be entertained, then led in turn through "the Castle wall" (22), "a stately Hall" (27), "the kitchin rowme" (28), and "a godly Parlour" (33) before climbing "a stately turret," moving through the outer rooms occupied by Phantases and (the unnamed) Reason, to enter—finally, and at great length—the chamber of Eumnestes (II.ix.47–53). Both this progression and the room's location as "inmost" establish the significance of Eumnestes's chamber, a significance borne out by both the texts Arthur and Guyon encounter there and, as we shall see, the heroic actions that those texts help enable.

Recent critical discussion of such inmost rooms has seen them occupied by a solitary individual. However such "private" spaces were commonly transactional.[16] As Angel Day describes the closet in 1592:

> The *Closet* in euery house, as it is a reposement [repository] of *secrets*, so is it onely . . . the owners, and no others commandement. The *Secretorie*, as he is a *keeper* and *conseruer* of *secrets*: so is he by his *Lord* or *Master*, and by none other to be directed. To a *Closet*, there belongeth properly, a doore, a locke, and a key: to a Secretorie, there appertaineth incidently, *Honestie, Troth* and *Fidelitie*.[17]

Here, tellingly, the position of the gentleman's closet in the household is invoked only to express as an extended metaphor the position of a secretary in relationship to his lord. This betrays, we suggest, the fact—attested to in numerous period documents—that the closet was a place not merely for the master, but for the master *and his secretary*. In Spenser's "inmost room" we find their analogues in Eumnestes and his "litle boy" Anamnestes:[18]

> Amidst them all [the papers] he [Eumnestes] in a chaire was set,
> Tossing and turning them withouten end;
> But for he was vnhable them to fet,
> A litle boy did on him still attend,
> To reach, when euer he for ought did send;
> And oft when things were lost, or laid amis,
> That boy them sought, and vnto him did lend.
> Therefore he *Anamnestes* cleped is,
> And that old man *Eumnestes*, by their propertis.
>
> (II.ix.58)

Eumnestes and Anamnestes develop through personification the Aristotelian division of "memory" and "recollection"[19]: the boy's functions therefore are in retrieval—in two senses: for items that are out of the reach of the old man; and for items that are lost or mislaid. At the same time, this relationship evokes that of master and servant.

While the details of this relationship are underdeveloped here, they are expanded upon in a dramatic gloss on *The Faerie Queene*, Book II. *Lingva: Or The Combat of the Tongue, And the fiue Senses For Superiority. A pleasant Comœdie* is a play that was first published anonymously by Simon Waterson in 1607 (internal evidence dates the play between 1602 and 1607), and subsequently went through at least four more editions before the end of the Civil War, with a Dutch translation appearing in 1648.[20] Sir John Harington owned a copy of the first edition, which he bound with eleven other quartos; in a manuscript note he alludes to "The combat of Lingua made by Thom: Tomkis of Trinity colledge in Cambridge."[21] Tomkis (c.1580–c.1634) is known to have published another play, *Albumazar,* which was acted before James I at Trinity on 9 March 1614/15 and published by Nicholas Okes in the same year.[22] It is therefore quite likely that *Lingua* was performed at Cambridge University in the opening years of the Jacobean era: sadly, the later story that the young Oliver Cromwell acted in the play is probably apocryphal.[23]

Lingua's plot owes much to Giorgio Alione's *Comedia de l'omo e de' soi cinque sentimenti,* and various aspects of the play are clearly indebted to works by Sidney, Shakespeare, John Heywood, du Bartas, Sir John Davies, and Rabelais, among others.[24] More importantly for our discussion here, as M. P. Tilley pointed out in 1927, crucial aspects of the play are drawn directly from Book II, Canto ix of *The Faerie Queene,* with additional borrowing from Cantos xi and xii.[25] In Tomkis's play Lingua (the tongue) desires to be named a sixth external sense, joining Tactus, Visus, Auditus, Olfactus, and Gustus. In the service of realizing her ambition, Lingua sets the senses against one another, generating civil strife in Microcosmus, Queen Psyche's domain. To restore order, Communis Sensus, with the aid of Phantastes and Memoria (or Memory), works to determine which of the five senses is chief. The play ends with Visus judged to be king of the senses, and with Lingua, her machinations having been exposed, punished by being imprisoned by the teeth of Gustus. The relation of this play to *The Faerie Queene* was succinctly articulated by Tilley: "[T]he Castle of Temperance in the *Faerie Queene* becomes in *Lingua* a Castle of Intemperance, in which the revolt of the Five Senses plotted by *Lingua* furnishes the major part of the action of the comedy."[26] Tilley also notes verbal echoes of Spenser, especially in Tomkis's presentation of Memory. Spenser's Eumnestes is "all decrepit in his feeble corse" (II.ix.55); *Lingua*'s Memory is more vividly "an old decrepit man, in a black Veluet Cassock, a Taffata Gowne furred, with white Grogaram, a white beard, Ueluet slippers, a Watch, Staffe, &c." (D3ᵛ). Eumnestes is "well remembred of King *Nine*, Of old *Assaracus*, and *Inachus* divine" (II.ix.56), while Memory declares how "I remember in the age of *Assaracus* and *Ninus*, and about the warres of *Thebes*, and the siege of *Troy* . . ." (D4ʳ).²⁷

In *Lingua*, Spenser's Eumnestes and Anamnestes are taken out of their hindmost room, and presented in the wider world of Microcosmus: in so doing, certain characteristics that are hinted at in Spenser are both developed and reinflected in Tomkis's play. As in *The Faerie Queene*, Anamnestes remains the boy charged with the task of retrieval, but in *Lingua* the retrieval is necessitated by Memory's forgetfulness: "Spretious I haue forgot something. O my purse, my purse, why, *Anamnestes*? Remembrance where art thou *Anamnestes* Remembrance" (D3ᵛ). Memory depends on Anamnestes to read, because he forgets his spectacles—although naturally "I Remember that I forgot my spectacles, I left them in the 349. page of *Halls Chronicles*, where hee tells a great wonder of a multitude of Mise which had almost destroyed the Country, but that there resorted a great mightie flight of Owles, that distroyed them, *Anamnestes* reade these Articles distinctly" (F3ʳ). (For the curious, in none of the editions of Hall's *Chronicles* does pagination reach 349.)²⁸ But whereas in *The Faerie Queene*, we might assume that the "litle boy" is passively obedient to Eumnestes, in *Lingua*, he is actively unhelpful, as Memory complains: "that vild boy is alwayes gadding, I remember he was at my heeles, euen now and now the vild Rascall is vanisht" (D3ᵛ). For his part, Anamnestes, commanded to "Goe sirra, runne, seeke euery where, I haue lost my purse somewhere," remarks in an indignant aside: "Go sirra, seeke, runne, I haue lost, bring, here's a Dogges life with a poxe, shall I bee always vsde like a water-Spanniell" (D4ʳ).

For dramatic purposes, and in the interest of turning these abstractions into recognizable social types, Tomkis presents Memory and Anamnestes in a way that evokes a number of relationships: master and servant, master and secretary, teacher and student. The homoeroticism latent in these relationships would have been highlighted by *Lingua*'s original performance within Cambridge's homosocial milieu (which also inflects the frankly misogynist treatment of the play's only female character, Lingua).²⁹ When a friend remarks that Anamnestes looks "leane," he replies, "Alas, how should I do otherwise that lie all night with such a Rawbond *Skelton* as *Memory* and runne all day on his Errands" (E3ᵛ-E4ʳ). But the situation is worse when Memory "fauoures best": "Thus when wee are friends, then must I come and bee dandled vpon his palsie-quaking knees, and he'le tell me a long story of his acquaintance with King *Priamus* and his familiarity with *Nestor* and how he plaid at blowe-point with *Iupiter* when he was in his side-coates and how he went to looke Birds-nests with *Athous*, and where hee was at *Deucalions* floud & 20. such old wiues tales" (E4ʳ). Here Memory plays teacher to Anamnestes's student, but the pedagogical experience constantly crosses the line into feminizing "old wiues tales," uncomfortable and discomfiting bed-sharing, and "dandl[ing]" on the knee, an image at once parental and amorous that irresistibly conjures "*Iupiter* dandling *Ganimed* vpon his knee" at the opening of Marlowe's *Dido Queene of Carthage*.[30]

Thus a resentful Anamnestes represents Memory as a potential sodomite. Enacting a fantasy revenge that fits the alleged crime, Anamnestes figuratively "gelds" his master, an act explicitly linked to and construed in terms of the art of memory. Anamnestes is sent on the errand of locating Memory's "lost" purse. This action parodies a common medieval notion of memory retrieval. Carruthers has discussed the "*sacculus* or compartmentalized money-pouch, in which coins of various sizes can be carried, each in its place without loss or confusion," as a "common variant of the archetype of memory as *thesaurus* or *arca*."[31] As she describes the structure of memory systems such as the *sacculus*,

> The fundamental principle is to "divide" the material to be remembered into pieces short enough to be recalled in single units and to key these into some sort of rigid, easily reconstructable order. This provides one with a "random-access" memory system, by means of which one can immediately and securely find a particular bit of information, rather than having to start from the beginning each time in order laboriously to reconstruct the whole system, or—worse—relying on simple chance to fish what one wants out from the murky pool of one's undifferentiated and disorganized memory.[32]

In a smoothly operating memory system, the remembering subject in an act of directed recollection calls up from a compartment in her memory purse the information she desires to recollect. In this instance, however, Anamnestes must find the purse itself—the very memory structure is lost to Memory. Moreover, orderly recollection is parodied through Anamnestes's decision upon finding the purse to "anatomize [it] in [Memory's] absence." Upon rifling through it, Anamnestes finds a set of paper memoranda:

Memorandum that Maister *Prodigo* owes mee foure thousand
pounds and that his lands are in pawne for it: *Memorandum* that
I owe; that hee owes? tis well the olde slaue hath some care of
his credit, to whom owes he trow I? that I owe *Anamnestes*?
What me? I neuer lent him any thinke; ha this is good, thers
som-thing comming to me, more then I look'd for. Come on,
what ist, *Memorandum* that I owe *Anamnestes*—a breeching; I
faith Sir I will ease you of that paiment (*He rendes the bill*)
Memorandum that when I was a childe *Robusto* tript vp my heeles
at foot-bale: what a Reuengfull dizard's this?

(E3ʳ)

Instead of purposeful recollection, we have an anatomization that
takes the form of the disorderly, chance pilfering and destruction of
the contents of the purse.

This scene also develops Memory's emasculation. Tomkis wittily
conflates the "purse" as *sacculus* with the more common slang of
"purse" as "scrotum," allowing Anamnestes (once again) to emascu-
late his master ("anatomize his purse"). Anamnestes is hoping for
"Iewells," so that he "may finely geld [his master's purse] of the
stones" (i.e., jewels/testicles), but when he gets to the bottom he
finds "nothing but a company of worme eaten papers." Where Memory's stones should be, Anamnestes finds only papers which are, naturally, memoranda or memorials. These memoranda are promises to
perform specific actions: the repaying of debts, the beating of Anamnestes, and so on. One of the implications of Memory's symbolic
castration, then, is that such actions have not been, and may never
be, performed. The gelding of Memory necessitates failures of performance that are not merely sexual.

Why exactly is Memory described in terms of impotence? One
answer lies in the sheer proliferation of materials he is now called
upon to store. As Memory himself explains,

I remember in the age of *Assaracus* and *Ninus*, and about the
warres of *Thebes*, and the siege of *Troy*, the[r]e was few things
committed to my charge, but those that were worthy the preser-
uing, but now euery trifle must be wrapped vp in the volume
of eternitie. A rich pudding-wife, or a Cobler cannot die but I
must immortalize his name with an Epitaph: A dog cannot
pisse in a Noblemans shoe, but it must be sprinkled into the

Chronicles, so that I neuer could remember my Treasure [trea-
sury] more full, & neuer emptier of honorable, and true heroycall actions.

(D4ᵛ)

The "Treasure" that Memory refers to is the *thesaurus* or treasury
discussed by Carruthers.[33] In this case the memory structure has never
been "more full, & neuer emptier of honorable, and true heroycall
actions." Fullness alone is not the problem: it is that Memory is
called upon to store actions that had previously been understood as
forgettable. As Carla Mazzio has observed, "Memory has become so
crowded with bits and pieces of culture that he has lost his sense
of history."[34]

And the culprits behind this insistence on recording every piece
of trivia and thereby compromising Memory's powers of retrieval?
Scholars. "[T]he most customers I remember my selfe to haue," he
claims, "are . . . Schollers, and now a daies the most of them are
become Critticks, bringing me home such paltry things to lay vp for
them, that I can hardly finde them againe." Critics, he explains
"tickle" him "[v]ery familiarly: for they must know of me forsooth
how euery idle word is written in all the mustie moath-eaten *Manuscripts*, kept in all the old Libraries in euery Cittie betwixt *England*
and *Peru*." Common Sense concurs: "Indeed I haue noted these times
to affect Antiquities, more then is requisite" (D4ʳ).

Memory is thus abused by new-fangled fashions on two fronts: the
scholarly vogue for pursuing minutiae and the new trend of recording
every piece of trivia in the printed Chronicles, also a complaint of
Lingua's page Mendacio: "I must confesse I would faine have logged
Stow and great *Hollings-head* on their elbowes, when they were about
their Chronicles" (Dʳ). *Lingua* is here clearly satirizing the new antiquarianism that was perceived as taking hold of scholarly life in the
last years of the sixteenth century—the antiquarianism that saw the
founding of the Society of Antiquaries in 1586, and prompted the
printed chronicles of John Stow and Raphael Holinshed, among others; as Anne Lake Prescott puts it, the play "laughs at newfangled
historiography: Memory rejects what he sees as a recent fashion for
depths and margins . . . *Lingua* does not wish to rethink traditional
hierarchies."[35] The play is not alone in its contempt for the new
fetishists of the archive: Philip Sidney wrote of the historian "loden
with old Mouse-eaten records,"[36] and John Earle's character of an
"antiquarie" is "one that hath that vnnaturall disease to bee en-
amour'd of old age, and wrinckles, and loues all things (as Dutchmen

doe Cheese) the better for being mouldy and worme-eaten."[37] These satirical attacks on antiquarianism suggest a mistrust of the manuscript archive's appropriation by scholars and of the print chronicles' failure to select events properly by importance—by which is meant rank, so that a nobleman's dog and a rich pudding-wife now share paperspace with the siege of Troy and the wars of Thebes. But there is a more serious concern in *Lingua*.[38] Whereas Sidney draws attention to "old Mouse-eaten records," Earle to "mouldy and worme-eaten" papers and Spenser to documents "worme-eaten, and full of canker holes," *Lingua* makes a direct link between the "company of worme eaten papers" (E3ᵛ) that Anamnestes finds in Memory's purse and scholars' "company of studious Paper wormes." In this *Lingua* effectively ascribes the destruction of memory's materials to actively paper-eating "leane Schollers" (E3ᵛ).[39] Antiquarianism, ostensibly a discipline devoted to memory, is revealed as in fact exploiting Memory, and in the process, disabling the proper functioning of memory, which, as *Lingua* and *The Faerie Queene* agree, is to present evidence of "honorable, and true heroycall actions."

In the context of Memory's own iteration of what he is called upon to remember, antiquarians and scholars disrupt the proper functioning of memory through their emphasis on that which was previously understood as forgettable. This is an impotent activity; it does not produce heroic action, but instead emasculates Memory. That is, *Lingua* suggests that, in an age of antiquarian excess, the remembering subject would not be able to perform specific actions because of the loss of historical exemplars. In their place in Memory's purse lie only the worm-eaten papers that record the trivial (and commercial) concerns that fill *Lingua*'s Memory. This scene makes plain the connection between memory and action, and it is this connection that is of central importance to *The Faerie Queene*'s representation of memory, a representation that extends in Book II as far as Guyon's destruction of the Bower of Bliss.

§

It is not surprising that critical discussion of memory in Spenser centers on Canto ix of Book II. What has gone largely unrecognized is that while Eumnestes makes only a brief appearance at the end of Canto ix, issues of memory are worked out throughout the remainder of Book II, and focus on the relation between memory, bodily deportment and purposeful action. Guyon moves from reading the

"*Antiquitie* of *Faerie* lond" (II.ix.60) in Canto x to voyaging to and destroying the Bower of Bliss in Canto xii. How do we connect these two episodes? Consider the famous model for reading advanced by Spenser in his *Letter to Ralegh* that introduces the poem: "The generall end therefore of all the booke is to fashion a gentleman or noble person in vertuous and gentle discipline." Like the *Faerie Queene*, the "*Antiquitie* of *Faerie* lond"—an obvious analogue to Spenser's poem itself—functions to fashion a gentleman; it forwards the process by which Guyon acquires the "vertuous and gentle discipline" necessary to defeat Acrasia. In other words, his reading of Eumnestes's chronicle is a precondition for Guyon's heroic action. His consumption of the text is a shorthand for the broader disciplinary process, represented throughout Book II, by which Guyon is made a model of temperance. Crucial here is the significance of memory and history to this process. Guyon's textual encounter with heroic exemplars is necessary to his becoming one himself. In his final battle with Acrasia, he is armed with a memory stored with his own valorous antecedents.

However, Guyon's memory is not all in his head. We need to take seriously Spenser's reference to "vertuous and gentle *discipline*." In this instance, such discipline seems to emerge from reading alone, but the kind of reading Spenser assumes here is itself the end result of a disciplinary process. As Richard Halpern has argued, English education subjected early modern students to disciplinary practices that made subjects of them. Such a process aimed to fashion not only one's patterns of thought, but also the comportment of one's body.[40] The fashioning of Guyon, then, should be understood in terms not only of the transmission of historical materials, but also of a more general shaping of his behavior, including the most basic forms of bodily self-regulation. The consumption of Eumnestes's texts builds upon and encodes this process of fashioning a gentleman.

The interpenetration of bodily self-regulation and specific reading practices is shown in Alma's correction of Arthur and Guyon for their intemperate study of the chronicles of Eumnestes:

> So long they red in those antiquities,
> That how the time was fled, they quite forgate,
> Til gentle *Alma* seeing it so late,
> Perforce their studies broke, and them besought
> To think, how supper did them long awaite.
> So halfe vnwilling from their bookes them brought,
> And fairely feasted as so noble knights she ought.
>
>   (II.x.77)

Arthur and Guyon are so absorbed by what they read that they neglect the claims of their bodies. They also "quite forgate" the passing of time: a problematic form of forgetting for the performance of a heroic quest. There is an obvious irony here, for in absorbedly reading the chronicles of memory, the knights neglect the claims of both time and the body. Such neglect is potentially catastrophic; inattention to his own body is one of the reasons that Guyon earlier faints (II.-vii.65–6).[41] Alma reminds them of these claims, however, and by Canto xii, Guyon's reading has been entirely "incorporated," both memorized and corporealized.

The lessons of memory manifest themselves not only in Guyon's defeat of Acrasia, but in his liberation of Verdant, whose lack of memory takes the form of his immoderate sleep.[42] While Guyon has incorporated the lessons of memory, Verdant is one who has, in words used to describe Grill, "forgot the excellence / Of his creation" (II.xii.87). This form of forgetting is apparent in Verdant's bodily comportment, depicted in tacit opposition to Guyon's. Verdant, at this point unnamed, is first described as Acrasia's

> new Louer, whom through sorceree
> And witchcraft, she from farre did thither bring:
> There she had him now layd a slombering,
> In secret shade, after long wanton ioyes:
> Whilst round about them pleasauntly did sing
> Many faire Ladies, and lasciuious boyes,
> That euer mixt their song with light licentious toyes.
>
> (2.12.72)

The logic of the quest is here parodied and overturned, as epic journeying is echoed and replaced by Verdant's enchanted travel "from farre"; the only toil he has recently experienced are "long wanton ioyes," which are followed by his "slombering."[43] Over the next eight stanzas, Verdant is repeatedly referred to in terms of sleep, but it is a specific indirect linkage of his character with sleep that is most important:

> His warlike armes, the idle instruments
> Of sleeping praise, were hong vpon a tree,
> And his braue shield, full of old moniments,
> Was fowly ra'st, that none the signes might see.
>
> (II.xii.80).

It is *praise* and her instruments that sleep here, the praise that would be granted to Verdant had he not abandoned his "warlike armes" and given himself over to Acrasia's morphic pleasures. Sleeping praise is coincident with the erasure of "old moniments" from Verdant's shield, an erasure that evokes Verdant's forgetting of "the excellence / Of his creation" (II.xii.87). Verdant has here forgotten himself.[44] In giving himself over to idleness, he has forgotten those attributes of his identity that mark him as a knightly hero, the signs of his quest and of his identity having been "fowly ra'st" in a way that is suggested by his initial namelessness. Indeed, Verdant remains unnamed until after Guyon captures and binds Acrasia (82)—until he is forced to remember himself.

Spenser's association of excessive sleep, forgetting, and indolence is a commonplace one in the early modern period, especially but not exclusively in religious texts.[45] In such texts, sleep is often associated with the active and sinful forgetting of God and/or divine precepts; it also metaphorizes the fallen state of man. For example, the author of *Physicke, to Cure the Most Dangerous Disease of Desperation* (1605) states that

> If [Satan] espieth a man to be rich, and to haue worldly bles-
> singes through the gift of God, then will he apply him earnestly
> by his prosperitie to lull him asleepe i[n] the forgetfulnesse of
> God, in world[ly] Pleasures, pleasant Vanities, and transitorie
> delights, comfortes, and solaces; and by trusting in his Riches
> to lift vp himselfe arrogantly aboue others; to swell in pride, &
> to contemne his brethren, committing . . . many fonde, palpa-
> ble, and grosse errours and follies, against Gods word, euen as
> if he should say, Who is the Lord?[46]

Sleep and "forgetfulnesse of God" are associated with "transitorie delights," a yoking that associates the first two with hedonism. Also, the end result of this appetitive sleep is a disastrous act of forgetting: so engrossed is the sleeper in "worldly Pleasures" that he finally acts as if he cannot remember who the Lord is. Such extreme acts of forgetting, modes of action that encompass psychic and somatic phenomena, would also presumably constitute for this author the eradication of identity, grounded as identity is in the subject's relationship to God. To forget God—to act as if you don't know who the Lord is—is to forget yourself, to have your identity "fowly ras't." Verdant's forgetting of "the excellence of his own creation" marks him as one who has also forgotten God.

Just as Guyon's reading of Eumnestes's books must be understood in terms of "vertuous and gentle" discipline, Verdant's forgetting encompasses the complete breakdown of a basic somatic discipline that governs both thought and action. Both sleep and forgetfulness here describe a mode of inactivity and a reluctance toward a decreed action or set of actions, those associated with "warlike armes" and Christian heroism. Verdant should be understood as the anti-Guyon, a figure whose abandonment of his heroic quest is inextricably linked with a sleep that encodes what Linda Gregerson has nicely described as the "perpetual subjugation to the flesh" experienced by Acrasia's lovers.[47] Arguably the "old moniments" function not only as markers of identity, but also emblematize those heroic exemplars in terms of which Verdant no longer shapes his actions. In their "ras't" state, they are the opposite of Eumnestes's books.[48] While memory engenders heroic action, forgetting connotes effeminized lassitude. It is immoderate, emasculating sleep that Guyon destroys along with the Bower of Bliss. In doing so, he causes Verdant and various unnamed others to remember themselves, and presumably to take up the "warlike armes" that they had, with Acrasia's encouragement, earlier sacrificed to forgetting.[49]

But Grill remains. Reluctant to give up his beastly state, Grill bemoans his transformation back from a "hoggish forme" (II.xii.86).[50] Intriguingly, in the final action of the entire book Guyon and the Palmer "depart," leaving "*Grill* [to] be *Grill*, and haue his hoggish mind" (87). Grill remains to suggest both the limits of temperance and failures of self-recollection: his is the undisciplined, forgetful body that resists the kind of discipline that Spenser sees as central to heroic masculinity; he adopts modes of behavior simultaneously beastly and (insofar as Grill and Verdant are conceptually linked) effeminate.[51] Moreover, these modes of behavior will not earn Grill a place among the ranks of those heroic exemplars Guyon encountered in Eumnestes's book. And yet, his is the last name uttered in Book II; self-forgetting is granted a priviliged place in Spenser's own exemplary text. What is finally, if fleetingly, acknowledged is self-forgetting's power to shape an identity—"Let *Grill* be *Grill*"—that, in heroic terms, seems an eradication of identity.[52]

§

In Canto x, Arthur and Guyon read what *Lingua*'s Memory bemoans as being crowded out of his "Treasure": tales of "true heroycall actions." Fifteen years after *The Faerie Queene*, *Lingua* registers the perceived threat of antiquarianism to the regime of exemplary history. As Memory is befuddled by and overrun by antiquarian scraps, the heroic action that history texts are understood as enabling is impossible: with a memory as impotent as that of either Verdant or *Lingua*'s Memory, Guyon could not have destroyed the Bower of Bliss. This would seem to posit an opposition between the smoothly functioning memory of Alma's castle, and the dysfunctional Memory of *Lingua*. However, we have been arguing that *Lingua* develops a view of memory latent in *The Faerie Queene* itself. Indeed, the heroic action enabled by memory does not emerge out of the seamless functioning of Eumnestes's memory system. The books read by Guyon and Arthur are not provided by Eumnestes, or retrieved by Anamnestes.[53] Instead, "There chaunced to the Princes hand to rize,/An auncient booke, hight *Briton moniments*" (II.ix.59); "Sir Guyon chaunst eke on another booke,/That hight *Antiquitie of Faerie* lond" (II.ix.60). The salient point here is that memory is properly full—the texts that enable Guyon's and Arthur's actions are indeed in Eumnestes's chamber—but they are "chanced" upon rather than retrieved. What this means is not entirely clear. On the one hand, as Harry Berger notes, "The word 'chaunce' has by this time come to have its resounding ironies: this is God's work, and it is shown as God's will that they chance on their respective chronicles."[54] At the same time, "chaunce" also obviously connotes randomness, a view confirmed by the fact that memorial materials in Eumnestes's chamber have not been filed away in an orderly fashion—as would be expected with any memory system—but "were lost, or laid amis" (II.ix.58). Indeed, the word "chaunce" wonderfully encapsulates the vacillations between disorder and transcendent order that we earlier located in our discussion of Eumnestes's chamber as both worm-eaten archive and immortal scrine.[55]

    In this essay, we have passed from Eumnestes's chamber into a discussion of aspects of textual and social history that that chamber evokes. However, we do not want to erase the idealizing tendencies of Spenser's texts, represented most vividly by the "immortal scrine." The point is, though, that *Lingua* can and does ignore such tendencies, thereby bringing into sharper relief Spenser's engagement with specific spaces (the "hind most" room) and social relations (master and secretary). In addition, it is through *Lingua* that we can begin to see all that is at issue in Spenser's depictions of memory and forgetting, tied up as each is in notions of impotence and action. And while Spenser finally spares Grill/forgetting, Tomkis goes even further by creating a minor character named Obliuio. Anamnestes asserts that the "very naming of [Obliuio] hath made me forget my selfe"; he also complains bitterly that Obliuio has been "preferred before [him]" (E4ʳ). In a play in which memory's exemplary force has been jeopardized by the activities of antiquarians, Obliuio, who never appears on stage, is represented as having achieved prominence: "that Rascall is so made-of euery where" (E4ʳ). The world of *Lingua* is one in which forgetting is much more than "let be." Tomkis's play reveals a potential latent in Spenser's poem by pushing it to extremes. In doing so, it illuminates Spenser's engagement with social and textual practices his poem both registers and downplays.

Birbeck University of London   *Pennsylvania State University*

NOTES

Earlier versions of some materials in this paper were presented at conferences of the Modern Language Association (Washington, DC, December 2000) and the Renaissance Society of America (Chicago, March 2001). For their comments and suggestions, we are grateful to Patrick Cheney, Richard Helgerson, Carla Mazzio, Gail Kern Paster, and Anne Lake Prescott.

1.   Edmund Spenser, *The Faerie Queene*, II.ix.57. All references are to *The Faerie Queene Book Two*, ed. Edwin Greenlaw in *The Works of Edmund Spenser: A Variorum Edition*, ed. Edwin Greenlaw, Charles Grosvenor Osgood, and Frederick Morgan Padelford (Baltimore: Johns Hopkins Press, 1933).

2.   "The metaphor of memory as a written surface is so ancient and so persistent in all Western cultures that it must, I think, be seen as a governing model." Mary Carruthers, *The Book of Memory: A Study of Memory in Medieval Culture* (Cambridge: Cambridge University Press, 1990), 16.

3.   Thomas Wilson, *The Arte of Rhetorique, for the vse of all suche as are studious of Eloquence* (London: Richard Grafton, 1553), Ee.iiii.ᵛ.

4.   Ruth Leila Anderson, *Elizabethan Psychology and Shakespeare's Plays* (Iowa City: University of Iowa Press [University of Iowa Humanistic Studies, vol III, no 4], 1927), 16–18, 38–39; E. Ruth Harvey, *The Inward Wits: Psychological Theory in the Middle Ages and the Renaissance* (London: The Warburg Institute, 1975), 1–2, 30; Nancy G. Siraisi, *Medieval & Early Renaissance Medicine: An Introduction to Knowledge and Practice* (Chicago: University of Chicago Press, 1990), 81–82.

5.   As David Lee Miller notes: "Eumnestes sits 'tossing and turning' his records 'withouten end'—that is, without any principle of closure to direct his research." Miller, *The Poem's Two Bodies: The Poetics of the 1590 Faerie Queene* (Princeton: Princeton University Press, 1988), 186.

6.   Judith H. Anderson, " 'Myn auctour': Spenser's Enabling Fiction and Eumnestes' 'immortall scrine,' " in *Unfolded Tales: Essays on Renaissance Romance*, ed. George M. Logan and Gordon Teskey (Ithaca: Cornell University Press, 1989), 16–31.

7. Carruthers, *Book of Memory*, 16.

8. John Willis, *Mnenomica; or, the Art of Memory* (London: Leonard Sowersby, 1661), B6^{r-v}. This passage does not appear in the earlier (1621) edition.

9. Pierre de la Primaudaye, *The Second Part of the French Academie . . . translated out of the second Edition, which was reuiewed and augmented by the Author* (London: G.B.R.N.R.B., 1594), K7^v-L2^v at K8^v.

10. The following section draws on Alan Stewart, "The Early Modern Closet Discovered," *Representations* 50 (1995), 76–100.

11. Alice T. Friedman, *House and Household in Elizabethan England: Wollaton Hall and the Willoughby Family* (Chicago and London: University of Chicago Press, 1989), 9, 146–47.

12. Indeed, Orlin proceeds with the "working notion" that the closet "was identifiably a *little* room . . . and perhaps an inmost room, within a bedchamber or last in a string of private apartments." See Orlin, "Gertrude's Closet," *Shakespeare Jahrbuch* 134 (1998), 44–67 at 65, 52.

13. Patricia Fumerton, *Cultural Aesthetics: Renaissance Literature and the Practice of Social Ornament* (Chicago: University of Chicago Press, 1991), 71–72.

14. Richard Rambuss, *Closet Devotions* (Durham and London: Duke University Press, 1998), 122–23 citing Edward Wettenhall, *Enter into thy Closet: or, A Method and Order for Private Devotion*, 5th edn. (London: R. Bentley, 1684), B3^v.

15. Sir John Harington to Sir Amias Paulet, [December 1603?]. *The Letters and Epigrams of Sir John Harington together with The Prayse of Private Life*, ed. Norman Egbert McClure (Philadelphia: University of Pennsylvania Press, 1930), 109–11.

16. For this argument, see Stewart, "Early Modern Closet," and for Orlin's critique of this conclusion, see "Gertrude's Closet," 57–58.

17. Angel Day, *The English Secretorie* (London: Richard Jones, 1592), Q^v.

18. Surprisingly, perhaps, given his focus on Spenser as professional secretary, Richard Rambuss does not mention the Eumnestes-Anamnestes relationship, but suggests that Eumnestes can be read as "a surrogate within the poem for the author in the Spenserian capacity as poet/secretary and now historian." Rambuss, *Spenser's Secret Career* (Cambridge: Cambridge University Press, 1993), 68.

19. Aristotle, "On Memory," trans. J. I. Beare, from *The Complete Works of Aristotle: The Revised Oxford Translation*, ed. Jonathan Barnes, 2 vols (Princeton: Princeton University Press, 1984), 1: 714–20.

20. *Lingva: Or The Combat of the Tongue, And the fiue Senses For Superiority. A pleasant Comœdie* (London: G. Eld for Simon Waterson, 1607). Other editions appeared in 1617, 1618, 1622, 1632, and 1657. For the Dutch translation, see *Lingua: ofte Strijd tusschen de tong en de vyf zinnen om de heerschappy* trans. Lambert van den Bos (Amsterdam: G. van Goedesberg, 1648). For a general account of the play see *The Cambridge History of English Literature*, ed. A.W. Ward and A.R. Waller, 15 vols (Cambridge: Cambridge University Press, 1932), 6: 315–17. Long neglected, this play has recently been brought back to critical attention by Patricia Parker, Carla Mazzio, and Anne Lake Prescott. See Parker, "On The Tongue: Cross Gendering, Effeminacy, and the Art of Words," *Style* 23 (1989), 445–63; Mazzio, "Sins of the Tongue" in *The Body in Parts: Fantasies of Corporeality in Early Modern Europe* ed., David Hillman and Carla Mazzio (New York and London: Routledge, 1997), 53–80; idem., "Of Sound

Mind: Speech Disorders and the Structure of Memory on the Early Modern Stage," unpublished paper delivered at the MLA conference, Washington, DC, December 2000; Prescott, *Imagining Rabelais in Renaissance England* (New Haven: Yale University Press, 1998), 73, 138–40. An on-line version is available: see http://www.indiana.edu/~letrs/index.html.

21.   British Library Additional MS 27632, fo. 30; cit. in F.J. Furnivall, "Sir John Harington's Shakspeare Quartos," *Notes and Queries* 7th ser., 9 (1890), 382–83 at 382. We follow Harington's attribution here.

22.   Thomas Tomkis, *Albumazar, a comedy presented before the Kings Maiestie at Cambridge, the ninth of March, 1614. By the Gentlemen of Trinitie Colledge* (London: Nicholas Okes, 1615); another edition appeared in 1634. See the edition by Hugh G. Dick, *Albumazar: A Comedy (1615)* (Berkeley: University of California Press, 1944); for an on-line version see http://www.indiana.edu/~letrs/index.html. On Tomkis see also E.K. Chambers, *The Elizabethan Stage*, 4 vols (Oxford: Clarendon, 1923), 3: 497; Gerald P. Mander, "Thomas Tomkis," *Times Literary Supplement* (31 March 1945), 151; G.E. Bentley, *The Jacobean and Caroline Stage*, 7 vols. (Oxford: Clarendon, 1941–1968), 5: 1225.

23.   *Cambridge History of English Literature*, 6: 317.

24.   M.P. Tilley, "The Comedy *Lingua* and the *Faerie Queene*," *Modern Language Notes* 42 (1927), 150–57 (on Alione); G.C. Moore Smith, "Notes on Some English University Plays," *Modern Language Review* 3 (1907–1908), 141–56 at 146–49 (on Sidney's *Arcadia, Julius Caesar, A Midsummer Night's Dream, Foure PP, Club Law, The Parnassus Plays*); F. S. Boas, " 'Macbeth' and 'Lingua,' " *Modern Language Review* 4 (1908–1909), 517–20; Tilley, "The Comedy *Lingua* and Du Bartas' *La Sepmaine*,"- *Modern Language Notes* 42 (1927), 293–99; idem., "The Comedy *Lingua* and Sir John Davies's *Nosce Teipsum*," *Modern Language Notes* 44 (1929), 36–39. For debts to Rabelais, see Prescott, *Imagining Rabelais*. See also Greenlaw's notes: *The Faerie Queene*, ed. Greenlaw, 299–300.

25.   Tilley, "The Comedy *Lingua* and the *Faerie Queene*."

26.   Tilley, "*Lingua* and the *Faerie Queene*," 152.

27.   As A. C. Hamilton notes, "Eumnestes's memory extends to the beginnings of biblical, classical and mythical military history": Ninus of Babylon was "the fyrst that made warre"; Assaracus was son of the founder of Troy, the great-grandfather of Aeneas; and Inarchus was a river god, the first King of Argos. See *The Faerie Queene* ed. A. C. Hamilton (London: Longman, 1977), 258.

28.   In all editions, "*Halls* Chronicles" are foliated in three sequences, none of which reaches fo. 349. Edward Hall, *The Vnion of the two noble and illustre famelies of Lancastre & Yorke*, various edns (London: R. Grafton for various, 1548–1560?).

29.   See Alan Bray, *Homosexuality in Renaissance England* (London: Gay Men's Press, 1981), esp. ch. 2; Bruce R. Smith, *Homosexual Desire in Shakespeare's England: A Cultural Poetics* (Chicago: University of Chicago Press, 1991), esp. ch. 6; Alan Stewart, *Close Readers: Humanism and Sodomy in Early Modern England* (Princeton: Princeton University Press, 1997), esp. chs. 3, 4 and 5; Mario diGangi, *The Homoerotics of Early Modern Drama* (Cambridge: Cambridge University Press, 1997), esp. ch. 2.

30.   Christopher Marlowe and Thomas Nash, *The Tragedie of Dido Queene of Carthage* (London: Thomas Woodcocke, 1594), A2^r.

31.	Carruthers, *Book of Memory*, 251.

32.	Carruthers, *Book of Memory*, 7.

33.	See Carruthers, *Book of Memory*, 34–35, 160–61.

34.	Mazzio, "Sins of the Tongue," 69.

35.	Prescott, *Imagining Rabelais*, 139.

36.	Philip Sidney, *An Apologie for Poetrie* (London: Henry Olney, 1595), D.ᵛ.

37.	John Earle, *Micro-cosmographie. Or, a peece of the world discovered; In Essayes and Characters* (London: William Stansby for Edward Blount, 1628), Cᵛ-C2ʳ.

38.	Richard Helgerson has noted other serious concerns about antiquarianism, arguing persuasively that the activities of late Elizabethan and Jacobean "antiquaries" were perceived as political and threatening, because "the individual autonomy of [the antiquarian] himself, the communal autonomy of the group to which he belonged, the national autonomy of the land he and his fellow chorographers represented . . . menace[d] the king's claim to absolute power." Helgerson, *Forms of Nationhood: The Elizabethan Writing of England* (Chicago: University of Chicago Press, 1992), 127–28.

39.	The *OED* cites only one later use of the term "paper-worm," which it explains as identical to "bookworm": "One who seems to find his chief sustenance in reading, one who is always poring over books." Its application in *Lingua*, however, is clearly designed to suggest something more destructive than a passion for reading. See *OED* s.v. paper-worme (11.162), book-worm 2. (2.398).

40.	Richard Halpern, *The Poetics of Primitive Accumulation: English Renaissance Culture and the Genealogy of Capital* (Ithaca: Cornell University Press, 1991).

41.	Harry Berger, Jr., focues on the pre- and post-faint phases of Book II. He argues that Guyon's faint occurs after his passing through Mammon's cave because Guyon has "[fed] his eyes at the expense of sustaining nature" (*The Allegorical Temper: Vision and Reality in Book II of Spenser's The Faerie Queene* [New Haven: Yale University Press, 1957], 23). This episode of Guyon's reading, then, offers another example of Guyon's potentially dangerous curiosity. In this instance, however, Guyon's near-repetition of Canto vii's faint is prevented through Alma's intercession in his reading of Eumnestes's books; the supper he then consumes presumably offers sustenance that complements Guyon's diet of heroic texts and helps nourish him for the struggles ahead. In the light of such near-repetitions, it is worth noting that what Berger says of the cave of Mammon is, from *Lingua*'s perspective on *The Faerie Queene*, also true when memory's matter is not applied to noble or heroic endeavors: it betrays a "perverted use of the raw materials of life" (*Allegorical Temper*, 25). For other influential accounts of Guyon's faint, see Frank Kermode, *Shakespeare, Spenser, Donne: Renaissance Essays* (London: Routledge, 1971), 60–83; Paul Alpers, *The Poetry of The Faerie Queene* (1967; rpt. Columbia: University of Missouri Press, 1982), 235–75. On the significance of diet to Book II, see Michael Schoenfeldt, *Bodies and Selves in Early Modern England: Physiology and Inwardness in Spenser, Shakespeare, Herbert, and Milton* (Cambridge: Cambridge University Press, 2000), 40–73.

42.	The composition of this paper coincided with a workshop at the 2001 International Spenser Society conference (Cambridge, England, July 6–8) devoted to memory, forgetting, and Spenser. A number of papers touched upon the significance of memory and forgetting to the final cantos of Book II; most relevant and helpful to this essay have been fine unpublished papers by Lisa Broome-Price, Chris Ivic, Grant Williams, and Jennifer Summit (a version of the last is forthcoming in *ELH*).

43. We encounter in Book II a precursor to Verdant in the figure of Cymochles, who has been "lulled fast a sleepe" by Phaedria on her floating island (6.18).

44. On self-forgetting, see Garrett A. Sullivan, Jr., " 'Be This Sweet Helen's Knell, And Now Forget Her': Forgetting, Memory and Identity in *All's Well That Ends Well*," *Shakespeare Quarterly* 50 (1999), 51–69.

45. The next two paragraphs draw on unpublished work by Sullivan on the conceptual connections between forgetting, excessive sleep, and lethargy.

46. W. W., *Physicke, to Cvre the Most dangerous Disease of Desperation* (London: Robert Boulton, 1605), E^v-E2^r.

47. Linda Gregerson, *The Reformation of the Subject: Spenser, Milton, and the English Protestant Epic* (Cambridge: Cambridge University Press, 1995), 120.

48. In his emphasis on sleep and forgetfulness and his depiction of a "braue shield, full of old moniments," Spenser draws heavily on books 16 and 17 of Tasso's *Gerusa-lemme* Liberata. Like Verdant, Tasso's Rinaldo is awakened from an immoderate sleep. Moreover, the shield that is used to awaken him evokes both the "old moni-ments" and the books of Eumnestes that are read by Guyon in Canto x. In this shield Rinaldo sees "the pedigree of worthies stout,/Who seem'd in that bright shield to live and move./ *Rinaldo waked up and cheer'd his face, /To see these worthies of his house and race. /To do like acts his courage wish'd and sought . . .* " (Torquato Tasso, *Jerusalem Delivered: The Edward Fairfax Translation [1600]* [Carbondale, IL: Southern Illinois University Press, 1962], book 17, stanzas 81–82, emphasis ours).

49. "The Bower of Bliss projects all of the erotic fantasies, the wishful thinking, the nostalgia for a lost age, the escapist impulses which all of us experience . . . They must be repressed and the Bower ruthlessly destroyed because they inhibit action and become a substitute for it. . . . [T]hey make us forget the Fall and the need to repair its ruins. Verdant's slumbering is one example of our forgetfulness, and Grill's contentment with his animal state another" (Maurice Evans, "Guyon," *The Spenser Encyclopedia*, ed. A. C. Hamilton, et al. [Toronto: University of Toronto Press; London: Routledge, 1990], 343–44, esp. 344). In an unpublished paper delivered at the 2001 International Spenser Society conference, "Wring out the Old: Squeez-ing the Text, 1951–2001," Harry Berger, Jr. argues that the Bower of Bliss episode stages the displacement of male desire onto female provocation. Read in this light, the self-forgetting of either Verdant or Grill betrays less Acrasia's debilitating sexual control over men than a male response, either hysterical or wishful (or both), to the possibility of release from the strictures of memory, history and temperance.

50. The linkage between beastliness, sleep, forgetting and the non-performance of specific prescribed actions is not unusual in this period, as evidenced by Hamlet's "bestial oblivion" soliloquy (William Shakespeare, *Hamlet*, ed. Harold Jenkins [Lon-don: Methuen, 1982], 4.4.32–66, esp. 40), in which the question is posed, "What is a man / If his chief good and market of his time / Be but to sleep and feed? A beast, no more" (33–35). This question, of course, is overdetermined for Hamlet by both the example of Fortinbras and his awareness of his own nonperformance of revenge for his father's death.

51. Michael Schoenfeldt describes Grill as "the negation of the ancestral memory that is read in Alma's turret. He is not so much the victim of Acrasia's powerful

magic as of his own forgetting; he is the beast that all are capable of becoming in a moment of moral relaxation" (*Bodies and Selves*, 72). At the same time, Supriya Chaudhuri notes that the character of Grill emerges out of Plutarch's dialogue from the *Moralia*, "Beasts Are Rational," in which Gryllus laments his return to human form in a way that foregrounds the notion that "beasts possess intelligence and excel man in natural virtues, notably temperance" ("Grill," *The Spenser Encylopedia*, 342).

52.   On self-forgetting as constitutive of identity, see Sullivan, "Sweet Helen's Knell." Chris Ivic ("Refashioning Gentlemen: Collective Memory in *A View*," unpublished manuscript) also discusses Verdant and self-forgetting. Grant Williams has in an unpublished essay discussed the sites of "amnesiac jouissance" that Guyon encounters and that Grill embodies ("Phantastes's Flies: The Trauma of Forgetting in Spenser's Memory Palace," ms. p.13). Williams's phrase nicely suggests the potent lure of forgetting in Book II.

53.   Neil Rhodes and Jonathan Sawday have recently read Eumnestes's chamber as a library that "functions imperfectly" because there is "no efficient, stable, method of classification and indexing." Rhodes and Sawday, "Introduction: Paperworlds: Imagining the Renaissance Computer," in *The Renaissance Computer*, ed. Neil Rhodes and Jonathan Sawday (London: Routledge, 2000), 1–17 at 9.

54.   Berger, *Allegorical Temper*, 80 n.3.

55.   In this regard, the description of Eumnestes's chamber confirms David Lee Miller's broader point that "Spenser's narrative hovers between the apparent randomness of chivalric errancy and the providential guidance of an allegorical foreconceit" (*The Poem's Two Bodies*, 170).

CLARE R. KINNEY

"Beleeve this butt a fiction": Female Authorship, Narrative Undoing, and the Limits of Romance in *The Second Part of the Countess of Montgomery's Urania*

Previous discussions of the manuscript continuation of the *Urania* have tended to offer general overviews of the differences in narrative content between the two parts of Mary Wroth's romance; this essay addresses some of the moments in Part II in which Wroth does seem to be returning to the familiar matter of the 1621 *Urania*, but in such a manner as to frustrate the interpretive expectations she has previously created. The continuation's intermittent containment or subversion of the significance of its female-voiced histories of desire complements the assault on illegitimate female authorship evident in its criticisms of the "poeticall furies" of the character Antissia and suggests a new anxiety in its author—presumably fueled by some of the scandalized responses to the publication of *Urania* I—about her own practices as a female fiction-maker. Wroth's revisionary designs, some of which are both comic and deflationary, seem to betray her impatience with the protocols of her chosen genre. Even as it copiously augments the 1621 text, Part II of the *Urania* comes very close to "undoing" romance.

*M*Y STARTING POINT IS A CURIOUS moment, early in Mary Wroth's manuscript continuation of the *Countess of Montgomery's Urania*, when King Selarinus of Epirus lends a sympathetic ear to a lady he has encountered at the house of the sister of the enchantress Melissea. The lady describes herself as a princess of Tartaria and relates the painful history of her ill-fated marriage, unhappy widowhood, and subsequent alienation from family and friends (a history which recalls

in its general outlines the melancholy narratives offered by several
female characters in the 1621 published portion of the *Urania*). But
as the mysterious beauty concludes her tale, she suddenly and surprisingly asks Selarinus to "beleeve this butt a fiction, and dunn to please
and pass the time away with."[1] Given that the 1621 *Urania* repeatedly
bears witness to the particular value its author confers upon the representation of woeful personal experience before an appreciative
and noble audience, *this* speaker's unexpected undercutting of the
authority of her own story is both puzzling and dismaying.[2] It is as
if the most basic assumptions and agendas governing Wroth's writing
of romance are being called into question.

I want to explore the implications of such moments of "narrative
undoing" in Part II of the *Urania*. Previous discussions of the manuscript continuation have offered illuminating overviews of the differences in narrative content between the two segments of Wroth's text.
Barbara Lewalski and Mary Ellen Lamb, for example, both discuss
Urania II's movement away from relating the complicated love interests of the 1621 *Urania*'s chief characters to deploying the familiar
motifs of quest romance in storylines addressing the adventures of
the lost children of the heroes and heroines of Part I.[3] This essay, by
contrast, will focus upon some of the moments in the work in which
Wroth *does* seem to be returning to the familiar matter of Part I, but
in such a manner as to frustrate the interpretive expectations she has
previously created.

The episode I've just described, with its unexpected subversion of
the authenticity of the history narrated, reverses the dynamics of a
striking moment in the 1621 *Urania* when the precise status of a
narrative is also put in question. In *Urania* I, Wroth's heroine Pamphilia tells the lady Dorolina the sad tale of Lindamira, "faigning it
to be written in a French Story"; she ends by rehearsing Lindamira's
own complaint which, according to Pamphilia, "because I lik'd it,
or rather found her estate so neere agree with mine, I put into Sonnets."[4] After Pamphilia concludes her recitation, we read that Dorolina "thought [it] was some thing more exactly related then a fixion"
(I: 505), and indeed, not only does the tale of Lindamira's false lover
echo Pamphilia's own situation, but as many readers have noted,
other details of Lindamira's history (including her exile from court)
also suggest a conflation of Lady Mary's own biography with both
Pamphilia's and Lindamira's.[5] When Pamphilia, speaking of Lindamira's faithless beloved, declares "I will with the story conclude my rage
against him" (I: 502) the "him" might as easily be Amphilanthus—or
Wroth's own philandering lover, William Herbert. The prose narrative of Lindamira's troubled affair with its coda of seven sonnets

offers a suggestive miniature version of the 1621 *Urania*'s own hybrid text (i.e., a prose romance followed by the *Pamphilia to Amphilanthus* lyrics). And like the *Urania*, it is a complicated act of simultaneous masking and disclosure, eliding the distinction between fiction and fact, romance and autobiography, even as it affords yet another of those characteristically Wrothian moments in which the history of an unhappy woman is granted a particular authority by sympathetic listeners.[6]

So what are we to make of the continuation's unwonted interest in subverting the significance of the female-voiced history of desire? The supposed princess of Tartaria's story involves a character who declares her own history to be a fiction, but a later episode in *Urania* II offers an even more telling undoing of female-voiced narrative. In an extended and teasing interlude, prince Philarchos recounts to his sister Pamphilia his adventures at the court of Lycia. The officially happily-married Philarchos sees from his bedroom window a garden full of lovely ladies. Recalling his amorous past and ruefully deploring his lost liberty, he decides to seek out their company, albeit insisting he desired no more "(honor and Vertu beeing my guide) then sivile conversation" (II: 123). But in attempting to find his way into the garden, he stumbles instead into the chamber of a lady whom he overhears lamenting her constant and unhappy love for none other than himself. Philarchos decides that the nobler course is *not* to retire: "showld I bee afraide, as thinking my undaunted spiritt cowld . . . - nott bee master of my passions? Beesides, what insivilitie it wowld bee nott to acknowledg thankfullnes" (II:125). When he reveals himself, the lady protests her chaste and honorable love for him and her astonishment at this "unlooked for adventure" (II:126). They begin to converse and Philarchos kisses her, "Butt this was all I wowld doe, and soe much was butt sivilitie" (II:125). The prince and the lady chat "of many matters, yett all of love" until dawn, when he asks her to tell him her story. She recalls an encounter with him many years ago, but as she describes the growth of her love, Philarchos interrupts her, insisting that her words of praise and devotion are "butt complements and Vanities; nott sound truths, butt only fictions nott substancies" (II:128). Apparently forgetting his pleasure in hearing her declare her love when she thought herself unobserved, he lectures her on female modesty and honor; when, in tears, she defends her "longe so-chaste love," he declares: "you butt maske desire under the guilded outside of a fained chastitie. For love is desire, and desire is nott worthy of the sweetest, noblest, and best-deservingst title of chastitie" (II:129). Arguing that "thes frensies of love . . . hath binn, are, and ever wilbee . . . the certaine ruin of any

(though the greatest woemen)" (II:130), he bids her return to her
home and be a comfort to her father in his old age.

Short-circuiting the lady's autobiography and declaring it to be
one of "fictions not substancies," asserting that her tale of chaste love
merely masks a story of transgressive desire, Philarchos in effect "de-
authorizes" her history. It is not a story that can be permitted to be
told (although his own framing story can be fully articulated—even
to a postscript in which he admits he "never was soe neere by temptation like to breake [his] faith" to his own wife [II:130]). Nor does
Pamphilia, his auditor, challenge his correction of the lady—although
it pains her to "heere love soe cruelly blamed," she still "thank[s]
her deere brother for the tale and sweete expressions in itt" (II:131).
But Philarchos's narrative comes very close to an indictment of everything Wroth herself has undertaken in lending a particular authority,
in the 1621 *Urania*, to women telling stories about the vicissitudes
of female desire, even as she encodes or masks her own erotic history
within her story of Pamphilia's perfect love for Amphilanthus.

One might compare Wroth's representation of Philarchos's "de-
authorizing" of the Lycian lady's history with *Urania* II's striking
assault on "illegitimate" female authorship in its comically brutal
criticisms of the "poeticall furies" of the character Antissia. We have
already seen Antissia writing unhappy poetry in *Urania* I in response
to being jilted by Amphilanthus; she takes up her pen again in the
continuation, where much of her later story is mediated by the distinctly unsympathetic voices of Rosindy (Pamphilia's brother) and
her own nephew Antissius. Antissia fancies herself an inspired poet,
dresses eccentrically, writes immodest hymns to Venus, speaks in
"raging, raving, extravagent discoursive language" and is likened by
Antissius to a "man in woemans clothes acting a sibilla" (II: 41)—
his words indict her both for her gender transgression and her usurpation of the vatic voice.

Urania II's treatment of Antissia has been much discussed, most
readers following Mary Ellen Lamb's suggestion that the text makes
her a "kind of lightning rod" to preempt and absorb criticisms of its
female author as well as perhaps a reflection of Wroth's own anxieties
about her project.[7] I entirely agree with this reading, but believe we
can push it a little further. In the 1621 *Urania*, Antissia is carefully
positioned as a foil to Pamphilia: both are wounded by the errancies
of Amphilanthus, and both frame their distress in poetry. But whereas
Pamphilia's poetry both contains and masks her unhappiness, and
her public demeanor remains impeccable, Antissia's poetry becomes
problematically and literally incontinent: its sentiments spill over into
her real time actions. Attempting to "put some of her thoughts in

some kind of measure," she composes a sonnet which concludes: "Restlesse I live, consulting what to doe,/And more I study, more I still undoe" (I:114). As soon as she writes these lines, "'Undoe,' cride she, 'alas I am undone, ruind, destroyd, all spoild by being forsaken,'" and only minutes later she makes a public spectacle of her jealousy when she mistakes Pamphilia's brother Rosindy for Amphilanthus and loudly berates him for infidelity. Eventually, in furious desperation, she persuades prince Dolorindus, who is desperately in love with her, to make an attempt on Amphilanthus's life—studies, in effect, to undo *him*.

In *Urania* I, the actions of this incontinent female poet do not seem in any way to reflect upon Pamphilia's own engagement in poetic making. Pamphilia and other women are represented approvingly within the published portion of the romance text as they write, and share with other writers and readers, their rather more hermetic poetry. In *Urania* II, however, Pamphilia no longer functions as the "legitimate female poet" counterpoising the negative example offered by Antissia. Indeed the manuscript continuation contains not one poem written by Pamphilia. She does, on the one occasion, sing a lyric in public, but it is one of Amphilanthus's poems (and even more tellingly, it is a poem not even authored by Wroth but by William Herbert [II: 30–31]).[8] In *Urania* I, the moment at which Pamphilia finally and unequivocally discloses her love for Amphilanthus coincides with her showing him her poetry: "she tooke a deske, wherein her papers lay, and kissing them delivered all shee had saved from the fire . . . unto him" (I: 320). This event is echoed and reversed in *Urania* II, when the man Pamphilia finally and reluctantly marries proposes to her. The King of Tartaria finds her surrounded by her books, and writing busily—but "when she parceaved him, she clapt her papers into her deske"(II: 271–72). Shortly after her wedding to Tartaria, alone at night in the same "secrett waulkes" whose trees she decorated with her poems in *Urania* I, Pamphilia suffers a kind of breakdown and acts with unprecedented extravagance: "she wept, she cride, nay she allmost roared out her commplaints." Eventually she recovers enough to "wring her conseites . . . into some od and unusuall (as her fortunes were turned) sort of verce: a thing she had nott in a pretty space dunn. . . . They were extreame sad and dolefull, and sertainly such as would have moved too farr in Amphilanthus, had hee then seene them" (II: 279). But neither Amphilanthus nor the reader sees the verses: Wroth's text does not rehearse them for us—and indeed the narrator's remark that they might have moved Amphilanthus too greatly hints that there is something excessive about their occluded content. The manuscript continuation does not reaffirm a Pamphilian model of "wringing" passion into poetry, does not reaffirm the consolations of female art: instead we must assume that even Pamphilia's creations may partake too much of the dangers identified by the contrite Antissia, when she eventually declares poetry to be even in its highest form "butt a delightfull frenzie" and at its worst "raptures and fixions able to turne a world of . . . woemens heads into a mist of noe sence" (II: 251).[9]

The very presence of Antissia's fervid recantation in *Urania* II is worth further consideration. We are given the story of her sins against womanly decorum twice over in the manuscript: once in the third person account of the events leading up to her healing on the isle of Delos by the enchantress Melissea, and again, considerably later in the text, in her own description of her extravagant behavior and subsequent recovery to the Queen of Bulgaria (II: 250–253). Antissia's restoration comes about after her long-suffering husband Dolorindus takes her on a sea voyage to the island of St. Maura, a location of particular significance within the larger narrative of Wroth's romance. In the 1621 *Urania* it is the place where several major characters are healed of problematic passions by being flung into the waters that surround the isle; their immersion erases their previous emotional history, permits them to enter wholeheartedly into new connections, to reinvent themselves as it were (I: 230–31). But Antissia never reaches St. Maura; her ship instead makes landfall at Delos where she is duly subjected to a magical water cure to rid her of her "poeticall furies," but must continue to live with the painful memory of her previous deeds. Significantly, her impassioned recitation of her own history only serves to reinscribe her lack of self-possession: she is described as all too "willing for the most part to heere her self speake" (II: 250), and we are told that her interlocutor, the Queen of Bulgaria, "could not often times forbeare smiling" at her garrulity and self-display (II: 253). Antissia's self-recollection only confirms her function within the text as a negative exemplar: she is not permitted to play any other role or author any other story.

Urania II's "undoings" of female authority and authorship in general and its erasure of Pamphilia's identity as exemplary female poet in particular suggest a new anxiety in its creator—presumably fueled by some of the scandalized responses to the publication of the 1621 text—about her own practices as a female maker. Indeed its portrait of Antissia speaks pretty exactly to the *ad feminam* criticisms leveled at Wroth in the vicious verses penned by Edward Denny, when he charged her with maliciously slandering himself and his family in her romance. Antissius's description of Antissia's behavior as "fittinger for a man in woeman's clothes acting a sibilla then a woeman" and her own husband's criticism of her "poetical furies . . . that in raving rime bury truth of modestie" (II: 51) recall Denny's description of Wroth as "Hermophradite in show, in deed a monster," a woman whose "witt runns madd," a woman who has made herself "a lying wonder."[10] But we are left with the paradox that even if Wroth does not publish her manuscript continuation, even if she composes in private a work that seems to chasten and censor the 1621 Urania's interest in authorizing acts of female narrative and lyric self-fashioning and in eliding the boundaries between fact and fiction, she nevertheless does not stop writing, and indeed produces a very copious text. So what *are* we to make of the different designs of the second part of the Urania?

The continuation, while apparently offering a more conventional romance narrative, also betrays a growing impatience with that mode. The plot lines concerning the lost and enchanted children of the main characters of the 1621 Urania repeatedly offer us monstrous foes (Urania II is seriously over-populated with giants) persecuting noble captives in hideous strongholds; at regular intervals questers storm these castles and release the prisoners, only to have the lost children once again disappear, mysteriously swept away to await the coming of some other designated rescuer. The virtuous enchantress Melissea appears at intervals to announce that a larger pattern of destiny is being worked out and to place various royal children in safe-keeping, but never clarifies the reason for their sequestration. There are repeated references to one particular knight who can alone complete these mysterious adventures, a young man who may be Amphilanthus's natural son and who goes by the name of Faire Design.[11] But if it is Faire Design who is to give us narrative closure, Wroth's *own* design nevertheless remains unfinished, and I would propose that it is far from a fair design. The history of the lost children is frankly incoherent (even by the standards of romance terminable and interminable); one of them, seen by Selarinus as a very small boy at the start of Urania II, is two hundred pages later admired as a noble youth in Tempe by Parselius, even though only a few months seem to have elapsed in the lives of Pamphilia and Amphilanthus in the interim.[12] While one might infer that the deeds and destinies of the younger generation are Urania II's main interest, they are recounted in such a fragmentary, almost improvisatory manner that it is difficult to believe that they represent the work's emotional core.[13] Indeed Wroth is not unwilling to subvert high romance seriousness with moments of comic anticlimax. At one point, Amphilanthus rescues a party of imprisoned royal children from their monstrous captors; when he is formally introduced to the youngsters we read "The

Emperour beeheld them, saluted them, and blessed them, butt had small discourse for them, seldome having had conversation with Children" (II:186).

Such a flickering moment of comic realism suggests to me a kind of romance burn-out. It is a phenomenon that I'd suggest is already manifesting itself towards the end of the last book of the 1621 *Urania* as Wroth recounts the adventures of a group of princely knights who are questing to discover the whereabouts of Amphilanthus (who has disappeared under mysterious circumstances). These exfoliating narratives include an extended and very acerbic account of the wooing practices of the philandering Duke of Brunswick (who courts naive young women by sending them poetry written by other men for other women), and the semi-subversive introduction of a grotesquely intrusive Talking Knight into the more serious tale of the Duke of Florence's attempt to woo the sad Lady of the Forest Champaign. Wroth's mixed tone in these pages even inflects, just a little, the book's concluding account of the restoration of Amphilanthus to the grieving Pamphilia: as Pamphilia runs to embrace her beloved, "forgiving, nay forgeting all injuries," the narrator dryly notes that "he with open armes received her, and with all unfained affection embraced her, and well might hee joyfully doe it, love thus exprest, besides a labour saved of asking pardon" (I: 660). In *Urania* II, these moments of near pastiche or comic anticlimax are even more salient. If Wroth has turned away from the narrative matter foregrounded in *Urania* I—the obsessive telling and retelling in the first person feminine of her ur-history of the ill-used but constant female subject—she does not seem to be entirely wholehearted in her construction of less inflammatory romance narratives. Moreover, when she does return to the histories of the main players of *Urania* I there is a continued suggestion that romance protocols are inadequate to her ends. As other readers have noticed, there is a distinct feeling of diminishment in her treatment of these characters.[14] Several of them die (one of them from an illness unromantically exacerbated by his obesity) and Wroth makes a point of occasionally mentioning the somewhat reduced powers of her aging warriors. One noble couple, Ollorandus and Melisanda, produce an unworthy son. Threaded through the business-as-usual of giants, enchantments, and knightly quests, counterpointing the hyperbolic praise lavished on various representatives of the younger generation, we have unidealizing testimonies to mortality, contingency, and loss.

This feeling of diminishment also inflects Wroth's ongoing narrative of Pamphilia and Amphilanthus. On the surface, we are in pretty familiar territory. Although united at the beginning of *Urania* II, and indeed going so far as to carry out a *verba de praesenti* marriage, hero and heroine are again separated when Amphilanthus departs to go jousting in Crete and begins an affair with the Queen of Candia. The lady, eventually tiring of Amphilanthus but reluctant to relinquish him to Pamphilia, conspires with his old tutor to persuade him that Pamphilia has abandoned him to marry the Tartarian King, Rodomandro; as a consequence, Amphilanthus is cajoled into marrying the Princess of Slavonia. Pamphilia suffers cruelly in his absence and is herself finally persuaded to marry the devoted Rodomandro. The semi-private contract between Pamphilia and Amphilanthus—perhaps Wroth's most striking fantasy of autobiographical wish-fulfilment—becomes oddly coterminous with the marriages of state engendered by Amphilanthus's errancies and other people's plots: quite late in *Urania* II, the Wrothian narrator actually refers to Pamphilia as Amphilanthus's wife (II: 381). This narrative doubleness is reinforced by the odd final pages of the manuscript continuation, which briefly flash forward to the King of Tartaria's death (II: 406) while also leaving Pamphilia and Amphilanthus eventually reconciled in a chaste and loving relationship while she is yet married and her husband still alive.

What most interests me here, however, and moves me to argue that Wroth's "undoings" extend even to the history of her favorite characters, is the curious tone of the reconciliation episode near the end of *Urania* II. It is an episode which faintly recalls events at the close of the 1621 *Urania* when the errant Amphilanthus finally makes his way back to a mourning Pamphilia and repledges his faith to her, but the manuscript continuation frames the lover's rapprochement rather differently. Pamphilia, although still loving Amphilanthus and suffering deeply when she herself marries Tartaria, has punished him for distrusting her constancy by refusing ever to speak to him directly. Only the deathbed confession of Amphilanthus's old tutor Forsandrus, in which he discloses just how he intercepted and confiscated the lovers' correspondence and falsely informed Amphilanthus that his lady had already married the King of Tartaria, permits a new understanding between the two.

Pamphilia, however, almost never hears Forsandrus's confession. In extremis, he sends a message begging that he may reveal to her something "which most conserned her honor." But "[s]he replyde that they all Very well know how nott ten days beefor she had a hawking hurt her leg soe much as she had nott ever since binn able to stand upon itt, nor goe much less" (II: 386). Only after Forsandrus renews his pleas does she consent to be carried into his chamber. The crucial revelation is almost thwarted by a sore leg, a leg which also makes its presence felt when Pamphilia, alone with Amphilanthus (in a episode which recalls her opening of her portable desk in *Urania* I to show him her love poems), unlocks the little cabinet in which Forsandrus has kept their stolen correspondence. The sight of the letters "strake poore Amphilanthus into such a passion as hee fell from the stoole, butt hapily neere Pamphilia. For her lamenes wowld nott have permitted her to have dunn him that willing service she wowld els have done"—namely take his head in her lap and revive him (II.388–89).

The jarring, almost comic, excessiveness and circumstantiality of the whole business of Pamphilia's injured leg, a leg whose pains come close to preventing the plot resolution which will reconcile the lovers, a leg which offers the reader the incongruous vision of a lame heroine unable (except for the happy accident of the trajectory of his swoon) to comfort and restore her prostrate knight, suggests that even when Wroth has returned to the very heart of her romance matter she is coming close to subverting it. Much earlier in *Urania* II, when Pamphilia suspects that Amphilanthus has strayed once more and opens her heart to her friend Veralinda, the latter offers comfort by saying that although Amphilanthus was ever inconstant, "when hee shall see you againe, bee assured hee will bee (nay, hee can bee noe other then) as truly ore att least as passionately loving you as ever" (II: 210). Pamphilia cries out in reply: "What care I for passion? Lett mee have truthe" (II: 210). I would like to suggest that Pamphilia's words might stand as a gloss on what Wroth herself is up to in her continuation. Wroth's self-censorship, her text's undercutting of the female voice which speaks its desire, its occlusion of Pamphilia's poetry, its suspicion of the "frenzies" of love lyrics, comes close to implying that there can be no "true fictions" of virtuous female passion. At the same time, the narrative "static" she creates within the Pamphilia-Amphilanthus story, her most privileged fiction of desire, suggests a disenchantment with her attempts to relate yet again the exemplary history which is also, being in some sense *her* story, something a little more exact than a fiction—as if she is weary of those unending rehearsals of loss and reconciliation. Hinting that there may be another story here, one in which the "truth" of the complaining, aging, lamed body insists on not being disturbed yet once more by the exigencies of passion, Wroth flickeringly undoes romance.

University of Virginia

NOTES

1. Lady Mary Wroth, *The Second Part of the Countess of Montgomery's Urania*, MRTS 211 (Tempe: University of Arizona Press, 1999), ed. Josephine A. Roberts, completed by Suzanne Gossett and Janel Mueller, 10. Subsequent citations of this work will be noted parenthetically.

2. The "undoing" of this female narrator's authority is further complicated, later in the continuation, when she is proved to be an enchantress; Selarinus reencounters her and she proceeds to seduce him and hold him captive to her charms for several years (II: 304–05).

3. See Mary Ellen Lamb, *Gender and Authorship in the Sidney Circle* (Madison: University of Wisconsin Press, 1990), 146ff; Barbara K. Lewalski, *Writing Women in Jacobean England* (Cambridge: Harvard University Press, 1993), 282–85.

4. Lady Mary Wroth, *The First Part of the Countess of Montgomery's Urania*, MRTS 140 (Binghamton: MRTS, 1995), 499, 502. Subsequent citations of this work will be noted parenthetically.

5. See, for example, Lamb, 187–88; Naomi J. Miller, *Changing the Subject: Mary Wroth and the Figurations of Gender in Early Modern England* (Lexington: University Press of Kentucky, 1996), 138; Maureen Quilligan, "The Constant Subject: Instability and Authority in Wroth's *Urania* Poems," *Soliciting Interpretation: Literary Theory and Seventeenth-Century English Poetry*, ed. Katharine Eisaman Maus and Elizabeth D. Harvey (Chicago: Chicago University Press 1990), 326–27.

6. Helen Hackett writes: "Fiction, like irony, has a 'double force,' at once saying and not saying; and like irony or private versifying, Wroth seeks to appropriate fiction as a means of 'safe' female expression." See "'Yet Tell Me Some Such Fiction': Lady Mary Wroth's *Urania* and the 'Femininity' of Romance," *Early Women Writers: 1600–1720*, ed. Anita Pacheco (London and New York: Longman, 1998), 64. On the blurring of narrative boundaries in the *Urania* between fiction and fact, romance and autobiography, see also Jennifer Lee Carrell, "A Pack of Lies in a Looking Glass: Lady Mary Wroth's *Urania* and the Magic Mirror of Romance," SEL 34 (1994): 79–107.

7. Lamb, 162; see also 168.

8. See note to *The Second Part of the Countess of Montgomery's Urania*, 30.39 (482–83).

9. For an alternative explanation of the silencing of Pamphilia as poet, see Lewalski, 296.

10. For Denny's verses, see *The Poems of Lady Mary Wroth*, ed. Josephine A. Roberts (Baton Rouge: Louisiana State University Press, 1983), 32–33.

11. It is as if we are in Wroth's own version of Malory's Grail Quest with Faire Design the Galahad figure. For a particularly interesting discussion of the significance of this character, see Mary Ellen Lamb, "The BioPolitics of Romance in Mary Wroth's *The Countess of Montgomery's Urania*," ELR 31 (2001): 121–30.

12. See *The Second Part of the Countess of Montgomery's Urania*, 2–3 and 204–05.

13. For an alternative discussion of the significance of the histories of the lost children in *Urania* II, see Sheila T. Cavanaugh, *Cherished Torment: The Emotional*

Geography of Lady Mary Wroth's Urania (Pittsburgh: Duquesne University Press, 2001), 195–218.

14.   See in particular Paul Salzman, "The Strang[e] Constructions of Mary Wroth's *Urania*: Arcadian Romance and the Public Realm," *English Renaissance Prose: History, Language and Politics*, ed. Neil Rhodes (Tempe: MRTS, 1997), 121; also Lamb, *Gender and Authorship*, 147.

FORUM

DAVID SCOTT WILSON-OKAMURA

Republicanism, Nostalgia, and the Crowd

Most accounts of English republicanism have located its initial phase in the middle decades of the seventeenth century. New work on the republican tradition has challenged that view and moved the date back. The question now is not whether to move the date but how far. Was Edmund Spenser a republican? Respected scholars have suggested that he was. This essay takes issue with that finding and argues that what sounds like proto-republicanism in Spenser's writing is actually a conservative response to the decline of the English aristocracy. Whether or not the decline was real, or merely perceived, is a question for historians. Our concern is with the poetry, and what the poet opposed was not monarchy, but the abuse of monarchy (i.e., tyranny). One index of the poet's stance on this topic is Arteg-all's encounter with the Egalitarian Giant in *FQ* V.ii. Another is his treatment of crowds; the essay concludes, therefore, with an attempt to place Spenser's crowd scenes in the classical tradition of epic and history-writing.

*U*NTIL VERY RECENTLY, REPUBLICANISM was not something that students of Elizabethan literature needed to worry about. According to traditional accounts, the first phase of English republicanism belongs to the Interregnum. David Norbrook, however, has shown that the language of classical republicanism was already well understood and in play by the late 1620s; by 1649, it was "at once excitingly new and as familiar as a dog-eared school-book."[1] According to Markku Peltonen, the seeds of English republicanism were sown even earlier, during the reign of Elizabeth I, and with special fertility in Spenser's Ireland.[2] Most recently, in an article provocatively titled "Was Spenser a Republican?" Andrew Hadfield has argued that the "author of the most significant work ostensibly devoted to monarchy in the sixteenth century was, in fact, a republican."[3]

But this is not a paper about early English republicanism; rather, it is a paper about things that look like republicanism but that turn out, upon closer inspection, to be something else.

Was Spenser a republican? A great deal will depend on how one defines the term. The problem, as J.G.A. Pocock observed, is that early modern English republicanism was "a language, not a programme."[4] Unfortunately, the historians have not always set a good example in this matter.

In 1986, Patrick Collinson delivered a lecture entitled "The Monarchical Republic of Queen Elizabeth I." After pointing out that many aspects of Tudor government were administered at the municipal, rather than the national, level, Collinson describes a manuscript in which Lord Burghley laid out a contingency plan for what should happen if Elizabeth were to die suddenly, without appointing an heir. Burghley proposed an interregnum of no more than a year, during which time a *Magnum Consilium* of thirty-four magistrates, selected by the Privy Council from the peerage, would choose the next king. In other words, England was to be governed by something like a small republican senate—for a year. As revolutionary as this sounds, Collinson himself is careful to point out that the suggested arrangement was (a) anomalous; (b) never proposed in parliament, and therefore never enacted into law; (c) temporary; and (d) emphatically not proleptic of the republican Interregnum of the 1650s.[5]

In 1997, John Guy reprinted Collinson's lecture in an undergraduate history reader and added an essay of his own, which was decidedly less cautious. What had been, in Collinson, a relatively modest statement—"when it came to the crunch, the realm took precedence over the ruler. So citizens were concealed within subjects"—becomes in Guy's contribution, "The intellectual avant-garde of Tudor England were the king's subjects, but inside every humanist was a citizen struggling to get out."[6] Resistance to absolutism is routinely labeled "republican" or "quasi-republican." In practice, though, what Guy means by the term *republican* is "a preference for constitutional or 'limited monarchy.'"[7]

Louis Adrian Montrose's use of the term *republicanism*, in a recent address to the International Spenser Society, is also indiscriminate. Noting that parliament overrules Mercilla in the matter of Duessa's trial and execution (*FQ* V.x.1–3), Montrose has argued that the trial episode marks a "bridling" or "circumscription" of the queen, and in consequence a form of republicanism.[8] Similar readings of the trial episode have been offered before, briefly by Angus Fletcher and in detail by Colin Burrow, who suggests that the outcome (if not the

description) of the trial represents the triumph of "Parliamentary justice" over regal clemency, the arbitrary exercise of which threatened
to become a form of tyranny.[9] Burrow and Fletcher, though, avoid
using the term *republican* in their readings, presumably because the
idea of limited monarchy was already a commonplace of political
theory in the period. Sir Philip Sidney, for example, was adamant in
his opposition to absolutism. He knew the works of Machiavelli,
and even adopted some of his political vocabulary. But his allegiance,
as Blair Worden has demonstrated, was not to republican government
(which he thought prone to "division"), but to limited monarchy
on the model of the Ancient Constitution.[10] Limited monarchy was
characteristic of the republican tradition in this period, but not distinctive of that tradition.[11]

This is a simple point, but one that sometimes seems to elude even
the most vigilant of scholars. Thus, in the process of arguing against
the patronizing idea that political resistance and criticism were "unthinkable" for Elizabeth and her subjects, Collinson draws our attention to what he calls the other face of Tudor ideology, the

> anti-monarchical virus which was part of the legacy of early
> sixteenth-century humanism. Had not Erasmus preferred the
> "lofty-minded beetle" to both eagle and lion, making the mean-
> ing of his imagery clear in a frankly mordant attack on "people-
> devouring kings"? "They must be called gods who are scarcely
> men, . . . magnificent when they are midgets, most serene when
> they shake the world with the tumults of war and senseless
> political struggles."[12]

"The references," as Collinson points out in a footnote, "are to the
adage 'Scarabeus aquilam quaerit.'" So far so good. Unfortunately,
Collinson goes on:

> To read this adage in connection with the allegorical passage
> in Spenser's *Shepheardes Calender* ("Julye," 213–28), in which
> the downfall of Archbishop Grindal is approximated to the clas-
> sical legend of the eagle dropping a shellfish (or tortoise) on the
> bald head of Aeschylus in mistake for a stone, is to appreciate
> Spenser's barely repressed republicanism. Erasmus uses this tale
> to demonstrate that the eagle, cruelly rapacious rather than truly
> courageous, is also myopic rather than "eagle-eyed." "Anyone

who considers all this will almost declare that the eagle is unworthy of being taken as an example of kingly rule."

"Barely suppressed republicanism"? Suppressed beyond all recognition is more like it. Collinson's quotations from Erasmus are apposite
in a general way (the eagle anecdote *is* critical of Elizabeth), but it
is not clear to me that they are apposite in a specific, much less a
specifically republican, way. Spenser uses the eagle to represent Elizabeth, not because he found the equation in Erasmus, but because (to
quote Erasmus) "the eagle has been found the suitable candidate to
be elected king, not only by the *phrêtrai* of the birds, but by the
senatus populusque of the poets and by universal acclaim."[13] It is, in
fact, another commonplace—as is the anecdote of the eagle and the
misplaced projectile.[14] Assuming for the sake of argument that Erasmus was a republican, there is, in short, no evidence in favor of an
Erasmian interpretation for Spenser's allegory. On the contrary, what
evidence we do have tells against such a reading: whereas Erasmus
(following Pliny) identifies the misguided missile as a tortoise,
Spenser describes it (twice) as a "shell fish" ("Julye," 224 and 225),
presumably because that was the way that Grindal himself told the
story in 1564, at a funeral sermon that Spenser probably attended as
a young man.[15]

   Hadfield's arguments are more serious—he does not attempt to
reclassify Spenser by redefining republicanism—and cannot be dismissed in a paragraph. His case comes down to four main points: (1)
Spenser praises the Venetian republic in a sonnet; (2) Spenser moved
in circles where republican ideas were current; (3) Spenser calls for
a broader, "more republican" distribution of power at the end of *A
View of the Present State of Ireland*; and (4) the "distributive justice"
advocated by the Giant with Scales in *Faerie Queene* V.ii.30–54 has
a sound basis in Aristotle's *Ethics*. In the rest of this essay, I shall
address each of these points in turn, concluding with some thoughts
of my own on the representation of crowds in the Giant with Scales
episode and elsewhere.

At the end of the sixteenth century, the republican tradition in Europe was represented in Europe by two states, Venice and the Netherlands (the republic of Florence, celebrated by Bruni and Machiavelli,
did not survive the fifteenth century). Venice was old, distant, and
Catholic; the Dutch republic new, proximate, and Protestant. Sidney,
of course, was chest-deep in Dutch politics and intimate with the
architects of the new government. Unfortunately, the States were

fractious. Prone to division, they were weak in themselves and therefore dependent on neighboring monarchies; Sidney and his circle
were not impressed.[16]

That left Venice, the republican government of which is apparently
celebrated by Spenser in the commendatory sonnet that he wrote for
Lewis Lewkenor's translation of *The Commonwealth and Government
of Venice* (1599), by Gasparo Contarini (1483–1542). The sonnet itself
is not a masterpiece by any measure; nevertheless, it is important to
consider the poem in its entirety:

The antique *Babel*, Empresse of the East,
Vpreard her buildings to the threatned skie:
And second *Babell*, tyrant of the West,
Her ayry Towers upraised much more high.
But with the weight of their own surquedry,
They both are fallen, that all the earth did feare,
And buried now in their own ashes ly,
Yet shewing by their heapes how great they were.
But in their place doth now a third appeare,
Fayre *Venice*, flower of the last worlds delight,
And next to them in beauty draweth neare,
But farre exceeds in policie of right.
   Yet not so fayre her buildinges to behold
   As *Lewkenors* stile that hath her beautie told.

On the other hand (and here I merely echo points made earlier, by
Jonathan Goldberg and Peter Platt), Spenser's enthusiasm for Venice
is less than emphatic. What really engages him, as we see in the
final couplet, is not the Venetian consitution, or even Contarini's
description of it, but the English translator's prose style. This is not
to say that Spenser finds nothing to praise in Venice herself: she is,
he says, the "flower of the last worlds delight," and she exceeds
Babylon and Rome "in policie of right." Given the status of Rome
and Babylon in Protestant mythography, this is not much of a compliment.[17]

Hadfield's second point, that Spenser moved in circles where republican ideas had some currency, is more difficult to refute because
it is, in practice, rather difficult to substantiate. Hadfield names four
men, three of whom were Spenser's neighbors in Ireland: Sir Walter
Ralegh; his protegé, Sir Thomas Harriot; Harriot's artist-friend, John

White; and Essex. That these men trafficked in dangerous opinions is not really in question. Ralegh and Harriot, for instance, both liked to talk, if not practice, atheism.[18] Ralegh's *Historie of the World* (1614), which was Oliver Cromwell's favorite book in college, was suppressed by Elizabeth's successor because it was "too sawcie in censuring princes."[19] Ralegh also composed a treatise on "The Perogative of Parliaments" (the title is posthumous), in which he defended both the history and the function of the institution, praised Elizabeth for taking suggestions on policy from commoners,[20] and welcomed the fact that a defeudalized nobility was no longer a military threat to the authority of the crown: "The force therefore by which our kings in former times were troubled is vanished away" (*Works* 8:183).

Like Machiavelli, Ralegh was strongly in favor of a citizen militia; he believed that "the strength of England doth consist of the people and yeomanry," the peasants of France, by contrast, having "no courage nor arms" (*Works* 8:163). Markku Peltonen has demonstrated, in persuasive detail, that the materials out of which an English republican tradition might have been fashioned were widely available from about 1570 on, in the form of books: especially books by Machiavelli. But books do not always produce the effects that we think they ought to, and Peltonen's attempts to identify actual republicans in this period have been less successful. As Vincent Carey demonstrates, Anglophone interest in Machiavelli did not usually translate into an enthusiasm for republican government.[21] On the one hand, the rhetoric of republican authors (like Machiavelli) was a commonplace in English writing about Ireland in this period. According to Carey, though, it was not used to advocate representative government in Ireland; instead, it was employed to urge military reform (substituting citizens for mercenaries and colonies for garrisons), to criticize the corruption of local magistrates, and to recommend a policy of colonial expansion. In the sixteenth century, then, quoting a republican and being a republican were sometimes two different things.[22]

This observation also applies to Hadfield's argument about power-sharing in *A View of the Present State of Ireland* (c. 1596). At the end of the *View*, Spenser makes Irenius say that

> this should be one principall in the Appointement of the Lord
> deputies aucthoritye that it shoulde be more ample and absolute
> then it is and that he should haue vncomptrolled power to doe
> anie thinge that he with the Advizement of the Councell
> shoulde thinke mete to be done . . . and this I remember is
> worthely obserued by machiavell in his discourse vppon Livie

wheare he Comendethe the manner of the Romaines gouernement in givinge absolute power to all their Consulls and gouernours which if they abused/ they shoulde afterwardes dearelie
Answeare and the Contrarye theareof he reprehendethe in the
states of *Venice* of florence and manye other principalities of
Italye whoe vsed to limitt theire Chief officers so streightly as
that thereby some times they haue lost suche happie occacions
as they coulde neuer come vnto againe, the like wheareof who
so hathe bene Conuersante in the gouernement of Irelande
hathe to often sene to their greate hurte.

(*Variorum* 10:229)

Hadfield makes two points about this passage. First, "Irenius could
easily have argued that governors need to have greater powers and
ended his discussion there" (173); instead, Spenser insists that Ireland's governors are to be held accountable for their actions.[23] Second,
Hadfield observes that Spenser's argument "takes the form of a familiar paradox: in order to defend the centre, power must be devolved
to the margins. In other words, in order for the monarchy to survive,
it must become more republican and allow a large section of the
amorphously defined political classes to seize the reins of government" (173). "In other words" is a little phrase, but in this case it
is doing a lot of work. In fact, what Spenser says (and Hadfield's
paraphrase obscures) is that he wants more power for the queen's
lord deputy. This was hardly an "amorphously defined political class"
and Spenser is not calling for a republican revolution (he refers, after
all, to Venice and Florence . . . and "other principalities"). What he
says he wants is more autonomy for provincial governors, for men
such as Sidney's father and the Lord Grey de Wilton. This might, as
Richard Helgerson has argued, translate into a return to the decentral-
ized government that characterized England before the Tudors,[24] a
revival, in short, of the old aristocracy (though not, and this is an
important distinction, a revival of serfdom).[25] But it does not suggest
an enthusiasm for "more republican" forms of government.

   In the event, the next lord deputy of Ireland was Robert Devereux,
the second earl of Essex. According to Hadfield, "republican ideas
and ideals were widespread within the Essex circle immediately prior
to his disastrous coup of 1601" (170). He cites, as his authority for
this statement, an article by the historian F. J. Levy.[26] The word
republican, however, does not appear in Levy's article; instead, Levy
shows that Essex and company were avid readers of Tacitus. The

problem, of course, is that Tacitus was useful to so many people in the Renaissance: not only to dissidents, but also to princes on the lookout for dirty tricks.[27] Essex, presumably, was a dissident; but dissidence can take many forms, not all of which involve republicanism. Tacitean history is, in large part, the story of how the senatorial class was deprived of its traditional authority by the first Roman emperors, Augustus and Tiberius. In other words, it was the prototype for the story of the Tudor monarchs and the crisis of the English aristocracy; or so it appeared to Essex and his followers.[28] The question was what to do next. Tacitus disliked tyranny, but he did not want to go back to the chaos of the late Republic, either. Essex, by contrast, did try to go back, but what he had to go back to was not a republic; his rebellion was a reassertion of the privileges and autonomy of the old aristocracy.

That rebellion, as everyone knows, did not succeed. This brings me to Hadfield's final point, the failed rebellion of the Egalitarian Giant, in *Faerie Queene* Book V. Hadfield cites several instances of anti-tyrannical sentiment in *The Faerie Queene*, all of which have received ample notice in recent criticism: the Mercilla episode, the Malfont episode, and the Mutabilitie cantos. But to show that Spenser was taking the next step and embracing republican structures of government Hadfield needs to show that the poet was really on the side of the Giant with Scales. Readers will recall that the episode closes with Talus elbowing the Giant off of a cliff and into the sea. Like many readers, Hadfield is unhappy about this ending. Hadfield, though, contends that Spenser didn't like the ending, either, and that he was secretly of the Giant's party, because the Giant is actually employing an argument from Aristotle's *Ethics*.

According to Aristotle, "the just is—the proportional; the unjust is what violates the proportion. Hence one term becomes too great, the other too small, as indeed happens in practice; for the man who acts unjustly has too much, and the man who is unjustly treated too little, of what is good" (*Nic. Ethics* 1131b). "This," says Hadfield, "is precisely what the Giant argues when he claims that he will curb the excesses of tyrants and Lords who overawe the commons and distribute wealth more equally" (178). I'd like to make several points here. First, it is probably significant that the Giant episode is directly preceded by allegorical encounters with bribery and local corruption; as Elizabeth Heale points out, "It was widely recognized that a major cause of the rebellion of the poor was their oppression by the rich";[29] whether or not Spenser approved of peasant rebellions, he was not unacquainted with their origins. Second: the Giant is proposing a

redistribution of wealth; he does not seem to be interested in changing the constitution. If, therefore, we are looking for evidence of
Spenser's republicanism, we should probably be looking somewhere
else. Third, the Giant's argument is not, in fact, a very good one by
Aristotelian standards. The Giant wants to weigh the wealth of the
world in a pair of balances, and distribute it evenly to the children
of the earth: a laudable goal, but not one that Aristotle approves of.
For according to Aristotle, the mean of justice is not an arithmetical
average; you don't find it by computing the midpoint (*Nic. Ethics*
1106). Some people really are better than others, and they *deserve*,
therefore, a bigger portion of the loot: "If the persons are not equal,"
says Aristotle, "their shares will not be equal" (*Nic. Ethics* 1131a).[30]
One law for the lion and the ox is oppression.

So runs the proverb in hell, according to William Blake. And Spenser
does comment explicitly on the Giant's disregard for "the meane"
(V.ii.49). In general, though, debating the philosophical merits of a
fictional argument is not a productive form of literary criticism. The
fact that Artegall's statements can be defended with reference to the
text of Aristotle is persuasive only for those who hold that, in all
subjects, "to think correctly is to think like Aristotle." That Spenser
admired Aristotle is beyond question, but on which side of idolatry
it is harder to decide. On the subject of justice versus the arithmetical
average, we do know that Gabriel Harvey was firmly on the side of
Aristotle.[31] But this does not settle the argument, either, because, in
addition to being friends with Edmund Spenser, Gabriel Harvey was
(as Dr. Johnson might have put it) a jackass; his name confers no
dignity on our cause, his opinion no authority.

 This leaves us with the poetry itself. Hadfield, very properly, has
directed our attention to the Giant who argues. But what of the
crowd that gathers to listen? After Talus shoulders the Giant into the
sea, Spenser tells us

> That when the people, which had there about
> Long wayted, saw his sudden desolation,
> They gan to gather in tumultuous rout,
> And mutining, to stirre vp ciuill faction,
> For certaine losse of so great expectation.
> For well they hoped to haue got great good,
> And wondrous riches by his innouation.
> Therefore resoluing to reuenge his blood,

> They rose in armes, and all in battell order stood.
> 　　* * * * * *
> 　　Yet nought they could him [*Talus*] hurt, ne ought dismay
> 　　But when at them he with his flaile gan lay,
> 　　He like a swarme of flyes them ouerthrew;
> 　　Ne any of them durst come in his way,
> 　　But here and there before his presence flew,
> And hid themselues in holes and bushes from his vew.
> 　　　　　　　　　　　　　　(*FQ* V.ii.51, 53)

At length, Talus dispatches the "raskall rout" (st. 54), and we turn our attention elsewhere. The crowd returns, however, towards the end of the book, when the Parisian mob takes up arms against its rightful sovereign, Sir Burbon of Navarre. Despite misgivings about his religious convictions, Artegall and Talus join forces with the French king, and defy the "troupe of villains" (V.xi.51),

> Who flocking round about them, as a swarme
> 　　Of flyes vpon a birchen bough doth cluster,
> 　　Did them assault with terrible allarme,
> 　　And ouer all the fields themselues did muster,
> 　　With bils and glayues making a dreadfull luster;
> 　　That forst at first those knights back to retyre:
> 　　As when the wrathfull *Boreas* doth bluster . . .
> 　　　　　　　　*　　　*　　　*
> But when as ouerblowen was that brunt,
> 　　Those knights began a fresh them to assayle,
> 　　And all about the fields like Squirrels hunt;
> 　　But chiefly *Talus* with his yron flayle,
> 　　Gainst which no flight nor rescue mote auayle,
> 　　Made cruell hauocke of the baser crew,
> 　　And chaced them both ouer hill and dale:
> 　　The raskall manie soone they ouerthrew,
> But the two knights themselues their captains did subdew.
> 　　　　　　　　　　　　　　(*FQ* V.xi.58–59)

Eventually, Talus drives the "scattred crew" into the deep (st. 65); as in the previous episode, "[t]he rebellious mob and their champions . . . return to the sea, the chaotic element."[32] Again, the crowd is likened, first to a swarm of flies, and then to a pack of burrowing rodents, seeking shelter in hedgerows, holes, and fields. In the humanist tradition, as explored by A. B. Chambers, the fly was associated with cynicism, with heresy, with lechery, and with impudence.[33] In this case, though, the image is probably more important than the history of its iconography. Flies are dirty, they congregate on dunghills, and they are easily dismissed as individuals; it is only when they assemble in groups that they become really bothersome. Ultimately, though, the crowd, like the swarm, is a nuisance rather than a menace:[34] real aristocrats, like Sir Burbon and Sir Artegall, leave "the baser crew" to Talus and concern themselves with the "captains," which I take to mean the officers, or perhaps the baronial sponsors who instigate the uprising in the first place.

Crowd scenes, of course, are not usually the stuff of classical epic, which prefers the catalogue. Where crowds do appear, the portrait is rarely flattering. Consider, for instance, a probable source for Spenser's mob/storm wind comparison, the first simile of the *Aeneid*. In this simile, Virgil (70–19 B.C.) compares Neptune, calming the storm, to an orator, calming a mob:

> Ac veluti magno in populo cum sæpe coorta est
> Seditio, sæuitque animis ignobile uulgus,
> Iamque faces & saxa volant, furor arma ministrat.
> Tum pietate grauem, ac meritis, si forte virum quem
> Conspexere, silent, arrectisque auribus astant;
> Ille regit dictis animos, & pectora mulcet.
> Sic cunctus pelagi cecidit fragor . . .
>
> (*Aen.* 1.148–54)[35]

And just as, often when sedition springs up in a great crowd, the mob goes mad, rocks and firebrands are flying, rage supplies weapons, then, if by chance they should catch sight of a certain man, ponderous with *pietas* and deserving, they fall silent, stand to and perk their ears, the man rules their minds with his words, and soothes their breasts. So now the din of the sea fell silent.

Virgil starts out with a neutral crowd word, *populus*. But this quickly gives way to another pair of crowd words, *ignobile* and *vulgus*. The crowning touch comes in line 153, where Virgil says that the people stop and perk their ears. According to Servius, ear-perking is something that animals do, "because their ears are moveable." As in

Spenser, the implication of the simile is two-fold: the crowd is wild and impersonal, like a storm, and like a dog, perking its ears at the call of its master, it is bestial and servile. According to his first biographer, Virgil avoided crowds: something that was hard to do in Rome, but it shows in the poetry.

The treatment of crowds in Roman history-writing admits of more variety than epic. Tacitus (A.D. 56–c. 120) is famous for his crowd scenes, but for Tacitus, as for Virgil, the crowd is usually a mob.[36] The following description of a street-fight between two armies is typical:

> The populace (*populus*) stood by watching the combatants, as if they were at games in the circus; by their shouts and applause they encouraged first one party and then the other. If one side gave way and the soldiers hid in shops or sought refuge in some private house, the onlookers demanded that they be dragged out and killed; for so they gained a larger share of booty, since the troops were wholly absorbed in their bloody work of slaughter, while the spoils fell to the rabble (*vulgus*). Horrible and hideous sights were to be seen everywhere in the city: here battles and wounds, there open baths and taverns; blood and piles of corpses, side by side with harlots and their partners. There were all the debauchery and passion that obtain in a dissolute peace, every crime that can be committed in the most savage conquest, so that men might well have believed that the city (*civitatem*) was at once mad with rage and drunk with pleasure. . . . As if this were a new delight added to their holidays, they gave way to exultation and joy, wholly indifferent to either side, finding pleasure in public misfortune (*malis publicis*).[37]

The problem here is not just that the *populus* is bloodthirsty; that is only a symptom of the real problem, which is that the people are indifferent to the *res publica*, the public welfare; their very numbers, he says elsewhere, cut them off from any interest in the state (*communium curarum*).[38] The historian's disdain is palpable, and characteristic.[39] It was not, however, inevitable in the history-writing tradition. Livy (59 B.C.–A.D. 17), for instance, writes of crowds that do not stand on the sidelines of history, crowds of bold deeds and noble sentiments, enamored of liberty but mindful of justice, "doing no harme to any creature as they passed along: following therein the modestie of their forefathers."[40] Although Livy was himself a member of the leisure class, the speeches that he places in the mouths of his senators suggest that he was sympathetic to the demands of the commoners, even when framed in the shape of armed insurrection:

> They wrung and wrested from our forefathers that power and authoritie fire new, and whereof they had as then, no proofe and experience: how thinke yee then, that having tasted now the sweetnesse of it, they will endure the want thereof? especially seeing, that we our own selves are not of so temperate carriage in our government and command over them, but that they have need of some succour and releese.[41]

This is an altogether different view of the crowd from what one finds in Tacitus. It is an important view, however, because it was Livy, rather than Tacitus, who prompted Machiavelli's influential meditations on republican liberty and Livy who made Milton a republican.[42] Spenser, by contrast, cites Machiavelli, but writes in the tradition of Tacitus and Virgil; his crowds are vulgar in both senses of the word.

At this point, it might seem natural to insist on the distinction between a republic and a democracy. Milton, too, had doubts about the *vulgus*;[43] indeed, this was typical of republicanism, both in Britain and on the Continent. But doubts admit of distinctions, some of which are important. On the one hand, republicans did not, in the words of Blair Worden, "envisage universal suffrage or anything like it." On the other hand,

> they did want to entrust a large measure of power to men outside the elite: power which would be mixed with or balanced by that of a higher group or class but which might be decisive nonetheless. They tended to draw, at least implicitly, a distinction between the people and the rabble: between responsible citizens who could safely be entrusted with power and the multitude which could not.[44]

Thus, for Milton, the essential sovereignty of "the people" is the keystone, not only of his defense of regicide, *The Tenure of Kings and Magistrates* (1649),[45] but also of his last-ditch effort to forestall the restoration of the monarchy, *The Readie and Easie Way to Establish a Free Commonwealth* (1660). Critics sometimes fault Milton for compromising on the issue of popular sovereignty in the latter treatise, because he wants to make membership in the Grand Council a lifetime appointment and because he limits the voting franchise to a small fraction of the population, observing that popular assemblies are historically unstable and give way in their extremity ("a licentious and unbridl'd democratie") to dictatorship.[46] But unlike most of his contemporaries (including the radical Levellers), Milton makes merit, rather than property, the deciding factor in who gets to vote.[47] Milton's greatest fear, at this juncture, was that, if given the chance, the majority of voters *would* make the wrong decision and invite the king to return. Indeed, sometimes the distinction between the people and the mob collapses altogether, as when Milton complains (in the preface to *Samson*) about the custom of introducing "trivial and vulgar persons" into tragedy, a practice "which by all judicious hath bin counted absurd; and brought in without discretion, corruptly to gratifie the people." Nevertheless, the idea that sovereignty inheres in "the people" is fundamental to the argument of *The Readie and Easie Way*: although Milton is reluctant to trust the majority, he insists that authority is still derived from "the people" and is not to be "transferrd, but delegated only, and as it were deposited" in the senate of principals;[48] this idea of "the people," as distinguished from "a misguided and abus'd multitude,"[49] he never surrendered.

There is no such distinction to be made in *The Faerie Queene*. There are mobs and there are crowds, some of which are occasionally benign: for example, the "rude rablement" that gather to inspect the dragon's corpse (*FQ* I.xii.5–12). But the people as such have no place in Spenser's poem.

Whether or not there was a crisis of the aristocracy, a crisis was perceived. Ralegh, as we saw earlier, welcomed it on the grounds that it effectively eliminated armed conflict between the barons. Algernon Sidney (1622–1683), the great republican martyr, was less optimistic. Like Ralegh, he perceived that the civil wars of the fifteenth century had delivered a fatal blow to the English aristocracy. For Sidney, though, this created rather than solved a problem: deprived of their feudal authority, "the lords have only more money . . . but no command of men; and can therefore neither protect the weak, nor curb the insolent. By this means, all things have been brought into the hands of the king, and the commoners." The observation was not a new one. What was different was the remedy: where Essex had tried (in vain) to revive the aristocracy, Sidney would strive (successfully) to remove the king.[50] In the meantime, Essex and Sir Philip kicked against the goads of consolidation and imagined or conspired to effect a Gothic revival of baronial autonomy. Theirs was a protest against absolutism, but it was a protest that looked backward, to the Ancient Constitution, to the English tradition of common law, to the demands and concessions of Magna Carta (1215), the Provisions of Oxford (1258), and the Ordinances of 1311. It was reform that they envisioned, not a revolution.[51] Such were the politics and such the style of *The Faerie Queene*, as well: archaizing with, as Helgerson observes, the aristocrats at center-stage and the monarch at the margins.

It is tempting to dismiss this archaizing impulse as nostalgia: lethal, in the cases of Sidney and Essex, but impotent in the grand scheme of things. The power of nostalgia, however, should not be underestimated. That there was such a thing as English republicanism in the first half of the seventeenth century, before there was an English republic, has now been established in detail by David Norbrook. But republicanism, as Worden points out, did not bring the republic itself into being.[52] Norbrook himself concedes that republicans were never numerous: "even at the high tide of the 1650s the proportion of committed republicans in the population was a very small one, and the quasi-republican regime that was toppled by the monarchy was probably the most despised government in English history."[53] Defenders of the common law, by contrast, were both more numerous and, in the long term, more successful.[54] Theirs was not the language of chivalry, but of the Ancient Constitution: unwritten, immemorial, irrecusable. That language, the language of the law, was archaic of necessity. But it was not impotent. For twenty-three years, it refused a king; then, in 1649, it put him on trial and deprived him at once of life and crown. Only then could the English experiment in republican government (which is still ongoing) actually make a beginning. Nostalgia, to be sure, did not *make* the republic. It only made the republic possible.

East Carolina University

NOTES

Spenser's epic is cited from the text established by Hiroshi Yamashita and Toshiyuki Suzuki in *The Faerie Queene*, ed. A. C. Hamilton, Longman's Annotated Poets, 2nd ed. (New York: Longman, 2001); the prose and shorter poetry are cited from

The Works of Edmund Spenser: A Variorum Edition, ed. Edwin Greenlaw, et al., 11 vols. (Baltimore: Johns Hopkins University Press, 1932–57), hereafter *Variorum*. A version of this paper was presented at The Place of Spenser: Words, Worlds, Works: A Conference of the International Spenser Society (7 July 2001, Cambridge, England). For suggestions and criticism I am grateful to Peter C. Herman, Thomas Herron, Roger Kuin, Richard Peterson, Tracey Sedinger, and Tricia Wilson-Okamura.

1.   David Norbrook, *Writing the English Republic: Poetry, Rhetoric, and Politics, 1627–1660* (Cambridge: Cambridge University Press, 1999), 14; for the 1620s, see ch. 1. On the revival of interest in classical republicanism as an alternative to "Whig, liberal, and marxist accounts of early modern England," see Steve Pincus, "Reconceiving Seventeenth-Century Political Culture," review of Markku Peltonen, *Classical Humanism and Republicanism in English Political Thought, 1570–1640* (1995) and Tony Claydon, *William III and the Godly Revolution* (1996), in *Journal of British Studies* 38 (1999): 98–111, at 98–101.

2.   Markku Peltonen, "Classical Republicanism in Tudor England: The Case of Richard Beacon's 'Solon his Follie,'" *History of Political Thought* 6 (1994): 469–504 and *Classical Humanism and Republicanism in English Political Thought, 1570–1640* (Cambridge: Cambridge University Press, 1995), ch. 2: "Classical Republicanism in the Margins of Elizabethan Politics."

3.   Andrew Hadfield, "Was Spenser a Republican?" *English* 47 (1998): 169–82, at 169.

4.   Quoted in Blair Worden, "English Republicanism," *The Cambridge History of Political Thought: 1450–1700*, ed. J. H. Burns (Cambridge: Cambridge University Press, 1991), 443–75, at 446.

5.   Patrick Collinson, "The Monarchical Republic of Queen Elizabeth I" (1986), *Elizabethan Essays* (London: Hambledon, 1994), 31–57.

6.   Collinson, "*De Republica Anglorum*: Or, History with the Politics Put Back," *Elizabethan Essays*, 1–27, at 19; John Guy, "Tudor Monarchy and Its Critiques," *The Tudor Monarchy*, ed. John Guy, Arnold Readers in History (London: Arnold-Hodder Headline, 1997), 78–109, at 81.

7.   Guy, "Tudor Monarchy and Its Critiques," 81–82; for "republican" and "quasi-republican," see 97–100. Pincus, "Political Culture," 102–105 makes a similar point about the "overly capacious" definition of republicanism employed by Peltonen.

8.   Louis Adrian Montrose, "'O Queen, the matter of my song,'" plenary lecture, The Place of Spenser: Words, Worlds, Works: A Conference of the International Spenser Society (8 July 2001, Cambridge, England).

9.   Colin Burrow, *Epic Romance from Homer to Milton* (Oxford: Clarendon, 1993), 132–39. Cf. Angus Fletcher, *The Prophetic Moment: An Essay on Spenser* (Chicago: University of Chicago Press, 1971), 208: "Mercilla's trial of Duessa takes place in what amounts to a parliament, and in this framework the monarch could not, except symbolically, assume absolute right in imitation of Julius Caesar." Spenser also seems to favor parliament in *Briton moniments*, according to which "The weary Britons" were subjected to pagan depradations "Til by consent of Commons and of Peares, /

They crownd the second *Constantine* with ioyous teares" (*FQ* II.x.62); in Holinshed, Constantine II is crowned by the army.

10.   Blair Worden, *The Sound of Virtue: Philip Sidney's* Arcadia *and Elizabethan Politics* (New Haven: Yale University Press, 1996), ch. 13; see also Debora Shuger, "Castigating Livy: The Rape of Lucretia and *The Old Arcadia*," *Renaissance Quarterly* 51 [1998]: 526–48 and Norbrook, *Writing the English Republic*, 12. For Sidney's political vocabulary, see Worden, ch. 2 (on *virtue*).

11.   To take but one instance, limited monarchy was also a feature of what John Guy calls the "feudal-baronial" tradition in English politics; see "The Rhetoric of Counsel in Early Modern England," *Tudor Political Culture*, ed. Dale Hoak (Cambridge: Cambridge University Press, 1995), 292–310.

12.   Collinson, "Monarchical Republic," 44, citing Margaret Mann Phillips, ed. and trans., *Erasmus on His Times: A Shortened Version of* The Adages *of Erasmus* (Cambridge: Cambridge University Press, 1967), 51.

13.   *Erasmus on His Times*, 49.

14.   See Louis S. Friedland, "Spenser as a Fabulist," *Shakespeare Association Bulletin* 12 (1937): 85–108, 131–54, 194–207 at 144–45.

15.   "Aeschilus the Poete lieng on slepe bare headed nere the Sea, a great seafowle, thinkyng his head to be a stone, wheron he might breake the shelfishe which he carried, lette it fall on hys heade, wherewith he was killed out of hand." Edmund Grindal, *A Sermon, at the Funeral solemnitie of the most high and mighty Prince Ferdinandus* (STC 12377; London: John Day, 1564), sig. Aiiiv (noted by Percy W. Long, "Spenser and the Bishop of Rochester," *PMLA* 31 [1916]: 713–35, at 734–35); the anecdote is one of several on the theme of *memento mori*. Thomas North's translation of *The Morall Philosophie of Doni* (STC 3053; London: Henry Denham, 1570) is also cited as a possible source for Spenser's shellfish, but the parallel is not exact; see the woodcut on 48 and *Variorum* 7:335–36). The substitution of "eagle" (in Spenser) for "seafowle" (in Grindal) was the occasion of some confusion for Long (734), none of it needful. The classical source for the anecdote is Pliny, *Natural History* 10.3.7, where the demise of Aeschylus contributes to a discussion of eagles that live in the vicinity of water; Spenser's eagle is probably, therefore, what is known as an erne or sea eagle.

16.   I am indebted for this point to Roger Kuin; for documentation, see Worden, *Sound of Virtue*, 228–31.

17.   Jonathan Goldberg, *James I and the Politics of Literature: Jonson, Shakespeare, Donne, and Their Contemporaries* (Baltimore: Johns Hopkins University Press, 1983) goes on to note that *policie* suggests "policing," i.e., spying, as well as politics (77). Peter G. Platt, "'The Meruailouse Site': Shakespeare, Venice, and Paradoxical Stages," *Renaissance Quarterly* 54 (2001): 121–54 adds that "flowers die, and 'last world' suggests both the most recent and the final world: ephemerality and the threat of apocalypse haunt the beauty of Venice" (135). Babylon was routinely identified as the location of the biblical Tower of Babel, the name of which means "confusion"; according to the Geneva gloss on Gen. 11.9, the tower's fall serves as an example of "Gods horrible iudgement agaynst mans pride and vaine glory." The association does not bode well for Venice.

18.   For atheism, see John W. Shirley, "Sir Walter Raleigh and Thomas Harriot," *Thomas Harriot: Renaissance Scientist*, ed. John W. Shirley (Oxford: Clarendon, 1974),

16–35. This essay is cited in Hadfield, 182 n. 49 as evidence of Ralegh and Harriot's radicalism; there is, however, no mention of republicanism.

19. John Chamberlain, in a letter to Dudley Carleton (22 Dec. 1614); quoted in Cyndia Susan Clegg, *Press Censorship in Jacobean England* (Cambridge: Cambridge University Press, 2001), 96. This sounds as if Ralegh got into trouble for challenging the divine right of kings; Chamberlain, however, goes on to say that Ralegh was disappointed in the book's reception, "for he thought he had wonne his spurres and pleased the King extraordinarilie." This, according to Clegg, makes "a veiled attack on [the King's] policies" unlikely; she goes on to argue that "the censorship of Ralegh's history derived more from the King's personal anxieties [about death] than from Ralegh's politics" (96–103).

20. Sir Walter Ralegh, *The Works of Sir Walter Ralegh, Kt.*, 8 vols. (Oxford: Oxford University Press, 1829), 8:195.

21. Vincent Carey, "The Irish Face of Machiavelli: Richard Becon's *Solon his Follie* (1594) and Republican Ideology in the Conquest of Ireland," *Political Ideology in Ireland, 1541–1641*, ed. Hiram Morgan (Dublin: Four Courts, 1999), 83–109. See also Richard Tuck, *Philosophy and Government 1572–1651*, Ideas in Context (Cambridge: Cambridge University Press, 1993), ch. 2 (37–41 et passim).

22. Cf. Blair Worden on the seventeenth century: "lettered Englishmen were fully capable of combining a sympathetic interest in Roman republicanism with conservative opinions about their own country's constitutional arrangement. Thus they could admire Brutus and Cassius without the thought entering their heads that Charles I should be slain or the monarchy removed." Review of David Norbook, *Writing the English Republic* (1999), *Times Literary Supplement* (29 January 1999): 5–6, at 6.

23. Debora Shuger makes a similar point in "Irishmen, Aristocrats, and Other White Barbarians," *Renaissance Quarterly* 50 (1997): 494–525, at 504–13.

24. Richard Helgerson, *Forms of Nationhood: The Elizabethan Writing of England* (Chicago: University of Chicago Press, 1992), 40–59. Shuger identifies a comparable tendency in Sidney's *Arcadia*; see "Castigating Livy," 533–37. Tobias Gregory points out, in response to Helgerson, that newly created barons like Leicester and Essex depended for wealth and influence on a strong central government; see "Shadowing Intervention: On the Politics of *The Faerie Queene* Book 5 Cantos 10–12," *ELH* 67 (2000): 365–97, at 386–91. Dependence was a fact of life for both men, but it chafed and eventually both of Spenser's would-be patrons took strong measures to secure their own autonomy: Leicester by going to the Netherlands, where he allowed himself to be appointed Governor-General of the United Provinces, a king in all but name; and Essex by going to Ireland. Neither attempt succeeded, but they are sufficient to indicate the general tendency of baronial ambition: the kind of independence that was enjoyed by the old nobility in the fifteenth century.

25. For Spenser's critique of baronial tyranny, see Shuger, "White Barbarians," 511–13. Shuger goes on to suggest Spenser's enchantment with the aristocracy was waning when he died; his new hero, as exemplified in late works like the *View* and *Mutabilitie*, was no longer the knight on horseback, but the bourgeois and the yeoman farmer (520 n. 25). The middle-class orientation of Spenser's life and poetry is also the subject of Michael Murrin, "The Audience of *The Faerie Queene*" *Explorations*

in Renaissance Culture 23 (1997): 1–21. Murrin, however, makes a distinction between the literature of chivalry, which continued to inspire "the middling sort," and the lifestyle of the Elizabethan aristocrat, which no longer resembled that of a knight errant.

26.   F. J. Levy, "Hayward, Daniel, and the Beginings of Politic History in England." *Huntington Library Quarterly* 50 (1987): 1–34.

27.   See Peter Burke, "Tacitism," in *Tacitus*, ed. T. A. Dorey, Studies in Latin Literature and Its Influence (London: Routledge & Kegan Paul, 1969), 149–71. For additional bibliography on Tacitus in the Renaissance, see David Scott Wilson-Okamura, "Spenser and the Two Queens," *English Literary Renaissance* 32 (2002): 62–84.

28.   Levy, "Beginnings of Politic History," 12.

29.   Elizabeth Heale, "Munera, Pollente," *The Spenser Encyclopedia*, gen. ed. A. C. Hamilton (Toronto: University of Toronto Press, 1990), 481.

30.   The first Aristotle quotation, cited from Hadfield, "Was Spenser a Republican?" 178, is from an unidentified translation. Subsequent quotations are from Martin Oswald, trans., *Nicomachean Ethics*, Library of Liberal Arts (New York: Macmillan, 1962). Cf. *Politics* 3.13.1284a3–18 on the circumstances under which monarchy is appropriate (cited by Shuger, "Castigating Livy," 534).

31.   For Harvey's argument against "arithmaticall proportion," see David Weil Baker, *Divulging Utopia: Radical Humanism in Sixteenth-Century England*, Massachusetts Studies in Early Modern Culture (Amherst: University of Massachusetts Press, 1999), 140–42.

32.   Fletcher, *The Prophetic Moment*, 246.

33.   A. B. Chambers, "The Fly in Donne's 'Canonization,'" *JEGP* 65 (1966): 252–59.

34.   See Hamilton's commentary on the musciform children of Error in *FQ* I.i.23: "The gnat, or fly, is an emblem of what is merely troublesome" (ad loc.). Compare the "vnruly rablement" (II.xi.17) that attacks the Castle of Alma in Book II: initially compared to "a swarme of Gnats" (II.ix.16; see also "swarmd" at st. 13), the Maleger's troops are easily dispatched by Guyon and Arthur and flee their blows "Like scattered Sheepe" (II.ix.14; see also "raskall flockes" at II.xi.19). As in Book V, the contest is framed in terms of class: Prince Arthur and Sir Guyon are knights, whereas Maleger and his "wicked bande" are "villeins" (II.ix.13; II.xi.5, 26, 29, and 35; see also "Carle" for Maleger at II.xi.16, 24, 33, 37, 43, and 46). Class antagonism surfaces again in V.iii.36: Artegall would be revenged on Braggadocchio, but Guyon pacifies him by pointing out that it would "dishonour . . . / . . . our iudge of equity,/To wreake your wrath on such a carle as he"; the point is not that vengeance is wrong, but that Braggadocchio is a peasant, and therefore beneath Artegall's notice. For more flies and sheep, see V.vi.29–30, in which the "raskall rout" that attacks Britomart in the house of Dolon is compared to "scattred sheepe"; VI.i.24, where Calidore's assailants in Briana's castle "flock" about him like sheep only to be brushed away like "bryzes" (gadflies); VI.viii.40, in which the Salvage Nation that prepares to sacrifice Serena "flocke[s]" about her, "like many flies"; and VI.xi.48, where the brigands who fight Calidore are likened to flies buzzing around a carcass in summer.

35. The Latin text of the *Aeneid* is cited from *P. Virgilii Maronis Opera* . . . (Venice: Heirs of Lucas Antonius Iunta Florentinus, 1543–44), facsimile reprint, The Renaissance and the Gods, 2 vols. (New York: Garland, 1976). The passage cited here appears on fol. 163r, as does the commentary of Servius quoted below.

36. Cf. Gian Biagio Conte: "Tacitus is a master at the description of masses, which is often haunting and frightening. He can be equally powerful when he depicts the crowd as calm, or threatening, or dispersing when gripped by panic. In his description of the crowd one notes the senator's fear mixed with disdain at the turbulence of the soldiers or the dregs of the capital. Yet the aristocratic historian manifests an almost equal disdain for his peers, the members of the Senate, whose behavior is described with a subtle malice that emphasizes the contrast between the facade and the reality of their feelings: their flattery of the emperor masks the hatred they secretly feel towards him and their concern for the public welfare conceals intrigue and ambition." *Latin Literature: A History*, trans. Joseph B. Solodow, rev. Don Fowler and Glenn W. Most (Baltimore: Johns Hopkins University Press, 1994), 537.

37. Tacitus, *Histories* 3.83; translation adapted from *The Histories*, trans. Clifford H. Moore, Loeb Classical Library (Cambridge: Harvard University Press, 1962).

38. Ibid., 1.89.

39. See also *Annals* 1.39, 4.74, 12.43, 14.14, 14.45; *Histories* 1.40, 1.72, 1.89–90, 2.29, 2.44, 2.87–91, 3.55, 4.20, 4.36–37, 4.49–50, and 4.67.

40. Philemon Holland, trans., *The Romane Historie Written by T. Livius of Padua* (STC 16613; London: Adam Islip, 1600), p. 122. The passage quoted here appears in Livy's description of the crowd that deposes the tyrannical decemvirate, *De urbe condita* 3.46–54.

41. Ibid., 123.

42. According to John Aubrey, "Whatever he wrote against Monarchie was out of no animosity to the King's person or out of any faction, or Interest but out of a pure zeall to the Liberty [of] Mankind, wch he thought would be greater under a free state than under a Monarchall goverment. His being so conversant in Livy and the Rom: authors and the greatnes he saw donne by the Rom: commonwealth & the virtue of their great Captaines induc't him to." *The Early Lives of Milton*, ed. Helen Darbishire (London: Constable, 1932), 14–15.

43. See Perez Zagorin, *Milton, Aristocrat and Rebel: The Poet and His Politics* (New York: D. S. Brewer-Boydell & Brewer, 1992). Milton's anxiety about the *vulgus* is also "a recurrent theme" in Norbrook; see *Writing the English Republic*, 19 et passim.

44. Worden, *Sound of Virtue*, 229.

45. See *The Complete Prose Works of John Milton*, gen. ed. Don M. Wolfe, 8 vols. (New Haven: Yale University Press, 1953–1982), 3:198–298; cited hereafter as *CPW*.

46. Milton, *CPW*, 7:438. That democracies need not be licentious and unbridled is indicated by his earlier reference to "a frugal and selfgoverning democratie" (*CPW*, 7:427).

47. Milton, *CPW*, 7:442–43. Cf. Christopher Hill, *The Century of Revolution: 1603–1714*, 2nd ed. (New York: Norton, 1980), 115: "some Levellers excluded paupers and wage labourers from the 'free people,' on the ground that their economic dependence precluded political independence. This view had something to be said

for it. . . . Nevertheless, the fact that the most radical political party even of the Revolutionary decades excluded over half the male population (and all women) from political life tells us much about seventeenth-century English society. In normal usage, 'the people' did not include the poor."

48.   Milton, *CPW*, 7:432; cf. *Tenure of Kings and Magistrates*: "The power of Kings and Magistrates is nothing else, but what is only derivative, transferr'd and committed to them in trust from the People, to the Common good of them all, in whom the power yet remaines fundamentally, and cannot be tak'n from them, without a violation of thir natural birthright" (*CPW*, 3:202; cited in *CPW*, 7:432 n. 114).

49.   Milton, *CPW*, 7:463. On the essential nobility of the English people, cf. 7:411–21, 428.

50.   See Blair Worden, "The Commonwealth Kidney of Algernon Sidney," *Journal of British Studies* 24 (1985): 1–40 and Jonathan Scott, *Algernon Sidney and the English Republic, 1623–1677*, Cambridge Studies in Early Modern British History (Cambridge: Cambridge University Press, 1988), 39–42.

51.   For Sidney and the "Gothic" ideal of a limited monarchy, see Worden, *The Sound of Virtue*, 239–43; and Peter C. Herman, "'Bastard Children of Tyranny': The Ancient Constitution and Fulke Greville's *A Dedication to Sir Philip Sidney*," forthcoming in *Renaissance Quarterly*.

52.   Worden, review of Norbrook, *Writing the English Republic*, 6.

53.   Norbrook, *Writing the English Republic*, 7.

54.   See J. G. A. Pocock, *The Ancient Constitution and the Feudal Law: A Study of English Historical Thought in the Seventeenth Century* (1957), reissued with three additional chapters of response to subsequent scholarship (Cambridge: Cambridge University Press, 1987); a briefer (but less pointed) account is available in Corinne C. Weston, "England: Ancient Constitution and Common Law," *Cambridge History of Political Thought: 1450–1700*, ed. Burns, 374–411. See also Guy, "Rhetoric of Counsel," esp. 307–309 on the role of "fuedal-baronial" tradition in the run-up to 1641–42. Spenser's evaluation of the common law tradition admits of a distinction: he thought it appropriate to England, but not to colonial Ireland; see Carol V. Kaske, *Spenser and Biblical Poetics* (Ithaca: Cornell University Press, 1999), 77–79.

ANDREW HADFIELD

Was Spenser Really a Republican After All?: A Response to David Scott Wilson-Okamura

*A*NYONE WHO WANTS TO ARGUE that there was rather more political argument in the literature of the past than has generally been recognized must surely welcome serious discussion of the politics of that literature in the present. While, on the one hand, I would want every reader to be persuaded by the force and truthfulness of my arguments, on the other, I am glad that there is a community of scholars and critics who consider them worth disagreeing with. David Scott Wilson-Okamura's challenge to what I had made as suggestions rather than conclusions is worthy of a detailed response partly because he scores a number of palpable hits, but also because he has made me wish to refine and rethink my original position rather than accept his claims. In the final analysis, we may both conclude that despite our differences we are not so far apart after all.

Professor Wilson-Okamura criticizes my suggestion that Spenser was a republican through a series of interrelated strategies. He argues that there was, in fact, virtually no republicanism before the execution of Charles II in 1649. What looks like republicanism to eager modern readers was invariably an attack on a variety of modes of tyranny with the goal of restoring older, more aristocratic forms of government. He then proceeds to show how my readings of Spenser's republicanism fall into these traps, before concluding with a fascinating and learned analysis of the crowd in the histories of Tacitus and Livy, and how Spenser's work fits into the historical tradition they inaugurated. Accordingly, I shall divide my response into two sections. First, I shall try to show that what looked like republicanism was more like republicanism than anything else. And, second, I shall respond to specific points made against my original article.

I

Professor Wilson-Okamura cites J. G. A. Pocock's claim that republicanism was "a language, not a programme." The first problem of his argument is that he does not actually define what the language—or languages—of republicanism actually were. Instead, he proceeds to attack what he sees as the vague and ill-defined ways in which historians—principally Patrick Collinson and John Guy—have abused our understanding of early modern history. Professor Wilson-Okamura is undoubtedly right to argue that support for limited monarchy cannot be considered as republicanism per se, although, as he admits, it is characteristic of republican arguments in the period. It is one thing to criticize imprecision, however, and quite another to try to remove all the constituent elements of a belief because they do not conform to an ideal that is never actually defined. My suspicion is that short of the discovery of a treatise proclaiming that Queen Elizabeth was an awful tyrant who deserved to be executed and a government based on the support of the people established in her place, Professor Wilson-Okamura will brook no republicanism before the 1640s (although he admits towards the end of his essay that David Norbrook's researches have established that "there was such a thing as English republicanism in the first half of the seventeenth century"). In other words, anything that falls short of this ideal is excluded as not republican. There are dangers inherent in hard-headed scepticism—which can easily slide into a type of gullibility—as there are in apparently ahistorical naïveté.

I would suggest that a republican tradition constituted a number of different elements and languages, not all of which were exactly congruent or fitted together perfectly. Furthermore, this cluster of beliefs, ideas, and identifiable modes of writing do not necessarily indicate republicanism or republican thought if produced in isolation.[1] First, there is a rhetoric against tyranny, often derived from Tacitus's *Histories* and *Annals*, but which also often stemmed from Protestant resistance theorists such as John Knox, John Ponet, and Christopher Goodman, writing in the 1550s.[2] Second, there is a strong commitment to the humanist program of educational reform and a concentration on the study of the classics. Through the study of Cicero, Aristotle, Plato, Polybius, Thucydides et al., came an interest in the political ideas they espoused, as well as an understanding of the institutions and forms of political organization they advocated. Such study led to a select group of highly educated men possessing the means and the confidence to understand different constitutions in the ancient world and contemporary Europe and so debate alternative forms of government, including varieties of mixed rule made up of elements of monarchy, oligarchy, and democracy, as well as republics such as Rome and Venice.[3] Third, there is a stress on the need for virtue in government officials or magistrates, often leading to the suggestion that hereditary monarchy was not the ideal form of government because one could not guarantee that the best would inherit the throne. Often such arguments would praise the constitution of Venice because official positions were not held for life or at the whim of a monarch but rotated every few years. Equally important to note, other arguments, often derived from Machiavelli, would praise republics as best equipped to pursue wars, and claim that active virtue was best achieved in the trying conditions of battle.[4] Fourth, there is a keen interest in histories of the republic and enthusiasm for Livy, who exhibited nostalgia for the lost republic and portrayed the opponents of and conspirators against Caesar—Brutus, Cassius and Pompey—in a positive light.[5] There is also enthusiasm for Lucan's *Pharsalia*, certainly a work against tyrants and arguably a republican classic.[6] The very representation of the founding of the republic, the story of the rape of Lucrece, can, of course, be read as a republican gesture.[7] Fifth, the language of natural rights is employed, often derived from Huguenot treatises and the opposing arguments made by Catholic "monarchomachs" such as Francisco Suarez.[8] This language grants citizens rights to relative autonomy and freedom from the oppressions of bad monarchs who they have the right to oppose if necessary. A treatise which argued this case and which had a significant influence in Elizabethan and Jacobean England is Innocent Gentillet's *A Discourse upon ther meanes of wel governing and maintaining in Gods Peace, a Kingdome, or other principalitie . . . Against Nicholas Machiavell the Florentine*, translated by Simon Patericke in 1602.[9] Gentillet's defence of the rights of the individual against the "policy" of the ruler defended and articulated in *The Prince* shows how complex and divided a republican tradition was (republicans concentrated far more on Machiavelli's political analysis in the *Discourses on the First Decade of Livy*).[10] The final element I would single out is the aspect of republicanism which forms the basis of both John Guy and Patrick Collinson's arguments, the importance of offices and positions of responsibility held by ordinary citizens/subjects.[11] Professor Wilson-Okamura gives their arguments short shrift, not without some good reason, because in themselves documents which stress the importance of churchwardenship or the village constabulary are not obvious proof of an enthusiasm for a new political order, let alone the grander claim that "inside every humanist was a citizen struggling to get out."[12]

The point is that there is a danger of dismissing or underestimating the extent of republican thought in Tudor and Stuart England because a hard and fast definition is sought. There is, as Mark Goldie has argued, a problem in "confining the idea of republicanism to outright rejection of monarchy, and of supposing that the monarchic idiom precluded the republican."[13] Such a definition of republicanism will, of course, make sure that nothing actually appears before the 1640s. Dr. Goldie's point is the same as that of Guy, and to a greater extent, Collinson, namely an attempt to make sure that early modern political consciousness is not simply limited to a circumscribed, elite class centered around the court, and, less significantly, parliament. Following Aristotle's definition of a citizen as "one who shares in government," Dr. Goldie seeks to shift arguments away from formal representation and constitutional issues to local activity and responsibility:

[T]here is a republican tradition in which the active involvement of the citizen rather than the passive exercise of the franchise was the essential feature of a good polity . . . This "republican" tradition has little to do with the presence or absence of a monarch. *Res publica* literally means . . . "the public thing", and was most often translated as the "common weal" or "commonwealth". Early modern England was neither a democracy nor, in our modern sense, a republic. It was monarchical. Yet it could be said to be an unacknowledged republic, or a monarchical republic.[14]

Professor Wilson-Okamura will undoubtedly respond that this definition is far too broad and will have the effect of making everyone a republican who participates in public life, producing an already-known answer to a loaded question (the equal and opposite objection to the one that Dr. Goldie has raised to critics such as Professor Wilson-Okamura).

However, the office-holding definition of the republic need not stand alone. Indeed, it is one of the problems of the debate that it has been made in isolation, I think. It is also a pity that Professor Wilson-Okamura refers to Markku Peltonen's *Classical Humanism and Republicanism in English Political Thought*, but does not really want to engage with any of his arguments (a further sign of how committed he is to a monolithic and restrictive definition of republicanism). Peltonen, while being careful not to collapse the distinctions between republicanism and humanism, argues that republicanism had its greatest impact in inaugurating a theory of citizenship a long time before the Civil War: "Although classical republicanism as a constitutional goal was not fully developed in early modern England, a theory of citizenship, public virtue and true nobility based on the classical humanist and republican traditions, was taken up, studied and fully endorsed throughout the period."[15] Nevertheless, Peltonen's actual discussion of Elizabethan republicanism in the works of John Hooker, John Barston, Richard Beacon, and Lewes Lewkenor's translation of Contarini, clearly links republican ideas to definitions of government that derived from the instigation and consent of the people and their ability to control and limit the actions of the monarch. Political power should come from below not above.[16] Peltonen points out that there are three particular features of the Venetian constitution that Lewkenor "found highly commendable": its "ability to hold corruption at bay"; the election of magistrates and the mechanisms of government, including the Venetian prince, the senate, which possesses supreme power but was unable to " 'tyrannize, or to pervert their country laws'," and the great council of 3000, which was in effect a " 'Democrasie or popular estate'" including a much wider section of the political nation. Lewkenor saw Venice as "the embodiment of the mixed constitution" and therefore "a touchstone for the governments of other commonwealths."[17]

As Professor Wilson-Okamura has pointed out, there are objections to Peltonen's rather all-inclusive definitions and analyses, notably Vincent Carey's counterreading of Richard Beacon's *Solon His Follie*, which he argues is less a republican political treatise than a work "in favor of the glorification and advancement of princely rule."[18] However, the two seemingly exclusive definitions are not necessarily diametrically opposed: in the process of representing a commonwealth designed to protect the liberty of English subjects, Beacon was clearly recommending the most severe oppression of the Irish. This is a familiar paradox of republican political thought and should remind us of Machiavelli's argument that war was the best way of maintaining the virtue and liberty of the republic. An established republic cannot reform itself so that "reform must be carried out by violent means."[19] If *Solon his Follie* is a work that recommends violence and destruction in the name of reform and liberty this does not make it a nonrepublican work. After all, the most aggressive policies and systematic slaughter in Ireland were carried out by English republicans, showing that republicanism was not always a good or a nice thing.[20] The work itself is full of republican examples and rhetoric, demanding that magistrates obtain the consent of the people before acting; placing emphasis on the need to persuade the people of the good of the commonwealth; citing the key example of Brutus's expulsion of the Tarquins as an example of the need for magistrates to act decisively; and stressing that the mixed constitution was the best and most stable form of government.[21] Moreover, Peltonen's study is not without pertinent definition and detail, as the example of Lewkenor's translation of Contarini indicates. An enthusiasm for a mixed constitution does not in itself constitute republicanism, but if notions of citizenship, liberty, and the need for active virtue are also present, then the case does look somewhat less flimsy. Can we label Sir Thomas Smith's *De Republica Anglorum* a republican—or quasi-republican—work, as Patrick Collinson would have it?[22] I have to confess that I am not sure about this issue and it is dangerous to assume that every time the words *res publica* or "commonwealth" are used we have evidence of a republicanism waiting to burst out. Nevertheless, it is clear that a large number of political ideas and elements of a republican political vocabulary had entered the mainstream of British politics in Elizabeth's reign and Spenser knew and used these.

One last, crucial point needs to be made before I try to answer Professor Wilson-Okamura's four specific points against my article. I did not mention in that work—although, on reflection, I should have done so—that one of Spenser's key sources in a *View* was George Buchanan, probably the foremost republican theorist in the British Isles in the sixteenth century. There is not really space here for a sustained discussion of the use that Spenser made of Buchanan's work, although one is urgently needed. I shall confine my argument to a few comments.

Spenser makes use of Buchanan's major work, the posthumously published *Rerum Scoticarum Historia (History of Scotland)* (1582) in his account of the origins of the Irish and Scots in a *View*.[23] In doing so he makes it clear that he has access to Buchanan's work, probably owning a copy ("Never the more are there two Scotlands, but two kindes of Scots were indeed (as you may gather out of Buchanan)"; "and even so do the wild Scots, as you may read in Buchanan").[24] Buchanan's writings were well known in the Leicester and Sidney circles to which Spenser had been attached all his adult life.[25] Buchanan's political ideas were expressed in a number of his works as well as the *History of Scotland*, including his Latin poetry, the famous dialogue *De jure regni apud Scotos: dialogue* and his vociferous condemnation of Mary Queen of Scots, *A detection of the Actions of Mary Queen of Scots*.[26] Buchanan argued that "kings are not ordained for themselves, but for the people." and he terrified his pupil, James VI, with endless examples of the fates of kings who had failed to heed this principle, had sought their own pleasures instead, and so become tyrants.[27] The worst of these was James's mother, Mary Queen of Scots.[28] Buchanan, probably the most secularized and classically oriented political theorist available for an Elizabethan reader, argued that kings were elected by the people and were answerable to them.[29] The king cannot rule without a council and the people provide the king with a model of government to which he is required to subscribe.[30] The people make the laws that the king has to obey, and he must never rule in his own self-interest or he can be deposed by anyone.[31] Hereditary kingship is an undesirable political form—although the Scots have surrendered to it with the accession of Kenneth III—because princes should really be chosen for their virtue not according to their birth.[32] And, like Lewkenor/Contarini, Buchanan admires Venice for its liberal and long-lasting constitution.[33]

Buchanan certainly looks far more like a republican than most of the political thinkers discussed so far and he has been accorded this status by some historians.[34] He cannot be termed a republican in the strongest possible sense of the word (desiring the replacement of the monarch by a representative body), but by any other definition he would appear to qualify as one. How much did he influence Spenser's writing? I would suggest that it is improbable that Spenser only used Buchanan as an antiquarian source, even if that is what he emphasises in a *View*. It is possible that the dialogue form of *De jure regni apud Scotos: dialogue* influenced Spenser's choice of form for a *View*, and that that work functions like Beacon's *Solon His Follie* as an analysis of political forms that ranges well beyond Ireland itself. Just as Buchanan used the figures of himself and William Maitland, a prominent Scottish politician with whom he disagreed, so might Spenser have cast Irenius and Eudoxus as a version of himself and an English humanist.

This connection remains to be proved and is highly speculative. Rather more concrete is the relationship between Spenser's representation of Mary Queen of Scots as Duessa, one of the key evil figures in *The Faerie Queene* and Buchanan's obsessive hatred of Mary. For Buchanan, Mary was keen to ignore council and was the cause of much dissension in the kingdom.[35] She was guilty of the murder of Darnley and so had committed crimes for which she deserved to be put to death.[36] Buchanan posed the obvious rhetorical question that if she had done this to the king, what would she do to her subjects?[37] She is compared to the witch, Medea.[38] Buchanan died before Mary and so did not represent her trial and execution. Nevertheless, it is quite possible that Spenser made use of Buchanan's portrait of Mary when representing her in *The Faerie Queene* as a foul, deformed witch who was guilty of capital crimes. Just as Buchanan argued that the monarch needed to be subject to the impartial laws established by the people so does Spenser represent Elizabeth having to bow to the justice of the demands of her powerful subjects in the trial of Duessa in Mercilla's palace (V, ix, 38–50). The connection is not immediately apparent, but, given the subject matter and Spenser's use of Buchanan as an authority elsewhere in his writings, it is plausible, and would therefore add more republican emphasis to Spenser's narration of the episode. When James VI tried to have *The Faerie Queene* suppressed, he may also have seen the connection, given that he also demanded that Buchanan's history was a work that he argued should be forbidden.[39]

II

I hope these points suggest that if republicanism is defined as a cluster of ideas, objectives, strategies, and arguments, then Spenser not only had access to republican ideas but, as I argued in my earlier article, he associated with those who were interested in republicanism and had reasons for taking republican rhetoric seriously. Professor Wilson-Okamura is right that advocation of the mixed constitution, which incorporates monarchy, aristocracy (or oligarchy), and democracy, does not make a republican, but it is clear that there is a significant difference between the political theories of Buchanan and those expressed by Sir Thomas Smith. To collapse these varieties of political thought as if they were all "a reassertion of the privileges and autonomy of the old aristocracy" (Wilson-Okamura, p. 260) is equally problematic. Republicanism did, of course, look back to ancient constitutions and political practices; but then, as Hannah Arendt and Karl Marx have both pointed out, so do all republicans and revolutionaries. It is never easy to make the content go beyond the form.[40] Hence, I think we have to be more nuanced in our political readings of specific authors, as well as recognizing that certain types of ideas—such as republicanism—may not have been clearly articulated. And, as Richard Dutton has recently argued, "works were allowed on to the stage and into print, with minimal apparent interference" from the authorities, indicating that the range and variety of seemingly subversive material available to readers in the late sixteenth and early seventeenth centuries was actually quite broad.[41] Articulating republican ideas did not necessarily bring the author to the hostile attention of the authorities. To do that you had to insult someone at court, such as Lord Burghley, or cause a diplomatic incident by slandering a foreign king's mother.

I shall respond to the four points that Professor Wilson-Okamura makes against my article in the order in which they were made. I think it ought to be borne in mind that one of the cornerstones of my argument, Spenser's allegory of the trial of Duessa, does not feature in Professor Wilson-Okamura's argument, as it has been commented on at length elsewhere. This is fair enough but it does have the effect of making my reliance on Artegall's defeat of the Giant with the Scales appear to be rather greater than it actually is because this is an episode that Professor Wilson-Okamura wants to analyze in detail (it occupies one and a half pages in an article of fourteen pages).

First, Professor Wilson-Okamura questions how significant is Spenser's sonnet prefacing Lewkenor's translation of *The Commonwealth and Government of Venice*. He is right that it is an odd sonnet which concentrates more carefully on the style of Lewkenor's translation than the content of the treatise. However, I am not sure that this detail has the significance that he places upon it. After all, it is a dedicatory sonnet meant to pay tribute to the translator and it does its job well. I don't think we can conclude that Spenser had no interest in Venice or disliked the contents of the work on this basis. It is, of course, possible that he had not read the work carefully, but, this would also seem unlikely. And I really cannot find anything unusual in Spenser seeing Venice as a city that will outlive Babylon and Rome: any modern commentary on Venice will explain that the longevity of the Venetian republic was a feature praised by historians of the city.[42] The apocalyptic imagery and tone of the poem fit in with other work Spenser appears to have been writing towards the end of his life such as "Two Cantos of Mutabilitie." Lewkenor's translation is singled out by Peltonen as a key republican work in English, and it was produced by an important figure in the Essex circle.[43] I think it is hard to accept Peter G. Platt's argument that Venice was a city that encapsulated and expressed the paradoxes of Renaissance thought.[44] Rather, Contarini/Lewkenor represents Venice as a beacon of liberty that should influence and inspire other European states to copy its social and legal practices, tolerance of strangers and constitution (although there are some problems about the excess of liberty available and on display there). Spenser's sonnet, if anything, expresses the fear that Venice may not last as long as Lewkenor's translation.

Second, Professor Wilson-Okamura questions whether the circles Spenser moved in were as republican as I have suggested. He is right to point out that some of my sources merely indicate an interest in radical ideas or a criticism of tyranny rather than republicanism as such. He is also right that it is hard to substantiate the claim (but then this, as I've already pointed out, is a central crux, and it is too easy to throw the baby out with bath water ...). Nevertheless, Spenser is directly linked to Lewkenor's translation of *The Commonwealth and Government of Venice*, which is a serious piece of evidence. He must also have known Beacon's *Solon His Follie*, given the close parallels between Beacon's and Spenser's careers in Munster, which, even if we accept Vincent Carey's interpretation of the work, does use and spread republican ideas, concepts and langauge.[45] He was closely linked to Sir Walter Ralegh who was an enthusiastic reader of Machiavelli, and, he also made substantial use of Buchanan. Add to these figures the Tacitean historians associated with Essex—not all of them, as Professor Wilson-Okamura points out, republicans or even critics of a powerful monarchy—and the point seems to be one that can be defended.

Third, Professor Wilson-Okamura argues that Spenser's use of Machiavelli in a *View* to suggest that the office of the lord deputy in Ireland needs to have increased powers but greater responsibility for his actions, is not, as I claimed, a sign of a republican political thought. Rather, it is an argument for the revival of the aristocratic autonomy that existed in England before the advent of the centralized Tudor state. This seems to me an inherently implausible argument given that one of the central contentions of a *View* is the need for the crown to bring over-mighty subjects to heel.[46] This is a theme that runs throughout the dialogue, and the need to stop rather than encourage the power of feudal lords, barons, and other oppressors of the people, is one of the main reasons for Irenius's citation from *The Discourses*. To take some examples which indicate the extent of Spenser's critique of the irresponsible aristocracy: the Wars of the Roses are seen to have led to anarchy and the degeneration of the English who have become Irish; the feud between the Butlers and Geraldines are seen to have helped destroy good government and plunge Ireland into anarchy; what Ireland needs is for the English invasion to succeed as fully as the Norman Conquest succeeded in England, establishing the proper rule of law.[47] Richard Helgerson's argument that Spenser was a poet whose work articulated "a Gothic ideology of renascent aristocratic power," cited with approval by Professor Wilson-Okamura, is interesting and provocative, but it risks reducing political arguments to questions of form.[48] Certainly it is hard, I think, to square the complex discussion of courtesy in *The Faerie Queene*, Book VI, which is translated from the court to the country ("a fayre flowre . . . though it on a lowly stalke doe bowre" (Proem, 4)), with a straightforward enthusiasm for old-fashioned aristocratic, chivalric values. A similar judgment might also be made of the "shepheards nation" in *Colin Clouts come home againe*. They are certainly not members of the "old aristocracy," but they are figures who are treated sympathetically in the poem and their discussions clearly make more sense than those produced at court by the vile figures who surround the queen.

I think the problem lies in Professor Wilson-Okamura's desire to visualize a straw republican man whom he thinks his opponents have created. The passage I cited from a *View* does make use of a republican argument, and it is noticeable that Professor Wilson-Okamura does not answer the point I made that "Irenius could easily have argued that governors need to have greater powers and ended his discussion there"—although he quotes these very words. I am not suggesting that Spenser wanted a "republican revolution," but showing how the use of republican military strategy was intimately bound up with forms of political organization. Anyone who recommended such proposals as a means of increasing English control over Ireland was automatically changing the nature of English political life. Of course, in one sense this is simply a means of proposing "more autonomy for provincial governors," but the link made to republican city-states and the increased responsibility of the office-holder concerned do, I would suggest, signal an important change.[49]

Finally, Professor Wilson-Okamura argues that my interpretation of Artegall's defeat of the Giant with the Scales is misconstrued. He suggests that the Giant's use of Aristotle to argue for more egalitarian means of the distribution of wealth has nothing to do with politics and is manifestly wrong. I learnt a great deal from Professor Wilson-Okamura's nuanced and subtle discussion of Virgil, Tacitus, and Livy's conception of the crowd. I agree with him that Spenser was nervous and often dismissive of the politics of mass democracy, and that he most frequently saw the crowd as the "many-headed monster."[50] However, it is a feature of much republicanism, just as it is of arguments in favor of a more inclusive mixed constitution, that widening the political nation is one thing, tolerating full-scale democracy or the rule of the mob/crowd is quite another. George Buchanan's *De Jure Regni Apud Scotos*, for example, opens with a ferocious assault on the evils of the mob and the worst types of subjects who must not be encouraged or permitted to take part in the political process. For Buchanan, government by the ignorant many is a form of tyranny and must be opposed by the judicious political thinker.[51] No one seriously equates republicanism and democracy.

Nevertheless, the thrust of Professor Wilson-Okamura's argument is that Spenser demonstrates that the political form produced by demands for equality is anarchic terror and that he wholeheartedly endorses Artegall's killing of the Giant. I agree that Spenser is nervous of the consequences of the Giant's arguments, and that they cannot be endorsed in the form they are given. It is obviously naïve to try and weigh everything in a balance and distribute wealth accordingly. But it is also naïve to believe as Artegall does that everything is simply ordained by God: "He maketh Kings to sit in souerainty;/He maketh subiects to their powre obey" (V, ii, 41). Given that Artegall derives his power and authority from Jove, a usurper, a point I made in my original article, this argument cannot be taken at face value. Furthermore, these lines are given an ironic force at the end of the book when the Faerie Queene recalls Artegall prematurely from the "salvage island" (Ireland) "ere he could reforme it thoroughly" (V, xii, 27). This is an action the poem quite explicitly condemns ("But enuies cloud still dimmeth vertues ray"), indicating that the monarch is not always right. Subjects who have to obey in such circumstances—especially given the high stakes involved in abandoning an unreformed Ireland—will have to accept the disasters that may result from the stupid actions of ill-informed monarchs. The Giant's followers precipitate chaos, but then so does the queen herself. A belief in the inalienable rights of hierarchy is no better in the end than a foolish trust in instant equality. The point is, perhaps, that elements of the Giant's thought, which does have a basis in Aristotelian philosophy and ethics, albeit imperfectly derived, have to be incorporated into the constitution or else the state will degenerate into tyranny. In effect, this is precisely what the mixed constitution was supposed to ensure.

There is a lot more to discuss about this episode as it raises numerous questions that may or may not be resolved elsewhere in the poem. The Giant's challenge to Artegall clearly fits into larger patterns of argument in the poem, which is why I am reluctant to accept Professor Wilson-Okamura's argument that we must read the Giant's fate only in terms of wealth and not politics (especially given Artegall's lines and his role throughout the book). I would also want to read the event in terms of Artegall's education as the Knight of Justice, the opening and the end of Book V, and, the radical questions raised by "Two Cantos of Mutabilitie," which provide a terrifying vision of chaos. *The Faerie Queene* is too capacious, inclusive, and, arguably, chaotic a work to be neatly compartmentalized.

III

I would like to conclude by thanking Professor Wilson-Okamura for his stimulating response. I have not only learnt a great deal from his observations but have been given the opportunity to clarify and revise my own ideas. I think there is a danger in his article of assuming that I claimed a certainty which I never intended; the interrogative of the title was genuine (as is that employed here). Nevertheless, there were times when I was obscure, vague, and satisfied with easy answers. I still think that Spenser was interested in republican thought and rhetoric. Like so many other Englishmen in the 1590s, he knew that maintaining the principle of hereditary monarchy was problematic, perhaps impossible, in the face of the childless Elizabeth's imminent death. He was also, I think, hostile to female rule and frustrated by what he saw as Elizabeth's inept political sense.[52] Whether readers are persuaded by my suggestion that we can see signs of republican thought in his writings, or whether Spenser is better defined as a nostalgic adherent of older forms of aristocratic culture, is, I hope, a matter we should debate further.

University of Wales, Aberystwyth

NOTES

1. See Blair Worden, "English Republicanism", in J. H. Burns, ed., *The Cambridge History of Political Thought, 1450–1700* (Cambridge: Cambridge University Press, 1991), 443–75. Worden, it should be noted, sees little that can be construed as republicanism in England before the 1640s.

2. See Rebecca W. Bushnell, *Tragedies of Tyrants: Political Thought and Theater in the English Renaissance* (Ithaca: Cornell University Press, 1990).

3. See Quentin Skinner, *The Foundations of Modern Political Thought*, 2 vols. (Cambridge: Cambridge University Press, 1978), I, pt. 2.

4. See J. G. A. Pocock, *The Machiavellian Moment: Florentine Political Thought and the Atlantic Republican Tradition* (Princeton: Princeton University Press, 1975), chs. 7–9; Worden, "English Republicanism," 446.

5. Gian Biagio Conte, *Latin Literature; A History*, trans. Joseph B. Solodow, rev. Don Fowler and Glenn W. Most (Baltimore: Johns Hopkins University Press, 1999, rpt. of 1994), 370.

6. See David Quint, *Epic and Empire* (Princeton: Princeton University Press, 1993), ch. 4.

7. As the versions of the story produced by William Painter and William Shakespeare suggest. On the former see "Tarquin's Everlasting Banishment: Republicanism and Constitutionalism in *The Rape of Lucrece* and *Titus Andronicus*" *Parergon* (forthcoming, Oct. 2002). On the latter see Andrew Hadfield, *Literature, Travel and Colonialism in the English Renaissance, 1540–1625* (Oxford: Clarendon Press, 1998), 147–62. See also Jonathan Bate's analysis of *Titus Andronicus*, in his edition (London: Routledge, 1995), introduction, where he claims that "Shakespeare's earliest tragedy may be shot through with an unexpected vein of republicanism" (21).

8. W. M. Spellman, *European Political Thought, 1600–1700* (Basingstoke: Macmillan, 1998), ch. 3; Robert M. Kingdon, "Calvinism and resistance Theory, 1550–1580" and J. H. M. Salmon, "Catholic Resistance Theory, Ultramontanism, and the Royalist Response, 1580–1620," in Burns, ed., *Cambridge History of Political Thought*, 193–218, 219–53. See also Worden, "English Republicanism," 448.

9. See Felix Raab, *The English Face of Machiavelli: A Changing Interpretation, 1500–1700* (London, 1965), 56–57, *passim*.

10. See Niccolò Machiavelli, *The Discourses*, ed. Bernard Crick (Harmondsworth: Penguin, 1970); Skinner, *Foundations of Modern Political Thought*, I: 158–62, 169–71.

11. Patrick Collinson, "The Monarchical Republic of Queen Elizabeth I," *Bulletin of the John Rylands Library* 69 (1986–7), 394–424; "*De Republican Anglorum*: Or, History with the Politics Put Back," in Patrick Collinson, *Elizabethan Essays* (London: Hambledon Press, 1994), 1–29; John Guy, "Tudor monarchy and its critiques," in John Guy, ed., *The Tudor Monarchy* (London: Arnold, 1997), 78–109.

12. Guy, "Tudor monarchy," 81.

13. Mark Goldie, "The Unacknowledged Republic: Officeholding in Early Modern England," in Tim Harris, ed., *The Politics of the Excluded, c.1500–1850* (Basingstoke: Palgrave, 2001), 195–232, 180.

14. Goldie, "Unacknowledged Republic," 154.

15. Markku Peltonen, *Classical Humanism and Republicanism in English Political Thought, 1570–1640* (Cambridge: Cambridge University Press, 1995), 12.

16. Peltonen, *Classical Humanism*, ch. 2. See, for example, 57, 67–70, 106–07.

17. Peltonen, *Classical Humanism*, 116–17.

18. Vincet Carey, "The Irish Face of Machiavelli: Richard Beacon's *Solon his follie* (1594) and republican ideology in the conquest of Ireland," in Hiram Morgan, ed., *Political Ideology in Ireland, 1541–1641* (Dublin: Four Courts Press, 1999), 83–109, at 109. See also Steve Pincus, "Reconceiving Seventeenth-Century Political Culture" (review of Markku Peltonen, *Classical Humanism and Republicanism in English Political Thought, 1570–1640* and Tony Claydon, *William III and the Godly Revolution*), *Journal of British Studies* 38 (1999), 98–111. I acknowledged this problem in my article, "Was Spenser a Republican?", *English* 189 (Autumn 1998), 169–82 at 170.

19. Pocock, *Machiavellian Moment*, ch. 7 (quotation 209); Machiavelli, *Discourses*, bk. 2.

20. See Willy Maley, "How Milton and some contemporaries read Spenser's *View*," in Brendan Bradshaw, Andrew Hadfield, and Willy Maley, eds., *Representing Ireland: Literature and the Origins of Conflict, 1534–1660* (Cambridge: Cambridge University Press, 1993), 191–208.

21. Richard Beacon, *Solon His Follie, or a Politique Discourse touching the Reformation of common-weales conquered, declined or corrupted*, ed. Clare Carroll and Vincent Carey (Binghampton, NY: MRTS, 1996), 48, 65, 85, *passim*.

22. Collinson, "*De Republica Anglorum*," 15–17. See also the careful and balanced discussion of Smith's text in A. N. McLaren, *Political Culture in the Reign of Elizabeth I: Queen and Commonwealth, 1558–1585* (Cambridge: Cambridge University Press, 1999), ch. 7.

23. Edmund Spenser, *A View of the State of Ireland*, ed. Andrew Hadfield and Willy Maley (Oxford; Blackwell, 1997), 45, 36, 51, 60, 63.

24. Spenser, *View*, 45, 63. For discussion see Arthur Williamson, "Patterns of British Identity: 'Britain' and its Rivals in the Sixteenth and Seventeenth Centuries" in Glenn Burgess, ed., *The New British History: Founding a Modern State, 1603–1715* (London: Taurus, 1999), 138–73, at 160–62.

25. James E. Philips, "George Buchanan and the Sidney Circle," *Huntington Library Quarterly* 12 (1948–9), 23–55; Blair Worden, *The Sound of Virtue: Philip Sidney's Arcadia and Elizabethan Politics* (New Haven: Yale University Press, 1996), *passim*.

26. There are numerous commentaries on the political ideas of George Buchanan, among the most useful being J. H. Burns, "The Political Ideas of George Buchanan," *Scottish Historical Review* 30 (1951), 61–68; J. H. Burns, *The True Law of Kingship: Concepts of Monarchy in Early Modern Scotland* (Oxford: Clarendon Press, 1996), ch. 6; Roger A. Mason, "James VI, George Buchanan and *The Trew Lawe of Free Monarchies*," in *Kingship and the Commonweal: Political Thought in Renaissance and Reformation Scotland* (East Lothian: Tuckwell Press, 1998), 215–41.

27. George Buchanan, *De Jure Regni Apud Scotos (or a Discourse concerning the due privilege of Government in the Kingdom of Scotland)* in *An Appendix to the History of Scotland* (1721), 181. On Buchanan as tutor of James see D. Harris Willson, *King James VI and I* (London: Cape, 1956), 19–27; I. D. McFarlane, *Buchanan* (London: Duckworth, 1981), 445–50.

28. George Buchanan, *A Detection of the Actions of Mary Queen of Scots in Appendix to the History of Scotland; The history of Scotland written in Latin by George Buchanan; faithfully rendered into English [by J. Fraser]* (1690), bks. 16–20.

29. Buchanan, *De Jure Regni*, 185. On the secular nature of Buchanan's thought, see Roger A. Mason, "*Rex Stoicus*: George Buchanan, James VI and the Scottish Polity," in John Dwyer, Roger A. Mason and Alexander Murdoch, eds., *New Prespectives on the Politics and Culture of Early Modern Scotland* (Edinburgh: John Donald, 1982), 9–33.

30. Buchanan, *De Jure Regni*, 200–03.

31. Buchanan, *De Jure Regni*, 210, 272.

32. Buchanan, *De Jure Regni*, 246–48; *History of Scotland*, bk. 19 (230–32).

33. Buchanan, *De Jure Regni*, 189–90.

34. Williamson, "Patterns of British Identity," 159 (Williamson finds "quasi-republicanism" in Buchanan's writings and argues that Buchanan imagined Scotland as "Livy's virtuous republic"); Roger A. Mason, "George Buchanan, James VI and the Presbyterians," in Roger A. Mason, ed., *Scots and Britons: Scottish Political Thought and the Union of 1603* (Cambridge: Cambridge University Press, 1994), 112–37, at 117.

35.   Buchanan, *History of Scotland*, bk. 16 (175–76).

36.   Buchanan, *History of Scotland*, bk. 18 (189–90).

37.   Buchanan, *Detection of the Actions of Mary Queen of Scots*, 89–90.

38.   Buchanan, *Detection of the Actions of Mary Queen of Scots*, 64.

39.   See Richard A. McCabe, "The Masks of Duessa: Spenser, Mary Queen of Scots, and James VI," *ELR* 17 (1987), 224–42; King James VI and I, *Basilicon Doron* in *Political Writings*, ed. Johann P. Somerville (Cambridge: Cambridge University Press, 1994), 1–61, at 46.

40.   Hannah Arendt, *On Revolution* (London: Faber, 1963); Edward Said, *The World, The Text and The Critic* (London: Faber, 1984, rpt. of 1983), 121–25.

41.   Richard Dutton, *Licensing, Censorship and Authorship in Early Modern England* (Basingstoke: Palgrave, 2000), 86. See also Cyndia Clegg, *Press Censorship in Elizabethan England* (Cambridge: Cambridge University Press, 1997).

42.   See, for example, David C. McPherson, *Shakespeare, Jonson and the Myth of Venice* (Newark: University of Delaware Press, 1990), ch. 2.

43.   Peltonen, *Classical Humanism*, 115–18; Andrew Hadfield, *Literature, Travel and Colonialism in the English Renaissance, 1540–1625* (Oxford: Clarendon Press, 1998), 46–58.

44.   Peter G. Platt, " 'The Meruailouse Site: Shakespeare, Venice, and the Paradoxical Stages,' " *Renaissance Quarterly* 54 (2001), 121–54.

45.   On Beacon's relationship to Spenser see Willy Maley, *A Spenser Chronology* (Basingstoke: Macmillan, 1994), 85; Alexander Judson, "Spenser and the Munster Officials," *Studies in Philology* 44 (1947), 157–73.

46.   See Deborah Shuger, "Irishmen, Aristocrats, and Other White Barbarians," *Renaissance Quarterly* 50 (1997): 494–525. Professor Wilson-Okamura cites Shuger's article, even though it seems to me to seriously undermine his point.

47.   Spenser, *View*, 91, 67, 21–22.

48.   Richard Helgerson, *Forms of Nationhood: The Elizabethan Writing of England* (Chicago: University of Chicago Press, 1992), 49.

49.   It is worth pointing out what a dangerous position the lord deputy or lord lieutenant of Ireland occupied; debt, disgrace and execution were often the deputy's lot, so it could be argued that Spenser was simply trying to rationalize a state that already existed. For details see Ciaran Brady, *The Chief Governors: The Rise and Fall of Reform Government in Tudor Ireland, 1536–1588* (Cambridge: Cambridge University Press, 1994); Steven G. Ellis, *Tudor Ireland: Crown, Community and the Conflict of Cultures, 1470–1603* (Harlow: Longman, 1985).

50.   Christopher Hill, "The Many-Headed Monster in Late Tudor and Early Stuart Political Thinking," in Charles H. Carter, ed., *From the Renaissance to the Counter-Reformation: essays in Honour of Garrett H. Mattingly* (London: Cape, 1966), 296–324.

51.   Buchanan, *De Jure Regni*, 167–70.

52.   John Guy, "Introduction: The 1590s: the second reign of Elizabeth I?," in John Guy, ed., *The Reign of Elizabeth I: Court and Culture in the Last Decade* (Cambridge: Cambridge University Press, 1995), 1–19.

GLEANINGS

RICHARD McNAMARA

Spenser's Dedicatory Sonnets to the 1590 *Faerie Queene:* An Interpretation of the Blank Sonnet

*T*HE 1590 *Fearie Queene* is concluded by an array of seventeen sonnets, of which fourteen are addressed to males and three to females. Two sonnets printed on a page, the whole sequence follows, as Carol A. Stillman has demonstrated, the rules of heraldic precedence in order of rank, social standing, official posts and titles, with senior officials of the crown preceding their juniors.[1] As indicated below in table 1, Hamilton in his new edition of the poem gives the order of the sonnets. These are numbered for ease of reference: [2]

DS 1	Hatton	*DS 10*	Grey
DS 2	Burghley	*DS 11*	Buckhurst
DS 3	Oxford	*DS 12*	Walsingham
DS 4	Northumberland	*DS 13*	Norris
DS 5	Cumberland	DS 14	Raleigh
DS 6	Essex	*DS 15*	Pembroke
DS 7	Ormond		
DS 8	Howard	*DS 16*	Carey
DS 9	Hunsdon	*DS 17*	Ladies

Under the one addressed to the Countess of Pembroke, Sidney's sister, the array includes a blank which has puzzled critics. The blank may simply be, as is generally assumed, the result of the confusion caused by the sudden decision to add new ones.[3] It seems to me, however, that the space is deliberately meant to be so as a tribute to the deceased poet, Sir Philip Sidney.

This assumption should be readily acceptable to those who are aware of the universal ritual of laying a "blank setting" in remembrance of the dead. The custom is seen even today, for instance, at military and high-risk sports club dinners. On such occasions, it is common to preserve an empty dinner place for the deceased, always at the seat where they would have sat if alive, between the closest individuals.

Sidney's death in 1586 was marked by a one-month period of official mourning and a state funeral at St. Paul's cathedral.[4] A few years later when Spencer published the poem, he would have certainly wished to have him among the recipients. But since he was dead, all Spenser was able to do was to give him a "blank" space, not among the men, but among the women right next to Lady Pembroke (Sidney's sister, Mary, and Spenser's Clorinda in "Astrophel)" and before Lady Carey (Elizabeth, daughter of Sir John Spencer of Althorpe and Spenser's Phyllis in *Colin Clout*) and all the ladies of the court.

It seems important to note that *DS 15,* unlike all the others,[5] does not directly praise the recipient: it is predominantly an eulogy of her dead brother in words of the highest rank: "The heuens pride, the glory of our daies, . . . Who first my Muse did lift out of the flore, . . ." Spenser expresses similar feelings in his dedication to the Countess of Pembroke in *The Ruines of Time* which was written in 1590; he writes: "there bee long sithens deepe sowed in my brest, the seede of most entire love and humble affection unto that most brave Knight your noble brother deceased. . . . But since God hath disdeigned the world of that most noble Spirit, which was the hope of all learned men, and the Patron of my young Muses, together with him both their hope of anie further fruit was cut off. . . ."[6] We may now assume that Spenser intends the blank under *DS 15* as a kind of poetic tribute to Sir Philip Sidney.

Kyushu Lutheran College, Japan.

NOTES

1.   See Carol A. Stillman, "Politics, Precedence, and the Order of the Dedicatory Sonnets in *The Faerie Queene*," *Spenser Studies* v (1984), 143–48.

2.   *The Faerie Queene,* ed. A. C. Hamilton (London, Pearson Education, 2001), 726.

3.   About the complicated situation of the printer when asked to cancel the first ten sonnets in the first issue and rearrange them, with seven new ones, in the order that we have them, see L. G. Black's entry in A. C. Hamilton (ed.), *The Spenser Encyclopedia,* (Toronto, 1990; repr. 1997), 293–94.

4.   Philip Sidney was knighted in 1583, but he was not a nobleman by birth. It is in this sense I think that the Sidney Internet Directory declares: "Elizabethan

poet, soldier and statesman Sir Philip Sidney was the first commoner to have a state funeral at St. Paul's cathedral, in London. The next to be honored in this way was Admiral Lord Nelson and then later, Sir Winston Churchill—who is descended from the Sidney family—and Lady Diana Spencer." See Cris Sidney. *The Sidney Internet Directory*. On-line Internet. 6 Feb. 2002. Available: http: //wwwi~way.-co.uk/~sid/directory.html.

5.   *The Faerie Queen*, ed., A. C. Hamilton (London, 2002) p. 734. Hamilton notes at 726 the impersonal character of the sonnets: "Except for *DS 10* and *DS 15,* most sonnets are impersonal and interchangeable."

6.   See W. A. Oram, et al. eds., *The Yale Edition of the Shorter Poems of Edmund Spenser* (New Haven: Yale University Press, 1989), 230.

ANDREW HADFIELD

Robert Parsons/Richard Verstegen and the Calling-in of *Mother Hubberds Tale*

Spenser scholars are familiar with the wealth of evidence that proves that *Mother Hubberds Tale* was "called-in" by the authorities soon after it was published in 1591 because of its thinly veiled attack on Sir William Cecil, Lord Burghley.[1] Comments in works by Gabriel Harvey, Thomas Nashe, John Weever, Thomas Middleton, and Thomas Scot demonstrate what a significant scandal the poem caused.

One of the most substantial comments on the affair occurs in a polemical pamphlet entitled *A Declaration of the True causes of the Great Troubles, Presupposed to be Intended against the Realme of England,* published in Antwerp in 1592:

> And because no man dare frame an endytement against him [Burghley], I will heere omit many other articles of highe treason, but yf any will undertake to justifie his actions in his course of government, let him know, that there is sufficient matter of reply reserved for him, which is not extracted out of *Mother Hubberds* tale, of the false fox and his crooked cubbes, but is to be uttered in plain prose, and shal lay open to the world, his birth, his lyf, and perhaps his death, seing his detestable actions are such, as do aske vengeance of heaven and earth.[2]

Spenser's poem is highlighted in italic as a marginal note, directing the reader to the passage, presumably because the author felt that the scandal generated by the poem's publication was so well known.

The tract, published without naming the author or the place of publication on the colophon, was probably written by either Robert Parsons or Richard Verstegen.[3] Parsons (1546–1610), one

297

of the most significant English Jesuits, became rector of the English College in Rome in 1588.[4] He was responsible for sending Jesuit missions to Britain and he constantly urged Philip II of Spain to invade England and depose Elizabeth. Verstegen (fl.1565–1620), a zealous Catholic antiquarian and polemicist, lived in Paris and Antwerp, where he published a series of works.[5] He was in "frequent correspondence with Cardinal Allen and Robert Parsons [at the English college in Rome], and for a time in their pay."[6]

A Declaration blames all of England's troubles on the regime of the Cecils, the evil councillors who have led Elizabeth astray from the true, old religion (8–9). In doing so they have caused her to support all the wrong causes in Europe: attacking the king of Spain, helping the Huguenots in France, and causing the Scottish wars (27–29, 14–16, 13–14). The development of Protestant factions in Britain has dispersed the unity of the Catholic faith and so caused misery for Elizabeth's subjects (40). Cecil is seen as an ambitious man of low birth (63–64) who has used his power to set up an Inquisition worse than the one in Spain (73) and wages his fanatical wars against the Spanish and the Jesuits without any popular basis of support (72–73). A Declaration fits neatly into a line of Catholic propaganda and has clear affinities with the earlier attack on the earl of Leicester, Leicester's Commonwealth: the Copy of a Letter Written by a Master of Art at Cambridge (1584).[7]

It is clear why the author of A Declaration would want to use Mother Hubberds Tale in his argument. Spenser's poem is mentioned casually but with calculated emphasis at a key moment. As the passage cited above indicates, the author's point is that Cecil's infamy is so widespread and well known that those who wish to find evidence of his nefarious dealings do not have to rely on what is written in verse, but can find numerous examples of nonliterary hostility. This indicates that Parsons/Verstegen knew that Mother Hubberds Tale had caused a major scandal and was widely consulted, being the first port of call for those keen to make the case against Cecil. The superficial reference to the substance of the poem, that it describes the deeds of "the false fox and his crooked cubbes," shows that the author of A Declaration had clearly not read the poem. It would be hard for even the most wilfully blind of readers not to recognize that the narrative describes the adventures of a fox and an ape and that the fox's cubs fail to make an appearance. The "crooked cubbes" must, of course, be a reference to the hunchbacked Sir Robert Cecil, but this only serves to emphasise the lack of engagement with the narrative of the poem. The author of A Declaration is guessing what the poem should contain. [8]

The question that needs to be asked is how did either Parsons or Allen come to refer to Spenser's poem if neither had read it, and what is the significance we should give to the reference? Some suggestions can be made. First, the substance of the passage and the fact that a marginal note directs the reader to it indicate that Parsons/ Verstegen saw *Mother Hubberds Tale* as the source that most readers in England were likely to know detailing Cecil's crimes. It is little wonder that *The Faerie Queene* ends with a reference to Spenser's previous writings having caused "a mighty Peres displeasure" (*FQ* VI.xiii.41). Second, the fact that news of the scandal reached the continent suggests that a community of Catholic readers kept each other informed of events in England. Richard S. Petersen's recent discovery of a letter from the recusant Sir Thomas Tresham to a Catholic friend in the country, dated 19 March 1591, shows that the "calling in" of Spenser's poem was widely reported among members of the Catholic community in England.[9] Clearly Catholic exiles in Europe learned of events in England from their coreligionists. It is possible, of course, that Tresham, who Parsons claimed had "reconcyled" to the Catholic faith, may have been the source himself.[10] Third, reference to a well-known work does not always mean that the author had read the book in question. And fourth, it might also be pointed out that there is a splendid irony in Spenser, a Protestant English poet with the ambition to compete with the greatest contemporary poets in Europe, appearing to be best known on the continent for his usefulness as a source of Catholic propaganda.

University of Wales, Aberystwyth

NOTES

1. The evidence is collected in *The Works of Edmund Spenser: A Variorum Edition: The Minor Poems, Volume II*, ed. Dorothy E. Mason (Baltimore: Johns Hopkins University Press, 1947), 580–85.

2. *A Declaration of the True causes of the Great Troubles, Presupposed to be Intended against the Realme of England* (1592), 68. Subsequent references to this work in parentheses in the text. The quotation is reproduced in *Minor Poems, II*, 581.

3. Verstegen is the more probable author and the second edition of the *STC* attributes the work to him (the first attributed it to Parsons). For (brief) comment see Anthony G. Petti, "Beasts and Politics in Elizabethan Literature," *Essays and Studies* (1963), 68–90, 80.

4. On Parsons's life see *DNB* entry; C. R. N. Routh, *Who's Who in Tudor England* (London, rev. ed., 1990), 331–34.

5.   On Verstegen's life see *DNB* entry.

6.   *DNB* entry.

7.   Ed. D. C. Peck (Athens, OH: University of Ohio Press, 1985). For the relationship between that work and Spenser, see Andrew Hadfield, "Spenser's *View* and *Leicester's Commonwealth*," *Notes and Queries* 246 (Sept. 2001), 256–59. *A Declaration* also weighs in with an attack on Leicester (52–54).

8.   This fact vitiates Brice Harris's interesting claim that the Ape in *Mother Hubberds Tale* was generally understood to be Robert Cecil and his argument becomes circular: see "The Ape in *Mother Hubberds Tale*," *HLQ* 4 (1940–41), 191–203, 198–200.

9.   Richard S. Peterson, "Laurel Crown and Ape's Tail: New Light on Spenser's Career from Sir Thomas Tresham," *Spenser Studies* XII (1998), 1–35. Petersen refers to *A Declaration* although his suggestion that "the fox and the ape in his [Spenser's] tale are identified respectively with Burghley and his son Robert Cecil" (14) is not borne out by the facts.

10.   Peterson, "Laurel Crown," 27.

Index

Abernathy, John, *A Christian and Heavenly Treatise Containing Physic for the Soul* (1615), 94
Aitchison, Jean, 144
Alençon, Duke of, 112
Alione, Giorgo, *Comedia de l'omo e de' soi cinque sentimenti*, 222
Alpers, Paul, 85, 103
Ammianus, Marcellinus, 200
Anderson, Judith, 133–47, 217–18
Antichrist, Islam and Catholicism as, 38–39
Antiquaries, Society of (1586), 226
Arendt, Hannah, 282
Ariosto, Ludovico, *Orlando Furioso*, 41, 58, 83, 113, 115, 124
Aristotle, 88, 261, 278
    Ethics, 256, 260
Ascham, Roger, 54–55
Asconius, 9
Augustus, Emperor (Octavian), 6–11, 17, 22, 25, 113, 115

Bakhtin, Mikhail, 108
Bale, John, 52–55, 57, 61
    Image of bothe Churches, The, 52–55
Barkan, Leonard, 138
Beacon, Richard, *Solon His Follie,* 279–80, 281, 284
Beecher, Donald, 102, 103
Bible, Books of :
    Corinthians, 79
    Ephesians, 56
    Ecclesiastes, 188
    Isaiah, 61
    1 Kings, 154
    Matthew, 79, 108
    Revelation, 17, 47, 59, 60, 61
    Romans, 61
Bible, figures in:
    Solomon, 154–55
Blake, William, 141
Boiardo, Matteo, *Orlando Innamorato,* 115
Bowman, Mary R., 151–76
Brant, Sebastian, 11
Bright, Timothy, 97, 98–99
Brink, Jean, 5
Buchanan, George, 280–82, 285–86
    Rerum Scoticarum Historia, 280–82
Buckman, Ty, 107–25
Bulger, Thomas, 108, 109, 152
Burghley, Lord, *see:* Cecil, William
Burrow, Colin, 154–55
Burton, Richard, 97
Burton, Robert, 78, 79, 86, 102
Bynneman, Henry, 20, 21

Caesar, Caius Julius, 277
Carey, Lady (Elizabeth Spencer), 294
Carey, Robert, 111
Carey, Vincent, 258, 279, 284
Carroll, Clare, 167
Carruthers, Mary, 218, 224, 226
Cavanagh, Sheila T., 176
Cecil, William, Lord Burgley, 24, 192–93, 204, 206–07, 254, 283, 297–98
Chambers, A. B., 263
Chansons de geste, 39
Charles II, 275
Cheney, Donald, 194
Cheney, Patrick, 2, 194
Chetwood, Knightley, 9
Cicero, Marcus Tullius, 18–19, 22, 25, 190
Collinson, Patrick, 254, 255, 256
Comes, Natalis, *Mythologica,* 187, 199, 202–03
Commons, House of (1566), 110

Contarini, Gasparo, Cardinal, *The Commonwealth and Government of Venice* (1599), 257, 279–80, 283–84. *Also see*: Lewkenor, Lewis (trans.)
Cooper, Thomas, 19–20
Counter-Reformation, 39
Cromwell, Oliver, 222, 258
Cyprus, 38

Dante Alighieri, 45
Darnley, Henry Stuart, Lord, 281
Daunce, Edward, 44
Day, Angel, 221
Declaration of the True causes of the Great Troubles (Parsons/Verstegen), 297–99
Denny, Edward, 244–45
Derrida, Jacques, 145
Despair, sin of, 92–96
Devereux, Robert, Earl of Essex, 184, 204, 258–59, 260, 267
Digby, Sir Kenelm, 183
Dobin, Howard, 108
Donatus, Aelius, 1, 5–7
Donne, John, 2, 4, 144
Dryden, John, 9, 11
Dudley, Sir Robert, Earl of Leicester, 19, 20, 21, 24, 26, 112
Dürer, Albrecht, 47, 48
Dutton, Richard, 282
Dyer, Sir Edward, 3, 20

Earle, John, 226, 227
Edwards, Thomas, 194
Eggert, Katherine, 136, 161, 162, 167, 172
Elisabeth I, 107–13, 118, 120, 123–25, 162, 170, 173, 174, 186, 187–88, 191, 276
Enterline, Lynn, 134–35
Erasmus, Desiderius, 256
Escobedo, Andrew, 75–88, 92
Evans, Maurice, 157

Fletcher, Angus, 254–55
Fletcher, Giles, the Elder, 206
Fogarty, Anne, 168
Foxe, John, 276
    Actes and Monumentes, 47, 52, 56
Fowler, Elizabeth, 152–53, 168
Fraunce, Abraham, 195

Freeman-Gilbert, Louise, 85
Friedman, Alice, 220
Frye, Susan, 143
Fulgentius, 203
Fulke Greville, 1st Lord Brooke, 3
Fumerton, Patricia, 220

Gallus, Cornelius, 9
Gascoigne, George, 3
Gentillet, Innocent, *A Discourse*, 277
Gerung, Matthias, 47, 49
Goldberg, Jonathan, 257
Goldie, Mark, 278
Graziani, René, 43
Greenham, Richard, 94–95, 96, 98, 102
Gregerson, Linda, 231
Gregory VII, Pope, 57
Grey de Wilton, Arthur, Lord, 21, 22, 23, 167, 173, 174, 259
Gruninger, Johann, 11, 12, 17
Guellius, 6
Guy, John, 254, 276–77

Hadfield, Andrew, 175, 253, 256–61, 275–87, 297–99
Hall, Edward, *Chronicles*, 223
Halperin, Richard, 228
Hamilton, A. C., 43, 58, 108, 140
Harington, Sir John, 194–95, 202, 220, 222
Harriot, Sir Thomas, 257
Harvey, Gabriel, 3, 18, 20, 21, 22, 23, 201–02, 261
Hatton, Christopher, 110–11
Heale, Elizabeth, 260
Healy, Thomas, 175
Helgerson, Richard, 3, 24, 259, 267
    Self-Crowned Laureates, 24, 284
Henri IV, King of France, 170
Henry VIII, 58
Highley, Christopher, 166, 167
Holinshed, Raphael, 226
Hooker, Richard, 82
Horace [Flaccus], Quintus, 5, 6
Hunter, G. K., 18

Ireland, 184, 257
Islam as Christian heresy, 45–46

James VI, King of Scotland, 11, 281, 82

Jerome, Saint, 40
Julius II, Pope, 52

Kaske, Carol V., 88
Keats, John, 139
Kelsey, Lin, 183–207
Kenneth III, King of Scotland, 281
Kierkegaard, Sören, 75, 81, 82, 84
  Sickness Unto Death, The, 81–83, 86
Kinney, Clare R., 239–48
Knight, W. Nicholas, 158–59, 160
Knox, John, First Blast of the Trumpet
  Against the Monstrous Regiment of
  Women (1558), 165, 166

Lamb, Mary Ellen, 242
Leicester's Commonwealth, 110, 298
Lepanto, Battle of (1571), 38
Lewkenor, Lewis, transl. of Contarini's
  Commonwealth and Government of
  Venice, 279–80, 283–84
Levinus, Lemnius, 86
Levy, F. J., 10, 259
Lewis, C. S., 119, 151
Livy [Titus Livius], 264–65
Luther, Martin, 39–46, 78, 79, 82
  On War Against the Turks, 46
  Table Talk, 47
Lyly, John, 18, 19

MacCabe, Colin, 175
Machiavelli, Niccolò, 255, 258, 265
  Discourses on the First Decade of Livy,
  277
Maecenas, 6, 9, 10, 11
Maley, Willy, 175
Malory, Sir Thomas, 122
Malta (1565), 42
Mareshal, Jacobo, 11, 13
Marlowe, Christopher, Dido Queene of
  Carthage, 224
Marx, Karl, 282
Mary I (Tudor), 110, 165
Mary Queen of Scots, 280–82
Mazzio, Carla, 226
McCabe, Richard, 109, 168, 173
McNamara, Richard, 293–94
Melancholy, 95–96
Memory in FQ, role of, 215–33
Meyer, Samuel, 194
Mildmay, Sir Walter, 20

Milton, John, 206–07, 265–66
  Readie and Easie Way, 266–67
  Tenure of Kings and Magistrates, The
  (1649), 265–66
Montrose, Louis Adrian, 254
More, Sir Thomas, Dialogue of Comfort,
  46
Moschus, 200
Munster County, 111
Muhammad, 45

Neff, Merlin, 43
Nelson, Herbert, 157
Netherlands, 169–70, 256–57
Newman, Karen, 165
Nohrnberg, James, 59
Norbrook, David, 207, 253, 267, 276

Ogilby, John, 11, 15
Oram, William A., 194
Orinoco river, 204
Orlin, Lena Cowen, 220
Ovid, [Publius Ovidius Naso], 5, 25, 83,
  134–35, 191
  Metamorphoses, 134–35, 137, 139,
  195–99, 203
  Tristia, 25

Parsons, Robert, S. J., 80–81
  A Declaration of the True causes of the
  Great Troubles, 297–99
Paster, Gail Kern, 99
Patterson, Annabel, 184
Pausanius, Description of Greece, 200
Pedianus, Asconius, 9
Peltonen, Markku, 258
  Classical Humanism and Republicanism
  in English Political Thought,
  278–79
Pembroke, Mary, Countess, 293–94
Perkins, William, 80, 81, 83, 95
Peterson, Richard S., 299
Petrarch, Francesco, 18, 140
Philip II, King of Spain, 37, 38, 43–44,
  170, 298
Pincius, Aurelius, 11
Platt, Peter, 257, 283
Pocock, J. G. A., 254, 276
Pollio, Asinius, 6, 9, 11
Ponsonby, William, 20
Predestination, 78–79

Primaudaye, Pierre de la, *Second Part of the French Academie*, 219
Purchas, Samuel, 57
Puttenham, George, 190

Quilligan, Maureen, 161, 176
Quitslund, Beth, 91–103

Ralegh, Sir Walter, 3, 4, 24, 26; nicknames for, 187, 191; 183–207, 257, 258, 284
    Historie of the World (1614), 258
    "Ocean to Cynthia," 183–91
Rambuss, Richard, 2–3, 9, 24, 220
Reformation, Protestant, 39
Republican tradition in 16th-century Europe, 256–57
Reynolds, Edward, 80
Ricoeur, Paul, 142, 145
Robinson, Benedict S., 37–61
Roche, Thomas P., 84, 133, 140
Romano, Giuliano, 198
Russia, 206

St. Paul's Cathedral, 294
Saladin, 39
"Saracen" romance, 37–61
Saracens as Protestant motif, 37–61
Scalingi, Paula Louise, 165
Schoenfeldt, Michael, 99
Servius, 4, 263–64
Shakespeare, William, 135, 144, 145
    Hamlet, 135
    Lucrece, The Rape of, 135
    Othello, 38
Shelley, Percy Bysshe, 139
Sidney, Algernon, 266–67
Sidney, Sir Philip, 205, 226, 255, 256, 293 - 294
Skelton, John, 79, 81, 82
    Magnificence, 76
Skulsky, Harold, 100, 103
Smith, Roland M., 157, 159
Smith, Sir Thomas, 20, 282
    De Republica Anglorum, 282
Snyder, Susan, 78
Song of Roland, 122
Sowdone of Babylon, The, *41*
Spenser, Edmund:
    Arthur-Gloriana as Tudor succession narrative, 118

Debate over women rulers, 164–66
Despair in Protestant literature and *FQ*, 75–88
Ireland, treatment by male and female voices in *View* and *FQ*, 169
Irish view, anachronistic criticism of his, 174–75
Justice, his conception of, 151–76
Mother Hubberds Tale and Catholic propaganda, 297–99
Poetic tribute to Sidney, 293–99
Republicanism and ES, 253–87
Vergil as a model, 1–26
Works of
Amoretti, 139, 141, 147
Colin Clouts Come Home Againe, 183–87, 192, 204–06
Complaints, 24, 25, 184, 192–93, 198, 206
Faerie Queene, Book II, 215–33, 151–76, *FQ* 1590, 293–94, Dedicatory Sonnets (1590), 293–94
    Figures and places in:
    Acrasia, 137, 138, 140, 176, 228–31
    Acrasia's Bower, 140–41
    Abessa, 58
    Acidia, 38
    Alma, 10, 216, 220, 229
    Alma, Castle of, 99, 122, 220, 232
    Amidas, 153, 156–57
    Amoret, 134, 140, 141–43, 145–47, 197
    Archimago, 57, 58, 78
    Artegall, 43, 60, 107, 134, 151–64, 170–76, 253, 261–63
    Arthur, 38, 42, 43, 44, 61, 118–25, 170, 216, 220–21, 231
    Astraea, 112, 154, 161
    Belge, 167, 168–70, 172, 173
    Belphoebe, 119, 121, 147, 188, 207
    Blandamour, 146
    Bower of Bliss, 136, 227, 231
    Bracidas, 153, 156–58
    Britomart, 13, 91–92, 93–94, 100, 107, 133–37, 140, 143, 146–47

Burbon, 170, 171–72, 173, 174, 262–63
Busirane, 141–42
Caelia, 101
Calidore, 125
Colin Clout, 162
Contemplation, 87
Cupid, 134, 140
Despaire, 87, 103
Diana, 134
Duessa, 53, 55, 56, 103, 111, 122, 146, 166, 176, 281–82
Egalitarian Giant, 260–61
Faerie Queene, 61, 119–25
Fidelia, 103
Florimel, 124, 140, 158, 159
Flourdelis, 167, 168, 171–72, 174
Furor, 6–7
Geryoneo, 168, 169–70
Glauce, 134
Gloriana, 118, 119–20, 123–24, 162
Grantorto, 168, 170–71, 173, 174
Grill, 231, 232
Guyon, 122, 123–24, 138–39, 155, 161, 220–21, 227–32
Hellenore, 88
House of Holiness, 88, 99, 103, 134
Irena, 167, 168, 172, 174
Kirkrapine, 58
Lucy, 158
Malbecco, 84–85, 103, 138, 140
Malecasta, 134, 137
Maleager, 99
Mammon's Cave, 138
Mammon's House, 139
Mercilla, 37, 43, 282
Merlin, 107–09, 120
Mount Acidale, 125, 162
Munera, 43, 153, 163, 167
Neptune, 158
Night, 55
Orgoglio, 58, 100, 102, 122
Palmer, The, 138, 231
Patience, 102
Phedon, 6
Philtera, 157
Pollente, 43, 153, 162
Pride, House of, 57, 134
Proteus, 158, 159

Pyrochles, 42, 122
Radigund, 160–66
Red Crosse, 37, 55–57, 58, 59, 60, 77, 78, 81, 84, 85, 86, 87, 99, 100, 101, 102, 103, 123, 146
Sanglier, Sir, 154
Sansfoy, 55, 56–57, 146
Sansioy, 55, 56
Sansloy, 55, 57
Scudamour, 91, 93, 94, 134, 140, 153, 197
Souldan, 38, 43, 44
Speranza, 87
Talus, 163, 172, 173, 261, 262–63
Temperance, House of, 216, 222
Terpine, 162
Timias, 120, 207
Una, 53, 55, 57, 59, 77, 88, 100, 103, 119, 123
Venus, 134
Venus, Temple of, 153
Verdant, 136, 229–31
Fowre Letters, 20–21
Hymn of Heavenly Beauty, 86
Letter to Ralegh, 56, 112–13, 119, 124, 161, 228
Mother Hubberds Tale, 192–93, 198, 205, 297–99
Muiopotmos, 137–38, 139
Mutabilitie Cantos, 260, 283, 286
Ruines of Time, 206, 294
Shepheardes Calender, The, 2, 20, 22, 25, 139, 255
Teares of the Muses, 191
View of the Present State of Ireland, 167, 169, 256, 258, 280
Spenser family, 22
Spenser Society, International, 254
Spira, Francis, 77, 82
Starke, Sue Petitt, 194
Staton, Shirley, 161, 176
Stewart, Alan, 215–33
Stillman, Carol A., 293
Stowe, John, 226
Strong, Roy, 111–12
Stubbs, John, 110
Succession anxieties, Tudor, 107–25
Sueraz, Francisco, 277
Sullivan, Garrett A., Jr., 215–33

Tacitus, Cornelius, 259–60.264–65
  Annals, 276
  Histories, 276
Tasso, Torquato, 39, 43, 44, 113
  Gerusaleme Liberata, 41–42, 61, 116,
    117
Teskey, Gordon, 85
Throckmorton, Elizabeth, 187
Tilley, M. P., 215
Tomkis, Thomas, *Lingua*, 215–16,
  222–23, 226–28, 231–33
Tresham, Sir Thomas, 193, 299
Turks, Ottoman, 38–40
Turler, Jerome, *The Traveiler*, 201

Urban II, Pope, 44, 57

Varus, 9
Venice, 256–57, 283
Vergil, 1–26, 107, 113, 263, 265
  Aeneid, 4, 9, 107, 113–15, 124, 262
  Bucolics, 9

Eclogues, 8
Georgics, 9

Wars of the Roses, 284
Wever, Richard, *Lusty Iuventus*, 76–77,
  82–83
Whetstone, George, 3
White, John, 258
Willis, John, 219
Willymat, William, *Physic to Cure the
  Most Dangerous Disease of Despair*,
  79–80, 93, 94
Wilson-Okamura, David Scott, 253–67,
  275–78, 280, 282–87
Wittreich, Joseph, 108
Wofford, Susanne, 135
Woodes, Nathaniel, *Conflict of
  Conscience*, 77, 83
Worden, Blair, 255, 265
Wroth, Mary, *Urania, The Second Part
  of*, 239–48

Young, Dr. John, 23